Setting
Domestic
Priorities

Setting Domestic Priorities

WHAT CAN GOVERNMENT DO?

Henry J. Aaron and Charles L. Schultze, editors

GORDON BERLIN
BARRY BOSWORTH
LINDA R. COHEN
JOHN J. DiIULIO, JR.
FRANK LEVY
WILLIAM McALLISTER
RICHARD J. MURNANE
ROGER G. NOLL
ISABEL V. SAWHILL
CLIFFORD WINSTON

The Brookings Institution
Washington, D.C.

Copyright © 1992 by
THE BROOKINGS INSTITUTION
1775 Massachusetts Avenue, N.W., Washington, D.C. 20036

Library of Congress Cataloging-in-Publication data:

Setting domestic priorities : what can government do? / Henry J. Aaron
  and Charles L. Schultze, editors.
      p. cm.
  Includes bibliographical references.
  ISBN 0-8157-0054-7 (cloth : alk. paper)
  ISBN 0-8157-0053-9 (pbk. : alk. paper)
  1. United States—Social policy—1980–   2. United States—Economic
policy—1981–   3. Government spending policy—United States.
I. Aaron, Henry J.   II. Schultze, Charles L.
HN59.2.S48   1992
361.6'1'0973—dc20   92-28464
                                                               CIP

9 8 7 6 5 4 3 2 1

The paper used in this publication meets the minimum
requirements of the American National Standard for
Information Sciences–Permanence of Paper for Printed
Library Materials, ANSI Z39.48-1984.

Foreword

DISCONTENT WITH government in general and with elected officials in particular is widespread among U.S. voters. Three successive presidents have run against Washington. Both Congress and the president have sunk in public esteem. More fundamentally, Americans doubt that government works.

This book is addressed to that perception. What *can* government do? Clearly, not everything. Numerous poorly conceived, badly designed, or ineptly executed programs have failed, and too many survive despite their shortcomings. Many social and economic problems cannot be solved by just one more governmental program and will require changes in private individual and group behavior.

At the same time, many governmental interventions have met their original objectives. Social security has saved millions of the elderly and disabled from economic destitution, and medicare has assured virtually all of them financial access to hospital and physician services. An interstate highway system links the forty-eight contiguous states. Federal support of university-based scientific research has made U.S. universities meccas for hundreds of thousands of foreign students. In these and many other areas, government has worked for the United States.

Just because some governmental programs have succeeded does not necessarily mean that more would be better, particularly when large and persistent federal deficits have eroded U.S. national saving. More spending on some programs requires either less spending somewhere else or higher taxes. And the sobering roster of failed governmental interventions reminds everyone that new initiatives should not be undertaken lightly.

This book deals with the question of what government can, and should, do to solve problems in seven important areas: health, homelessness, crime, families and young children, education, research, and infrastructure. Authors examine whether new or improved government

vii

interventions can address problems in these areas more effectively than current efforts are doing. Typically, the authors are cautious in their claims for what can be accomplished by changes in government policies. But they all argue that government can play a part in finding solutions.

Setting Domestic Priorities: What Can Government Do? was edited by Henry J. Aaron, director of the Brookings Economic Studies program, and Charles L. Schultze, senior fellow in Economic Studies. The authors from Brookings, in addition to Aaron and Schultze, are senior fellows Barry P. Bosworth and Clifford M. Winston. Other authors include Gordon L. Berlin, Manpower Demonstration Research Corporation; Linda R. Cohen, University of California, Irvine; John J. DiIulio, Jr., Princeton University; Frank Levy, Massachusetts Institute of Technology; William McAllister, John Jay College of Criminal Justice at City University of New York; Richard J. Murnane, Graduate School of Education at Harvard University; Roger G. Noll, Stanford University; and Isabel V. Sawhill, the Urban Institute.

Each of the chapters in this book was reviewed by outside commentators at a conference. Serving as commentators were John H. Bishop, Cornell University (education and training); Richard T. Gill (families and young children); Marvin H. Kosters, American Enterprise Institute (health); Richard R. Nelson, Columbia University (science); James M. Poterba, Massachusetts Institute of Technology (infrastructure); John C. Weicher, Department of Housing and Urban Development (homelessness); and James Q. Wilson, University of California, Los Angeles (crime).

Diane Maranis, Valerie M. Owens, David J. Rossetti, Evelyn M. E. Taylor, and Kathleen Elliott Yinug helped prepare the manuscript for publication. Nancy D. Davidson, Patricia Dewey, Venka Macintyre, James R. Schneider, and Theresa B. Walker edited the manuscript. Roshna M. Kapadia and Laura A. Kelly checked the manuscript for accuracy, and Susan L. Woollen prepared it for typesetting.

The views expressed here are the authors' alone and should not be ascribed to the commentators or to the trustees, officers, or other staff members of the Brookings Institution.

BRUCE K. MAC LAURY
President

August 1992
Washington, D.C.

Contents

Tables

Figures

Setting
Domestic
Priorities

1

HENRY J. AARON
AND CHARLES L. SCHULTZE

What Can Government Do?

FEW PEOPLE THINK the United States is doing very well these days. The slow recovery from the recession of 1990–91 is painful enough, but workers' earnings have grown little for two decades. Families have struggled to maintain or raise living standards by having both spouses work or by having fewer children than their parents, but there is little more they can do along those lines. Violent crime is plaguing the inner cities. More people, especially children, are poor than twenty years ago. Homelessness and public begging are commonplace in U.S. cities. Family bonds are weakening. Urban riots result not only from justifiable resentment and rage but also from a contempt for life and civil decency. Meanwhile, U.S. voters have become increasingly cynical about government, elected officials, and bureaucrats.

But we are far from helpless. There are ways to begin to turn things around. This book is a pragmatic blend of conservative and liberal approaches to that task. It is not built on the belief that government can fix every problem. But it is grounded in the idea that government can take specific actions to make some things better. Some of these actions require higher spending. Some merely depend on spending more intelligently. In some areas current government spending can be cut. The book is also based on the proposition that the United States should pay now—through tax increases and spending cuts—both for current programs and for any new government spending and should not try to push the costs off onto the future by borrowing.

It deals with three major areas of national life: health care, social policy (homelessness, crime control, problems of families and children, and education and training), and public investment (research and infrastructure). The authors were not asked to state how to wholly eradicate the problem they were addressing, but were requested to identify which government actions work and which do not. They were asked to identify shortcomings in the organization of government activities, to recommend changes, and to identify programs that should

1

be curtailed. If they concluded that increases in public expenditures would help solve important problems, they were asked to explain why and to estimate the costs of the expansion.

The results varied. The chapter on health care examines three quite different alternatives to reforming the health care system and recommends the one that most nearly builds on the present system. Additional federal expenditures would be required to extend health care to those who do not now have access, and rigorous controls on both private and public health care spending are proposed. In contrast, the most important improvements in government policy regarding infrastructure and research involve reforms in program structure, in how government allocates funds to research, and in how it designs highways and airports and sets prices for their use. If such changes were made, the nation could reap substantial benefits by spending modest additional sums on infrastructure and related investments, far less than often proposed.

The four chapters on social policy reject many existing and proposed federal policies as ineffective or unproven. These chapters focus on those in which results have already been demonstrated or where evidence is strong that new programs are likely to be effective. The net cost of the social programs the authors recommend is relatively modest, but looms larger in the context of a federal budget already badly out of balance. The authors provide evidence that the recommended measures will improve the conditions they are addressing. But in no case do they claim that those measures will "solve" the problems.

We hold the conviction that taxes generally distort private economic decisions, but large government deficits do such serious economic damage that increases in current tax rates are imperative. By siphoning off private saving from investments at home or abroad, deficits retard growth and pile up unpaid bills for this generation and those to come.

We present a budget program that not only pays for suggested changes in domestic policy but effectively achieves a balanced budget in ten years. It would be economically desirable to go further and achieve a modest surplus, but the magnitude of the budget deficit currently puts that goal beyond reach. Our program includes expansions in some current government activities. We also suggest expenditure cuts in defense and civilian programs. To pay for the extension of health insurance to those who do not now have it and to meet the fiscal goals we set forth, we show that taxes will have to be raised and by how much.

Health Care

Over the past fifteen years the number of people without health insurance has risen from 27 million to 35 million. Sharp and continuous increases in costs have brought financial crises to U.S. businesses that sponsor health insurance for 150 million workers and their families, to governments whose budgets are being wrecked, and to individuals who fear loss of insurance coverage.

Henry J. Aaron outlines these problems and describes the major alternative proposals for extending coverage and controlling costs. He takes for granted a public consensus that essentially all Americans should have health insurance. Three major approaches to this goal have been advanced: national health insurance, under which government would sponsor coverage for a defined list of services and pay for them through increased taxes; tax credits, under which everyone would be required to buy health insurance and the government would provide refundable tax credits that would cover all of the costs for the poor and a declining share for those better off; and extended employer-sponsored health insurance with a public backup plan for people not covered through their own work or that of a family member.

Aaron points out that all three approaches achieve universal coverage through government mandates that increase the share of national health costs financed by the public sector. They differ in the degree to which costs currently borne by private payers are shifted to government budgets. He suggests that the greater the proportion of health care costs shifted from private to public budgets, the greater will be the redistribution of income and the more intense and protracted the debate about reform. He urges that reform of health care financing not be held hostage to protracted debates about income redistribution. Instead, he recommends that Congress seek universal coverage by extending and building on the current system of employer-sponsored health insurance, rather than by replacing it.

Too much is spent on health care because insurance encourages patients to demand costly care and physicians to provide it even when the benefits are small. This problem cannot be entirely avoided under any system in which patients are spared most of the cost of care when they are ill. Since extension of insurance coverage will only aggravate this problem, new methods of controlling growth of health care spending are essential. Increased competition can do some of the job, but it alone is unlikely to control growth of low-benefit, high-cost health care because it leaves the incentives of patients and physicians unchanged. In contrast, governmentally enforced local and regional budget limits on private health care spending would force providers to weigh the effectiveness of various medical interventions. But budget limits must be converted into specific decisions limiting health care spending by individual insurers and providers. This process carries a risk of bureaucratic rigidity and public opposition as some health care procedures are curtailed or delayed. A combination of budget caps on both public and private health care outlays, together with policies to improve information for those who buy health insurance and use health services (often called "managed competition"), offers the best hope of limiting growth of health care spending while preserving flexibility in insurance and health care systems.

Social Policy

This book examines policies addressed to four major social concerns: homelessness, crime, problems of families and children, and education. These problems have emerged over many years, reflect broad social and economic trends that will be difficult and slow to reverse, and have defied the best efforts of well-meaning people, inside government and out, to solve them. But even if complete solutions lie beyond reach, in each case, the situation can be improved. Doing so will require changes in a variety of policies, no one of which will stand out as decisive. As emphasized in some of the chapters below, many actions must be undertaken simultaneously for any to make much difference. They may take many years to bear fruit. Elected officials who tell the American public that policy changes will bring quick improvements mislead their constituency and are unsuited to guide the nation on these issues. Impatience is not a substitute for commitment.

Homelessness

Homelessness was not a serious public problem fifteen years ago. But now roughly half a million people are homeless on any given day. Most are single men or mothers with young children. Many are simply too poor to afford housing. Some cannot be housed because they are severely mentally ill, abusing alcohol or drugs, have physical disabilities, or have some combination of these problems.

Several trends have converged to create the problem. The supply of low-cost housing, including flophouses and single-room occupancy hotels, has dwindled. Earnings at the lower end of the wage distribution have fallen, and inflation has eroded the value of welfare grants. As a result, fewer people can afford today's more costly housing. Increased cocaine abuse, especially crack, has added to the number of people unable to function in the family or at work. State mental hospitals no longer house and care for the indigent mentally ill. The community health services that were supposed to replace the hospitals were not developed or were insufficient, and the housing in which some of the poor mentally ill lived disappeared. And changes in the law or in its interpretation denied local authorities the power they once had to jail vagrants or to hospitalize the mentally ill.

Gordon Berlin and William McAllister describe government attempts to help the homeless and the reasons these efforts failed. Because affordable, standard-quality, permanent housing and services are scarce, making them available only to homeless people could induce precariously housed people to become homeless, overwhelming local governments and worsening the problem. Efforts to identify and assist those who are likely to become homeless will not work because homelessness is a relatively rare event and policymakers cannot accurately predict who will become homeless or which interventions will be effective.

Berlin and McAllister outline three options for dealing with homelessness. The first—to boost all low incomes and increase the supply of low-rent housing for everyone or to drastically lower housing standards—would end homelessness but is unlikely to be adopted because it is too expensive or politically unfeasible. The second—to continue to treat homelessness as a temporary problem requiring only emergency programs—has the virtues of lower costs and greater political attractiveness, but makes sense only if the problem is truly temporary. Berlin and McAllister argue that it is not.

Under these conditions, the authors propose a third strategy. This aims first to get the homeless off the streets and into temporary housing and then to provide services that move people into permanent housing and allow them to function with as much independence as possible. Because most of those who enter temporary shelters eventually find permanent housing on their own and because resources to help the homeless will always be scarce, Berlin and McAllister urge that government-supplied permanent housing be provided only to the homeless who have been in temporary shelters for an extended period.

For the mentally ill and the alcohol- or drug-dependent, assistance with permanent housing should be given only after they have received appropriate social services and, for the alcohol- and drug-dependent, only after they have adhered to residential rules and to treatment regimens for an extended period. Delayed permanent housing assistance and stiff behavioral standards for the chemically dependent are essential both to deter people from entering shelters to qualify for housing and to mitigate the pathologies that contribute to remaining homeless.

Housing subsidies will be necessary for many of the homeless who will never be able to earn enough to afford even the most basic standard housing. The federal government should provide housing or vouchers for about 380,000 single adults and families. In addition, local governments should relax local housing codes to enable the construction or conversion of housing that would be below current standards, including single-room occupancy hotels.

The total cost of this strategy would run approximately $5 billion annually (in 1992 dollars). While state and local governments should contribute to these efforts, the total cost is too great for them to absorb. In addition, each locality hopes that if it refuses to provide services, the homeless will tend to move elsewhere and impose costs on some other community. For these reasons, the federal government will have to bear most of the burden if the job is to be done.

Crime

Two wars on crime have been fought since the mid-1960s, reports John DiIulio. The first war, waged from 1967 to 1980, aimed to eradicate what were then thought to be root causes of crime: poverty and unemployment. Whether the war was never really fought, poorly executed, or flawed in conception remains in dispute. That it was not won is beyond doubt. Rates of incarceration and lengths of sentences declined. Crime rates did not.

The second war, initiated by the Reagan administration in 1981, was directed against criminals. It is still under way. The administration called states and localities into the battle against crime, but itself remained outside the fray, except for efforts to interdict the flow of drugs, restore the death penalty, and exhort lower-level governments. Rates of incarceration and lengths of sentences increased, but crime rates and convictions climbed so fast that the number of convicts on parole or probation skyrocketed.

The problem, DiIulio points out, is that evidence does not support the effectiveness of most commonly recommended interventions. Advocates of longer sentences, gun control, increased use of probation and other forms of supervision, increased interdiction of drugs, or measures to combat poverty cannot cite good evidence that these methods actually curb crime. In contrast, evaluations suggest that two other interventions would produce benefits worth an increase in public expenditures.

The first responds to the dramatic increase in the proportion of the prison population incarcerated for drug-related crimes. Although strong theoretical arguments can be adduced to support legalization of drugs, DiIulio does not recommend it. The arguments in favor of legalization rest on the proposition that if drugs were legal, street prices would fall, eliminating the enormous profits that lure suppliers into an illegal business. With lower prices, the rewards to criminal distribution would be slashed, and fewer users would rob, steal, and kill to sustain their habits. Nevertheless, DiIulio characterizes legalization as nonviable, partly because it gives insufficient weight to the increased use that lowered prices might induce, but more fundamentally because a large majority of the public has repeatedly and strongly expressed opposition to such a policy.

DiIulio recommends instead drastically expanded drug treatment programs for prisoners. Because recidivism among released convicts is so high and because the average criminal commits so many crimes a year, even a very small reduction in recidivism would easily justify the costs of drug treatment for all inmates with drug histories. Evaluations do not indicate that these programs would cause a dramatic fall in the national crime rate, but do show that they would reduce it enough to justify greatly expanded treatment. The cost of such a program in federal and state prisons, DiIulio estimates, would be approximately $500 million annually.

The second intervention that, on the evidence, works well enough to justify expansion is community policing in inner cities: the regular use of patrols, on foot or in cars, to put the police in routine contact with neighborhood residents. This would replace the style of policing that many police departments, such as that in Los Angeles, have developed (sometimes called "911 policing"), in which the police are largely invisible to residents except when summoned to deal with complaints. Experiments with intensified patrolling indicate that it helps reduce crime and increase neighborhood security. Since the exact method of community policing that works best is unclear and may vary from city to city, additional evaluations are still warranted. But expenditure of an additional $1 billion a year in federal assistance to cities for the hiring of more police would support a doubling in community policing in poor urban neighborhoods and would greatly improve safety. While DiIulio stresses that policing is and should remain primarily a local responsibility in the United States, the federal government, by initiating two wars on crime, has assumed a role in assisting localities. By channeling assistance into community policing, the federal government could make it effective.

Children and Families

Just as family incomes have become more unequal, so have the lives and prospects of young children. Isabel V. Sawhill points out that while some indicators of the average well-being of children are improving, others portray serious problems. Average family incomes are at historic highs. Parents are better educated than ever before. At the same time, child poverty has risen since the early 1970s. Divorce rates have stabilized but are higher than in the past, so that children are more likely to spend part or all of their early lives in the care of only one parent. Two-thirds of black children and one-fifth of white children are born to unmarried women. Television brings not only educational entertainment but a ceaseless montage of violence into the lives of children.

Sawhill examines three strategies to help families and young children. The first would emphasize increased incomes, through such instruments as family allowances or refundable tax credits. Providing substantial assistance to all families entails large increases in spending or reductions in revenues that would have to be paid for by higher tax rates, higher deficits, or other means. Sawhill argues that public policy can do more for less cost to help families and children in other ways. The one form of income support she endorses is the earned income tax credit, which she would increase to enable virtually all of the full-time working poor to move above official poverty thresholds. The net cost to the federal budget would be $9 billion annually when fully effective.

The second approach consists of interventions to help families function better. Such public programs include support for food and health care under the women, infants, and children (WIC) program, childhood immunization, and home visiting. The most costly element of this strategy is a large expansion of Head Start into a day-long, year-round program providing services to children starting at age 3. To maintain quality, it will be necessary to boost salaries and training. The net cost of all these expansions will be $7 billion annually when fully effective.

The third approach is to encourage parents to plan their families, to do a more adequate job of both nurturing and supporting financially any children who are born, and to make sure that government policies themselves do no harm. Because life prospects for both teenage mothers and their children are so poor, public efforts to discourage teenage pregnancy and childbearing are particularly essential. Making contraception more readily available is effective and saves money in short order. Prohibiting abortions would damage life prospects of young women and increase public spending. By one estimate it would result in 75,000 additional births to teenagers and cost $500 million annually in higher cash assistance payments. It is striking that the U.S. teenage pregnancy rate is three times higher than that in Canada or in any Western European country and that the U.S. teenage birthrate is two to six times higher, although U.S. teenagers are no more sexually active than teenagers in Canada or Europe.

These interventions will help millions of American families. However, Sawhill stresses, powerful forces, largely beyond the influence of policies such as these, are shaping family structure. First, economic changes have made the one-earner family a luxury that only the most educated can afford. Wages paid to young men with low skills and little education have fallen sharply, so that the economics of supporting a family have become much harsher. Second, major cultural changes have affected society as a whole. Women have entered the labor force, lengthened their working lives, and intensified their commitments to careers outside the home. All fifty states have enacted no-fault divorce laws. Divorce and out-of-wedlock births are increasingly accepted. In general, differences between the lives of men and women have narrowed, and the old order is unlikely to be reestablished. These changes have brought profound benefits, especially to adult women who have been freed from stifling restrictions of earlier ages. But they also entail costs. Sawhill makes clear that while trying to reverse history is fruitless and undesirable, ignoring the costs, especially for children, and refusing to do something about them is shortsighted.

Education and Training

Between 1948 and 1973, earnings of fully employed 40-year-old men almost doubled. Since 1973 those earnings have fallen 4 percent. In 1979, 25- to 34-year-old male college graduates earned 13 percent more than high school graduates of the same age. By 1989 the gap had widened to 43 percent. Growth of average earnings has virtually stopped and inequality has widened. The reward to being well educated has dramatically increased, not primarily because the well educated are earning more, but because the less educated are earning less.

These facts underlie the recommendations Richard J. Murnane and Frank Levy make for improving the U.S. educational system and on-the-job training. Because of the changing demands of modern technology, the labor market will increasingly reward workers who have the skill to participate in complicated production processes and office procedures and to solve problems as well as perform rote tasks. American elementary and secondary students score lower on standardized tests than do students from most other countries, rich and poor. To educate workers for future labor market demands, as well as to correct current flaws, American schools will have to change.

The key to reform of U.S. schools is across-the-board change: the development of new curricula and examinations that require students to solve problems, not just learn facts; the ability to attract teachers with higher skills in math, science, and other subject areas; the establishment of standards that students and teachers must meet; and a change in incentives to make sure that students who take demanding courses and do well in them derive tangible benefits, even if they do not go on to selective colleges and universities. For example, Murnane and Levy urge that the skills of graduating high school seniors be assessed and that the results be made available to potential employers for use in determining initial assignments and starting wages.

Systemic reform will be advanced by increased parental choice among public schools. Such choice will provide information about which programs parents value and can help generate support for innovative educational practices. But choice is no substitute for direct efforts to improve each school. Murnane and Levy see little evidence to suggest that giving parents vouchers to pay for private, as well as public, schools will make much difference in educational achievement. Past studies indicate far more variation in educational quality within public schools than between public and private schools. Furthermore, the difference between average educational performance of students in private and public schools is tiny relative to the gap between current overall performance and the standards that students will have to meet if they are to operate effectively in the labor market.

Murnane and Levy place particular stress on the need to implement all parts of a program for systemic reform. Better curricula mean little if students have few incentives to study or if teachers are unable to teach them. All schools must have sufficient resources to innovate. The value of improvements in the school will be undercut if employers are unaware of student performance.

Murnane and Levy address their recommendations for educational reform mostly to state and local governments because education is and will remain primarily their responsibility. Nonetheless, they stress, the federal government can help. It can maintain and increase aid for disadvantaged students and remove impediments in current law to the best use of this support. They recommend increasing 1992 federal aid for educationally disadvantaged children from its current $6.1 billion to $8 billion as a means of supporting extra services in schools with high concentrations of low-income children.

The federal government could help states recruit teachers. The primary attraction for better trained teachers will be a combination of higher pay and improved working conditions. Although these are principally matters for the states, the federal government can help by supporting experimental programs seeking to find ways to meet some of the most critical needs, especially more science and math teachers and more teachers from minority groups. The federal government can also help, both with research and through coordination, in developing educational standards for student achievement and testing techniques to assess that achievement. Not enough is known currently about how to reconcile the legitimate interest of society in exercising some control over what is taught with the need to treat teachers as professionals, not as functionaries. Murnane and Levy recommend federal support for research on how to reconcile these two objectives.

Only training and increased experience, not school reform, can upgrade the skills of workers already in the labor force. The American economy does not provide private employers optimal incentives for training, and the country invests less in training than do many competitor nations. As increasing numbers of U.S. companies adopt new production processes that stress worker responsibility for problem solving and quality control, the rewards to higher skills will increase. To date, publicly sponsored programs to train disadvantaged workers have produced benefits more consistently for women than for men. Expansion of public support for training is warranted to help support management initiatives. Murnane and Levy recommend an increase in the federal budget for worker training.

Public Investment

Since the founding of the republic, the federal government has invested in what now is called "infrastructure." Before the twentieth century the federal government's role in promoting science was small. Since World War II, the federal government has assumed primary responsibility for funding basic research and a major role in applied research. In recent years, critics have alleged that the federal government spends too little in support of public investment and science.

Research and Development

Output per worker has increased in part because the amount of capital workers use and their educational attainment have grown over time. Much of the increased productivity, however, arises from scientific advances, generated by basic and applied research and managerial improvements. The annual return to society from expenditures on research and development (R&D) is estimated to run as high as 30 to 50 percent. Market economies tend to do too little R&D because many of the benefits accrue to people or businesses other than the sponsor. Governments try to offset this bias by awarding patents, directly supporting research, and providing tax incentives.

Linda R. Cohen and Roger G. Noll emphasize that much can go awry between the recognition of this governmental role and the implementation of policies to support research and development. Public support for R&D can undermine market competition, and pork barrel politics can distort the allocation and design of research support. The government may select projects that have low return, support projects just because they boost employment, and sustain projects long after the chances they might reveal anything useful have vanished.

Over the past quarter century the U.S. private sector has increased R&D investment faster than government has done. After comparing the U.S. research effort with that in other countries, the authors conclude that this nation does not appear to be a laggard, either in the size of its overall R&D effort or in government support for R&D. If there is a problem with the U.S. R&D effort, they say it is with respect to how the nation allocates and manages R&D, not with how much it spends.

Cutbacks in expenditures on national defense make some reallocation of R&D inevitable and desirable, even if defense R&D is cut less than outlays on hardware, operations, and personnel. These cuts will mean most in civilian industries, such as microelectronics, that have important defense and nondefense applications. Although the defense cutback creates an opportunity to shift R&D support to activities that will boost civilian productivity, Cohen and Noll stress a serious risk: much R&D has won congressional support because of its connection to defense and could not have won approval on its civilian technological merits alone. Indeed, even R&D with primarily civilian benefits has often been characterized as necessary for national defense to secure approval. They emphasize the need for Congress to begin to accept purely civilian justifications for federal support of R&D.

Health research is a second area, Cohen and Noll suggest, where reallocation should be considered. This issue is difficult because scientific opportunities in biomedical research are unusually rich and the potential benefits to humanity extraordinary. On the other hand, the United States is now troubled by high and rising expenditures on medical care. Most other countries do not use the fruits of medical R&D nearly as much as the United States does. With reform of health care financing, U.S. practices will come to resemble those abroad. Cohen and Noll suggest that a shift of research support to other fields might yield increased benefits.

The practical question is how to reallocate effectively. The principal vehicles for publicly supported civilian research are research joint ventures, groups of companies that join together to address a defined set of problems, and generic research centers, which carry out research of potential benefit to a broad range of companies. Cohen and Noll stress that research centers should focus on problems no single company or small group of companies would pursue and joint ventures should include whole industries, so that government subsidies do not put excluded companies at a disadvantage. Research subsidies should be limited to R&D that will not be immediately appropriable by foreign companies. The government should prevent joint ventures from undertaking research that would tend to foster monopoly. Finally, the government should bear most of the cost of R&D so that companies will participate willingly even if most of the benefits accrue to others.

Cohen and Noll point to a pervasive and dangerous bias in political management of R&D: the tendency to support big projects for which congressional and executive sponsors can take credit, such as the supersonic transport, the Clinch River breeder reactor, and a number of large energy development projects. This tendency is exacerbated by fragmented jurisdiction over R&D among many congressional commit-tees and executive agencies. Accordingly, Cohen and Noll recommend that jurisdiction over technology research should be consolidated in one executive agency and one committee in each house of Congress and that such research should be separated from such glamorous demonstration projects as the space shuttle and synthetic fuels plants.

The federal government provides grants and contracts that directly support research at universities. In addition, by paying overhead charges on grants and contracts, it indirectly supports other university-based activities. Cohen and Noll stress the importance of finding an alternative to current arrangements for overhead reimbursement that does not undermine the contribution of university-based research in making U.S. universities preeminent in the world. They urge an end to the ultimately futile effort to calculate precise fractions of the costs of libraries, electricity, building maintenance, and other general overhead items to be attributed to specific research projects. The federal government should simply add to research grants a reimbursement fee calculated in advance to approximate estimates of overhead costs. Both the universities and the government could share the substantial savings from reduced accounting costs necessitated by current rules.

In short, Cohen and Noll hold that the government need not spend more to support research and development, but should spend more wisely.

Public Infrastructure

Federal spending on infrastructure—roads, airports, conservation projects, school buildings, and other structures—fell from 4 percent of gross national product in the 1960s to 2 percent in the late 1980s. This drop, together with perceived shortcomings in the adequacy of public capital, has led some analysts to call for large increases in public investment. Some have estimated returns from such expenditures that vastly exceed returns available on private investment.

Clifford Winston and Barry Bosworth examine these claims. They find justification for some additional public investment, but not for huge increases. There are large potential gains from correctly pricing the use of public capital, especially for roads and airports, and from correcting certain engineering errors in the original design of the interstate highway system. Their principal finding is that the major need is not for additional federal dollars, but for radical reform in the way the nation now designs highways and airports and prices their use. Moreover, unless use of public capital is correctly priced, the benefits from investing more will be reduced.

One approach to assessing the needs for investment in public infrastructure is to calculate the annual investment that would be required to maintain the ratio of the stock of public capital to GNP. The authors estimate that to meet this goal 1990 outlays ($55 billion) would have to be increased by a relatively modest $8 billion for what is called "core" infrastructure—roads, bridges, public utilities, airports, and mass transit. To achieve the same result for all the rest of the public infrastructure, such as school buildings and public offices, 1990 outlays ($130 billion) would have to be raised by an additional $3 billion.

To achieve the more ambitious goal of restoring the ratio of public capital to its historic 1970 peak level over the next ten years would require an additional $33 billion a year in annual investment outlays. And to accomplish the same goal for the total public stock of capital, including school buildings, would require infrastructure investment to rise by $83 billion. But, the authors point out, this latter objective has little rationale. The appropriate stock of school buildings, for example, depends upon the size of the school-age population, which reached historic highs several decades ago and has fallen dramatically since then. The annual cost of maintaining the interstate highway system is much smaller than the cost of building it.

An alternative source of estimates for infrastructure needs are engineering studies and surveys of what it would cost to achieve specified physical standards for the nation's highways, bridges, airports, and other infrastructure. The authors' analysis suggests that for the core infrastructure, studies produced by various federal agencies generate investment needs roughly equivalent to those required to preserve the ratio of infrastructure to GNP—that is, little additional investment would be required to maintain the status quo, but much larger amounts are needed to make up deficiencies and improve the current infrastructure.

All calculations of investment necessary to reach some ratio of the public capital stock to GNP or some set of physical standards ignore the growing evidence of waste and inefficiency in the present system and do not weigh costs against benefits. The needs of the country could be better served by modifying the system of prices imposed on users of roads and airports, rather than by sharply boosting investment.

Road damage is a steeply increasing function of vehicle weight per axle, yet current road user charges encourage trucks with high weights per axle. Furthermore, no additional charge is imposed on drivers who choose to travel at peak hours despite the costs from increasing congestion they impose on other drivers. Instituting road use taxes based on axle weight and on use of roads during times of peak use would bring substantial benefits. Congestion charges at airports would reduce delay by spreading flights more evenly throughout the day. Collectively, these benefits would take many forms: reduced resurfacing costs, reduced vehicle damage from potholes, and a reduction in time lost waiting in traffic jams or in planes awaiting takeoff or stacked up for landing. Potential benefits from efficient pricing could rise to an estimated $25 billion annually by also thickening roads, since thicker roads cut maintenance expenses far more than they raise resurfacing costs, and by adding runways to busy airports, thereby cutting the costs of delay. If these various reforms were undertaken, the estimated benefits could be achieved with only a slight increase—$3 billion a year—in the current level of highway and airport investment.

Winston and Bosworth also decry the same kinds of political ineffi- ciencies in the allocation of infrastructure investment that Cohen and Noll find in the allocation of support for science. The pork barrel is stuffed mainly with public infrastructure. The result is the selection of projects on the basis of political, rather than economic, considerations. Increased investment will not eliminate this influence. Pricing reform will mitigate its effects.

Paying the Bills

When fully phased in (by 1997), the programs recommended above would require about $90 billion in federal expenditures ($78 billion in today's purchasing power), two-thirds of which ($60 billion) is required to pay for the extension of health insurance. But under current policies and programs, the federal budget deficit is already projected to be $265 billion, or 3.4 percent of GDP, by 1997 and rising. In the chapter on the federal budget, Charles Schultze sets forth the economic reasons why the financing of any new or expanded federal programs should be considered only in conjunction with the much larger budgetary actions needed to eliminate the deficit.

Schultze proposes a comprehensive series of budgetary and program- matic measures with five components. The first is enactment of a health care reform package, with tough cost controls on both private and public spending, along the lines recommended by Henry Aaron. Cost controls that gradually pare 2 percentage points from the annual growth of health care costs would reduce projected federal budget outlays by $21 billion in 1997 and $86 billion in 2002. The second component is the institution of a special value-added tax of 4 percent on consumer goods and services (rising to 5 percent by 2002), with revenues earmarked for the federal costs of medicare not covered by payroll taxes and premiums and for the cost of extending health coverage to the uninsured. Under this scheme, the value-added tax rate would have to be raised (as would the current payroll tax for hospital insurance) if health care cost controls failed to slow cost growth as projected. Schultze argues that this feature of the proposed financing would set up political pressures to adopt tough and effective cost controls.

The third element in the overall budget program consists of large cuts in federal spending: a $47 billion cut in 1997 defense spending below the currently planned path, a $20 billion cut in civilian spending, and a substantial increase in the premium charged for part B medicare physicians' benefits. The fourth component of the package is a proposal to tax social security benefits more like private pension funds; this proposal would bring in $17 billion annually. The final component of the package is $25 billion in increased spending to finance the bulk of the programs (other than health care reforms) recommended in the preceding chapters.

Adoption of all five sets of proposals would reduce the federal budget deficit by $180 billion in 1997 and virtually eliminate it by 2002. These projections depend on achievement of the 2-percentage-point reduction in the rate of growth of health care spending. If the growth of health care costs is not reduced, the payroll and value-added taxes and beneficiary premiums would have to be raised by $75 billion in 2002, and a modest $40 billion deficit would still remain.

Summing Up

For the quarter century following World War II, the United States was distinguished by can-do confidence. Earnings rose strongly. The members of each generation justifiably expected to earn more than their parents had. Most young people emerged from school able to do what employers asked of them. Financial access to health care steadily expanded as most Americans secured health insurance through work, and public programs covered most others. American science and technol-

---

What Government Can Do

Health care
- Mandate employer-sponsored health insurance for full-time workers.
- Control health care costs with managed competition, backed up by a cap on total spending.

Social policy
- Increase temporary housing for the homeless and treatment for mentally ill and substance abusers.
- Give federal subsidies for 380,000 housing units allocated only to homeless who obey strict rules in residences and adhere to treatment regimens.
- Require treatment for all federal and state prisoners with drug problems.
- Give federal funds to double community patrolling in high-crime urban areas.
- Increase earned income tax credit to eliminate poverty among fully employed families.
- Provide day-long Head Start to all preschool children age 3 or older.
- Increase federal availability of services to support families, prevent teenage pregnancies, and protect the right to abortions.
- Reform education: develop new curricula, upgrade teacher skills, establish performance standards for teachers and students, develop and administer tests of student skills that are made available to employers.
- Increase federal aid for educationally disadvantaged students and give school districts using this aid greater flexibility.

---

ogy led the world in most fields. An interstate highway system, unique in the world, laced the North American continent.

Not everyone shared this progress. The civil rights revolution removed the most blatant legal shackles that suppressed blacks, but full economic equality remained only a dream. Efforts to reduce workplace discrimination against women had just started. The movement to end discrimination against homosexuals had not even begun. Civil disorder swelled during the 1960s but subsided in the 1970s. Nevertheless, most of the nation shared in the feeling that America was on the right track.

That vaunted American optimism is now in hibernation. Large tax cuts and increases in defense spending created deficits during the early

- Allow limited parental choice among public schools.
- Offer federal support for teacher recruitment, educational experiments, and development of educational standards.

Public investment
- Reallocate federal R&D support from defense to civilian research other than biomedical research, avoid large "pork barrel" R&D, consolidate political control of R&D in one executive agency and one committee in each house of Congress.
- Replace cost accounting for reimbursement of indirect research costs at universities with a simple percentage formula.
- Build thicker highways, charge users on basis of damage to highways and congestion costs, add runways and air traffic control devices at airports and impose congestion charges.

Budget reform
- Balance the budget by 2002
  —impose health care cost controls (− $86 billion)
  —reduce spending on selected domestic federal programs
  (− $25 billion)
  —reduce defense spending further (− $85 billion)
  —tax social security more like private pensions (− $21 billion)
  —impose value-added tax earmarked for health programs
  (− $194 billion)
  —lower interest costs because of smaller federal debt
  (− $105 billion)
  —increase top-bracket tax rate from 31 to 34 percent
  (− $11 billion)
  —and increase spending for actions above (+ $121 billion)

and mid-1980s. High and rising interest payments on the debt and federal health care spending, now rising at 12 percent a year, are perpetuating those deficits. They have done double damage, siphoning off private saving that could have financed productivity-enhancing investment and stifling federal efforts to do anything to address the country's social problems that might cost money. Political leaders, fearful of punishment at the hands of their constituents, have shrunk from tax increases and spending cuts that would end deficits and provide the means for the federal government to deal with the nation's problems.

Behind political timidity is ideological division. Conservatives have promoted the idea that government typically is inefficient and ineffective, and the less of it the better. They have argued that policies motivated by the desire to do good instead do harm, that taxes seriously distort economic decisions and depress economic incentives, and that any tax increase to balance the budget or finance new social spending would be the most damaging blow that could be delivered to the American economy. More recently these themes have been enlarged to encompass the view that erosion of family values has caused social deterioration in America, and that government is helpless to improve the lot of the poor and the downtrodden without changes in those values.

The traditional liberal view, that an appropriate federal program backed up by enough money can solve almost any social problem, has not been much in evidence lately. Previous program failures and large federal deficits have silenced most traditional liberals. But a new view has gained ground that savings from cuts in defense spending and possibly revenues from additional taxes on the rich should be used not for deficit reduction, but for investments in "infrastructure." This term is sweepingly defined to include outlays not only for roads, airports, bridges, and other traditional forms of public capital, but also for education, training, urban reconstruction, and other social programs and for revitalizing older industries and promoting new high-tech enterprises. Where conservatives see great economic harm in even small tax increases, especially on the well-to-do, liberals see none even in large ones, as long as they are levied on the well-to-do.

Both liberals and conservatives see only part of what is needed to reverse the sense of helplessness sapping American will. The problems confronting the United States are large and complex, solutions to many of them remain elusive, and government policy cannot be expected to make more than a small contribution to their solution. But solid research establishes that many government programs are effective and worth their cost and that reforms can improve the effectiveness of others. Still others are not worth what they cost and should be curtailed.

Drug treatment for prison inmates and increased community policing will not solve the crime problem, but they will help. Powerful social and economic trends buffet families and children, but children can be prepared for school and parents can be provided work-enhancing income support. Homelessness will exist as long as people are poor, low-cost housing is scarce, and mental illness and drug abuse abound; but many of the homeless can be housed and assisted with the problems that made them become homeless. Large improvements in the educational achievement of American children may require parental insistence that children watch less television and work harder, but broad school reforms can encourage those changes. There is no good reason why the United States should spend so much more on health care than other countries do and yet have so many more citizens without access to health care. Pork barrel politics may be an inescapable consequence of representative democracy, but government can support research and development more efficiently than it does. And instead of spending huge additional sums on highways and airports, imaginative policies can reduce congestion and maintenance costs at only modest budget cost.

A common thread that runs through this book is the theme of mutual responsibility—responsibility on the part of citizen-taxpayers to help those who need it, and responsibility on the part of those who need assistance to help themselves. Drug rehabilitation for prisoners is something society should offer, but it will not work unless prisoners use it. Society should provide treatment and services for homeless substance abusers, but should also make it more difficult for them to refuse help and continue panhandling. The chances for effective systemic reform in education can be improved with federal incentives and technical assistance, but parents, school boards, and teachers' unions must take responsibility for seeing it through. And expansion of the earned income tax credit is a way society can help those who work hard but earn too little to escape poverty.

This book stems finally from the belief that all citizens of this nation share an interest in confronting each of these problems. The bonds of nationhood are weakened for all by homelessness, untreated illness, crime, family decay, and poor education, even when these problems seem to afflict only strangers. Unless all Americans come to see the children in a public housing project murdered by random gunfire as their own children, or to feel a personal identity as Americans with people who are unlike themselves in class, color, geography, or life-style, they will easily lose heart and withdraw when attempts to help "others" seem to fail. Americans have traditionally displayed fortitude, grit, and stubborn determination when trying to help themselves, their friends, and their neighbors. Now they must use these admirable qualities to deal with their nation's problems.

2 HENRY J. AARON

Health Care Financing

THE HEALTH CARE financing system is plagued by two major problems. First, costs are high and soaring. Currently, health care absorbs 15 percent of net domestic product and is claiming an additional 1 percent of net domestic product every two and one-half years. If this pace continues, the share of net domestic product spent on health care will reach 16 percent in 1994 and 18 percent in 1998. Second, roughly 35 million people are uninsured, and most who are currently insured fear loss of coverage, curtailment of health benefits, and the prospect of greatly increased out-of-pocket expenses.[1] In addition to these overriding financial problems, many medical procedures are untested and of doubtful efficacy. For people in poor neighborhoods, services are unavailable, hard to reach, or available only from impersonal and expensive hospital emergency rooms.

Although rising costs and actual or feared lack of coverage have produced widespread calls for reform and an outpouring of specific proposals, no consensus has emerged on the character of reform. All major plans recognize that government compulsion is necessary to achieve universal coverage, although they differ on the form of compulsion and in the way they seek to control rising costs.

The emergence of such a popular consensus is of urgent importance, both to reduce the expenditure of vast sums on low-benefit health care and to extend financial access to those now without it. The plan that is adopted is likely to build on current employer-sponsored health insurance,

Marvin H. Kosters was the discussant for this chapter. The author wishes to thank Karan Singh for research assistance.

1. Perhaps twice as many lack coverage at some time over a period of one or two years, but 50 percent of those found to be uninsured on any given day are insured six months later. Katherine Swartz and Timothy D. McBride, "Spells without Health Insurance: Distribution of Durations and their Link to Point-in-Time Estimates of the Uninsured," *Inquiry*, vol. 27 (Fall 1990), pp. 281–88; and " 'Survey Shows Widespread Public Concern about Health Insurance Coverage and Costs," press release (Menlo Park, Calif.: Henry J. Kaiser Family Foundation, April 8, 1992).

not replace it. The principal reason is that radical changes in the way
the United States pays for the roughly $750 billion now spent on health
care would require a massive redistribution of income among income
classes, industries, and regions. Redistribution is always highly controversial and sometimes desirable, but the more reform of health care financing
is tied to income redistribution, the harder it will be to develop agreement
on how to achieve the primary goals of this reform: reducing excessive
outlays and assuring financial access. These objectives can be achieved
much faster if issues of income redistribution are left for another forum.

To achieve cost control, it is necessary to change the way physicians
and especially hospitals are paid. In particular, for reasons set forth
below, market-based competition alone cannot control growth of health
care spending. Effective control will require the imposition of budget
limits on hospitals and fee controls on other providers to overcome the
incentive of insured patients and their physicians to disregard cost in
choosing care, even when benefits are slight.

Breaking the Bank

U.S. expenditures on health care have three major characteristics: they
are large; they are growing fast; and they are highly concentrated on a
small fraction of the population.

What Is the Problem?

The facts of high outlays in the United States are widely known. The
United States spends more per capita on health care than any other
country: $2,354 in 1989, compared with $1,683 in Canada, the second
highest spending country, $1,232 in Germany, and $1,274 in France.
The United States spends 3 percentage points more of its total production
on health care than Canada.[2] U.S. medical outlays rose 5.5 percent per
year (after adjustment for general inflation) between 1985 and 1991,
widening the health care spending gap between the United States and
Canada. Despite greater outlays in the United States, satisfaction with
health care financing is higher abroad.

One reason the United States spends more on health care than other
countries is that per capita income remains higher in the United States

2. George J. Schieber, Jean-Pierre Poullier, and Leslie M. Greenwald, "Health Care
Systems in Twenty-Four Countries," *Health Affairs*, vol. 10 (Fall 1991), pp. 22–38.

than in any other developed nation, and the share of income devoted to health care rises with income. However, health care spending in the United States is unusually high even after adjusting for per capita income.

Rising outlays on a technologically dynamic sector are not usually a source of concern, but part of the increase in health care outlays is widely seen as wasteful. This view is soundly based, because sick patients who are insured do not have to pay most of the cost of health care. In such circumstances, the physician who acts as the patient's agent sees that the patient gets as much care as the patient would want if the patient knew as much about health care as the physician. The patient who pays nothing for care will want to use medical services that yield any benefit at all, regardless of the cost to society. This situation is a recipe for unnecessarily high but not necessarily rising expenditures.

Health care expenditures have been rising in the United States principally because of technological transformation of medical care.[3] New diagnostic techniques, such as computed tomography and magnetic resonance imaging, nuclear medicine, and sonography, are commonplace today, providing vastly improved information at little or no discomfort to the patient. New methods of treatment, such as organ transplants, coronary artery surgery and angioplasty, and artificial skin were also developed in recent decades. Nor is the development of new technology slowing: waiting in the wings are a host of new pharmaceutical agents (some designed independently and at considerable cost for each patient), implantable defibrillators for victims of heart disease, positron emission tomography, and many other advances.

The United States is not alone in facing rising costs of a rapidly expanding menu of beneficial diagnostic and therapeutic procedures financed so that patients face few costs at time of care. The incentives of patients and their physicians to demand low- as well as high-benefit care is the same whether governments or private insurers pay the bills. The United States has not imposed spending limits on physicians and hospitals, while other countries have done so, typically through budget limits on hospitals and fee controls on physicians. In the absence of any such limits, patients do not face what economists call a *budget constraint* when consuming health care, as they do in the purchase of other goods. The central issue in cost control is how to create arrangements that serve this function.

3. See Joseph Newhouse, "Medical Care Costs: How Much Welfare Loss?" *Journal of Economic Perspectives*, forthcoming.

In the absence of a budget constraint, health care spending is bound to grow quickly as science advances. While it is possible in principle for medical advances to replace costly procedures with less expensive ones, such advances are relatively uncommon. More typically, innovations expand the list of what medicine can do (replace joints with prostheses, transplant organs, or crush deposits in coronary arteries to improve circulation, for example) or replace painful and invasive procedures with less painful ones (lithotripsy in place of surgery to remove kidney stones, or CT scans to replace pneumoencephalograms, for example). Typically, as pain and invasiveness fall, the number of cases in which the procedure can be used increases, often so much that total costs increase even if the price per patient falls.

Not only do financial incentives encourage demand for essentially all beneficial care, but in addition physicians are not agreed on the need for various diagnostic and therapeutic procedures. As a result, many costly services are provided in situations where many physicians believe they are inappropriate and even harmful.[4] This interaction among a payment system that creates incentives to do everything that is beneficial regardless of cost, a technologically dynamic field with rapidly growing beneficial interventions, and a lack of clear and agreed indications for intervention jointly accounts for most of the increase of health care costs in the United States.[5] Various other factors that contribute to such high outlays are widely and incorrectly blamed for their rapid increase. These factors include high administrative costs, defective rules for compensating victims of medical negligence, and bad health habits.

Some analysts suggest that the United States could save as much as $95 billion in administrative costs by paying physicians and hospitals the way Canadians do.[6] More sober calculations suggest that offsetting costs under a reformed financing system would cancel most of the savings

---

4. See, for example, Robert H. Brook and Mary E. Vaiana, *Appropriateness of Care: A Chart Book*, report prepared for George Washington University, National Health Policy Forum (Washington, June 1989); and John Wennberg, "Outcomes Research, Cost Containment, and the Fear of Health Care Rationing," *New England Journal of Medicine*, vol. 323 (October 25, 1990), pp. 1202–04.

5. The rate of growth is slightly increased by the gradual aging of the U.S. population, which can be expected to add about 12 percent to total U.S. health care spending by 2020. This increase should be set against the annual growth in real per capita health care spending, which has been averaging over 4 percent in recent years.

6. Steffie Woolhandler and David U. Himmelstein, "The Deteriorating Administrative Efficiency of the U.S. Health Care System," *New England Journal of Medicine*, vol. 324 (May 2, 1991), pp. 1253–58.

in administrative outlays.[7] The opportunities for savings from reform of malpractice insurance and from improvements in health habits are even smaller. Total physician malpractice premiums absorbed only $5 billion of personal health care spending in 1990. The benefits of curtailing defensive medicine that confers no medical benefits whatsoever, but is prescribed to avoid litigation, are unlikely to approach even one year's growth in health care outlays.[8]

Improvements in health habits are highly desirable, but not because they would lower costs. Estimates of the economic consequences of a cessation of smoking, for example, indicate that it would generate small net medical savings at best and would on balance impose overall social costs. Those spared premature deaths from smoking-induced cancers, heart disease, or other sicknesses would eventually die from other more costly illnesses. Alzheimer's disease, for example, would generate costs even larger on average than those associated with deaths from smoking-induced illnesses. Premature deaths from smoking typically occur when working lives and associated payroll tax payments are largely complete but claims on social security retirement benefits have not yet begun. Many such deaths are from sudden and lethal coronaries and are therefore medically inexpensive. In addition, the costs of antismoking campaigns further offset any medical savings from reduced smoking. Similar problems are associated with other campaigns to improve health habits.[9]

Curtailing administrative outlays may save resources. Improving the malpractice compensation system would improve equity. Living healthier

7. Government Accounting Office, *Canadian Health Insurance: Lessons for the United States,* HRW-91-90 (June 1991); and J. F. Sheils and G. J. Young, "National Health Spending under a Single-Payor System: the Canadian Approach" (Washington: Lewin/ICF Staff working paper, November 21, 1991).

8. The Congressional Budget Office estimates that defensive medicine boosted physician outlays by $15.1 billion in 1989. The CBO estimate is based on James W. Moser and Robert Mussachio, "The Cost of Medical Professional Liability in the 1980s," *Medical Malpractice Management* (Summer 1991). Reform of malpractice insurance is highly desirable for other reasons, however. One reason is to assure that the estimated 99 percent of victims of medical negligence who now receive no compensation at all are assisted in some fashion. A second reason is to assure that the few physicians who account for a disproportionate share of medical negligence either improve or are removed from practice. See *Patients, Doctors, and Lawyers: Medical Injury, Malpractice Litigation, and Patient Compensation in New York: The Report of the Harvard Medical Practice Study to the State of New York* (Harvard Medical Practice Study, 1990), pp. 7-29, 7-39 to 7-40; and A. Russell Localio and others, "Relation between Malpractice Claims and Adverse Events due to Negligence—Results of the Harvard Medical Practice Study," *New England Journal of Medicine,* vol. 325 (July 25, 1991), p. 248.

9. Louise B. Russell, *Is Prevention Better Than Cure?* (Brookings, 1986).

lives is worthwhile because it makes people feel better and live longer. Although desirable, any savings from these sources are not answers to controlling the growth of health care spending. At best, these savings can be achieved only once. But real health care spending is now rising each year by about $40 billion. The plausible savings from all of these sources can only briefly offset the steady increase in medical costs.

Why Rising Costs Matter

Rising costs constitute a genuine economic problem for business, labor, and governments. They also lie at the root of discontent over current financing arrangements.

The economic problem. Producing health care uses capital, such as costly medical equipment and buildings, and skilled workers, such as physicians, nurses, technicians, and administrative staff. When health care is worth less than the other goods and services that could have been produced with those resources, there is a real economic loss. The current financial system virtually guarantees such losses.

When insured patients incur expenses greater than their deductibles, they pay only a small fraction of the cost of care—usually 10 or 20 percent when they are subject to coinsurance, or none at all when total expenses exceed the stop-loss limit that puts a cap on total liability of the insured. Such patients have an incentive to consume not only care that brings large benefits, but also care that brings benefits worth as little as 20 cents or perhaps even less to them, but that costs society resources worth $1. The result is economic waste.[10]

For workers whose productivity is rising slowly and for their employers, the rapid and partly wasteful increase in the cost of a major fringe benefit paid by employers means that either of two unfortunate consequences must follow: the growth of cash wages or other fringe benefits of employees is retarded, or prices of goods must increase. Both slow growth of real incomes.

---

10. Note that waste does not imply that the medical services in question are of no value, merely that the value is smaller than the benefits that could have been realized. Nor does waste of medical resources imply that resources are not wasted elsewhere in a market economy. Everyone has a list of wasteful consumption (usually consumption by someone else) or wasteful government expenditures. The United States might be better off if waste in sectors other than health care were eliminated before, or at least simultaneously with, the elimination of wasteful medical outlays. The point is simply that welfare improves if waste is reduced wherever it is found.

Cost shifting. Those who pay directly for health care strain mightily to shift costs to others. Whether these efforts succeed or fail, someone ends up stuck with the growing health care bill. This homely fact largely explains the spreading disenchantment with the current system of health care payment.

Employers are paying a declining share of the cost of health care under employer-sponsored insurance. Insurance that pays for care from the first dollar of expenses is vanishing, replaced by plans that impose sizable deductibles, frequently of $250 per year or more per person. Many plans pay for a reduced proportion of cost if patients refuse to select providers from a list of physicians who have agreed to provide care at a cash discount. Employers are requiring employees to pay a larger share of premiums for health insurance they sponsor.[11]

	1985	1991
Employers pay all premiums	*Percent of plans*	
Individual	61	45
Family	36	23
Average employee share of premiums	*Percent of premiums*	
Individual	6	10
Family	15	18

Meanwhile, premiums have risen rapidly, at a rate of 11 percent annually from 1986 to 1991.[12] Rapid growth in both the quantity and quality of health services partly explains premium growth.[13]

Meanwhile, governments have shifted costs to private payers. According to one recent study, medicare and medicaid paid only 90 percent

11. *Hay/Huggins Benefit Report: Annual Survey of 1000 or More Employers* (Philadelphia: Hay Huggins, 1985, 1991).

12. The averages conceal huge variations in annual rates that arise in large part because of lags in recognition of rising costs by insurers. Annual real premium increases ranged from 2 to 17 percent over the period from 1980 through 1989. Jon Gabel and others, "Tracing the Cycle of Health Insurance," *Health Affairs*, vol. 10 (Winter 1991), pp. 48–61.

13. Distinguishing price from quantity is often difficult in health care services. When patients receive a broadened range of services that enables them to spend fewer days in a hospital for a given illness, has the quantity or the price of care risen? Although a good case can be made that the quantity of care has risen, official statistics measure this development as an increase in price. See Henry J. Aaron, *Serious and Unstable Condition: Financing America's Health Care* (Brookings, 1991), pp. 103–07. See also Joseph P. Newhouse, "Measuring Medical Prices and Understanding Their Effects: The Baxter Foundation Prize Address," *Journal of Health Administration Education*, vol. 7 (Winter 1989), pp. 19–26.

TABLE 2-1. Health Care Expenditures as a Share of Earnings
and of Federal and State-Local Government Expenditures, 1980, 1991

Health expenditures	1980	1991	Percent of change in real compensation, outlays, or revenues absorbed by health expenditures
Privately financed (as a percent of employee compensation)	13.3	20.0[a]	58[b]
Federal (as a percent of total federal outlays)	10.9	15.5	29[c]
State and local government (as a percent of state and local revenues)[d]	12.9	17.6	29[e]

SOURCES: Author's calculations based on *Economic Report of the President*, February 1992, tables B-3, B-10, B-56, B-77, B-80; Katharine R. Levit and others, "National Health Expenditures: 1990," *Health Care Financing Review*, vol. 13 (Fall 1991), pp. 43–44; and Sally T. Sonnefeld and others, "Projections of National Health Expenditures through the Year 2000," *Health Care Financing Review*, vol. 13 (Fall 1991), p. 22.
   a. Estimated.
   b. Deflated using consumer price index.
   c. Deflated using deflator for nondefense government purchases.
   d. State and local revenues equal personal tax and nontax receipts, corporate profits, tax accruals and indirect business tax, and nontax accruals.
   e. Deflated using deflator for state and local government purchases.

and 80 percent, respectively, of the hospital costs their patients generated, while private payers paid 128 percent.[14] Despite such cost shifting, public expenditures on health care are among the most rapidly rising components of federal and state budgets (see table 2-1). In short, sharply rising costs are simultaneously placing heavy financial burdens on governments and private businesses. Both are trying to shift costs to individuals by making them pay a larger share of health costs and by curtailing benefits.

The effort of employers to shift costs to workers has a number of predictable consequences. Disputes over health care plans have become the leading cause of strikes.[15] Some private businesses have dropped insurance coverage altogether.[16] Continued cost increases that are shifted to workers will undermine insurance coverage for the majority of employed Americans who now receive good coverage where they work.

14. Prospective Payment Assessment Commission, *Optional Hospital Payment Rates: Congressional Report*, C-92-03 (March 1992), table 2-1, p. 40.
15. Chris John Miko and Edward Weilant, *Opinions '90* (Detroit: Gale Research, 1991).
16. Katharine Levit, Gary Olin, and Suzanne Letsch, "Changes in America's Health Insurance Coverage 1980-1991," *Health Care Financing Review* (forthcoming). Over the period from 1980 through 1991, the proportion of workers insured through employer-sponsored plans fell by 6 percent; the proportion of their dependents insured fell by 13 percent.

Access

Americans lack health care for two distinct reasons. Workers and their dependents may lack health insurance because their employer does not sponsor a health insurance plan or they elect not to participate in an insurance plan their employer offers. Those who do not work may lack insurance because they are not eligible for public support through medicare (serving the aged and disabled) or medicaid (serving some of the poor and near poor) and cannot afford or do not buy insurance on their own. Popular concern about potential lack of financial access extends beyond the currently uninsured, however, because millions who are now insured fear loss or restriction of coverage.

Any reform plan that credibly promises universal financial access to care must deal with three central facts. First, some people are too poor to pay for health insurance and must be subsidized. This group includes not only those who lack the skills or disposition to work, but also full- or part-time workers who earn so little that health insurance is simply beyond their means. Second, some people with adequate incomes elect not to be insured. They may refuse coverage for themselves or their dependents, even when their employers sponsor insurance plans or they could easily afford to buy coverage individually. They may refuse coverage because of shortsightedness, because of a rational understanding that some public program or private group will pay for their care in the event of serious illness, or because they can afford to pay directly for the costs of treatment of even serious illnesses. If this group is to be insured, it must be required to do so. Third, a serious problem economists call *adverse selection*—that those most likely to use above-average amounts of health care are most likely to seek health insurance—has intensified in recent years, leading to the breakdown of private insurance markets for small groups and obstructing job mobility even in large groups.

Low Incomes and High Insurance Costs

The cost of standard health insurance for large groups averages $5,000 a year for family coverage and $1,925 for individual coverage.[17] Depending on place of residence, age, occupation, and medical history, premiums can be much lower or many times higher for individuals or

17. These estimates are based on the premium costs as reported in *Hay-Huggins Benefit Report*, 1991, increased by 12 percent.

small groups. Even the average is high enough to prevent many families—especially those who are both poor and out of the labor force—from buying insurance. Such households typically buy health insurance only if someone else pays for it.

Employer sponsorship seems to offer a way to extend coverage to workers too poor to pay for it themselves. Standard economic theory indicates that private employers base their demand for workers on the total cost of employing them. Some employers of workers who produce output worth little more than the minimum wage will find the combined cost of cash wages and fringe benefits including health insurance exceeds the value of what the worker produces. The average premium for large-group family coverage comes to about $2.50 an hour for full-time year-round employees, roughly two-thirds of the minimum wage and a sizable fraction of compensation of low-wage workers; for members of small groups rates are often far higher. If all workers and their dependents are to be insured through their employers, it will be necessary either to subsidize insurance for low-wage workers or to find some other way to support coverage for them. In either case, universal coverage will not result if workers and employers are left to pursue private incentives.

Voluntary Lack of Insurance

Of the 35 million Americans without insurance, few have enough income to pay for a serious illness—only 22 percent had annual incomes more than three times official poverty thresholds in 1991.[18] But except for the poorest households or those for whom premiums would be particularly high, health insurance is not literally unaffordable; it is simply less valuable to the households than other things that they can afford to buy. A decision by a household with sufficient income not to buy insurance is not necessarily irrational. In the name of personal freedom a case can be made to allow individuals to make such a choice and bear the consequences.

The argument that voluntary decisions not to buy insurance are optimal fails for two reasons. First, people who do not buy insurance do not bear the full consequences. The United States has arrangements, loosely described as the *social safety net*, to assure that people in dire need of health care receive it. These programs excuse households from

18. The percentage was calculated using three times the 1990 poverty threshold and money income pertaining to a family of four in 1990.

the full consequences of a decision not to buy health insurance, by having society subsidize that decision.[19] Second, people who elect not to have insurance frequently do so not just for themselves, but also for spouses and children, people who may not be adequately involved or capable of participating fully in the decision. While many would let individuals bear even unfortunate consequences of their own decisions, requiring spouses and dependent children to do so is another matter.

The Breakdown of Small-Group Insurance

A small minority of the population accounts for most health care outlays. The loss to any insurer who gets stuck with a disproportionate share of high-cost cases is potentially ruinous. Companies of all sizes deal with this problem partly by trying to curb financial loss in easy-to-identify cases. Many companies exclude new workers from coverage for preexisting conditions for several months. Such restrictions can effectively bar workers from changing jobs when they or family members are receiving costly therapy. The average cost of insuring employees of large companies ordinarily does not differ widely from the average cost in the community where the workers reside, although such factors as age, sex, race, and work-related risks can cause premiums even of large companies to vary significantly around community averages. But variations in per capita health care costs among small groups may be vastly larger.

Two developments have aggravated these problems in recent years. First, costs of medical treatment have risen far faster than prices of other commodities. Second, insurers have become increasingly adept at identifying potentially high-cost customers. A history of illness is an excellent indicator that in the future a person is likely to use more medical services than average. In addition, certain high-cost illnesses are correlated with occupation. Florists and beauticians find it hard to buy insurance at any price because they are thought to employ disproportionate numbers of gay men among whom AIDS is epidemic. Employees in bars and gas stations are deemed to be at particular risk of armed robbery or other workplace injuries. Construction and logging companies often cannot buy insurance because of physical dangers associated with these

---

19. The exclusion of employer-financed insurance from personal income tax is a strong incentive for the acquisition of insurance by those for whom the tax incentive is significant; but for many the tax incentive is irrelevant because they would pay little or no tax in any event.

occupations.[20] An instinct for financial survival, not venality, explains this outcome, which reflects the simple fact that insurance companies know less about their prospective customers' demands for health care than the customers know. This problem cannot be avoided entirely in a market system. Even well-intentioned efforts by states to improve coverage can work perversely; a state that requires all insurance plans to include generous mental health benefits, for example, may make insurance for somatic illness prohibitively costly for people currently receiving psychotherapy.

Insurance companies increasingly use various other strategies to shield themselves from potentially ruinous losses on high-cost patients. They exclude preexisting illnesses from insurance, condition group insurance on the removal of identified, high-risk patients from the group, and curtail coverage after the onset of high-cost illnesses, for example by imposing reduced maximums on total payments by the insurance company. And for some groups, they simply set exorbitant premiums or refuse coverage altogether.

Once again, these practices do not in general reflect greed or selfishness by insurers. Rather they are an inescapable response when companies that do not want to commit business suicide confront competitors who are free to use these techniques. An agreement by all companies to forgo these business practices would serve everyone, but would be unstable, because a violator could corral low-cost customers, cut rates, and then use reduced rates to attract additional customers and increase profits. Since no company can afford to be the last to break the agreement, all would persist in practices understood to be contrary to the public interest. An agreement not to use these common underwriting practices can be made stable only if they are prohibited by law—that is, by increased governmental regulation of insurance companies. A remarkable degree of consensus exists about the urgent need for reform of the small-group insurance market. As one commentator observed, "The small-group market . . . is currently in a death spiral."[21]

For the majority of employees who work in groups of one hundred or more, the problem of access to insurance is rather different. In these

20. Some might see poetic justice in the fact that the groups insurers are most likely to shun are lawyers (because they are too litigious) and physicians (because they use much more health care than average). Wendy K. Zellers, Catherine G. McLaughlin, and Kevin D. Frick, "Small-Business Health Insurance: Only the Healthy Need Apply," *Health Affairs*, vol. 11 (Spring 1992), p. 177.

21. Mark A. Hall, "Reforming the Health Insurance Market for Small Businesses," *New England Journal of Medicine*, vol. 326 (February 20, 1992), p. 565.

cases, employers have reacted to rising costs by increasing premiums employees must pay, especially for dependents, and by increasing deductibles and copayments. Although the proportion of workers in these groups who are insured has declined minimally, the range of coverage for dependents has narrowed. On balance, therefore, private insurance coverage has narrowed, especially for small groups and dependents.[22]

Summary

Most participants in the health insurance debate have concluded that universal insurance coverage is both important and desirable. It is important because, for reasons set forth below, control of the growth of health care spending requires that the budgets of hospitals and the fees of physicians be subject to overall control. Such controls must apply to all patients who are served and cannot be divorced from payments for the services patients receive. All participants in the health insurance reform debate recognize that large increases in coverage cannot be achieved without increased government involvement. The principal issue concerns the nature of the involvement. Apart from large cost savings, universal coverage would be desirable because it would bring financial access to health care to all U.S. residents, a perquisite of modern civilization long ago instituted in every other major industrial nation.

Reform

The debate on health care financing reform concerns how government power should be used to deal with the two central problems: controlling spending growth and extending financial access. First, should the current sharing of financial responsibilities among government, private businesses, and individuals be changed, and, if so, how? Second, how should current government regulation of health care services be changed?

The Role of Government in Health Care

Governments directly provide health care services and regulate insurance companies, hospitals, physicians, and pharmaceutical companies.

---

22. Between 1988 and 1990, the proportion of workers who were uninsured rose in every two-digit industrial group except public administration. The largest increases were in wholesale trade, where the proportion uninsured rose from 13.1 percent to 18.3 percent, and entertainment and recreation, where the proportion uninsured rose from 21.3 percent to 26.1 percent. Data from Fu Associates, Arlington, Va.

TABLE 2-2. Sources of Payments to Major Health Care Providers, 1992[a]

Source	Hospitals	Physicians	Other[b]
	Billions of dollars		
Government			
Federal	125.3	45.4	47.9
State and local	47.9	11.1	26.4
Direct payments	15.8	31.6	112.8
Private insurance	110.1	77.4	41.9
Other private	14.8	0.1	8.4
	Percent		
Government			
Federal	39.9	27.4	20.1
State and local	15.3	6.7	11.1
Direct payments	5.0	19.1	47.6
Private insurance	35.1	46.8	17.7
Other private	4.7	0.1	3.5

SOURCE: Sonnefeld and others, "Projections of National Health Expenditures through the Year 2000."
a. Estimated.
b. Includes dental services, other professional services, and home health care; drugs and other medical nondurables; vision products and other medical durables; and nursing home care and other personal health care.

But governments play their largest role by paying an estimated $304 billion for health care, or 42 percent of all health care spending in 1992– 55 percent of hospital services and 34 percent of physician bills.[23] The United States relies on a mix of public and private payment for medical care, mostly through insurance or government programs (see table 2-2). In addition, the exclusion of health insurance premiums paid by employers from personal income tax of employees, which is worth $39 billion in 1992, is a major reason why most group insurance is provided through places of employment.[24]

Health care consists of several activities in which the share of the public and private sectors differs. Providers have to be educated and

23. Author's calculations based on Katharine R. Levit and others, "National Health Expenditures: 1990," *Health Care Financing Review*, vol. 13 (Fall 1991), table 8; and *Budget of the United States Government, Fiscal Year 1993*, pt. 2, p. 27.

24. Even without these incentives, much private insurance would be sold to groups because insurers can offer lower premiums to groups than they can to individuals. Groups typically contain people who generate different levels of medical cost, from which a single average premium can be set. If the same premium were offered to individuals, those not likely to be sick would be most likely to buy insurance, forcing insurers to boost premiums or face losses. This factor helps explain why group insurance is cheaper than individual insurance. The other reason is that selling and other administrative costs are typically lower with group plans than with individual plans.

trained, certified, and licensed. Health care has to be produced. And research, experimentation, innovation, and evaluation must be supported. Although important debates are now proceeding in most of these areas, current controversy centers on how to change methods of payment for health care.[25]

Marginal Changes in the Current System

Since a consensus on major reforms has not yet emerged, many proposals have been advanced to amend the current system to extend insurance to some or all of the uninsured and to control growth of expenditures.

Small-group insurance reform. The widespread recognition of the need to reform the small-group insurance market is reflected in the similarity of proposed reforms to deal with three distinct issues. First, insurers would be required both to sell insurance to all groups with fewer than a designated number of members that apply for coverage and to generally renew insurance. They would be prohibited from excluding some individuals or particular illnesses from coverage, except for a brief period after a person is covered initially. Workers who move from one job with insurance to another with insurance would be exempt from such exclusions on all jobs after the first. Second, limits would be placed on allowable variations in premiums. The third reform would allow insurers to buy reinsurance for risky patients or groups, a mechanism whereby the losses on high-cost patients are distributed among all insurers.

Whether the federal government or the states acting independently will enact these reforms remains unclear. More than twenty states have enacted some variant of small-group insurance reform. More than fifty bills were submitted in Congress during 1992. Sponsors of federal

25. Medical educators debate whether medical schools place too much emphasis on narrow specialties and too little on pediatrics, family medicine, and other forms of primary care. Public health experts argue over whether more resources should be devoted to school-based medical services for children, health clinics in low-income or thinly settled areas, or decreased reliance on fee-for-service physician payment. Reform of the malpractice system is a fashionable topic for discussion among physicians, lawyers, and many others. Huge variations in the use of various medical procedures across regions have led to research, largely under public sponsorship, to measure the medical benefits of procedures that have never been adequately evaluated and whose use varies widely. Although public support of biomedical research has increased, scientists argue that more should be spent because of unprecedented opportunities for major discoveries; meanwhile, payers tremble at the financial consequences of scientific success.

reform include President Bush, the chairmen of both the Senate Finance Committee and the House Committee on Ways and Means, and other leading members of both parties. Small-group insurance reform is a standard component of all plans to restructure health care financing other than those that would do away with private insurance altogether. A major appeal of small-group insurance reform for legislators is that it directly adds little to public expenditures at any level of government.

Unfortunately, it is also unlikely to add many people to the ranks of the insured. Evidence indicates that few business owners who refuse to sponsor insurance will do so if the premiums they face are reduced. Many small businesses do not sponsor insurance because they employ workers with below-average wages (meaning insurance costs are a large fraction of total compensation) and above-average turnover rates, which causes unusually high costs of workers moving into and out of the plan. The mean life span of small firms (twenty or fewer employees) with insurance is less than twenty-eight months.[26] Furthermore, those led to buy insurance by small-group reform are likely to generate particularly high medical costs. Covering them will push up premiums for those who are currently insured, who will then respond by dropping coverage. Those who retain coverage are likely to be sicker than average, which will further boost average premiums for small groups.[27] The paradoxical conclusion emerges that small-group reform will probably change coverage little and could actually reduce the numbers of people who are insured.

On balance, however, small-group reform is a desirable innovation because current arrangements tend to exclude from insurance those who need coverage most, the sick and those at high risk of becoming ill. Such reforms marginally increase the role of governments in the administration of the health care system. Quite simply, the small-group insurance market has become an instance of a private market that cannot survive under free competition; its continued existence requires added government

26. Kenneth E. Thorpe, "Administrative Costs in the U.S. Health Care System: Getting Inside the Black Box," paper prepared for the Robert Wood Johnson Conference on Administrative Costs in the U.S. Health Care System: The Problem or the Solution, Washington, D.C., February 12-13, 1992.

27. This feature of small-group reform accounts for opposition to the reforms by some insurers and small businesses. While the Health Insurance Association of America and the National Federation of Independent Businesses support small-group insurance reforms, two smaller groups, the National Association of Self-Employed and the Council of Smaller Enterprises, oppose it on the ground that reforms would raise the average cost of small-group insurance. *Medicine and Health*, vol. 46 (April 13, 1992), p. 1.

regulation. In the end, however, small-group reform will do little to extend insurance coverage or to control growth of medical costs.

Extending insurance coverage. President Bush supports reforms to the current system intended to bring insurance within the financial reach of some low-income households. The Bush plan would initiate refundable tax credits for low-income families: $1,250 for single persons, $2,500 for tax units of two people, and $3,750 for tax units of three or more. The credits would be reduced quickly as incomes exceed thresholds at which households become subject to personal income tax, which are estimated at $6,050 for a single person in 1993, $10,150 for a head of household with one child, and $15,600 for a married couple with two children.[28] All taxpayers would be entitled to deduct health insurance costs in computing taxable income if the deduction were worth more than the credit. The deduction would also be $1,250 per person (up to a maximum of three people).[29] Individuals with annual incomes below $50,000 would be eligible to claim the deduction, as would heads of household and couples with incomes below $65,000 and $80,000, respectively.

How much the credit and the broadened deduction would extend health insurance is unclear. The Congressional Budget Office estimates that about one-half of all tax units with no health insurance in 1989 would have been eligible for the full credit, another one-sixth for partial credit, and almost all of the rest for the deduction. The president's plan would require insurance companies to develop a bare-bones plan that would cost no more than the maximum credit. However, the credit is

28. Congressional Budget Office, "Appendices for the Testimony of Robert D. Reischauer before the Committee on Ways and Means, U.S. House of Representatives, March 4, 1992" (CBO, 1992), app. A., p. 2. These tax entry points take no account of the earned income tax credit, which is paid to families with children with modest earnings. People at the income levels listed in the text are still eligible for earned income tax credit. In 1992 this credit offsets income tax up to $1,324 for a head of household with one child and $1,384 for a married couple with two children. Single people are not eligible for the earned income credit. The combination of the phaseout of the health insurance credit and the earned income tax credit, payroll taxes, federal personal income taxes, and state income taxes cumulates to tax rates as high as 100 percent for families with earnings in the range of $12,000 to $18,000. See C. Eugene Steuerle, "Why the Health Care Debate Stagnates—And How to Focus its Attention on Children," paper prepared for the National Tax Association Symposium, May 18–19, 1992.

29. Deductions are worth less than credits of the same amount, because the saving from a deduction equals the amount of the deduction multiplied by the relevant tax rate, while the credit is worth its face value. A $3,750 credit reduces taxes by $3,750; a $3,750 deduction reduces taxes by a maximum of $1,050. The maximum tax rate in the income ranges where the deduction can be claimed is 28 percent (0.28 x $3,750 = $1,050).

less than the average cost of currently available insurance. By covering a population with above-average costs, the president's plan would cause some increase in the average. In addition, the president proposes to adjust the credit not for increases in medical prices, but in the consumer price index, which increases much less rapidly.[30] Nonetheless, the credit would doubtless cause many people who currently find insurance unaffordable to buy it, especially those eligible for the full credit.

Paradoxically, the president's plan could narrow insurance coverage by making it easier for employers to cancel insurance they now sponsor. Employers who now face large annual increases in premiums must choose among trying to hold down use of services, trying to shift those costs to employees, or dropping sponsorship of health insurance. For employers with disproportionate numbers of low-wage workers, the president's plan increases the relative attractiveness of the third option. Such employers would be tempted to cancel insurance plans, distribute some or all of their current premium payments to workers as higher wages, and remind workers of the new credits or deductions. Some employees would buy insurance with the added wages and credit (or deduction); others would elect to take the higher wages and forgo insurance.

The president's plan does nothing, however, to deal with the increase in expenditures on low-benefit, high-cost medical care. President Bush embraces small-group insurance reform. But as noted above, small-group insurance is not likely, on net, to materially broaden the affordability of health insurance, although it will increase access for high-risk groups. The president proposes to limit malpractice awards for pain and suffering, but the malpractice system has little to do with rising medical costs.[31] Insured patients and physicians acting in their interests would continue to face the same incentives that now lead them to seek essentially all beneficial care regardless of cost.

Achieving Universal Coverage

In the current debate on how to increase financial access to care, nearly all major participants advocate an increase in the public role.

30. Over the ten-year period 1982–91 the price index for health care rose 36 percent more than the consumer price index. (Author's calculation based on *Economic Report of the President, February 1992*, table B-56.) Pegging the increase of the credit to the consumer price index over such a period would have necessitated a cutback in insurance coverage of a similar amount.

31. The extent of defensive medicine is in dispute, but probably does not exceed about 4 percent of acute care outlays. For further discussion of this issue see Aaron, *Serious and*

Unlike President Bush's plan, most others, implicitly or explicitly, seek universal coverage both to increase financial access to care and to establish the conditions for effective cost control. They also recognize that market-generated incomes and voluntary individual action cannot materially extend coverage or even maintain it. This consensus is noteworthy, but little noted, perhaps because it is obscured by conflicting visions of exactly how the government should enforce universal coverage and how the costs of this coverage should be distributed and by divisive rhetoric on the virtues of one institutional arrangement over another.

Three broad approaches to universal coverage are described. Each embraces mandatory health insurance coverage financed by required premiums or taxes paid by individuals and businesses.

National Health Insurance

Under national health insurance all citizens (or residents) are entitled to a stipulated list of services from physicians, hospitals, and selected other providers.[32] Patients face limited cost sharing at the time of illness. Other costs of covered services are met through payments by government to providers. Taxes would be increased sufficiently to cover the added costs. Central issues revolve around the range of services covered, the degree of cost sharing required of patients, and the types of taxes used to pay for health services. In all cases, however, the uniform entitlement to care under the plan is independent of economic or employment status.

This approach to universal coverage is linked to major changes in the way health care providers are paid. Hospitals would operate on budgets periodically negotiated with public authorities, federal or state. Fee schedules would govern payments to physicians. Most costs of care currently met through premiums would be met instead from taxes.

This approach to financing health care shifts most current acute health care outlays from private to public budgets. Most insurance premiums paid by employers and individuals would be eliminated, replaced by

---

Unstable Condition, pp. 45–48; and Patricia Danzon, *Medical Malpractice: Theory, Evidence, and Public Policy* (Harvard University Press, 1985).

32. National health insurance proposals include the Comprehensive Health Care for All Americans Act (sponsored by Representative Mary Rose Oakar, Democrat of Ohio), the National Health Insurance Act (sponsored by Representative John Dingell, Democrat of Michigan), the Mediplan Health Care Act of 1991 (sponsored by Representative Pete Stark, Democrat of California), and the Universal Health Care Act of 1991 (sponsored by Representative Mary Russo, Democrat of Illinois).

taxes levied on businesses and households to cover increased public payments for health care (see table 2-3). Under any plausible set of taxes, a huge amount of income redistribution results, not only across income classes, but among regions, industries, and occupational groups.

Redistribution among income classes is highly progressive. Standard economic theory holds that all of the cost of health insurance paid by employers ultimately leads to reduced wages or other fringe benefits and is therefore borne by workers. Under this line of argument, workers bear the burden of health insurance premiums whether they or their employers pay them. Thus health insurance premiums, which vary little with income, are a kind of head tax.[33] In contrast, all taxes that might be used to pay for health insurance rise with income. Thus replacing premiums with any tax is progressive. Those now without insurance are helped by extended health coverage and pay little of the cost.

While some voters favor increased income redistribution in favor of the poor, others resist any extension, and some think current redistribution policies have gone too far. The current tax and transfer policies reflect a lengthy and rancorous history of negotiation and compromise on such issues. Income redistribution associated with the replacement of employer-financed health insurance would exceed that associated with any other major national policy now in existence and would dwarf any modification in policy that has been seriously discussed.

A movement to national health insurance would also cause huge additional random income redistribution across industries and occupational groups. Currently, few employers in entertainment and recreation or in retail trade sponsor insurance for their employees, while all employers in the auto and steel industries do. Instituting national health insurance would relieve the auto and steel industries of most or all of the premiums they now pay. The gains would initially flow to employers. But economic theory holds that they would eventually accrue to workers as higher cash wages, pensions, or other fringe benefits. These gains are offset by the higher taxes that would be imposed in some fashion on businesses and individuals. The ultimate burden or incidence of the taxes typically will differ from that of the premiums they replace. The final incidence pattern estimated by economists depends on which kinds of taxes are used, for example, sales taxes or payroll taxes. It is certain that the distribution of burdens will differ from that of current premiums

---

33. The only variations arise because employer-financed health insurance is more generous on the average for highly paid than for poorly paid workers.

TABLE 2-3. Effect of Alternative Plans for Universal Coverage
on Private and Public Budgets, 1992[a]

Billions of dollars

Plan	Physicians, hospitals, and drugs	Other	Total	Change in total from current plan
Current				
Private	322	126	447	...
Public	247	68	315	...
Total	569	194	763	...
National health insurance				
Private	54	126	180	−267
Public	538	68	606	291
Total	592	194	786	23
Tax credits				
Private	161	126	287	−160
Public	431	68	499	184
Total	592	194	786	23
Employment-based, public backup				
Private	310	126	435	−12
Public	282	68	350	35
Total	592	194	786	23

SOURCES: Author's calculations; and Sonnefeld and others, "Projections of National Health Expenditures through the Year 2000." Totals may not add due to rounding.

a. Calculations are based on the following assumptions: All plans increase the use of acute care services by $23 billion. National health insurance shifts five-sixths of private outlays for physicians, hospitals, and drugs to public budgets. Tax credits shift half. Employment-based plans shift 3 percent of current private outlays, but cover all incremental costs of added services directly or through subsidy to private sponsors.

and that the shifts cannot reflect any rational set of principles. It is also certain that most people will notice that they are paying taxes for benefits they regarded as free and that their employers are spared all premiums.

The huge amount of redistribution entailed in a shift from employer-financed to tax-financed health insurance is a major obstacle to the adoption of full national health insurance. In addition to the host of difficult and controversial decisions about what benefits to cover and how to control spending and the widespread fear of expanded government bureaucracy, supporters of a national health insurance plan have to persuade critics not only of the virtues of their plan, but also of the need for massive income redistribution, much of which would be capricious.

Tax Credits or Vouchers

Another approach to universal coverage requires everyone to carry private insurance.[34] Tax credits would cover all of the cost of health insurance coverage for low-income families. The credit tapers off as income rises, although not so sharply or at such low incomes as President Bush's plan does.[35] Unlike the president's plan, all families would be required to carry insurance. Under one proposal, people without insurance would be assessed an income tax surcharge equal to the health insurance premium, payable on their annual tax return.[36]

While individuals and families would be the direct objects of the requirement to carry insurance, incentives would remain for employers to sponsor, but not to pay for, insurance plans and to assist their employees in securing group discounts. However, such groups are generally unstable, because groups of people with low expected costs have strong tendencies to band together to secure low premiums or broader-than-average coverage for a given premium. Alternatively, groups might form linked by such other characteristics as religion, recreational affinities, or place of residence. If groups are formed by various self-designated collections of individuals, however, the insurance market becomes unstable, because some subgroup within any group typically has expected costs below the average for the group as a whole, and insurers face strong market incentives to sell insurance only to these subgroups.[37] For that reason, the tax credit approach has to be accompanied by legislated rules regarding the formation of groups.

34. Health insurance reforms based on tax credits include the Affordable Health Insurance Act of 1991 (sponsored by William Dannemeyer, Republican of California), the Comprehensive Health Care Access Improvement and Cost Containment Act of 1991 (sponsored by Representative Michael Bilirakis, Republican of Florida), the Health Equity and Access Improvement Act of 1992 (sponsored by Representative Amo Houghton, Republican of New York), and the Comprehensive American Health Care Act (sponsored by Senator Mitch McConnell, Republican of Kentucky). For a justification of this approach and a detailed plan, see Mark V. Pauly and others, *Responsible National Health Insurance* (Washington: American Enterprise Institute, 1992).

35. President Bush's proposal quickly and sharply reduces the value of the credit, starting at the income level where taxpayers first face positive personal income taxes and dropping to $125 per person when income reaches 150 percent of the tax entry point ($15,200 for a family of four in 1992).

36. Pauly and others, *Responsible National Health Insurance*.

37. This point is well established in the analytical literature on problems in the insurance market. Peter Diamond comments on a system under which premiums are restricted to fall within a narrow range, regardless of expected losses. "This would leave a large incentive to be in a large (possibly self-insured) group, in order to escape the cross subsidization of

How groups are formed is crucial also for administrative costs. The costs of selling and other administrative costs associated with small groups claim a disproportionate share of small-group premiums.[38]

Number of employees	Administrative costs as percent of claims
1 to 4	40
5 to 9	35
10 to 19	30
20 to 49	25
50 to 99	18
100 to 499	16
500 to 2,499	12
2,500 to 9,999	8
10,000 plus	5.5

To minimize administrative costs, one analyst has proposed that groups should be formed geographically. Each group would consist of 10,000 to 100,000 people who choose among a small number of competing health plans.[39]

The tax credit plan suffers from a difficult political dilemma. If credits phase out low in the income distribution, most families are left with a seemingly unattractive option. They will confront higher out-of-pocket costs for benefits they already enjoy, while employers would be relieved of responsibility for financing health care. While a rapid phaseout would require few added taxes to replace lost revenue, most households would face a sharp increase in the share of costs they would bear for insurance they already have. If the credit extends far into the income distribution,

---

less healthy people lumped into the open enrollment pools. This also maintains . . . much of the large transaction costs associated with individual insurance. It is unclear how much could be accomplished by the combination of direct regulation of the insurance market and income redistribution." "Organizing the Health Insurance Market," paper prepared for the 1991 meeting of the Econometric Society, p. 7. If the variation in premiums was not restricted, premiums would vary intolerably: people with active illnesses or chronic disabilities, for example, would face premiums many times those charged healthy young people. For a more technical exposition, see Michael Rothschild and Joseph Stiglitz, "Equilibrium in Competitive Insurance Markets: An Essay on the Economics of Imperfect Information," *Quarterly Journal of Economics*, vol. 90 (November 1976), pp. 629–49.

38. *Cost and Effects of Extending Health Insurance Coverage*, Committee Print, Subcommittee on Labor-Management Relations and Subcommittee on Labor Standards of House Committee on Education and Labor, Subcommittee on Health and the Environment of House Committee on Energy and Commerce, and Senate Special Committee on Aging, 100 Cong. 2 sess. (Government Printing Office, October 1988), p. 46, table 2.21.

39. Diamond, "Organizing the Health Insurance Market."

the tax increase necessary to replace lost revenues would become sizable. Again, most households would see themselves as paying more taxes so that their employers and other businesses could enjoy savings in health insurance premiums.

If the credit is large enough to shift a sizable portion of premium costs currently borne by the private sector to public budgets, the problem of large-scale income redistribution associated with full national health insurance arises, although on a somewhat smaller scale (see table 2-3).

Mandatory Employer-Sponsored Health Insurance

Employers now sponsor insurance covering about 56 percent of the U.S. population. Universal coverage can be achieved by requiring employers to sponsor health insurance plans for all full-time workers and their dependents and by extending public coverage to serve people with little or no connection to work.[40] Rules would be established concerning the proportion of premium costs paid by employees and employers, the range of services covered, the kinds and amounts of cost sharing, and the definition of full-time workers. People not insured through work would be covered by public plans under rules similar to those governing employer-sponsored plans. All workers would be entitled to a common set of benefits, but businesses would be entitled to retain or introduce additional coverage and workers would be entitled to buy supplemental coverage as individuals. Physicians might be prohibited from charging more than allowed under a fee schedule.

The added costs of insurance for those currently uninsured would be met in the first instance by businesses and workers forced to buy insurance. However, some of these burdens would shift to others. Affected businesses might raise prices or slow growth of wages, or public subsidies might be used to relieve some of the costs for businesses unduly burdened by the sudden requirement to pay health insurance premiums. Alternatively, such businesses might be excused from providing insurance if they paid a payroll tax to the public plan, which would then cover workers and their dependents. This approach invites companies facing

40. Plans that would mandate employer sponsorship include the Pepper Commission Health Care Access and Reform Act of 1991 (sponsored by Representative Henry A. Waxman, Democrat of California), the U.S. Health Program Act of 1991 (sponsored by Representative Edward R. Roybal, Democrat of California), and the Health Insurance Coverage and Cost Containment Act of 1991 (sponsored by Representative Dan Rostenkowski, Democrat of Illinois).

unusually high premiums or paying low average wages to choose a less costly option than sponsoring insurance. The tax has to be set high enough—roughly 10 to 11 percent of payroll—to encourage most firms to sponsor health insurance rather than pay the tax. Since employers would tend to exercise this option only if insurance costs exceeded the tax they would be required to pay, additional public revenues would be necessary to cover these workers and their families. Taxes would have to be raised to pay for these subsidies and to insure the currently uninsured who are not connected to a household with an insured worker.

This method of achieving universal coverage would not shift costs from one set of payers to another nearly as much as would both national health insurance and the tax credit plan (see table 2-3). Some businesses would experience increased expenses, and some that now sponsor insurance plans would enjoy savings. For example, many companies pick up part or all of the coverage costs for dependents of employees, even when the dependents are employed elsewhere. But most costs for workers and their dependents who are now insured at work would continue to be paid by their employers.

Summary

The similarities of the three plans to achieve universal coverage outnumber the differences (see table 2-4). All mandate coverage for everyone. All require some combination of new taxes or required payments by individuals and businesses to cover the costs of the newly insured. All stipulate minimum benefits to be provided under all plans, public or private, including covered services and patient cost sharing. All could assure a large or small menu of benefits. All permit individuals to buy services in addition to those required under the plan, although the rules could be designed to discourage or facilitate such supplemental coverage.[41]

The three plans differ principally in the degree to which costs of services rendered to those who are now insured would be shifted among payers. In 1992 private spending (through insurance and out-of-pocket individual expenses) on hospital and physician services and on drugs and other medical nondurable products will exceed $300 billion. An

41. For example, premiums of supplemental plans could be tax deductible, nondeductible, or subject to special taxes under any of the three broad approaches.

TABLE 2-4. Types of Universal Coverage

Plan	Coverage	Insured group	Payment for new groups	Redistribution of payments for previously served group	Required core of services	Individual can buy added services
National health insurance	Mandatory	Nation	New taxes	Very large (tax-financed public expenditures instead of premiums and individual payments)	Yes	Yes
Tax credits	Mandatory	Individual or self-constituted groups	New taxes and enforced direct payments by individuals	Large (tax-financed public expenditures instead of premiums and individual payments)	Yes	Yes
Employment-based, public backup	Mandatory	Place of employment or nation	New taxes and enforced premiums on business	Small (mostly among businesses)	Yes	Yes

additional $126 billion will be spent privately on other medical services.[42] All health care plans would shift some of these costs from the private to the public sector and all would cause some redistribution within the private sector of remaining outlays.

The precise amounts of both shifts are impossible to estimate apart from specific plans, but the three broad outlines entail widely varying amounts of redistribution. Table 2-3 illustrates these differences under stylized but plausible assumptions. A full-blown national health insurance plan, drafted on the model of the Canadian system, shifts roughly $270 billion in spending from private to public budgets. A generous tax credit–based scheme shifts roughly three-fifths as much.[43] An extension of employment-based insurance, with a public backup plan for those not connected to the labor force, shifts comparatively little. The implied tax increases vary from large (for the public backup to employment-based plans) to huge (for tax credit–based plans) to staggering (for national health insurance).

These illustrative calculations do not take into account the economic adjustments that any of the plans generate. For example, national health insurance or a tax credit plan that relieves employers of current health insurance costs would enable employers to pay higher wages. Economic theory strongly suggests that most would do so, although with indeterminate delay. Thus employees might eventually be at least as well off financially under these approaches as they are under current law even if they have to pay higher taxes to support national health insurance or higher premiums under a tax credit scheme. Indeed, the likelihood that they would be better off is high. Under standard economic theory, health insurance results in lower money wages or other fringe benefits than would be provided if the employer did not bear the costs of health insurance. The immediate effect, however, would be to relieve employers of part or all of the cost of health insurance they now bear and to shift financing to some combination of taxes; part of those taxes would fall

42. Author's calculations based on Sally T. Sonnefeld and others, "Projections of National Health Expenditures through the Year 2000," *Health Care Financing Review*, vol. 13 (Fall 1991), p. 22.

43. Some tax credit plans would require no added taxes beyond the revenues generated by terminating the current exclusion of employer-financed health insurance from personal income tax. Such plans confront most workers with an unattractive trade: they would receive credits worth only a small fraction of the cost of insurance they would be required to carry, while their employers would be relieved of all or most of the cost of current insurance. Any possible offsetting gain from higher wages would appear speculative and uncertain.

on the currently insured, who pay little or none of the premiums for their coverage.

Such redistribution among payers generates large numbers of both winners and losers from health insurance reform. Exactly who wins and who loses depends on the particular taxes used to finance each type of plan. Well-insured workers are likely to lose, as they will face higher taxes and possibly some restrictions on benefits they now enjoy.

The greater the amount of this redistribution, the greater the opposition to reform, because those who think they may lose will tend to be more vocal in their protests than those who think they might gain will be in their support. The amount of this redistribution is clearly greatest in the case of national health insurance, still considerable for tax credit plans, and least for employment-based reforms. Moreover, although some of the redistribution of health insurance costs—from low- to high-income groups, for example—has other justifications, much of the redistribution would be without any obvious rationale.

Controlling the Growth of Health Care Costs

Business and government have tried various devices to counter rising costs. Private insurers have negotiated discounts with groups of physicians and hospitals (so-called preferred provider organizations), and have implemented rules to guide physicians on when patients should and should not receive costly diagnostic and therapeutic procedures (so-called managed care). The government has replaced payments to hospitals under medicare based on costs incurred with payment of fixed fees based on primary and secondary diagnoses at time of admission (the diagnosis related group, or DRG system). The government has recently instituted physician fee schedules to reduce growth of spending and to reallocate funds from high-cost, procedure-based specialties to primary care. Administrative and financial assistance has been given to encourage development and expansion of health maintenance organizations, provider groups that promise to provide a stipulated list of services to patients for a fixed fee and that are able to provide care at lower total costs than can other providers.

Health care costs rose at about the same rate in the 1980s as in the preceding three decades. Costs include out-of-pocket outlays paid by patients and their families at the time of illness, services provided by physicians and hospitals for which they are not reimbursed, and various payments made by third parties, including insurance companies, businesses, and governments. Whether this trend reflects the failure of cost control efforts or the increased strength of forces driving up costs is not clear. What is increasingly obvious is that payers, private and public, are finding health care costs increasingly burdensome and even insupportable. Projections by the Congressional Budget Office indicate that even with a one-third reduction in defense and other discretionary spending, total government spending will claim a growing share of gross domestic product and the deficit will begin to rise in 1996 largely because of rising federal health care expenditures.[44]

Three broad approaches to controlling health care costs have been advanced. One relies on competition in various markets, including those for insurance and for the purchase of various medical services. A second manages this competition to offset certain aspects of the health care market that are inconsistent with free competition. A third relies on budget limits imposed on hospitals and other controls on physicians. No necessary connection exists between cost control and extension of coverage, but most who advocate national health insurance espouse budget limits to control costs, and most who advocate tax credits support market competition to control costs. Advocates of extending employment-based insurance support managed competition or budget limits.

What Is the Solution?

Proposed reforms to curb the excessive and rapidly increasing expenditures on health care all seek a device to impose on health care the discipline that limited consumer budgets enforce in most other markets. This constraint is largely absent from health care because most bills for acute care, roughly 90 percent of hospital bills and 76 percent of national health expenditures, are paid by some third party, either private insurer or government program. Moreover, the extension of health insurance will only intensify this problem.

Competition

One approach to cost control relies on competition among insurers on the basis of their skill at supervising providers to assure efficient provision of services; monitoring usage to minimize provision of low-benefit,

44. Congressional Budget Office, *An Analysis of the President's Budgetary Proposals for Fiscal Year 1993* (March 1992).

high cost care; holding down fees to providers; and processing claims efficiently and inexpensively. Those who best balance cost control with delivery of high-quality care and convenience in paying bills will attract customers and induce other insurers to emulate their methods.

Terminating or capping the exclusion of employer-financed health benefits from personal income tax would add to the willingness of households to buy insurance with significant deductibles and cost sharing. This shift strengthens financial incentives to economize on demands for care. Increasing cost sharing leads to sharp reductions in demand for care.[45] But most insurance already includes considerable cost sharing, and the goal of preventing serious illness from imposing excessive financial burdens places limits on total liabilities that most households can be asked to bear. High-deductible health insurance would reduce administrative costs of insurers by avoiding the high costs of processing many small claims. An increasing proportion of households might be induced to join health maintenance organizations and other prepaid group practices that can provide care at lower cost than fee-for-service providers have done.[46]

The market-based approach to cost control minimizes the role of government in controlling health care costs. It is likely to achieve some limited economies, but it does not deal with the fundamental source of excessive health care spending or of its rapid growth, and it may actually increase costs.[47] This approach suffers from four problems: the temptation of each payer to shift costs, instability in competitive markets, costliness of supervisory control, and failure to attend to the underlying cause of growing health care expenses.

Programs to hold down premiums through managed care succeed in part by shifting costs to other payers, rather than reducing real resource use.[48] Such cost shifting is possible, for example, because the cost of serving each additional patient in an uncongested hospital is below the average cost of serving all patients. Many overhead expenses rise less than proportionately or not at all as caseload increases. Furthermore,

45. Willard G. Manning and others, *Health Insurance and the Demand for Medical Care: Evidence from a Randomized Experiment* (RAND, 1988).

46. Congressional Budget Office, *The Effects of Managed Health Care on Use and Costs of Health Services* (June 1992).

47. One study reports that an increase in cost sharing of 10 percentage points would have reduced health care spending $6 billion to $12 billion (1 to 2 percent) in 1989. Congressional Budget Office, *Rising Health Care Costs: Causes, Implications, and Strategies* (1991), p. 35.

48. CBO, *Effects of Managed Health Care.*

most hospitals are currently operating far below capacity.[49] Accordingly, a hospital can increase profits or reduce losses by attracting patients from other hospitals, as long as payments at least cover incremental cost. Payers who are most effective at securing discounts from physicians and hospitals will be able to offer insurance for below-average premiums and to attract customers. These savings are of no benefit to society, however, because overhead costs will be shifted to payers less adroit at negotiating discounts.

Such cost control techniques as preadmission review and prior authorization for various procedures may save health care resources but use real resources themselves. Private payers willingly incur these administrative costs as long as the incremental private savings exceed incremental private costs, a condition that can be satisfied even if added administrative costs offset all or most of the savings from reduced resource use and even if the savings are achieved at the expense of some other payer. The practical question is whether alternative methods of cost control can achieve greater net savings by operating at lower administrative cost.

As noted earlier, private health insurance markets are prone to instability and fragmentation. Insurers can offer discounted premiums to groups with below-average expected medical costs. Since any group contains some members expected to generate costs below the average for that group, other insurers have the pervasive temptation to market selectively to them. Insurers have become increasingly adept in pinpointing low- and high-cost customers, a practice that is the source of problems in the small-group insurance market. Thus the result of rational behavior by individual insurance companies is a socially inferior market outcome.[50]

Ordinary market competition in the sale of insurance cannot be expected to control costs for a more basic reason. Most outlays are concentrated in a small minority of cases: 1 percent of patients account for about 30 percent of all acute care outlays at an average cost per episode of about $80,000; 5 percent account for more than half of outlays at an average

49. The average daily occupancy of hospital beds in 1989 was 66.2 percent. Health Insurance Association of America, *Sourcebook of Health Insurance Data* (Washington: HIAA, 1991), table 5-1, p. 82.

50. This practice need not occur when companies charge every customer a separate premium based on expected losses. But such experience rating is costly to administer for small groups and individuals and rests on behavior many regard as odious, such as setting exorbitant premiums for customers with a history of illness or for groups such as the elderly, the disabled, or ethnic or racial groups that are sicker than average.

cost per episode of about $30,000.[51] Because medical outlays are so highly concentrated, plausible high-deductible, high–stop-loss plans will not change the incentive of insured patients and their physicians to demand all beneficial care regardless of cost during episodes of illness that account for most medical outlays. To be sure, if insurance carried deductibles of $30,000, nearly half of all outlays would occur during episodes in which total spending was below the deductible. But such deductibles would expose most households to precisely the financial losses they buy insurance to avoid. An inescapable dilemma exists: if deductibles are low enough to be acceptable to most households, the incentive of patients to overconsume health care will be unaffected for episodes of illness accounting for the large majority of health outlays; if deductibles are high enough to blunt this incentive, most households will face unacceptable financial loss from illness. High-deductible insurance policies cannot be used to control excessive health care spending.

The Chimera of Contractual Cost Control

If it were possible to specify in advance which procedures would be available in which situations, patients could purchase insurance for defined services in specific situations. But such contracts cannot in fact be written because there are so many distinct diagnoses (about 10,000), so many variations in patients' characteristics that bear on treatment (age, health history, and prior treatment), and so many possible treatments given for patients with particular diagnoses. As a result, a contract to specify when and under what circumstances various medical interventions would be employed would have to deal with hundreds of thousands of contingencies. The task of compiling such a list would be herculean, and even if compiled, it would be too cumbersome to use. The resulting large number and variety of health insurance plans and the need for individual purchasers to choose among them and perhaps to negotiate specific restrictions and conditions based on their own circumstances would befuddle purchasers and bedevil vendors.

51. This pattern is similar in the United States, Canada, and France, and over time. See Aaron, *Serious and Unstable Condition*, pp. 51–52. Estimates of costs per episode have been updated to 1992 to account for rising medical costs. MEDSTAT Systems, Inc., reports that the distribution of charges among a group of private companies for which it gathers data was even more concentrated. They report that in 1990, 3 percent of patients accounted for 54 percent of all charges. Data from Medstat Health Policy Research Sample Database, Ann Arbor, Michigan.

Furthermore, neither patients nor physicians would have any incentive to abide by previously negotiated restrictions. On the contrary, patients would have strong motives to buy restrictive insurance when healthy, in order to minimize premiums, and to report and slant information so as to increase access to all services when sick, regardless of originally stated purpose or intent.[52] Physicians would have every incentive to help them out.[53]

Managed Competition

To meet these problems, some analysts have advocated *managed competition*,[54] an arrangement in which a few competing agents or health insurance purchasing corporations (HIPCs) assist in both the sale of health insurance and the purchase of health care.[55] Several HIPCs would be authorized in each area so that they would both promote competition among insurers and providers and compete among themselves. They would encourage plans that eliminated services providing few or no benefits, require acceptance of any applicant individual or group, and receive subsidies for members of groups expected to generate especially high costs. They would also negotiate costs with hospitals and physicians. Because of their size they would be able to afford to collect information, do research, and identify providers that supply high-quality care at reasonable prices.

52. This is a clear example of the problem of time inconsistency, a difficulty noted by Kydland and Prescott, which arises when policies that are optimal at the time they are negotiated cease to be optimal later, when elements of that policy must be put into effect and no practical device exists for enforcing adherence to the original agreement. See Finn E. Kydland and Edward C. Prescott, "Rules Rather than Discretion: The Inconsistency of Optimal Plans," *Journal of Political Economy*, vol. 85 (June 1977), pp. 473–91.

53. The same line of argument explains why the Oregon plan for rationing services under medicaid is flawed. This plan divides all medical services into 714 categories, ranked in terms of expected medical benefit per dollar of cost. The state will set a medicaid budget and pay for services, starting with those ranked highest, until funds are exhausted. Services below the cutoff line would be unavailable under medicaid. Because the medical categories are so gross, some patients will be denied highly beneficial care while others will be provided low-benefit care. The number of categories should be considered against the number of diagnoses and the fact that patients in many diagnostic categories differ widely in the likelihood that they will benefit from care. Furthermore, simple categorization does not address the issue of how *intense* the therapy should be.

54. For examples of plans espousing managed competition, see Alain Enthoven and Richard Kronick, "A Consumer-Choice Health Plan for the 1990s," *New England Journal of Medicine*, vol. 320 (January 5 and 12, 1989), pp. 29–37, 94–101; and John Garamendi, "California Health Care in the 21st Century: A Vision for Reform" (Sacramento: California Department of Insurance, February 1992).

55. Enthoven and Kronick, "A Consumer-Choice Health Plan for the 1990s."

Managed competition would avoid or mitigate many of the problems with ordinary insurance competition, including the tendency for insurance markets to fragment, the high administrative costs associated with many competing groups, and confusion for insurance buyers. It could save on administrative costs by reducing the number of competing insurance plans.[56]

Unless managed competition is backed up by limits on total health care spending, however, it is unlikely to succeed in significantly reducing the amount of low-benefit, high-cost care, because it leaves unchanged the tendency of insured patients and their physicians to overuse medical services. A particular managed competition plan developed in California would create a form of total budget control by regulating health insurance premiums and limiting the maximum addition to premiums that insurers can charge for optional extra services. Alternatively, all groups paying for health care can unite, rather than compete, to achieve a degree of control over health care expenditures similar to that possessed by health care plans in other countries where the government or government-sponsored entities control health care spending.

Expenditure Caps

The simplest way to slow the growth of health care spending is to cap resources available to health care providers. Governments in most other industrial countries impose such restrictions. Typically, hospitals operate under budget limits, subject to adjustments for special circumstances. Hospital administrators and physicians must match hospital services to available resources, which means tailoring to available resources the criteria for hospital admission and for access to various diagnostic procedures and therapies.[57] Hospitals may elect to specialize in some services, and rely on neighboring hospitals for others. Physicians

56. Peter Diamond has proposed a variant of this approach under which every person and family would be assigned to various groups of intermediate size on a geographical, but not on an employment, basis. Insurance companies would compete with each other on the basis of cost and service to insure each group. The objective would be to achieve groups of sufficient size to minimize administrative costs and mute the incentives of adverse selection. Diamond, "Organizing the Health Insurance Market."

57. Confronted with severe limits on equipment and staffing that necessitates denial of beneficial care to patients in Britain, one physician stated that there are always some reasons for not treating particular patients. He remarked that the physician "states the reason for not going forward in medical terms . . . but that formulation in many instances is in no small part conditioned by the fact that there really aren't enough resources to treat everybody." Quoted in Henry J. Aaron and William B. Schwartz, *The Painful Prescription: Rationing Hospital Care* (Brookings, 1984), p. 102.

are reimbursed under widely varying rules. Some countries establish fee schedules, which are expected to be consistent with a total spending target. If actual use of physician services exceeds that assumed in setting the fee schedule, rates for the succeeding year are reduced. Some countries pay physicians a fixed sum, or capitation payment. In most countries, physicians cannot prescribe the full range of diagnostic procedures for as large a proportion of their patients as U.S. physicians can.

The administration of spending caps would start with the establishment by the federal government of a ceiling on U.S. health care spending. A national budget would be parceled out among regions or states and then to substate units. The budgets would be allocated among hospitals and other providers by quasi-political entities. No one has described in detail how such expenditure caps would be calculated, what organization would determine allocations among and within the states, and how the limits would be enforced. The objective is the imposition of budget discipline on health care providers. A combination of a budget cap and managed competition would be attractive because it preserves some consumer choice and flexibility in the provision of health care.[58]

Can caps succeed in slowing spending growth, and is governmental involvement necessary? The answer to both questions is yes. A country's health care spending is inversely related to the share covered through government budgets. A 10 percent decrease in the percentage of health care outlays financed privately is statistically associated with a drop in health care spending of 3.1 percent, after controlling for population, per capita gross domestic product, and the governmental employment of physicians.[59] This relationship between source of financing and spending creates a presumption that increased public spending on health care need not be more inflationary than private financing. The share of health care spending that is financed privately is higher in the United States than in

58. Some supporters of employer-sponsored insurance plans have linked these plans to cost control based on spending targets, which would look like spending caps but would not be backed by enforcement authority. What would happen if actual outlays exceeded these targets is not clear, however. If the targets were merely indicative goals, they would have little effect, since incentives would be unchanged. If penalties were imposed, they would become caps in fact, and only targets in name.

59. See Aaron, *Serious and Unstable Condition*, pp. 107–08. Patricia Danzon argues that hidden costs imposed on patients, which arise under publicly financed systems, offset much or all of the supposed savings as indicated by official statistics. Thus costs associated with queues, which serve to curtail demand much as managed care does, are not recorded, while administrative costs are reported. See Danzon, "Hidden Overhead Costs: Is Canada's System Really Less Expensive?" *Health Affairs*, vol. 11 (Spring 1992), pp. 21–43.

any other major industrial country. It is not clear why elected officials in the United States are more likely to succumb to constituent pressure to boost health care spending than are those in other countries.

Some analysts hold out the hope that increased reliance on HMOs would produce a sustained slowdown in the increase of health costs. The record to date is not encouraging. First, spending by HMOs, although somewhat lower than that of fee-for-service providers, has been rising at about the same rate. Second, most recent HMO enrollees have joined the type of HMO that does not have lower costs than fee-for-service providers. Third, states where HMOs have a large share of the insurance market do not appear to have lower per capita health costs than do states where HMOs have a small share.

The Political Economy of Cost Control

The choice of instruments to control growth of health care spending will influence not only the speed at which health care spending rises, but also the political forum in which health care decisions are made.

Markets and flexibility. The distinguishing characteristic of current financing arrangements is decentralization. Outlays are determined by millions of providers and patients, business sponsors of health insurance, hundreds of insurers, and various governmental agencies. Individual patients, physicians, and other professionals generate demands for services by physicians or other professionals themselves, and by hospitals, laboratories, and testing centers.

These methods of paying for health care have been highly flexible in promoting innovative ways of delivering acute care. The most notable is the health maintenance organization, which has become the object of study and admiration by foreign experts. This innovation is well established, will persist, and may well expand under any of the methods of health care reform that have been advanced. An additional innovation is managed care—the variety of instruments insurers have developed for controlling use of health care and securing discounts. Extending insurance coverage and relying on competition in the marketplace to control cost will permit other such innovations to develop.

Limits on market flexibility. Although this system is highly flexible within its domain, it is surrounded by rigid boundaries. In particular, it does not permit resources to be shifted from traditional modes of delivering acute care to nontraditional health care or health-related activities that are widely thought to have important advantages for particular population groups: school-based clinics for children, neighborhood health clinics for residents of poorly served communities, health guidance to pregnant teenagers and counseling to young mothers on raising healthy children, or subsidies to encourage providers to practice in underserved areas. Under current arrangements, such activities require separate and explicit authorizing legislation and appropriations. Reliance on competition among insurers, on managed care, or on managed competition would not break down the financial walls between traditional acute care and these nontraditional methods of improving health.

Empowering state and local entities to allocate fixed budgets breaches these barriers. Such bodies would be free to shift resources from ordinary, acute care to alternative, nontraditional services. Physicians and other providers would continue to make clinical decisions at the time care is rendered, but budget limits and their method of allocation would determine the constraints within which these decisions would be made.

The chief arguments against budget caps concern potential bureaucratic rigidity. Traditional recipients of budget allocations will fight to retain their current shares. Those administering budget limits would confront the same pressures in trying to close an underused hospital that Congress faces when it seeks to close redundant military bases. On the other hand, the allocation of budgets for all health care services to geographical entities creates an opportunity for considerable reorganization in the delivery of care. The combination of budget limits with elements of managed competition would further reduce the likelihood of perpetuating outmoded facilities and organizations.

The need for decentralization. Considerable variation in the delivery of care exists within the United States. HMOs are a major force in California and Hawaii, a significant element in a few other states, but a negligible factor in others. Hospital utilization, lengths of stay, and use of various procedures differ widely among regions, states, and substate areas. Certain procedures are used far more frequently in some areas than in others. Clear evidence is lacking on which approaches are superior. These and many other differences are likely to persist indefinitely. It will be vital, therefore, for any reform to accommodate actual arrangements across the United States.

Painless Cost Control: The Impossible Dream

Whatever mechanism of cost control the United States chooses, the nation will rather quickly have to recognize that sustained reductions in the growth of health care spending can be achieved only if some beneficial care is denied to some people. While experts disagree on how much can be saved by such reforms as streamlining administration, reform of the malpractice system, or eliminating medically ineffective care, no one disagrees that these savings can be achieved only once. They may contribute to an explanation of why U.S. health expenditures are high; they cannot explain why expenditures are growing. When all practicable savings have been achieved from these sources, the growth of health care spending will resume at current rates unless services are restricted.

Summary and Recommendations

The chief characteristic of the financing of health care in the United States and all other developed countries is that patients bear little of the cost of health care when sick. No market-based health care reform would significantly change this situation for illnesses that account for the large majority of health expenditures. Facing little cost, patients have the incentive to seek care, even if it produces small benefits at great cost; physicians have every incentive to see that patients get what they want. At the same time that the interaction of financing and scientific advances are driving up costs, increasing numbers of U.S. residents find themselves without health insurance or afraid they will lose it.

Large-scale changes in an institution like health care, which absorbs more than one-seventh of net production and generates more than one-seventh of all incomes, are bound to create winners and losers and to be highly controversial. On balance, reforms that build on current insurance arrangements to provide universal coverage have the greatest chance of extending health insurance to those who now lack it. Linked to a single federally sponsored program covering all families and individuals not connected to the labor force, such workplace coverage could serve essentially all Americans. To achieve cost control, some form of budget limit is essential. This plan creates the opportunity to reallocate resources to nontraditional ways of delivering health care, but it also carries the risk of bureaucratic rigidity. This danger could be reduced if health insurance purchasing corporations and other elements of managed competition were used in the selection of insurers and care providers.

Whatever plan is adopted, additional government spending will be necessary just after its inception. The smallest increase in government spending would occur under plans that mandate employer sponsorship and provide public backup coverage. The on-budget costs of extending acute care coverage ran approximately $35 billion in 1991.[60] Of these costs, about two-thirds would go to cover uninsured nonworkers and one-third to subsidize premiums for low-wage workers. Part of these added federal outlays would offset current private expenditures. The budgetary costs would increase significantly if the plan includes some long-term care benefits.[61]

If acute care reform slows the growth of health care spending, the added front-end costs would rapidly be offset by reductions in future outlays. Although reform will boost costs initially, it will save money in short order if cost control is effective. A reduction in the rate of growth of health care spending by 1 percentage point would generate savings in three years that would offset the initial increase in national health care spending as a result of covering the uninsured. A reduction of 2 percentage points would offset the initial increase in less than two years. Since most health care spending is financed privately, most savings would accrue in the private sector. It would therefore take much longer before federal outlays returned to their baseline levels. But federal health care spending is projected to rise fast under current policy. Just a 2 percentage-point slowdown in the growth of medicare and medicaid projected under current law would reduce spending more than enough by the year 2000 to offset the added costs of providing universal coverage. In the future, the United States would enjoy lower health care spending than now confronts the nation, and all Americans would be assured a standard perquisite of citizenship in modern developed nations: access to health care they can afford.

60. For example, the plan developed by the National Leadership Coalition for Health Care Reform would result in added federal government expenditures of $35 billion in 1991. *Report of the National Leadership Coalition for Health Care Reform: Excellent Health Care for All Americans at a Reasonable Cost* (Washington, 1991), p. 29.

61. While reform of acute care financing does not logically require provision of added long-term care benefits, the effort to forge a political coalition for reform may lead to such a linkage. Simple acute care reform offers little to the elderly and disabled, who are currently covered by medicare, other than the prospect of paying higher taxes to support improved benefits for others. Adding long-term care benefits, a serious concern of the elderly, would offer them something of considerable value.

3

GORDON BERLIN
AND WILLIAM McALLISTER

Homelessness

JUST FIFTEEN years ago, homelessness was not a common feature of American life. Women and men were not sleeping on city streets; children and mothers were not crowding emergency shelters; and the word itself was barely known.

Currently, perhaps 1 million people become homeless in a year and a half million are without homes at any one time. The awareness that so many people are in such desperate straits furthers the belief of many Americans that government cannot solve social problems. Why has homelessness been so intractable? Why don't the obvious solutions work? What can government do?

Numbers and Characteristics

To be homeless is to be without adequate housing. But are the homeless only those "literally homeless," living on streets or in shelters? Or do they include the "hidden homeless," living in abandoned buildings or otherwise out of sight, or the "precariously housed," living in doubled- or tripled-up circumstances or in unsafe, substandard, or otherwise physically inadequate buildings?[1] Defining homelessness is thus an ethical and political act, not just an analytic one.

John C. Weicher was the discussant for this chapter. We thank Diane Baillargeon, Sar Levitan, Sy Malach, Peter Rossi, the editors, and especially Christopher Jencks for their critiques; Nancy Andrews, Susan Gewirtz, Paul Leonard, Frank Lipton, Andy Sum, and Barry Zigas for sharing their knowledge and numbers; and Mark Unger for his research assistance.

1. The phrases are from Peter H. Rossi, *Down and Out in America* (University of Chicago Press, 1989), p. 12; for a detailed review of definitional differences, see pp. 10–13, 47–48. See also Martha R. Burt and Barbara Cohen, "Review of Research on Homeless Persons: Literature Review Prepared for Food and Nutrition Service, USDA and the Interagency Council on the Homeless" (Washington: Urban Institute, March 1988), pp. 1–3. For an example of just how greatly the number can increase by including different kinds of precariously housed people, see Peter Marcuse, "Homelessness and Housing

TABLE 3-1. National Estimates of the Number of Homeless People

Study	Year of study	Estimated number of homeless
Census Bureau[a]	1990	228,000
Urban Institute[b]	1987	496,000–600,000
HUD[c]	1983	250,000–350,000

SOURCES: Department of Commerce, "Census Bureau Releases 1990 Decennial Counts for Persons Enumerated in Emergency Shelters and Observed on Streets," CB91-117, n.d., pp. 1–2; Martha R. Burt and Barbara E. Cohen, *America's Homeless: Numbers, Characteristics and the Programs That Serve Them* (Washington: Urban Institute Press, 1989), pp. 27–31; and Department of Housing and Urban Development, "A Report to the Secretary on the Homeless and Emergency Shelters" (Office of Policy Development and Research, May 1984).
  a. A count of the number of street and shelter homeless on the night of March 20–21, 1990.
  b. Based on a probability sample of 1,704 homeless service users, such as shelters and soup kitchens.
  c. Relies on several methods, all of which hinge on the estimates of key informants such as shelter providers and local activists.

Because definitions and measuring techniques vary greatly, population estimates differ.[2] Table 3-1 reports estimates from the only national studies, each based on a different methodology. The most widely accepted number is the Urban Institute's estimate that, at any one time, 600,000 people are homeless. The only nationwide study using a consistent methodology to estimate change over time suggests that the homelessness rate across 182 cities tripled from 1981 to 1989, with the rate of increase slackening slightly toward the end of the decade.[3]

In their location at the bottom of the housing market, the currently homeless are successors to the urban migrants and vagrants of the 1950s and 1960s who lived in the cheap hotels and flophouses of skid row districts. More than 80 percent of the "old" homeless were white and male, and about two-thirds were over 45.[4] They survived on pensions or earnings from casual labor, which usually paid enough to rent the cheapest accommodations—less than a dollar a night, at the time. Almost none lived on the streets. At least a quarter were alcoholics, and

---

Policy," in Carol L. M. Caton, ed., *Homelessness in America* (New York: Oxford University Press, 1990), pp. 138–59. Most researchers, ourselves included, tend to use the more limited definition, that is, those on streets and in shelters.

2. For a review of this controversy, see Anna Kondratas, "Estimates and Public Policy: The Politics of Numbers," *Housing Policy Debate*, vol. 2, no. 4 (1991), pp. 631–47.

3. Martha R. Burt, *Over the Edge: The Growth of Homelessness in the 1980s* (New York and Washington: Russell Sage Foundation and Urban Institute Press, 1992), pp. 130–39.

4. This description of the "old" homeless relies on Rossi, *Down and Out in America*, pp. 27–33; and Donald J. Bogue, *Skid Row in American Cities* (University of Chicago Press, 1963).

TABLE 3-2. Estimates of the Number of Different Kinds
of Homeless People

Subgroup	Percent	Number of people
Children	15	90,000
Parents	8	48,000
Married, no children	2	12,000
Single adults	75	450,000
Total	100	600,000

SOURCE: Martha R. Burt, *Over the Edge: The Growth of Homelessness in the 1980s* (New York and Washington: Russell Sage Foundation and Urban Institute Press, 1992), pp. 13–16.

perhaps similar proportions were mentally ill and suffered from physical disabilities.

The currently homeless differ from the old homeless in two crucial ways: they are literally without a dwelling, and they are poorer. The self-reported monthly income of homeless single adults in 1987 averaged $147, less than one-third that of men living on skid row in the 1950s. Families averaged $360 a month, excluding food stamps.[5] These incomes are 30 and 48 percent of the 1987 poverty levels, respectively.

Mothers and children are now homeless as they were not in the past (see table 3-2), and over half the homeless are minorities. Most single adult males have a work history, but fewer than 10 percent were working when surveyed, and 50 to 75 percent had not had a "steady job" for more than one year. These rates are lower than those of the old homeless. Additionally, the current homeless are younger than those in the past: 75 percent of the mothers are under 34, and the average age of single adults is in the mid-thirties.[6]

About one-third of homeless people suffer from severe and persistent mental illness, somewhat more than among the old homeless.[7] Today,

5. Authors' calculations based on Burt, *Over the Edge*, p. 57. Only half the families and less than 15 percent of homeless single adults received food stamps in 1987; the average benefit per person was $34 for families and $60 for single adults. Ibid., p. 20.

6. The numbers are from Burt, *Over the Edge*, pp. 14–19. For reviews of local and state studies on these and other dimensions, see Burt and Cohen, "Review of Research on Homeless Persons"; and Randall K. Filer and Marjorie Honig, "Policy Issues in Homelessness: Current Understanding and Directions for Research" (New York: Manhattan Institute, March 1990).

7. A "severely and persistently mentally ill" person has been suffering from schizophrenia, bipolar (manic-depressive) and depressive affective or schizoaffective disorders for a long time and as a result is unable to function in daily life. See Deborah L. Dennis, Irene S. Levine, and Fred C. Osher, "The Physical and Mental Health Status of Homeless

one homeless adult in three, as in the past, has an alcohol problem.[8] And both the old and the new homeless tend to be disaffiliated from relatives and friends.[9]

Drug abuse is a new phenomena. One review of studies found that 48 percent of homeless people reported using illegal drugs or having been treated for drug abuse.[10] In 1989, 75 percent of Baltimore's homeless men and 38 percent of its homeless women had a substance abuse disorder.[11] And a 1992 New York City study found that at least 57 percent of single adult shelter users and at least 26 percent of mothers with children tested positive for illegal drugs, mostly cocaine.[12]

Not surprisingly, the homeless frequently have combined problems of mental illness, alcohol and drug abuse, and physical disabilities.[13] For example, half of all homeless mentally ill people are chemically addicted, and perhaps 33 to 60 percent of homeless drug addicts also have a drinking problem.[14]

The coincidence of many problems makes help harder to give. The treatment for mental illness conflicts with that for drug abuse. Housing someone who is both mentally ill and crack addicted is more difficult

---

Adults," *Housing Policy Debate*, vol 2, no. 3 (1991), pp. 815–35. The range of estimates around the consensus of one-third can be great; for example, the Institute of Medicine's review of twelve studies found that 25 to 50 percent of homeless people were severely and persistently mentally ill. A. A. Arce and M. J. Vergare, "Identifying and Characterizing the Mentally Ill among the Homeless," in H. Richard Lamb, ed., *The Homeless Mentally Ill: A Task Force Report of the American Psychiatric Association* (Washington: American Psychiatric Association, 1984), pp. 75–89. Rossi estimates prevalence rates are 50 percent greater than in the past. Rossi, *Down and Out in America*, pp. 41–42.

8. Rossi, *Down and Out in America*, p. 156. See also Burt and Cohen, "Review of Research on Homeless Persons"; and Filer and Honig, "Policy Issues in Homelessness," pp. 15–17 and table 1.

9. Measuring social disaffiliation is not straightforward, and the degree to which it is found among the old and new homeless is much debated.

10. Burt and Cohen, "Review of Research on Homeless Persons," p. 41.

11. William R. Breakey and others, "Health and Mental Health Problems of Homeless Men and Women in Baltimore," *Journal of the American Medical Association*, vol. 262 (September 8, 1989), pp. 1352–57.

12. Authors' calculations based on data from New York City Commission on the Homeless, *The Way Home* (New York, 1992), pp. B-17, C-2, table 6.

13. Institute of Medicine, Committee on Health Care for Homeless People, *Homelessness, Health, and Human Needs* (Washington: National Academy Press, 1988), pp. 65–66.

14. National Institute of Mental Health, *Two Generations of NIMH-Funded Research on Homelessness and Mental Illness: 1982–1990* (Rockville, Md., 1991); and Institute of Medicine, Committee on Health Care for Homeless People, *Homelessness, Health, and Human Needs*, p. 65.

than if he were just the former. And as disabilities mount, employment becomes more unrealistic and public assistance more difficult to sustain.

Causes: Becoming and Remaining Homeless

Extreme poverty, low earnings, and social isolation are common to past and current homeless. And current levels of disability among homeless people may not be so different from those of a previous era. Why, then, have some poor people now become *literally* homeless—on the street—when an earlier, similar population avoided that fate?

For policymakers, answering this question is only partly instructive. The conditions causing someone to become homeless are not always the same as those causing that person to remain homeless. A lack of affordable housing may generate homelessness, but the failure to treat alcoholism, mental illness, drug addiction, physical disability, or other problems among those who have become homeless causes these afflictions to worsen, reducing the possibility of *simply* rehousing them. Unless these problems are also addressed, some currently homeless people will be unable to obtain and retain permanent housing even if it becomes available.

There is no evidence that can conclusively identify why people become or remain homeless. But changes in the economy, in government policies, and in social behavior in the 1970s and 1980s suggest some answers. Changes begun earlier also culminated during this time.

Poverty

During the 1970s and 1980s, urban job opportunities for unskilled workers and incomes for young males both took a beating. Between 1970 and 1984, nine major cities lost 683,000 low-skilled jobs, while they gained 742,000 high-skilled jobs.[15] Concomitantly, earnings collapsed among young males. Average earnings for the bottom 40 percent of all male high school dropouts, aged 20–29, plummeted from $5,816 in 1973 to $1,922 in 1986 (1990 dollars). Young black male dropouts did even worse, as earnings dropped from $4,172 in 1973 to $1,130 in 1986. More acutely, the percentage of all dropouts reporting no earnings rose

15. John D. Kasarda, "The Regional and Urban Redistribution of People and Jobs in the U.S.," paper prepared for the National Research Council, Committee on National Urban Policy, National Academy of Sciences, 1986.

from 12 percent to 19 percent between 1973 and 1979 and doubled to 38 percent in 1982.[16]

Declines in job opportunities and earnings may not only cause young men to become homeless but might also contribute to family homelessness as young mothers are left without financial support from the children's father. The feminization of poverty also may explain the development of family homelessness. The women and children in female-headed households made up 24 percent of those in poverty in 1966; they now constitute about 38 percent. And the poorest of these families have been hit hardest. In 1989 the average single-mother household in the bottom quintile had only $2,563 in cash income, about $1,000 (or 26 percent) less than in 1973. No other quintile dropped as much.[17]

Housing

At one time, poor single men lived in single-room occupancy hotels (SROs), rooming or lodging houses, cubicle or cage hotels, or flophouses.[18] But over the 1970s and 1980s, much of what remained of this housing disappeared; for example, perhaps 1 million SRO rooms—half the national total—were lost during this time and the number of other kinds of cheap rooms also declined (see table 3-3).[19] Tellingly, vacancy rates dropped; for example, vacancies in New York City's SRO hotels dove from 26 percent in the mid-1970s to 0 percent in 1981.[20]

Families may have become homeless because of the decrease in the supply of affordable housing for families with incomes below 50 percent

16. Current Population Survey, Public Use Tapes, March 1974, 1980, 1983, and 1987; and tabulations by Center for Labor Market Studies, Northeastern University.

17. *Overview of Entitlement Programs, 1992 Green Book, Background Material and Data on Programs within the Jurisdiction of the Committee on Ways and Means,* Committee Print, House Committee on Ways and Means, 102 Cong. 2 sess. (Government Printing Office, 1992), pp. 1274, 1371. (Hereafter *1992 Green Book.*) These statistics exclude female-headed households with no children.

18. These kinds of lodging differ in room size, building quality, privacy, amenities, and cleanliness, each of which correlates in obvious ways with cost. Historically, SROs were most expensive, and flophouses, which are akin to congregate homeless shelters, were least costly. For a description and history of these different kinds of housing, see Charles Hoch and Robert A. Slayton, *New Homeless and Old: Community and the Skid Row Hotel* (Temple University Press, 1989).

19. Lynda V. Mapes, "Faulty Food and Shelter Programs Draw Charge That Nobody's Home to Homeless," *National Journal,* March 2, 1985, pp. 474–76.

20. Philip Kasinitz, "Gentrification and Homelessness: The Single Room Occupant and the Inner City Revival," in Jon Erickson and Charles Wilhelm, eds., *Housing the Homeless* (Rutgers University, Center for Urban Policy Research, 1986), p. 249.

TABLE 3-3. Loss of Single-Room Occupancy, Rooming House, and Cubicle Hotel Units, Selected Cities

City	Years	Number of lost units[a]	Percent of stock[b]
Boston	1965–85	963[c]	96
Chicago	1960–80	31,396	n.a.
Chicago	1973–84	18,000	19
Chicago	1958–80	8,000[d]	100
Cincinnati	1970s	2,083	42
Denver	1976–81	28[e]	62
Los Angeles	1970–85	n.a.	50
Los Angeles	1969–86	2,300	n.a.
New York	1975–81	30,385	60
New York	1970s–80s	30,000–100,000	n.a.
New York	1960–90	24[f]	65
Portland	1970s	1,700	n.a.
San Diego	1976–84	1,247	26
San Francisco	1975–79	5,723	17
Seattle	1960–81	15,000	n.a.

SOURCES: Thomas Fodor, "Toward Housing the Homeless: The Single Occupancy Alternative" (1985), p. 3, cited in James D. Wright and Julie A. Lam, "Homelessness and the Low-Income Housing Supply," *Social Policy*, vol. 17 (Spring 1987), p. 51; Department of Planning, City of Chicago, "Housing Needs of Chicago's Single, Low-Income Renters" (1985), cited in Peter Rossi, *Down and Out in America: The Origins of Homelessness* (University of Chicago Press, 1989), p. 182; Charles Hoch and Robert A. Slayton, *New Homeless and Old: Community and the Skid Row* (Temple University Press, 1989), p. 175; Hamilton, Rabinowitz and Alschuler, Inc., *The Changing Face of Misery: Los Angeles' Skid Row Area in Transition—Housing and Social Service Needs of Central City East* (Los Angeles: Community Redevelopment Agency, 1987), cited in Burt, *Over the Edge*, p. 33; Joy Horowitz, "The Savior of Skid Row," *Los Angeles Times Magazine*, November 10, 1991, p. 16; "Making More Homeless," *Wall Street Journal*, January 24, 1992, p. A14; and Neighborhood Planning Workshop, Hunter College/CUNY, "Commercial Lodging Houses," New York, September 29, 1989, pp. 10–11.
 n.a. Not available.
 a. Unless otherwise indicated, units refer to SRO rooms.
 b. Based on stock existing at first time point.
 c. Number of rooming houses.
 d. Number of cubicle hotel rooms.
 e. Number of SRO hotels.
 f. Number of lodging houses in the Bowery district.

of the area median and because of the increase in the number of poor, unsubsidized renter households.[21] The number of unsubsidized units with rent plus utilities below $300 (1989 dollars) declined dramatically from 7.8 million occupied units in 1974 to 5.3 million by 1985. Over this period, the number of poor, unsubsidized renter households increased from 4.2 million to 5.5 million.[22] Fewer low-rent housing units, more households, and lowered incomes spell heavier rent burdens. Between

21. The poverty level is about 40 percent of the area median income and, of course, the incomes of homeless families are far below poverty.
22. William C. Apgar, Jr., and others, "The State of the Nation's Housing, 1991" (Harvard University, Joint Center for Housing Studies, 1991), pp. 16, 35. Some studies argue that vacant units, those with no cash rent, and assisted units with rents above $300

1975 and 1983, the number of very low-income households spending more than 70 percent of their gross reported annual income on rent rocketed from 2 million to 3.7 million—an 84.5 percent increase.[23] Between 1974 and 1985, the number of nonelderly, very low-income families that were "worst cases" rose from 1.1 million to 2.3 million before declining to 2.1 million by the end of the decade. Also over these years, the percentage of families that were "worst cases" because of their severe rent burden increased from 57 percent to 75 percent. And by 1989, 62 percent of these families were headed by single women.[24]

By the early 1980s, single-mother families were increasingly forced to choose between shelter and other necessities and so became homeless. Too, some families may no longer have been financially able to support young adult children who could not contribute to the household, forcing these children to leave and perhaps become homeless.[25]

Public Assistance

Between 1970 and 1992, median benefits to families with dependent children (AFDC) for a mother of two with no income declined 43 percent, with most of the decrease occurring in the 1970s. And although the combined average AFDC and food stamp benefit for such a mother fell

should be included in counts of affordable housing. See Kathryn P. Nelson and Jose M. Calzadilla, "Measuring Changes in Affordable Low-Rent Housing with AHS Data," paper prepared for the 1991 annual meeting of the American Statistical Association. However, vacant units are likely to be substandard and in the process of being taken off the market; units with no cash rents tend to be in rural areas and occupied by tenant farmers and workers whose rent is taken from wages; their increase in number from the 1970s to the 1980s was largely due to changes in measurement; and counting assisted units still results in a decline from 10 million to 8.1 million affordable units between 1974 and 1989. On vacancies and assisted units, see William C. Apgar, Jr., "An Abundance of Housing for All but The Poor," Working Paper W91-2 (Harvard University, Joint Center for Housing Studies, 1991); on zero cash rent units, personal communication with Apgar.

23. General Accounting Office, *Changes in Rent Burdens and Housing Conditions of Lower Income Households*, RCED-85-108 (April 23, 1985), p. 4. As Anthony Downs notes, very poor households typically spend more than their current income, and as Apgar and others point out, households tend to overstate their housing expenditures. Thus the number of households in these categories may be less than reported, but this does not necessarily mean the percentage change is less. Anthony Downs, *Rental Housing in the 1980s* (Brookings, 1983), p. 146; and Apgar and others, "State of the Nation's Housing," p. 17.

24. Department of Housing and Urban Development, "Priority Housing Problems and 'Worst Case' Needs in 1989," PDR-1314 (June 1991), pp. 21, 26–27.

25. Rossi, *Down and Out in America*, pp. 188–90.

only one-quarter, this still left her with just $623 to spend each month in 1991. More broadly, changes in means-tested programs caused 2.2 million more people to be poor in 1989 than in 1979.[26]

Care for the Mentally Ill

In 1955 about four-fifths of the persistently and severely mentally ill lived in state mental hospitals.[27] Now perhaps 5 percent do. These institutions were to be replaced by community mental health centers providing comprehensive, continuous, high-quality medical and psychiatric care and relying heavily on the use of new classes of psychotropic drugs to control the disease. However, only about a third to half of the centers envisioned were created, and they were not connected to the discharge planning of state hospitals. Partly as a result, the centers tend to serve the "worried well" and not the severely mentally ill.[28]

Moreover, no thought was given to housing those released from state institutions, and many found their way to the cheap lodging that has since disappeared. No single governmental agency is held accountable for providing services, as responsibility is fragmented among half a dozen agencies and three levels of government. And tightened mental hospital admissions standards exclude people who would previously have received treatment.

As a result, many homeless people are not able to maintain treatment. Roughly half of those released from mental hospitals are rehospitalized within one year (and then discharged after being stabilized).[29] Since the 1970s, a generation of chronically mentally ill patients has come of age who have never been inside a psychiatric hospital for more than thirty days, if at all, and often know little about their illness or medication requirements. This group is particularly at risk of becoming homeless.[30]

26. See *1992 Green Book*, pp. 641, 643 (1991 dollars), 1317.

27. Martha R. Burt and Karen J. Pittman, *Testing the Social Safety Net* (Washington: Urban Institute Press, 1985), p. 64; authors' calculations based on Burt, *Over the Edge*, p. 120; and comments by E. Fuller Torrey, in "Rethinking Policy on Homelessness," Heritage Lectures 194 (Washington: Heritage Foundation, 1989), p. 11.

28. Department of Health and Human Services, *Outcasts on Main Street: Report of the Federal Task Force on Homelessness and Severe Mental Illness* (Washington: Interagency Council on the Homeless, 1992), pp. 15–17.

29. E. Fuller Torrey, *Nowhere To Go: The Tragic Odyssey of the Homeless Mentally Ill* (Harper and Row, 1988), p. 25.

30. Several studies suggest the direct homeless effects of these changes. Studies in Massachusetts, Chicago, Ohio, New York State, and Boston found from 17 to 50 percent of patients released from mental hospitals were homeless or in unknown living arrangements

Legal Rights

As treatment for alcoholics and mentally ill people changed, new laws and judicial decisions decriminalized public inebriation and extended the civil rights of the mentally ill. In many cities, street alcoholics and drug addicts are ignored by the police, and a person must be both mentally ill *and* likely to harm himself or others before being involuntarily hospitalized. In an earlier era, these people would have been institutionalized or jailed.

Homeless Services

As homelessness worsened in the 1980s, the supply and quality of such homeless services as shelters, soup kitchens, and drop-in centers improved.[31] As cheap housing and cash assistance, such as general assistance benefits for single men, became scarce, homeless services became increasingly available. The perverse result is that some people may have become homeless to obtain help.

Single-Mother Families

Almost all homeless families are headed by young mothers, most are from minority groups, and, typically, the mothers have never married. Between 1970 and 1990, the number of households headed by never-married women soared from 248,000 to almost 2.8 million. Among blacks, the number increased from 173,000 to almost 1.6 million.[32] And between 1970 and 1989, the annual number of households formed

---

soon after their release. Many were released homeless. See Robert E. Drake, Michael A. Wallach, and J. Schuyler Hoffman, "Housing Instability and Homelessness among Aftercare Patients of an Urban State Hospital," *Hospital and Community Psychiatry*, vol. 40 (January 1989), pp. 46–51; Society for the Psychological Study of Social Issues, "Worlds That Fail: A Longitudinal Study of Urban Mental Patients," *Journal of Social Issues*, vol. 45, no. 3 (1989), pp. 79–90; John Belcher and Beverly G. Toomey, "Relationship Between the Deinstitutionalization Model, Psychiatric Disability and Homelessness," *Health and Social Work*, vol. 13 (Spring 1988), pp. 145–53; Frank R. Lipton, Suzanne Nutt, and Albert Sabatini, "Housing the Homeless Mentally Ill: A Longitudinal Study of a Treatment Approach," *Hospital and Community Psychiatry*, vol. 39 (January 1988), pp. 40–45; and Virginia Mulkern and others, "Homeless Needs Assessment Study: Findings and Recommendations for the Massachusetts Department of Mental Health" (Boston: Human Services Research Institute, 1985).

31. Burt, *Over the Edge*, p. 135.
32. *1992 Green Book*, p. 1078.

by unmarried young women almost tripled, from 190,000 to about 500,000.[33]

Drug Abuse

The problem of homeless drug dependents may be largely a development of the past five years. For example, detoxification facilities, which once served only those with alcohol problems, began to have to contend with drug problems in the mid-1980s.[34]

The problem of homeless drug addicts coincides with the rise of crack, which causes more violent behavior, is more addictive, and may cost more to use than previously popular drugs. Central-city emergency room episodes involving cocaine increased from 0.12 to 1.06 per 1,000 episodes between 1975 and 1985, even as all emergency room drug episodes declined from 8.83 to 7.64 per 1,000. A 1992 New York City study found that 54.0 percent of sheltered single adults tested positive for crack cocaine, whereas only 2.6 percent tested positive for opiates.[35] And an increasing proportion of mentally ill homeless people are becoming drug users.

The Descent into Homelessness

The single most important difference in the housing opportunities facing the old and new homeless is the loss of very cheap, and, by current standards, generally inadequate housing.[36] Compounding this loss is both the decrease in income for poor people and the increase in the number of poor. In view of these trends, why so few are homeless may be less of a puzzle than how so many stay housed.

Against this backdrop of a declining affordable housing supply, homelessness may have occurred in overlapping waves. In the late 1970s, non- and deinstitutionalization may have been the primary contributor to homelessness. In the early 1980s, the recession, combined with a

33. Authors' calculations based on Department of Health and Human Services, "Monthly Vital Statistics, Report of Natality Statistics," report 40, no. 8, supplement (National Center for Health Statistics, 1989); and Bureau of the Census, *Statistical Abstract of the United States, 1989, 1990* (Department of Commerce, 1989, 1990).

34. Dennis McCarty and others, "Alcoholism, Drug Abuse, and the Homeless," *American Psychologist*, vol. 46 (November 1991), p. 1142.

35. New York City Commission on the Homeless, *The Way Home*, pp. 44, C-2, C-3.

36. For every quality rental unit lost during the 1970s and 1980s, two substandard units were lost. Apgar, "An Abundance of Housing," pp. 31–32.

decade of falling income, pushed young men and young families out the
door. And in the mid- to late 1980s, the burst in crack use may have
added to the problem.

The odyssey that individuals and families travel in becoming homeless
suggests these larger changes do not immediately cause people to show
up at a shelter or to sleep on the street. Each story begins with a set of
predisposing conditions, usually severe poverty. Then comes a precipitat-
ing event or events—a worker loses a job, a mentally ill person decom-
pensates, drug users turn homes into crack houses, or abandonment,
arson, or conversion empties the building.

In most cases, this is not enough to put people on the street. Evicted
or pushed out of their homes, they travel a circuit of friends, relatives,
and others willing and able to provide temporary shelter or to lend
money. After a while, most people can contribute enough to the household
to remain, or they find a place of their own. But others, having exhausted
the goodwill and resources of kin as well as friends, finally arrive at a
shelter or the streets.[37]

Why Simple Solutions Sometimes Backfire

The solution to homelessness seems straightforward. For those already
homeless, provide the necessary permanent housing or services. To avoid
new homelessness, identify those at risk and provide housing, income,
or services. However, doing the first can make the problem worse. And
our knowledge is insufficient for effectively doing the second.

Dynamics of Homelessness

Every day, some people begin and others end a spell of homelessness.
Some spells are brief, others protracted. Many are permanent. Policies
that decrease the number of people who initially become homeless,
shorten spells, or reduce the return to homelessness help reduce the
problem. But well-intentioned measures can easily have perverse effects.

Recent data from New York City, for instance, show that an average
of 850 families became homeless—entered a shelter—each month. By
themselves, 15 percent found housing within a week, 32 percent within
a month, and half within three months. However, 30 percent remained

37. Rossi's evidence leads him to draw a similar sketch. Rossi, *Down and Out in
America*, pp. 188–90.

TABLE 3-4. Distribution of Stays in New York City Family Shelters When Families Leave on Their Own
Percent unless otherwise specified

Length of stay (days)	Distribution of completed stays for entering families
30	30.5
60	12.8
90	7.1
120	5.2
150	2.0
180	1.3
210	2.1
240	2.8
270	2.0
300	1.2
330	0.4
360	1.9
360 + [a]	30.6
Total	100.0
Average (months)	12.8

SOURCE: Authors' calculations based on data from City of New York Human Resources Administration.

a. Assumes an exit probability of 0.039 for those sheltered more than 360 days. This is based on the average of the five 30-day periods after 360 days. At this rate, no shelter stay would last more than nine years. Data from January 1990 show no families had been sheltered longer than seven years. But these shelters only began operating in 1983, and the data reflect New York City's provision of permanent apartments for long-staying families. Thus nine years does not seem an unreasonable assumption.

homeless at least a year and would have stayed homeless if they had not been provided with permanent housing (table 3-4). Thus, of the 10,200 families who became homeless in a year, only 3,060 would have remained homeless indefinitely.[38]

Giving permanent housing to those homeless the longest reaches a group that otherwise has a nearly 100 percent chance of remaining homeless. Targeting these persons reduces the likelihood that people will enter shelters or that those already homeless will extend their shelter stay in the hope of eventually qualifying for subsidized housing.

In contrast, allocating permanent housing to those who are recently homeless and likely to leave on their own creates an incentive to stay in shelters until they qualify for permanent housing. It also might induce an "entry effect" as people who are doubled-up enter a homeless program

38. Even after a year, a very small percentage would leave homelessness on their own, but to clarify the discussion, we ignore this group as well as mortality.

to gain access to scarce permanent housing. And just as important, giving housing today to someone who would find housing tomorrow, instead of to someone who would never find housing, "wastes" scarce resources.[39]

Events in New York City illustrate these principles. That city's policy was to build permanent housing and to give this housing to families homeless one year or more. From June 1988 to April 1990, the number of sheltered families decreased from 5,300 to 3,545. No significant change occurred in the rate at which families entered shelters or left on their own. In the spring of 1990, New York City altered its policy and began giving permanent housing to families who had been homeless just three months, sometimes less, in order to reduce the homeless family population as quickly as possible. From April to October 1990, the monthly number of families becoming homeless increased an average of 16.9 percent, and the rate at which families left on their own fell 2.3 percent compared with the same months the previous year. As a result, New York City sheltered 30.8 percent more families in June 1991 than if it had not altered its policy.[40]

The principle that policies aimed at shrinking the homeless population should reduce the number of people becoming homeless and increase the rate at which people leave homelessness is obvious. But it can easily and unknowingly be ignored.[41]

Prevention

In theory, the number of homeless could be reduced by identifying people before they become homeless and treating their problems to

39. The behavioral assumptions underlying this policy are controversial. Advocates and others argue that people do not become homeless or stay homeless to get government aid, particularly scarce housing. However, programs for poor people are being cut back at all levels of government while money for homeless programs has been growing. Depending on the condition of a person's current housing and on the conditions of and benefits from being homeless, it might be rational for some people to become homeless or to stay homeless longer than they otherwise would.

40. See Gordon Berlin and William McAllister, "Policy Analysis into Policy Management: It's Not What You Know That Counts" (City University of New York, Criminal Justice Research Center, 1992), pp. 4–9.

41. St. Louis and Massachusetts experienced similar problems when they made permanent housing available to homeless families. Personal communication with Dorothy Daily, coordinator of homeless services, City of St. Louis; and Michael A. Stegman, "Remedies for Homelessness: An Analysis of Potential Housing Policy and Program Responses," in Julee H. Kryder-Coe and others, eds., *Homeless Children and Youth: A New American Dilemma* (Transaction Publishers, 1991), pp. 225–69.

prevent homelessness.[42] Unfortunately, little is known about who is likely to become homeless and what services help people avoid that fate.

Homelessness is a rare event. Even if all homeless people are from the "extremely poor," only one extremely poor person in twenty is homeless at any one time.[43] Any program randomly targeted to this impecunious population would miss its target 95 percent of the time. Identifying families or people who are about to lose their homes or who have recently done so does not solve the problem. People may double up or find other housing. A New York City study, for instance, reported that 75 percent of evicted families stayed with friends and relatives until they found new housing.[44] They did not enter a shelter.

Some evidence suggests identification can be improved, but only with great effort. Using survey data that was costly and difficult to obtain from families entering New York City's shelters, one study suggested practical criteria that targeted 3 percent of the public assistance population to identify 30 percent of sheltered families. But still, 70 percent of those becoming homeless were not known in advance.[45]

Many programs to prevent homelessness exist, but their effectiveness is unknown.[46] They offer one-time rent, utility, or mortgage payments and counseling or mediation. Comparative data on what proportion of those aided would have stayed housed without the program and follow-up data reporting whether assisted clients remained housed are unavailable.[47]

42. The policy effectiveness of prevention depends, in part, on how one defines homelessness. One definition could incorporate people on streets and in shelters and another would also include those doubled-up. Because doubling-up is a more common strategy in the face of losing one's home than living on the streets or in shelters, the second definition would prevent more people from becoming homeless.

43. Assuming 450,000 single homeless people (excluding families) in 1987 and using Rossi's calculation of 7.2 million "extremely poor" single people (76 percent of the poverty level) in 1986, about 5 percent of those extremely poor are homeless at any one time. Burt, *Over the Edge*, p. 16; and Rossi, *Down and Out in America*, pp. 76–77, 143.

44. Richard I. Towber and Camilla Flemming, "The Housing Alert Program: A One Year Evaluation" (City of New York, Human Resources Administration, 1989), p. 6.

45. James R. Knickman and Beth Weitzman, "A Study of Homeless Families in New York City: Risk Assessment Models and Strategies for Prevention" (New York University, Health Research Program, 1989), vol. 3.

46. For descriptions of seven such programs, see David C. Schwartz, Donita Devance-Manzini, and Tricia Fagan, "Preventing Homelessness: A Study of State and Local Homelessness Prevention Programs" (New Brunswick, N.J.: American Affordable Housing Institute, 1991).

47. The GAO reports follow-ups in only eight of the forty-two programs it reviewed, and these were not done well enough to support program success claims. Government

In sum, not enough is known about what kinds of prevention programs work or whom to target. The evidence does not support claims that these efforts reduce the number of people becoming homeless (though they undoubtedly help those in need). As a result, claims for additional funding, especially if that funding were effectively diverted from programs that do work, like permanent housing, cannot be supported.

Local Policy Constraints

In making and implementing homeless policy, local decisionmakers confront four important constraints: legal advocacy and judicial decisions, federal funding regulations, reliance on nonprofit organizations, and the attitude of "not in my backyard" (NIMBY). The advocates and the courts may want any and all homeless people, not just the long-term homeless, to be immediately given scarce permanent housing. Federal funds intended only for emergency situations make long-term strategies difficult to implement. Nonprofits would prefer to help the least difficult cases. And communities will fight against locating services or housing in their neighborhoods.

Advocacy and Judicial Decisions

Because local governments have tried to avoid dealing with homelessness, policymaking often takes place in the courts.[48] In West Virginia and New York City, state courts ordered cities to open or expand emergency shelters. In St. Louis and Los Angeles, the threat of lawsuits caused local governments to sign consent decrees establishing shelters or providing temporary assistance. But court-made policy often ignores the dynamics of homelessness, and advocacy lawsuits on behalf of some homeless people can have the unintended consequence of making conditions worse for a larger number of homeless.

For example, to end New Haven's use of motels to house homeless families, the Connecticut State Supreme Court ordered the city to give 300 vacant public housing units to all the families in motels, regardless

---

Accounting Office, *Homelessness: Too Early to Tell What Kinds of Prevention Assistance Work Best*, RCED-90-89 (April 1990), pp. 26–27.

48. To see why this has been the case in New York City, see Donna Wilson Kirschheimer, "Sheltering the Homeless in New York City: Expansion in an Era of Government Contraction," *Political Science Quarterly*, vol. 104 (Winter 1989–90), pp. 607–23.

of how long each had been living there.[49] However, New York's experience showed that allocating permanent housing to those who had just entered shelters would have less impact, and perhaps a counterproductive one, on the long-run size of the homeless population than would limiting assistance to long-term shelter residents.

Court-ordered remedies have also not worked in New York City. In the early 1980s, the courts forced the city to guarantee emergency housing for single adults and for families. In response, the city opened dormitory shelters for both groups that met only the letter of the law, if that. Nevertheless, the fact that these facilities filled rapidly makes clear the housing market's inability to provide minimally adequate housing.

Court rulings and state regulatory decisions raised shelter standards, particularly for families, with regard to square footage, kitchen facilities, and private baths. To meet these standards, the city relied on welfare hotels. But because some of these hotels did not meet state standards for housing children, the courts ruled that the city could not use them.

When demand was heavy, families stayed overnight in welfare intake units or substandard hotels. Violations mounted, and contempt proceedings were filed. The courts joined in federal efforts to end using hotels entirely, setting a deadline for them to be emptied. To provide alternatives, the city began building permanent housing and transitional facilities, something it probably would not have done without these pressures. Legal advocates, however, continued to challenge hotel quality and they and the courts failed to take dynamics into account in meeting the goal of emptying the hotels.

Under these pressures, the city government ignored dynamics in allocating housing, and a once-diminishing hotel population began to increase. Scrambling to house a growing number of families but unable to meet the demand, the city was charged with 1,300 violations of judicial orders, and advocates sought to have the mayor and his top officials held in criminal contempt and jailed. After thirteen years of court battles, more homeless live on the streets in 1992 than in 1979.

Lawsuits have made the public aware that very poor people live in very inadequate housing. And they have forced local governments to commit emergency resources. But lawsuits are not a way to end homelessness and can make it worse.

49. Stephen Winzer, "Homelessness: Advocacy and Social Policy," *University of Miami Law Review*, vol. 45 (November–January 1990–91), pp. 387–405.

Funding and Claiming

Two central issues for homelessness policymaking are, where will the money come from and what can it be used for? Despite the deep, national origins of homelessness, the federal government has made policy as if the problem is temporary and solutions are local. The 1983 emergency food and shelter program provided emergency shelters with funds for food, consumable supplies, and emergency rental and utility assistance. It located the program in the Federal Emergency Management Agency (FEMA), an organization geared to provide temporary relief from earthquakes, hurricanes, and other disasters. In 1986 the emergency shelter grants program of the Department of Housing and Urban Development (HUD) provided funds to convert, renovate, or rehabilitate buildings into emergency, but not longer-term, shelters. With the 1987 McKinney Act, the government initially showed a realization that homelessness was neither a temporary nor a local problem. This act provided money for permanently housing the handicapped homeless, renovating buildings for homeless people, integrating homeless veterans into the work force, and putting needed services into permanent housing.

However, McKinney remains more a laundry list of programs distributed across at least seven departments or agencies, with little money available for each program.[50] These are a congeries of competitive and formula grant programs awarded to state and local agencies and to nonprofit organizations, making service integration unlikely. Many grants are for one-time experiments that will continue only with state support. And although McKinney appropriations have increased from $490 million in 1987 to $882 million in 1992, these levels are unlikely to have a long-term effect on the problem, even if the money were properly allocated.

Local and state governments bear the bulk of responsibility for dealing with homelessness but are unable or unwilling to spend the money to counter the problem. As a result, some look to the federal government.[51] However, mismatches between program requirements and homeless

50. For a criticism of how widely and thinly these programs are spread, see comments by Kenneth Beirne in "Rethinking Policy on Homelessness," pp. 28–31. One example of funding is the "safe havens" program, which would create intake housing and services for the mentally ill. The appropriations requested for fiscal year 1993 would house and serve less than 1 percent of all homeless mentally ill people.

51. This is because spending for poor people is redistributive, while city governments must maintain a city's competitiveness. Paul E. Peterson, *City Limits* (University of Chicago Press, 1981).

needs require local policymakers to stretch the meaning of existing federal programs. For example, cities maintain the fiction that families living in shelters for years are there temporarily in order to use the emergency assistance for families and the AFDC special needs programs. These are intended to provide help in emergency or temporary situations. Since every state in recent years has spent more money providing services to poor people than the federal block grant for social services provides, emergency assistance and special needs are the only other federal sources of support. The eight states using these funds to assist homeless families contain most of the homeless families.[52]

But stretching the meaning of existing programs commonly precipitates federal audits and threatened cutoffs. To avoid these, some cities do not use emergency assistance funding but cobble together money from the community development block grant (CDBG), along with state and local funding, to support the homeless. But from 1978 to 1988, CDBG appropriations were cut 74 percent (in constant dollars), effectively slowing federal support for homeless programs.[53]

In sum, the federal government has tried to play a small role in ending homelessness by assuming the problem has a short duration and thus requires only temporary assistance. But the lack of federal involvement partly explains why we have had fifteen years of homelessness. And fifteen years of a problem undermines the second assumption.

Nonprofit Organizations

Nonprofit organizations are key providers, and in most cities the sole providers, of transitional housing and services to the homeless. Compared with the public sector, nonprofits are thought to be remarkably cost effective in helping the homeless. In Washington, D.C., and in New York

52. Department of Health and Human Services, "Use of the Emergency Assistance and AFDC Programs to Provide Shelter to Families," p. 3. Six states rely on emergency assistance for families or special needs funding to pay 41 percent of their total temporary shelter program costs, but Health and Human Services (HHS) has consistently tried to limit using this funding source for most homeless families. In 1989, for instance, it proposed to limit emergency assistance funds to thirty days and to stop using special needs funds to pay for the higher rental costs of welfare hotels and shelters. Congress prevented this at the time, but HHS continues to try to impose such limits. Additionally, there is no ongoing federal support for social services for single men and women.

53. Morton J. Schussheim, "U.S. Housing: Problems and Policies," IB89004 (Congressional Research Service, June 28, 1991).

City, commissions have recommended that the local government get out of the homeless service business and turn responsibility over to nonprofits.

In part, nonprofit organizations seem comparatively efficient because they are more willing than government to turn away people who cannot or will not abide by their rules and because they select people who are less troubled.[54] By controlling access, these organizations avoid problems or costs government agencies cannot escape. In New York City's public shelters, for example, security costs can account for a third of shelter operating expenditures.

By relying on nonprofits, government effectively agrees to turn away the "hard" cases. Many communities may oppose this outcome, since many of the homeless will remain on the street. And it will be difficult to build a comprehensive, coordinated system when independent organizations, each with its own program philosophy and services, control intake and exit. Where government has funding leverage, one traditional resolution to this problem has been to require nonprofits to take a certain proportion or all of the difficult cases. However, this raises costs and threatens programmatic success.

NIMBY

Few communities welcome facilities to service homeless people. Residents fear a decline in property values, worry about public safety, or express racial, ethnic, or class prejudices.

Delays in finding sites can postpone implementing programs or cause their outright rejection. In some instances, NIMBY can be dealt with by negotiating with the community over projects from the outset, providing opportunities for the community to buy into the program and to integrate it into the community. This often means scaling back the size of the project, altering the building's configuration, having community members participate in client selection, or allowing the community to use the facility.

But some of the negotiated terms result in the need for even more facilities, as the number of clients is reduced or the scope of the program is changed or contracted. In the end, state and local government intervention will be required to force communities to accept facilities.

54. Good examples are the St. Frances and Heights supported housing programs for the mentally ill in New York City, Lazarus House for recovering substance abusers in Washington, D.C., and the Weingart Center for single men needing transitional housing in Los Angeles.

Policy Options

Ending homelessness requires housing that meets minimum quality standards at a price homeless people can afford. Since standards are higher now than ever before and incomes of homeless people are pitiably low, housing the homeless means approving large public expenditures, redefining minimum standards, or creating inequities between the homeless and other poor people.

Policymakers face several options. First, they can deal with the underlying low-income housing shortage. The federal government can help poor people pay for standard housing by subsidizing the earnings, incomes, or housing of all poor people. Or, local governments can lower housing standards sufficiently to permit recreating very cheap, lower-quality housing. Second, policymakers unable or unwilling to make either of these choices can continue the present policy of denying the severity or permanence of the problem. Or third, with relatively modest federal resources, state and local officials can target the homeless and create transitional housing facilities to provide controlled access to permanent housing.

Addressing Underlying Causes: Broad-based Programs

One way to make standard housing affordable is to raise earnings through economic growth, wage subsidies, a rise in the earned income tax credit (applied only to family breadwinners), public job creation, or an increase in the minimum wage. Another way is to increase income assistance by, for example, raising AFDC grants and establishing a federal general assistance program for individuals, or to provide large general rental subsidies by, for instance, expanding the rental voucher program.

These approaches are very expensive. Furthermore, by their nature, these programs would provide most of their benefits to people who are not homeless. In 1988, the Congressional Budget Office estimated that a housing entitlement program for all low-income families that relied on vouchers and retained current eligibility standards would cost $11.1 billion a year.[55] HUD estimated that housing vouchers to reduce rent burdens to 30 percent of adjusted income for 5 million very low-income

55. Congressional Budget Office, *Current Housing Problems and Possible Federal Responses* (December 1988), p. xxiii.

families and nonelderly individuals would cost $16.9 billion a year.[56]
And the supply of housing suitable for single individuals may be
inadequate. We estimate that the cost of building 750,000 SRO-type
units would be about $19 billion.

A related method of ending homelessness would be to restore AFDC
grants to their 1970 levels, liberalize the earned income tax credit, and
create a large-scale public employment program. The latter alone would
cost $5 billion or more a year.

These approaches have two obvious problems. First, they are costly.
With the current budget deficit and economic climate, garnering needed
political support for such subsidies, especially for nonelderly single
persons, is hard to imagine. Second, homelessness itself may have so
worsened the disabilities of some people that housing and income, while
necessary, are no longer sufficient to end homelessness.

Addressing Underlying Causes: Changing Housing Standards

Another way to address the housing shortage would be to relax
housing codes and zoning rules. This would enable entrepreneurs or
nonprofit organizations to recreate the lower-quality housing destroyed
in the past twenty years.[57]

This option has a negligible budget cost and, like the first option, is
equitable in that homelessness is not a prerequisite for gaining housing.
It is not clear, however, that most homeless single adults could afford
housing even of drastically reduced quality. SROs, for example, would
be very costly. Even when San Diego relaxed some standards to build
the Baltic Inn, the average monthly rent for a room was $270, well above
the average monthly income of a homeless person.[58] Cheaper cubicle

56. This program would be limited to those who receive federal housing assistance
and could obtain housing that met HUD's voucher quality standards. Relaxing these
standards would allow another 3.5 million families and single individuals to be eligible,
raising total annual costs to about $23 billion. Personal communication with Barry Zigas,
President, Low Income Housing Information Service, Washington.

57. On the necessity of current quality standards and some housing implications for
relaxing these standards, see Anthony Downs, "The Advisory Commission on Regulatory
Barriers to Affordable Housing: Its Behavior and Accomplishments," *Housing Policy
Debate*, vol. 2, no. 4 (1991), pp. 1095–1137.

58. Howard Husock, "Replicating Innovation: Judy Lenthall and SRO Housing
Construction in San Diego" (Harvard University, Kennedy School of Government, 1992),
exhibit D. However, homeless drug addicts probably have greater incomes than they report.
A heroin addict normally requires $50 to $100 a day for his habit and a typical crack
addict may need as much or more.

hotels, which are not as clean, comfortable, or private as SROs, cost $6 to $8 a night in New York City.[59] Prices would have to decline significantly before most homeless single adults could afford such housing.

Also, this strategy might bring back housing currently viewed as inadequate. In 1958, Chicago's cage hotels consisted of hundreds of five-foot-by-seven-foot spaces with a chicken wire ceiling, an iron bed, a light bulb, maybe a locker, and, at best, one toilet for twenty men. These floors were unventilated and commonly infested with vermin. Building and fire code violations were not unusual.[60]

Nevertheless, these facilities did provide independence and privacy as well as a sense of community, apparently much sought after by homeless people then as now.[61] And current shelter conditions in some cities are no better, and perhaps worse, than in those Chicago hotels.

It is unlikely that either of these strategies—broad-based housing and income programs or the recreation of the cheapest housing—would be politically feasible: one because it is too expensive, the other because it risks creating squalid housing. But the country has to choose some version of one or the other to end homelessness.

Treating Homelessness as a Temporary Emergency

Localities have usually treated homelessness as a temporary, emergency condition best left to charities, missions, and nonprofit shelter providers. Single adults receive few services, and families may be aided for a short time before being expected to find permanent housing. This strategy evades long-term public responsibility.

The policies of Los Angeles City and County are a case in point. There are no public shelters. Almost all of the public funds that nonprofit shelter providers and the missions normally receive are from federal programs, like CDBG, FEMA, or McKinney Act monies. Nonprofit organizations limit stays for single adults, and when shelters reach capacity they turn people away. Thousands of homeless people live in a few-square-block area, shuttling between the street and missions with seven-day-stay limits or nonprofit shelters with sixty-day limits.

For families, Los Angeles provides $30 a day, up to three weeks, for a stay in a welfare motel while families look for a home. If they find

59. Neighborhood Planning Workshop, Hunter College/CUNY, "Commercial Lodging Houses," New York, September 29, 1989, p. 12.

60. Bogue, *Skid Row in American Cities*.

61. Hoch and Slayton, *New Homeless and Old*.

one, the city pays the last month's rent and a security deposit; if they don't, families must find their way to nonprofit shelters, return to doubled-up situations, live in garages, or otherwise make do on their AFDC grant. The shelters provide services that move families toward the permanent housing that nonprofits are increasingly building. But room in the shelters is scarce, and there is no overarching public plan or monetary commitment to resolve the problem.

Specific policies differ among locales, but the goal of limiting claims on public resources is the same. For example, some communities do not allow people to "self-certify" their homelessness simply by requesting shelter. In St. Louis, for instance, the city investigates and certifies a person's homelessness before he or she can enter a shelter.

These local governments are effectively concluding that they cannot afford to create enough housing or to raise public assistance grants enough to end homelessness. A second assumption is that "no" public shelter is better than "any" public shelter, even as a shelter of last resort. Public shelters are expensive to operate, politicize the problem, can create their own demand, and may harm users more than help them. And areas with public shelters, even those with a right to shelter, have a substantial number of street homeless. Thus, from the perspective of most cities, public shelters are not a viable option.

But this strategy has obvious flaws. Quite simply, many people are left homeless, literally or effectively. They end up on the street or they return to housing arrangements that, by definition, were worse than the temporary shelter or welfare hotel they came to. A population of chronically homeless people accumulates, with no long-term strategy to meet their needs.

Targeting Homeless People

A third option would require active state and local intervention and modest new infusions of federal dollars targeted on those already homeless.

In practice, homelessness must be solved at the state and local level. But officials at these levels cannot effectively address the problem unless they can pay for permanent, as well as transitional, housing and services. And they are unable or unwilling to provide these things on a large enough scale without help from the federal government. But even if local voters were predisposed to house the homeless, doing so would put the locality at a competitive disadvantage with communities that kept taxes low by their refusal to support the homeless.

The challenge in designing local policy is to provide assistance efficiently without increasing the incidence or duration of homelessness. Thus such policies must pay attention to the dynamics of homelessness.

One policy that meets this test is a tiered structure of either public or nonprofit intake and shelter-based transitional services that serve as the gate to permanent housing. The policy has four elements: assured temporary housing; a "length of stay" criterion for allocating permanent housing; a "progress in treatment" or "service receipt" criterion; and legal pressures to assist outreach efforts in getting people off the streets and into service and treatment programs or some kind of housing.

Treatment progress would consist of meeting program goals: for an addict, remaining drug free; for a mentally ill person, taking medication regularly; for a drug-addicted head of family, completing a life skills class and attending regular drug treatment sessions. Requiring people to meet such tests reduces the chance that services themselves would cause the number of people becoming or remaining homeless to grow. Only those meeting the criteria get permanent housing.

Families and Single Adults without Other Problems

At entry, everyone would be assessed and intensive efforts would start to help them find alternative housing. The purpose of assessment is to learn why people are homeless, whether they have alternatives to shelter, and what services they need. Those able to find an alternative would be provided assistance, such as child care or help finding a job.

Those remaining after a month would be moved into transitional facilities. These may be better than the housing in which many homeless people previously resided. To ensure the facilities remain transitional, residents would be required to participate in services, to meet goals, and to abide by facility rules. Such rules might prohibit drinking and drug use, require children to attend school, and ban overnight guests. Services would teach money management and social living, parenting, and housekeeping skills and assist in searching for jobs. Help in finding alternative housing would continue.

Families. Families that meet basic service goals and that remain continuously sheltered for, say, one year (the length-of-stay criterion) would be given priority for publicly provided permanent housing. Long-term homeless families should be targeted first. Once the number of these families has been substantially reduced, eligibility should be broadened to include repeat shelter users with a *cumulative* shelter stay equal to the length-of-stay criterion. Since a third or more of those who become homeless have already been homeless, targeting previous shelter users will reduce the flow of people into homelessness.

Single adults. Many homeless single adults, even those with disabilities, are able and willing to work. For these people, transitional shelter can link them to help in finding a job and in saving money so that they can rent a place of their own. For example, the job training projects for the homeless supported by the McKinney Act have serviced 7,400 people. Some 4,600 have received training and 2,400 have obtained unsubsidized employment with an average wage of more than $5 an hour. About 2,000 participants have received help with their housing.[62]

Younger men often benefit from long-term education and training in a residential environment. For example, homeless men and women, aged 17-24, in a residential Job Corps site completed the program at the same rate as other young people. Upon graduation, most obtained jobs and found affordable housing.[63]

But many homeless people cannot find unsubsidized employment. For them, states and cities should enlist federal support to create a jobs program for homeless single adults sheltered at least sixty days. Individuals could qualify after completing a shelter work experience program. The work would be day labor jobs paying 90 percent of the minimum wage and could be administered using a hiring hall where work would be assigned and pay received on a daily basis. Jobs would last no more than twelve months. Full-time, year-round earnings at this rate would support a monthly rent of about $200 (30 percent of present earnings). Where basic housing costs more than this, single adults with good job attendance could be given access to subsidized SRO housing.

Some evidence suggests this approach is feasible. Studies of AFDC community work experience programs in seven cities concluded that individuals working off their benefits, and thus not receiving paychecks, did useful work that was valued by their bosses.[64] New York City's work relief employment project, which offered a paycheck instead of general assistance, had much higher attendance than did the regular general

62. Lawrence Bailis and others, *Job Training for the Homeless: Report on Demonstration's First Year* (Department of Labor, 1991), pp. iv–v.

63. Personal communication with Stanley Belza, regional director, National Job Corps Program, New York.

64. Gregory Hoerz and Karla Hanson, "A Survey of Participants and Worksite Supervisors in the New York City Work Experience Program" (New York: Manpower Demonstration Research Corporation, September 1986).

assistance work experience program.[65] And in the Vera Institute's neighborhood work project, ex-offenders, some of whom were homeless, called in for assignments and received a check on a daily basis. Thus the mechanics of a hiring hall approach appear feasible.[66]

To make this approach work, the federal government should take four steps. First, the Department of Health and Human Services should modify regulations to allow using funds from the emergency assistance for families program for more than thirty days per family per year. Alternatively, upon entering shelters, all families should be processed for medicaid eligibility so that medicaid case management funding can be used for services. We estimate this would cost $400 million a year when fully funded.

Second, McKinney Act money should be made available for services to homeless single adults and for capital construction of transitional facilities for both families and single adults. Funding should continue to grow at the annual rate of the last five years, about 20 percent, resulting in an annual cost of $1 billion when fully funded.

Third, up to 66,000 permanent units should be made available to homeless families, using a combination of public housing units (by giving homeless families priority) and rental assistance. The annual cost would be $213 million.

Finally, the federal government should provide support for the full-time equivalent of 68,000 time-limited, transitional public service employment jobs. The annual cost would be $540 million.

The Chemically Addicted

Of all the second-order problems complicating homelessness, none is likely to be more prevalent, persistent, and difficult to treat than substance abuse. Although many homeless substance abusers could conceivably manage their addiction and remain housed, many will need more than housing and a job. To end homelessness for these people, a system of

65. State of New York, Department of Social Services, "An Evaluation of the Work Relief Employment Project in New York City" (New York, 1975).

66. On the other hand, compared with a control group, former addicts and offenders in the supported work experiment did not show any net difference in employment and earnings. However, average employment rates in the control group were relatively high— 50 percent over the three-year follow-up. And there was some indication that the most disadvantaged participants with the least prior work history benefited more than a control group. Manpower Demonstration Research Corporation, *Summary and Findings of the National Supported Work Demonstration* (Cambridge, Mass: Ballinger, 1980).

services and strict performance standards is essential. Services would include outreach, detoxification, shelter-based or transitional drug-free residences, case management, substance abuse services, jobs or job training, help in finding permanent housing, and after-care services. Permanent housing should not be available to this group until and unless they have stayed drug free for an extended period, perhaps one year.

The Uniform Alcohol and Detoxification Act of 1971 created community-based "detox" centers that provide services to homeless alcoholics and, increasingly, drug abusers. However, homeless people report having difficulty gaining access to these and other substance abuse programs.[67] Funding for these centers should be tied to accepting some proportion of homeless people. Alternatively, shelters could develop their own detoxification units.

After ten days to two weeks in detoxification, clients would move to specially created drug-free transitional residences that would initiate therapy. Some people will be able to obtain their own housing and will require only short-term outpatient treatment; others will need long-term transitional housing and case management—possibly followed by supported housing.

Most people drop out of substance abuse programs and most graduates go back to drugs. The effectiveness of treatment improves with the length of stay in a therapeutic community. Stays lasting at least nine months are especially important for poor, isolated individuals without support networks, jobs, and housing. Since alcohol or drug abuse is never "cured" but only in remission, the goal would be to develop programs that keep graduates and dropouts connected to continuing treatment, integrate clients with family, work, school, and community, and lengthen the time between relapses.[68]

After meeting the goals set by the transitional shelter, individuals would receive help in finding work and permanent housing. Some of those unable to locate housing on their own could be eligible, after satisfying the length-of-stay criterion of one to two years, to move into

67. Barbara Lubran, "Alcohol and Drug Abuse among the Homeless Population: A National Response," in Milton Argeriou and Dennis McCarty, eds., *Treating Alcoholism and Drug Abuse among Homeless Men and Women: Nine Community Demonstration Grants* (New York: Haworth Press, 1990), pp. 19–20.

68. On dealing with narcotic addicts as mental health professionals deal with the chronically mentally ill, see M. Douglas Anglin, "The Efficacy of Civil Commitment in Treating Narcotics Addiction," *Journal of Drug Issues*, vol. 18 (Fall 1988), p. 535. On programmatic goals, see Jerome J. Platt and others, "The Prospects and Limitations of Compulsory Treatment for Drug Addiction," ibid., p. 512.

supported SROs that were managed by nonprofits. Preferably, individuals who find jobs could band together to obtain housing and to provide a "self-help" drug-free, peer-supported after-care environment.[69]

Would comprehensive services encourage housed, low-income substance abusers to become homeless in order to obtain services? Transitional shelter goals and requirements diminish this risk. Since an individual must enter a homeless transitional residence to receive treatment, only those who are serious and making progress in treatment are likely to enter and stay. In short, no one who was not homeless and sheltered would be treated.

Because many drug users will refuse treatment and others can function with their addictions, not all homeless addicts will be treated. We estimate that drug treatment services, shelters, and transitional residences serving 71,000 people for an average of twelve months would cost $554 million.

The Mentally Ill

Chronic mental illness is usually more or less treatable. To end their homelessness, some mentally ill people require intensive outreach, acute care hospitalization services, and transitional living, followed by highly structured and supported permanent housing. Others can go from the streets to a short-stay transitional facility and then to permanent housing. Those who are already in shelters and reliably take medication can go quickly to permanent housing.[70]

The structure of the system for mentally ill people would be similar to that of other groups.[71] Initial entry, from outreach services or other sources, would be into small, short-stay, service-intensive, residential

69. The 1988 Omnibus Drug Act encouraged the replication of Oxford Houses—drug-free, financially self-supporting, democratically controlled residences for former addicts. See McCarty and others, "Alcoholism, Drug Abuse, and the Homeless."

70. A comprehensive response to homelessness among the mentally ill must also come to grips with the residential instability of the population. Mentally ill people can randomly become disoriented, hear voices, wander the streets, and otherwise show the effects of their illness. These episodes and the absence of family relationships or social networks can result in hospitalization or homelessness and the likely loss of residence for failure to pay rent.

71. The policies suggested here are based on similar recommendations from the Institute of Medicine Panel, the American Psychiatric Association Task Force on the Homeless Mentally Ill, the American Psychological Association's Council of Representatives, and the Federal Task Force on Homelessness and Severe Mental Illness. See Deborah L. Dennis and others, "A Decade of Research and Services for Homeless Mentally Ill People: Where Do We Stand?" *American Psychologist*, vol. 46 (November 1991), pp. 1129–38.

"safe havens." These would provide psychiatric assessment, evaluation, and detoxification and would address acute psychiatric episodes.

Transitional shelters would be small and provide case management, training in daily living activities, medication monitoring, general medical services, and psychiatric and psychosocial treatment. Stays could last from three months to a year.

Permanent housing would range from independent living (for those who can manage complete independence) to structured community residences with complete services (for those who require intensive supervision and support) to long-term asylum (for those most severely mentally disabled who cannot function in the community). No transitional length-of-stay criterion would be imposed for access to permanent housing. Community mental health services—case management and acute care crisis intervention services—would have to be provided to those living independently.

Preliminary data from the National Institute of Mental Health (NIMH) community support programs, from McKinney-funded demonstration programs, and from similar local projects suggest this approach may work. New York State, for example, runs an intensive care management program for mentally ill people who are homeless or have a history of homelessness. One study, reporting on a sample of seventy program participants, found that fifty-five had been stabilized and were living in permanent housing twelve months after entering the program.[72]

In addition, New York City has developed three service-intensive, short-stay reception centers (or safe havens) that can house and treat individuals from the streets who are too afraid to enter a shelter or other standard setting. After stabilizing patients, these centers transfer individuals to the community or to transitional shelters. These provide intensive rehabilitation services, prepare individuals to live in the community, and place them in appropriate permanent housing. After operating for eighteen months, these centers have served one hundred individuals and graduated forty.[73]

But can community mental health services do what is necessary for people to remain housed? Since 1990, a New York City program has placed more than 636 people into newly developed permanent supported housing. A one-year follow-up of 284 of those placed found that 78

72. Data from New York State Office of Mental Health, Bureau of Evaluation and Services Research, Albany, N. Y., 1992.

73. Personal conversation with Frank R. Lipton, deputy commissioner, Human Resources Administration, City of New York.

percent had remained in their placement, while 21 percent were no longer in residence and could not be located.[74]

In another study, forty-nine homeless chronically mentally ill patients who were discharged from a psychiatric institution were randomly assigned to either a control group or a permanent supported housing program. Half the control group was discharged to a shelter or to an unknown place; all the experimental group went to live at a supported SRO. The residence offered individual case management, medication monitoring, money management, and meals and activities and had access to on-site psychiatric treatment. After one year, 69 percent of the experimental group were still in permanent housing and another 16 percent were in either an acute care or state hospital. Only 30 percent of the control group were permanently housed, and 26 percent were hospitalized.[75]

However, even "successful" interventions fail to permanently assist a significant proportion of those helped. In the study just described, of those referred to the SRO, 15 percent could not be located one year later and another 5 percent were homeless. Residential instability can be reduced but may remain a problem for a fourth of those housed.[76]

To implement this strategy for large numbers of homeless mentally ill, the federal government has to take the following actions. First, the eligibility and verification processes for supplemental security income (SSI) and disability benefits (SSDI) should be revised to accommodate the special problems of the mentally ill. Greater use of representative payee structures, simplification of the application process when hospitals and other mental health professionals certify illness, and relaxed verification processes for ongoing recertification of eligibility are necessary.

Second, to make serving the severely and persistently mentally ill their primary mission, the funding stream and the charters of community

74. New York City Human Resources Administration, "Summary Client Placement Report of the New York–New York Agreement to House Homeless Mentally Ill Individuals," New York, March 6, 1992, tables 12, 13.

75. Lipton and others, "Housing and the Homeless Mentally Ill." Although rehospitalization rates were similar for both groups, the length of stay for the experimental group was one-third of that for the control group (55 versus 168 nights). Because hospital stays cost about $300 a day and supported SROs about $70, the savings—while only suggestive, given the study's scale—are impressive.

76. The 20 to 50 percent of the homeless mentally ill who are also drug dependent pose particular difficulties. Neither traditional mental health nor drug abuse treatment programs are likely to be effective for many of these people, and programs often exclude them. Although experimental integrative approaches are being tested, there is no adequate intervention. The mentally ill who use illicit drugs will continue to be homeless even if housing and services are available.

mental health centers (CMHCs) should be revised. Federal funds should flow through states to communities, and each state should be required to develop a comprehensive service plan linking community mental health centers to state mental hospitals. This would tie the discharge plans of all state hospitals and all short-stay psychiatric hospitals to the service plans of the CMHCs and so fix responsibility for the care of the mentally ill in communities and states.

Third, a presidential commission should be appointed to review laws determining whether to commit individuals for shorter or longer stays when they suffer from illnesses that impair their judgment. Fourth, demonstration programs for different kinds of transitional housing and services should be started. In preparation for statewide expansion of these initiatives over the next decade, these efforts should include evaluation and ways to disseminate the lessons learned.

The estimated annual cost of this proposal would be $900 million. However, if the government can redirect CMHCs to serve the severely and persistently mentally ill, most of these costs would be offset.

This transitional system, like that for substance abusers, might attract people who are mentally ill but housed and not currently receiving services. Ideally, care of the homeless mentally ill would be embedded in a larger effort to establish the community mental health systems that were originally envisioned. But even if this is not possible, entry effects would be modest.

Two to four million Americans suffer from severe and persistent mental illness.[77] Almost all live in the community and are not homeless. They receive SSI or SSDI, rely on medicaid or medicare to pay for treatment, and have support from family and friends. By contrast, only 150,000 to 200,000 are homeless at any one time. These are, by most accounts, long-term homeless people. Thus it seems unlikely that many would become homeless to receive mental health services.

Outreach and Legal Pressure

For most Americans, solving the homelessness problem means clearing streets of panhandlers and parks of cardboard tents and sending somewhere else the sad people with shopping carts full of belongings. But this requires initially lending a helping hand, and then, if the hand is refused,

77. Burt, *Over the Edge*, p. 120; and HHS, *Outcasts on Main Street*, p. 18.

using city ordinances to prohibit sleeping in public spaces. This policy offers services and shelter, followed by legal pressures if necessary.

The rationale for outreach is obvious: people living on streets, especially many who are mentally ill or chemically dependent, cannot be expected to act on their own to improve their situation. They are disoriented, mistrustful, fearful, and resistant. An intensive and persistent outreach and referral program should be part of any intake facility for the mentally ill or the chemically dependent.

The outreach efforts of the NIMH community support program show that successful outreach requires intensive, skilled, protracted effort.[78] In one program, staff members contacted 4,500 people but provided meaningful case management for only about 1,500, while fewer than 750 were connected to programs and services. Project administrators speculated that a third of their clients could not be helped without changing the involuntary commitment laws.[79]

A 1989 review of five outreach programs reported that large numbers of contacts with homeless mentally ill clients yielded few who eventually were sufficiently engaged to receive intensive services. Another review concluded that "outreach and case management programs that promise to contact and link large numbers of individuals to existing services with relatively brief follow-up can expect limited long range success for clients."[80] To reduce the numbers of street dwellers, other measures will be needed as well.

Problems in dealing with drug abusers living on the street are worse. Although a substantial number are chronically addicted and resemble the mentally ill, some prey upon others and engage in criminal, sometimes violent, activities.

For transitional housing and services to work, shelter providers must be able to assign people to the appropriate shelter and to enforce residential rules of conduct. These practices cause some people to refuse shelter. For example, when New York City began assessment and assignment, a men's shelter population that had been growing annually at a 3 percent rate immediately began to decline at a 9 percent rate. Obviously, such people would refuse outreach as well.

To encourage or, in some instances, force people to take advantage of outreach help, a complementary policy that enforces laws against

78. Dennis and others, "A Decade of Research and Services."

79. Robert C. Coates, *A Street Is Not A Home: Solving America's Homeless Dilemma* (Buffalo, N.Y.: Prometheus Books, 1990), p. 174.

80. Dennis and others, "A Decade of Research and Services."

sleeping in public places, loitering, and perhaps begging will be necessary. The threat of jail may encourage addicts to remain in a therapeutic program or in transitional shelters or to get housing on their own. Such action, however, can and should be taken only if alternatives other than incarceration exist.

This policy may seem retrograde for a society that has tried to move away from coercion and punishment and toward treating substance abuse and psychological problems as illnesses. And the legal ascendance of individual rights makes such a policy difficult to implement. Antiloitering statutes have been struck down as too vague. The rights to travel and to freely associate in public spaces and the freedom of speech have all been used to defend against police actions taken against homeless men and women.

However, members of the psychiatric health community have questioned whether the balance between these rights and the needs of mentally ill persons has been lost in the case of the mentally ill.[81] Moreover, this proposal looks toward treatment, not punishment. Some evidence suggests that enforced drug treatment is as successful as voluntary treatment, and that legally enforced, close supervision in the community may be effective in reducing drug use.[82]

SROs

To permanently house many homeless single adults, a limited number of single-room occupancy hotels and targeted vouchers are necessary. Although transitional length-of-stay and service requirements will limit access to this housing, it is also important to just meet minimal housing standards for the units because higher quality will boost demand and increase costs.

Nonprofits have recently developed supported SROs for homeless people, consisting of small rooms in clean, rehabilitated or renovated buildings, which may also have a common kitchen and other amenities. Each SRO has a different service package, depending on the needs of clients. Such facilities help provide the continuity of care that professionals

81. See for example, E. Fuller Torrey, "Thirty Years of Shame: The Scandalous Neglect of the Mentally Ill Homeless," *Policy Review*, no. 48 (Spring 1989), pp. 10–15; and H. Richard Lamb, "Deinstitutionalization and the Homeless Mentally Ill," *Hospital and Community Psychiatry*, vol. 35 (September 1984), pp. 899–907.

82. George De Leon, "Legal Pressure in Therapeutic Communities," *Journal of Drug Issues*, vol. 18 (Fall 1988), pp. 527–45; and Anglin, "The Efficacy of Civil Commitments."

from mental health to drug addiction increasingly see as necessary for many homeless people.

Nonprofits in San Diego, San Francisco, and New York have already developed 1,700 of these units. These organizations are key in developing supported SROs, as both developers and owners. Policy should be directed at both helping nonprofits develop the necessary expertise and encouraging the birth of organizations to tackle these projects. But policy should also encourage private, nonprofit development of SROs. State and local governments could help lower construction costs by relaxing local building codes and density standards while still requiring SROs to meet health and safety standards.[83]

Although most SRO rooms should be reserved for the homeless, setting aside some for people who could afford higher rents than the homeless would enhance the financial ability of nonprofits to meet maintenance costs. Including residents who are not homeless would help establish norms for behavior other than those associated with homelessness and would create a social community.[84] Using rent vouchers could serve the goal of housing people who had not been homeless with those who had been.

To house the homeless adults coming out of the transitional shelter programs would require creating about 300,000 supported and nonsupported SRO units. What mix of government spending would be most effective and efficient—paying development costs outright, subsidizing low- or no-interest loans, or providing vouchers—is uncertain. The difficulties homeless families have had trying to use vouchers and the problems of homeless adults, however, make it unlikely that vouchers alone would be sufficient. We estimate the government would have to subsidize the development of at least 75,000 units at a cost of about $2.2 billion (a one-time outlay) and could provide vouchers for the rest at a cost of approximately $1 billion a year.

Problems with the Structured Shelter Option

This option has flaws. It creates inequities, as the long-term homeless gain better housing than some who never become homeless or who find

83. For example, cities could emulate San Diego by employing an "equivalency" standard in which the building code governing SRO construction was compared with that of hotels or current SROs to ascertain which requirements could be eliminated while still meeting health and safety standards. See Husock, "Replicating Innovation."

84. Hoch and Slayton, *New Homeless and Old.*

housing after a brief spell of homelessness. Access to housing and services through shelters and transitional facilities creates a path to scarce resources and develops structures that threaten to institutionalize homelessness. Open admissions allows individuals to self-certify their homelessness, threatening to overwhelm local budgets. And intensive services may encourage client dependency.

Although inequity is present in this strategy, the gate structure should reduce inequity, and those who get housing will have successfully met a "progress in treatment" standard. In addition, the efficiency gains from focusing aid on the long-term homeless are high, and the mentally ill have a legitimate claim over others.

The entitlement and institutionalization risks are endemic in any strategy that specifically targets a subpopulation. Avoiding these problems requires adopting a strategy that addresses the shortage of housing for all poor people. Such a strategy seems unlikely to be implemented. Self-certification allows people to compare the lowest-quality private housing they can obtain with the quality of public shelters. This effectively and publicly establishes the housing floor and so can politicize the quality of housing at the bottom of the private market. Services do not necessarily generate dependencies; they can promote self-sufficiency. Also, this strategy would not provide services for all mentally ill, chemically addicted, or otherwise impaired individuals. Those who can work or otherwise get by without such services are free to do so, but not on the streets.

Conclusion

Homelessness has many dimensions and many parts. Advocates see a simple problem—a safety net frayed by structural macroeconomic and national policy changes—and propose a simple answer: expand entitlements to income and housing.

Service providers and professionals think the problem lies in the particular needs of individuals—the mentally ill, the substance abuser, and the multiproblem family—and recommend a complex response involving services, treatment, and supported housing for everyone with a particular problem. Local officials, who have inadequate resources with which to act, see only the most difficult cases and blame the victim. They try to ignore the problem or severely limit their responsibility. And federal officials view homelessness as an aberration, the result of something peculiar to localities rather than a national problem requiring national solutions. Because each of these essential players has acted on its peculiar understanding of the problem, homelessness continues to plague America's poor.

Homelessness is not easy to understand or solve, but neither is it impossible to address. By paying attention to dynamics and to the medical and mental problems of some homeless people, administrators with access to permanent housing and a service-screening structure can reduce the problem. But this strategy can only work if other key players buy into it. Advocates must be willing to protect individuals from the failings of the system but should not use them as a lever to force local governments to take on the housing and income needs of all poor people. The federal government must recognize the national dimensions of the problem and agree to provide ongoing support. Service providers must be able to build a system, rather than just a few exemplary models, to meet the needs of the mentally ill and substance abusers, something they have not been able to do in the past.

Under these conditions, one could be cautiously optimistic that option three could reduce homelessness substantially among families, the mentally ill, and those willing and able to work, but less so among substance abusers and the dually diagnosed. The caution follows from our lack of knowledge about treatments that work for those with crack addiction, for some severely mentally ill, and for those who are both drug addicted and mentally ill. But even allowing for some failure here, government can make a difference.

This option does not stop people from becoming homeless. It can end homelessness for some, especially those for whom available affordable housing is not enough, and assuage the problem for others. But to stop producing homelessness, the country has to come to grips with the dilemmas posed by expensive housing, low incomes, and equity. It has to decide whether to provide the resources necessary for everyone to have decent housing or to define anew a lower minimum housing standard.

4

JOHN J. DiIULIO, JR.

Crime

NEAR THE END of his term, President Lyndon B. Johnson appointed the National Commission on the Causes and Prevention of Violence. Chaired by Milton S. Eisenhower, the commission issued its final report in December 1969.[1] The report, *Violent Crime*, contained three main findings. First, violent crimes are "chiefly a problem of the cities of the nation, and there violent crimes are committed mainly by the young, poor, male inhabitants of the ghetto slum." Second, "increasingly powerful social forces are generating rising levels of violent crime which, unless checked, threaten to turn our cities into defensive, fearful societies." And third, "only progress toward urban reconstruction can reduce the strength of the crime-causing forces in the inner city and thus reverse the direction of present crime trends."[2] The commission embraced the ten-point plan set out by Daniel P. Moynihan, then a counselor to President Richard M. Nixon, in his article "Toward a National Urban Policy." With Moynihan, it urged the federal government to take the lead in ameliorating the nation's urban ills, chiefly crime.[3]

Crime in the Inner City

In the 1980s the inner-city problem with drugs and crime became the urban nightmare about which the Eisenhower commission had warned, intensifying what Moynihan had described as the "poverty and social

James Q. Wilson was the discussant for this chapter.

1. National Commission on the Causes and Prevention of Violence, *Violent Crime: The Challenge to Our Cities* (New York: George Braziller, 1969), pp. 47–60, 82. The official title of the report was *Violent Crime: Homicide, Assault, Rape, and Robbery.* (Hereafter National Commission, *Violent Crime.*)

2. National Commission, *Violent Crime*, p. 82.

3. National Commission, *Violent Crime*, pp. 1–30, 74–81. Moynihan's "Toward a National Urban Policy" first appeared in *Public Interest*, no. 5 (Fall 1969), pp. 3–20. It was reprinted as the foreword to the Braziller edition of the national commission's report.

isolation of minority groups in central cities."[4] This grim urban reality was reflected in a variety of statistics on crime and corrections. For example, by 1980 one of every one hundred residents of some inner-city census tracts was behind prison bars. In 1990 in New York State and other jurisdictions nearly one-quarter of all teenage and young adult African-American males were under some form of correctional supervision (in prison, in jail, on probation, or on parole), and more than 10 percent of them were incarcerated. They were about twenty times more likely to be imprisoned than teenage and young adult white males.[5]

Of all Americans, inner-city African-American male teenagers and young adults from low-income urban families were at greatest risk of being victimized by violent crime. In 1989, for example, about 52 percent of the nation's 10.7 million African-American males, and 25 percent of its 83.4 million white males, lived in metropolitan central cities.[6] The violent crime rate (number of victimizations per 1,000 resident population for persons 12 years of age and over) for African-American males living in these areas was 61.5, compared with 46.8 for white males. The murder victimization rate for African-Americans was about six times the rate for whites, and blacks experienced much higher rates of rape, robbery, and aggravated assault than did whites. In Washington, D.C., for example, from 1985 to 1988, about three-quarters of all homicides were committed by young black males against other young black males. In 1991 several big- and mid-sized cities set new homicide records, and police related most of the increases to the drug trade.[7]

4. National Commission, *Violent Crime*, p. 10. See also Daniel P. Moynihan, "The Underclass: Toward a Post-Industrial Policy," *Public Interest*, no. 96 (Summer 1989), pp. 16–27, and (in the same issue) John J. DiIulio, Jr., "The Underclass: The Impact of Inner-City Crime," pp. 28–46, and Isabel Sawhill, "The Underclass: An Overview," p. 3–15.

5. DiIulio, "Impact of Inner-City Crime," p. 37, note 6; and Robert Gangi and Jim Murphy, *Imprisoned Generation: Young Men under Criminal Justice Custody in New York State: A Report* (New York: Correctional Association of New York, 1990), p. 1. Prisons are institutions for the incarceration of persons convicted of serious crimes, usually felonies. Most prisons are run by state governments. Jails are facilities authorized to hold, for periods longer than forty-eight hours, pretrial detainees and misdemeanants. Most jails are run by county governments.

6. Calculated from Department of Justice, *Criminal Victimization in the United States, 1989: A National Crime Survey Report* (Washington: Bureau of Justice Statistics, June 1991), p. 34.

7. Department of Justice, *Criminal Victimization, 1989*, p. 34; Department of Justice, *Violent Crime in the United States* (Washington: Bureau of Justice Statistics, March 1991), p. 7; Government of the District of Columbia, *Homicide in the District of Columbia* (Washington: Office of Criminal Justice Plans and Analysis, December 1988), pp. 8–9;

But there was little evidence that street crime from poor and minority inner-city neighborhoods had spilled over into affluent and white suburbs of the cities. To cite one representative example, in 1990 Philadelphia's total crime rate was about twice that of the four surrounding suburban Pennsylvania counties, and its violent crime rate was over three times that of those counties. Forty-two percent of all violent crimes committed in Pennsylvania occurred in Philadelphia, which contains only 14 percent of the population.[8] Nationally, in 1989 three-quarters of all single-offender crimes committed by whites were committed against whites, 76.3 percent of all such crimes committed by blacks were committed against blacks, and most black-on-black crime was committed in the inner cities.[9]

The decent, aspiring, law-abiding residents of inner-city neighborhoods lived in fear of being murdered, mugged, and extorted. They were reluctant to send their children to school or let them go out to play for fear that drug dealers and gang members would prey on their young. And they suffered indirectly but tangibly from the crime-induced depression of their local economies.

What Is to Be Done?

There have been, and continue to be, political, administrative, budgetary, and intellectual limits on federal crime policy. These limits are intractable; they cannot be wished away. But well within these limits, the federal government can do at least two sets of things to help state and local governments respond to the nation's crime problem.

—One, provide technical assistance and financial support to big cities that want to institute or expand community policing efforts, whether as part of the federal Operation Weed and Seed or independent of that program.

—Two, expand drug treatment programs in the federal prison system and provide the legal mandate, technical assistance, and funds necessary to operate and evaluate such programs in every state prison system in the country.

---

and for two reports on the increase in homicides, see Michael Isikoff, "Street Violence Surges Across U.S.," *Philadelphia Inquirer*, December 30, 1991, p. 2A, and "Homicide Records Set in Big Cities," *New York Times*, January 3, 1992, p. A14.

8. Calculated from *Uniform Crime Report, Commonwealth of Pennsylvania, Annual Report—1990* (Harrisburg: Pennsylvania State Police Bureau of Research and Development, 1991), pp. A2–A4.

9. Department of Justice, *Criminal Victimization 1989*, p. 53.

Over a decade's worth of research and practical experimentation has yet to show that, other things being equal, community policing reduces crime. But plenty of anecdotal evidence shows that community policing has reduced crime in some jurisdictions where it has been tried, and a good deal of systematic evidence shows that it makes citizens feel less threatened by crime and improves relations between the police and the community. Moreover, community policing can bridge the gap between traditional law enforcement activities (detect, arrest, prosecute, convict, incarcerate) and efforts to address the social and economic problems of drug-ravaged, crime-plagued urban communities.

In 1991, for example, the federal government gave local U.S. attorneys a central role in coordinating intergovernmental law enforcement activities that target drug traffickers and violent criminals and that address the social and economic problems in communities where drug trafficking and violent crime are serious problems. Known as Operation Weed and Seed, as of mid-1992, this strategy had been tried on a pilot basis in only two cities (Trenton, New Jersey, and Kansas City, Missouri). As the program's federal architects and state and local implementers quickly recognized, community policing is the key to operating any such program.[10]

In the wake of the 1992 Los Angeles riots, the Bush administration extended the program to sixteen other cities and asked Congress for $500 million to fund the effort. But unless and until community policing becomes the organizational norm in big-city police departments, it is difficult to suppose that any such effort can do much to contain the epidemic of drug and crime or to help cure the social and economic maladies of distressed big-city neighborhoods.

The sixty-two-year history of federal leadership in prison-based drug treatment programs is a checkered one. Between 1985 and 1992, the federal prison system made great strides in drug treatment. But, over this same period, the federal government has done little to help the states improve or expand their prison-based drug treatment programs.

Most but not all of the evidence on the effects of prison-based drug treatment programs on prisoners' postrelease behavior suggests that prisoners who participate in such programs commit fewer crimes in the future than otherwise comparable prisoners who do not participate. The programs' effects on prisoners' institutional behavior are clearer:

---

10. Michael Chertoff and others, "Weeds and Seed Program," Trenton, N.J.: Department of Law and Public Safety, May 21, 1992, pp. 2–3.

prisoners who participate in these programs are less violent behind bars and have fewer problems of other kinds than otherwise comparable prisoners who do not participate.

By increasing its role in community policing and in prison-based drug treatment, the federal government can probably make big-city streets safer than they are now, invigorate local law enforcement efforts, repair drug-ravaged lives, and possibly save money in the long run. The federal government could help in at least two other areas: testing the efficacy of certain types of gun control programs through sponsoring a national pilot project, and launching a large-scale research program into the causes, consequences, and prevention of crime.

Some may judge these recommendations overly ambitious and others may judge them paltry or timid. But all should judge them in light of the history of federal crime policy and with due consideration of competing perspectives on the effects of current federal crime policy.

The Two Federal Wars on Crime

Historically, Americans have been profoundly ambivalent about the goals of criminal justice. They have wanted a criminal justice system that apprehends and visits harm upon the guilty (punishment); makes offenders more virtuous, or at least more law abiding (rehabilitation); dissuades would-be offenders from criminal pursuits (deterrence); protects innocent citizens from being victimized by convicted criminals (incapacitation); and invites most convicted criminals to return as productive citizens to the bosom of the free community (reintegration). They want the criminal justice system to achieve these multiple, vague, and contradictory public goals without violating the public conscience (humane treatment), jeopardizing the public law (constitutional rights), emptying the public purse (cost containment), or weakening the tradition of state and local public administration (federalism). Thus, for example, Americans have wanted more prisons without additional corrections spending or sites for prison construction, jobs for prisoners without any loss of jobs to free workers, stern treatment of prisoners without any damage to prisoners' rights, and reintegration of offenders into the community without any threat to public safety.[11]

11. For a discussion of the complex ends of the American criminal justice system in relation to the role of corrections executives, see John J. DiIulio, Jr., "Managing a Barbed-Wire Bureaucracy: The Impossible Job of Corrections Commissioner," in Erwin C. Hargrove and John C. Glidewell, eds., *Impossible Jobs in Public Management* (University Press of Kansas, 1990), chap. 4, especially pp. 52–57.

There is no way to reconcile these conflicting public goals and mandates. What subnational criminal justice policymakers and administrators have generally done, therefore, is to let the programmatic pendulum swing with the public mood between liberal and conservative approaches to crime prevention and control.[12]

Only in the last quarter century have these practical and moral tensions in the American approach to criminal justice been played out nationally. Before 1964, crime was not a big issue in American national politics. With the 1968 presidential contest, however, crime became one of "the most emotionally charged of all domestic issues" and it has remained high on the national political agenda ever since.[13]

Between 1967 and 1992, the federal government waged two wars on crime. The first war (1967–80) was against poverty, the second one (1980–92) against criminals. In the first war the social and economic "root causes" of crime were attacked; in the second war the likelihood that criminals would be detected, arrested, prosecuted, convicted, and incarcerated was increased. The chief strategists in the first war were liberals who believed that the federal government should play a central role in crime control. They emphasized the goals of offender rehabilitation, reintegration, humane treatment, and constitutional rights. The chief strategists in the second war were conservatives who believed that the federal role in crime control should be kept to a minimum. They emphasized the goals of punishment, deterrence, cost containment, and federalism.

In February 1967 the nineteen-member President's Commission on Law Enforcement and the Administration of Justice, led by Attorney General Nicholas deB. Katzenbach, issued its final report, a 340-page document entitled *The Challenge of Crime in a Free Society*.[14] The report covered adult and juvenile crime trends, police, courts, corrections,

12. As William G. Mayer has concluded from analyses of public opinion data, between 1960 and 1965 public opinion on crime and punishment became more liberal, and between 1965 and 1988 it became increasingly conservative; see his "Shifting Sands of Public Opinion: Is Liberalism Back?" *Public Interest*, no. 107 (Spring 1992), pp. 3–17. Interestingly, Mayer's analysis of public opinion concurs very well with trends in criminal justice program administration such as the rise, decline, and, in many jurisdictions, official or de facto abolition of paroling authorities. On parole, see Edward E. Rhine, William R. Smith, and Ronald W. Jackson, *Paroling Authorities: Recent History and Current Practice* (Laurel, Md.: American Correctional Association, 1991).

13. Robert A. Diamond and Arlene Alligood, eds., *Crime and the Law: The Fight by Federal Forces to Control Public Problem Number One in America* (Washington: Congressional Quarterly, 1971), p. 1.

14. President's Commission on Law Enforcement and Administration of Justice, *The Challenge of Crime in a Free Society* (Government Printing Office, February 1967).

narcotics and drug abuse, control of firearms, and more. Nine detailed task force documents on topics ranging from juvenile delinquency to organized crime backed up the main report.[15]

The Katzenbach commission argued that the federal government could "make a dramatic new contribution to the national effort against crime by greatly expanding its support of the agencies of Justice in the States and in the cities." More broadly, the commission concluded that "the great social programs" financed and administered by the federal government were "America's best hope of preventing crime and delinquency."[16] It offered this ringing declaration of purpose: "Warring on poverty, inadequate housing and unemployment, is warring on crime. A civil rights law is a law against crime. Money for schools is money against crime. Medical, psychiatric, and family-counseling services are services against crime. More broadly and most importantly every effort to improve life in America's 'inner cities' is an effort against crime."[17] Beyond social programs, it recommended an eight-point "program of Federal support" in criminal justice that included state and local planning, scientific research, and grants-in-aid for operational innovations.[18]

Behind a thick fog of antiliberal political rhetoric on crime, the Nixon administration adopted virtually every major crime policy of the Johnson administration. It acted on most of the Katzenbach commission's proposals and executed many of the Eisenhower commission's recommendations. For example, it lavished federal support on state and local law enforcement agencies by way of the Law Enforcement Assistance Administration (LEAA).

A brainchild of the Katzenbach commission, the LEAA was proposed by President Johnson and established by title I of the Omnibus Crime Control and Safe Streets Act of 1968. In real terms, the LEAA's fiscal 1972 budget was greater than the total budget for the Justice Department

15. Though dated, many of these task force reports remain unsurpassed. For example, see President's Commission on Law Enforcement and Administration of Justice, *Task Force Report: Crime and Its Impact—An Assessment* (Government Printing Office, 1967). Chapters 3 and 4, "Economic Impact of Crime" and "Crime and the Inner City" respectively, anticipated many subsequent findings about the costs and contours of crime in America. Appendix A of this report, "Ecological Correlates of Crime and Delinquency," highlighted urban-rural and intercity differences in crime and delinquency rates. As the report hinted would happen, these spatial differences have become more pronounced over the last quarter century.

16. President's Commission, *Challenge of Crime*, p. 283.

17. President's Commission, *Challenge of Crime*, p. 6.

18. President's Commission, *Challenge of Crime*, p. 285.

in fiscal 1968.[19] During the Nixon years, the LEAA launched massive new intergovernmental criminal justice programs, including federally sponsored law enforcement personnel training institutes, national criminal justice data-gathering and information-sharing networks, ambitious offender rehabilitation programs, and community-based crime control initiatives. The Ford administration continued these initiatives and did little to change the crime policies that it inherited.

Between 1976 and 1980, however, a political and intellectual consensus emerged that these policies had failed. As measured by the Federal Bureau of Investigation's (FBI's) Uniform Crime Report (UCR), crime rates were much higher in 1976 than they were in 1968. For example, between 1968 and 1976 the total annual crime rate (number of crimes per 100,000 resident population) rose from 3,370 to 5,287; over the same period, the violent crime rate rose from 298 to 468. Between 1976 and 1980 the total crime rate rose to 5,950 and the violent crime rate rose to 597.[20] Thus, between 1968 and 1980 the total crime rate rose 45 percent and the violent crime rate doubled. Meanwhile, the perception took hold that the LEAA's statewide criminal justice planning initiatives were almost a total bust. The federal government was awash with data on crime and criminals, but nobody seemed to know what to do with it. In short, by 1980, the LEAA had spent about $8 billion, but the nation's criminal justice system did not seem demonstrably better for it.

During his 1976 presidential campaign, Jimmy Carter charged that the LEAA had wasted billions of dollars "while making almost no contribution to reducing crime." When Democrats in Congress kept him from abolishing the agency, he reorganized it in ways that spelled a drastic reduction in its functions and funding. The LEAA's fiscal 1980 budget was about 20 percent smaller than its fiscal 1979 budget, and it lost most of its research functions to other agencies.[21]

Three Views of the First Federal War on Crime

In the late 1970s liberal, moderate, and conservative schools of thought gave their views on why the LEAA and the entire Johnson-Nixon-Ford war on crime had failed.

19. Calculated from figures in Diamond and Alligood, *Crime and the Law*, p. 30.

20. Kathleen Maguire and Timothy J. Flanagan, eds., *Sourcebook of Criminal Justice Statistics, 1990* (Washington: Bureau of Justice Statistics, 1991), p. 353.

21. Quotation in Charles W. Hucker, "LEAA Funding Controversy Deciding Agency's Future," *Congressional Quarterly Weekly Report*, March 3, 1979, p. 366; see Charles W.

The liberals believed that the war had never really been fought. Under the block grant provision of the Omnibus Crime Control and Safe Streets Act of 1968, as much federal money had gone to low-crime rural areas as to high-crime urban areas. The Nixon administration had targeted most of the LEAA's budget on police departments, and little of it on programs to rehabilitate offenders or address the underlying socioeconomic causes of crime.

But the liberal view had a silver lining. Many analysts predicted that crime rates would decrease as the 90 million baby boom Americans born between 1946 and 1968 aged out of their most crime-prone years. Thus demographics might succeed where politics and policy had failed; get-tough anticrime measures would become patently indefensible, and a national moratorium on prison construction could be adopted.

The moderates said that the war had been more or less sound in conception but necessarily flawed in execution. Whatever President Johnson had wanted or President Nixon had done, the American criminal justice system was a prisoner of federalism, a loose administrative confederation of thousands of different agencies operating under a mind-boggling array of political, legal, and budgetary constraints. Even under the best conditions, neither the LEAA or any other federal agency could enforce an effective national crime control strategy. The LEAA's much-publicized leadership problems, including frequent vacancies in top positions, frequent changes in mission statements, and low morale, eliminated any remaining chance that it could do so.

The conservatives decided the war had been fought according to an intellectually and morally bankrupt strategy. The LEAA aside, plenty had been spent on what the Katzenbach commission called "the great social programs that are America's best hope of preventing crime and delinquency."[22] But the money was wasted and not merely because of intergovernmental administrative problems. Rather, a profound lack of scientific knowledge about the "root causes" of crime hampered efforts to reduce crime. Nobody really knew how to fashion large-scale programs that would reduce crime or have other predictable and desirable social or economic consequences. This was especially true for criminal rehabili-

Hucker, "Full Senate, House Panel Vote Major Restructuring, Extension of Embattled LEAA," *Congressional Quarterly Weekly Report*, May 26, 1979, pp. 1009–11; and Nadine Cohodas, "Emphasis on White-Collar Crime and Drug Trafficking Reflected in Justice Budget," *Congressional Quarterly Weekly Report*, February 2, 1980, p. 272.

22. President's Commission, *Challenge of Crime*, p. 283.

tation programs, which the best empirical research of the day had suggested were ineffective.[23]

In the conservative view, the intellectual hubris of *The Challenge of Crime in a Free Society* was exceeded only by its moral sophistry. In the lines that came directly before its famous "Warring on poverty . . . is warring on crime" passage, the Katzenbach commission had suggested that slum dwellers did not "have the ability to assume responsibility" for their actions, because "society" had "let too many of them grow up untaught, unmotivated, unwanted."[24] But most slum dwellers were not criminals; they deserved to be praised for their good citizenship, just as the criminals among them deserved to be punished for their criminal misdeeds.

The conservative view also had its silver lining. The maturation of the baby boomers might or might not push crime rates down, and there was no good reason to tear down the walls of the nation's prisons and jails. Rather than focus on the "root causes" of crime, the penalties could be made more swift, certain, and severe. If crime did not pay, or paid less well, then fewer crimes would be committed. If prisons could not rehabilitate offenders, then at least they could protect the public by incapacitating criminals.

The Second Federal War on Crime

In 1981, based on this conservative view of federal crime policy, the Reagan administration launched a second federal war on crime. In this war, Reagan asserted, the "battle flag" would replace the "surrender flag."[25] The federal government would sound the charge, but the states and localities would have to do most of the actual fighting—and spending. The administration's fiscal 1983 budget asserted, "Public safety is primarily a state and local responsibility. This Administration does not believe that providing criminal justice assistance in the form of grants or contracts is an appropriate or effective use of federal funds."[26]

23. For an overview of that research and how it was interpreted, and a discussion of how subsequent research has rendered more positive findings, see John J. DiIulio, Jr., "Getting Prisons Straight," *American Prospect*, no. 3 (Fall 1990), pp. 54–64.

24. President's Commission, *Challenge of Crime*, p. 6.

25. Quoted in Dick Kirschten, "Reagan's Crime-Fighting Proposals—Shoot First and Then Load the Gun?" *National Journal*, November 13, 1982, pp. 1934–36.

26. "Administration of Justice Escapes Deep Spending Cuts in New Reagan Budget Plan," *Congressional Quarterly Weekly Report*, February 13, 1982, p. 275.

In 1982, the Reagan administration phased out the LEAA. Two years later, the administration won sweeping changes in the federal criminal code. The Comprehensive Crime Control Act of 1984 was the most important anticrime package enacted since the Omnibus Crime Control and Safe Streets Act of 1968. Among its key provisions, the law required federal judges to] follow new sentencing guidelines; permitted pretrial detention of dangerous defendants; restricted the use of the insanity defense; and increased penalties for drug trafficking. Four years later, Congress approved the $2.8 billion Anti-Drug Abuse Act of 1988. The bill allowed the death penalty for major drug traffickers; provided even stiffer penalties for drug dealers; denied federal grants, loans, and contracts to repeat drug offenders; and created a cabinet-level drug czar position.[27] The administration's opponents in Congress found there "was no effective answer to Reagan; trying to quarrel with him about who had the best ideas for fighting crime didn't work. And no member wanted to look as though he was for crime."[28]

During the 1988 presidential contest, supporters of George Bush ran the now famous Willie Horton television ad. The ad showed the mug shot of Willie Horton, a convicted murderer and Massachusetts prisoner, and the voice-over told of how Horton committed a sexual assault in Maryland during an unsupervised furlough from prison. No empirical evidence proves that the ad made any significant difference in the election results. But the ad did have some nontrivial political consequences. As one close observer noted, "Ever since George Bush so effectively used murderer-rapist Willie Horton against Michael S. Dukakis, Democrats have been determined to project a tough-on-crime stance."[29]

---

27. Contrary to some popular accounts, the Reagan administration provided no political push for a cabinet-level drug czar position. The push came from Democrats in Congress. In fact, in January 1983 President Reagan vetoed an anticrime bill cleared by Congress because it contained a provision establishing a cabinet-level drug czar position. The Reagan administration accepted the drug-czar provision of the 1988 bill as a compromise.

28. Nadine Cohodas, "Reagan Leadership the Margin for Passage," *Congressional Quarterly Weekly Report*, October 20, 1984, p. 2762.

29. Joan Biskupic, "Crime Fight Delayed in Senate; Biden Offers His Own Plan," *Congressional Quarterly Weekly Report*, November 25, 1989, pp. 3248–49. For the most part, however, Democrats in Congress did not match George Bush's anticrime rhetoric, much of which, it seems, was drawn directly from Reagan-era speeches. In his 1992 State of the Union Address, for example, Bush stated that "a tired woman on her way to work at 6 in the morning on a subway deserves to get there safely." (Transcript of President Bush's State of the Union Address, *New York Times*, January 29, 1992, p. A16.) In his

In September 1989 the administration announced its "war on drugs." Among the principal provisions of the $7.9 billion plan were an increase in federal aid to state and local police, and a tripling in economic and military aid to reduce coca crops and fight drug traffickers in Bolivia, Colombia, and Peru. The Bush antidrug plan came under heavy fire from several quarters. A strange-bedfellows coalition of liberal and conservative critics argued that the plan relied too heavily on interdicting foreign supplies and incarcerating petty traffickers, tactics they viewed as failed, futile, and a threat to civil freedoms.[30] Congressional Democrats charged that the plan put too much emphasis on antidrug law enforcement and not enough emphasis on drug abuse prevention and treatment. They also insisted that, even on its own terms, the plan was woefully underfunded.

Between 1990 and 1992, the administration resurrected several Reagan-era anticrime proposals, including an expansion of the federal death penalty, speedier execution of condemned prisoners, and a "good faith" exception to the rule against illegally obtained evidence. Congressional Democrats batted around these proposals and pushed various death penalty and gun control measures of their own.[31] The political pressures surrounding the federal anticrime policy debate grew more intense. In October 1990, Representative William Hughes, Democrat of New Jersey, stated, "I hope we never, ever bring up a crime bill again a month before an election."[32] By March 1992, it seemed that he would get his wish. A Republican filibuster over a week-long waiting period for the purchase of handguns had derailed an election-year crime bill that would impose the death penalty for more than fifty federal crimes,

---

1985 State of the Union Address, Reagan had spoken of a "tired, decent cleaning woman who can't ride a subway home without being afraid." (Text of address, *Congressional Quarterly Weekly Report*, February 9, 1985, p. 269.) In the 1989 address, in which Bush outlined his first major crime plan, he stated that street criminals had become America's "privileged class." (Text of speech, *Congressional Quarterly Weekly Report*, May 20, 1989, p. 1211.) Reagan had used the same language in 1982. (Quoted in Kirschten, "Reagan's Crime-Fighting Proposals," p. 1936.)

30. White House, *National Drug Control Strategy* (GPO, September 1989). The second drug-control strategy report was released on January 25, 1990, and got much the same reception as the first Bush antidrug plan. W. John Moore, "Dissenters in the Drug War," *National Journal*, November 4, 1989, pp. 2692–95.

31. Joan Biskupic, "Taking Tough Stance on Crime, House Boosts Death Penalty," *Congressional Quarterly Weekly Report*, October 6, 1990, pp. 3223–25, and Biskupic, "Death Penalty, Other Hot Issues Dumped from Crime Bill," *Congressional Quarterly Weekly Report*, October 27, 1990, p. 3615.

32. Quoted in Biskupic, "Taking Tough Stance," p. 3223.

reduce death-row appeals, and authorize $3.5 billion in criminal justice assistance to state and local governments. In the months following the Los Angeles riots, however, election-year crime bills floated to the top of the federal domestic policy agenda.

During the second half of Bush's first term, a national political and intellectual consensus began to emerge that the second federal war on crime had failed, especially in relation to the urban drug-and-crime problem.[33] Dozens of states issued blue ribbon commission reports on crime and corrections. Each claimed that the get-tough strategy of the 1980s had not succeeded where the war-on-poverty strategy had ostensibly failed.[34] But disagreement about the effects of the second federal war on crime still continues.

Competing Views of the Second Federal War on Crime

Two schools of thought prevail about the effects of the ongoing second federal war on crime and the direction that future federal crime policy ought to take. At the heart of the debate are hard-to-reconcile interpretations of the statistics on post-1980 trends in imprisonment, criminal victimization, and antidrug law enforcement. On the one side are those who maintain that, together with mandatory sentencing laws, drug-law enforcement has resulted in inhumane, crowded conditions behind bars, unwarranted increases in corrections spending, and no reduction in crime. By and large, they oppose any expansion in the nation's prison stock, support a greater use of probation and parole programs, and are open to arguments for the legalization of some or all drugs. On the other side are those who maintain that the "prison bulge" of the 1980s was merely relief from a "starvation diet" that began in the 1970s. They argue that prison conditions have not worsened, that more prisons have spelled less crime, and that the increased spending on prisons has been beneficial. For the most part, they support a further

33. For a good overview, see W. John Moore, "Crime Plays," *National Journal*, May 25, 1991, pp. 1218–22.

34. Two examples are California's *Blue Ribbon Commission on Inmate Population Management, Executive Summary* (Sacramento, Calif.: Prison Industry Authority, January 1990); and Governor's Management Review Commission, *Corrections in New Jersey: Choosing the Future* (Trenton, N.J., October 1990). As of mid-1992 the principal recommendations of these reports had not been enacted. The same holds for the dozens of other such reports issued in as many states.

expansion in the nation's prison stock, oppose a greater use of probation and parole programs, and oppose legalization of some or all drugs.[35]

There is something to be said for each school of thought. In the 1980s the nation's correctional population did increase steeply. In 1989 a record 4,054,000 persons—2.2 percent of the United States adult population— were in prison (17 percent), in jail (10 percent), on probation (62 percent), or on parole (11 percent). Between 1980 and 1991, the nation's prison population rose by 149.7 percent, from 329,821 to 823,144, and the national imprisonment rate (number of prisoners with sentences of more than one year per 100,000 resident population) rose from 139 to 310.[36]

But calculating the imprisonment rate relative to the number of serious crimes committed and arrests made produces a different, and quite unsensational, trend. The number of commitments to state prisons for each 1,000 serious crimes (murder, nonnegligent manslaughter, forcible rape, robbery, aggravated assault, and burglary) was 62 in 1960, 23 in 1970, and 25 in 1980. In the 1980s, it inched back to its 1960 level, reaching 62 again in 1989. Similarly, the number of commitments to state prisons per 1,000 arrests for serious crimes dropped from 163 in 1964 to 100 in 1970. In the 1980s it hovered between 130 and 150.[37]

Mandatory sentences, including the enforcement of tough antidrug laws, doubtlessly increased the nation's corrections population and boosted spending in the 1980s. For example, new sentencing guidelines and antidrug laws pushed the federal prisoner population from 24,805 at the end of 1984 to 62,764 by mid-1991. As a result, between 1981 and 1989, the Federal Bureau of Prisons annual operating budget grew faster than that of any other federal nondefense agency, from $500 mil-

---

35. These two schools do not break down cleanly along traditional ideological lines; for example, some conservatives who support the decriminalization of some drugs also support an expansion in the nation's prison stock. Similarly, some conservative supporters of strict drug-law enforcement, in the pursuit of this goal, are willing to relax their preference for state and local public administration, up to and including support for the federal government's use of national military forces in civilian law enforcement. See David C. Morrison, "Police Action," *National Journal*, February 12, 1992, pp. 267–70.

36. Department of Justice, *Correctional Populations in the United States, 1989* (Washington: Bureau of Justice Statistics, October 1991), p. 5; and Tracy L. Snell and Danielle C. Morton, "Prisoners in 1991" (Washington: Bureau of Justice Statistics, May 1992), pp. 1, 2.

37. Robyn L. Cohen, "Prisoners in 1990" (Washington: Bureau of Justice Statistics, May 1991), p. 7; and Snell and Morton, "Prisoners in 1991," p. 8.

lion to $1.6 billion.[38] Similarly, in California, from the end of 1980 to early 1990, mandatory sentencing, new drug laws, and increased imprisonment for parole violations drove the state's prisoner population from about 22,500 to over 86,000, and its annual corrections budget for 1994–95 is expected to be nearly $4 billion. Over the 1980s the New Jersey prison population tripled and the corrections budget quintupled, largely because of a change in the penal code and the enforcement of new drug laws.[39]

But sentences have not lengthened since 1973 even though mandatory sentencing laws have authorized or required longer sentences, and most felons continue to spend only a fraction of their sentences behind bars. For example, in 1986 the median sentence for a felony conviction was forty-eight months, compared with sixty months for most of the period between 1960 and 1980.[40] In 1986 the median time served in confinement was fifteen months, the same as it was in 1976, and in 1984 most felons served less than half of their time behind bars (jail and prison)—about 45.4 percent for all offenses, 50.5 percent for all violent offenses, and 44.0 percent for all property offenses. In many states, the likelihood of being sentenced to prison if convicted after an arrest has remained under 50 percent for all crimes except homicide.[41]

The large increase in corrections spending in the 1980s was money well spent. While money spent on prisons is not available for schools and other intrinsically more satisfying uses, every expenditure, public or private, means opportunity costs. By the same token, rhetorical statements such as "It costs more to keep a young man behind bars for a year than to send him to Princeton University for a year" obscure the fact that society may gain something important from keeping a violent criminal away from ordinary citizens.

38. The 1984 figure is from Patrick A. Langan and others, *Historical Statistics on Prisoners in State and Federal Institutions, Yearend 1925–86* (Washington: Bureau of Justice Statistics, May 1988), p. 13. The mid-1991 figure is from Department of Justice, *Monday Morning Highlights* (Washington: Federal Prison System, June 24, 1991), p. 20; and John Cogan and Timothy J. Muris, "The Myth of Domestic Spending Cuts," *Wall Street Journal*, September 6, 1990, p. A14.

39. *Blue Ribbon Commission*, pp. 2–3; and *Corrections in New Jersey*, pt. 1.

40. Patrick A. Langan, "America's Soaring Prison Population," *Science*, March 29, 1991, pp. 1568–73.

41. Langan, "America's Soaring Prison Population," p. 1570; Stephanie Minor-Harper and Christopher A. Innes, "Time Served in Prison and on Parole, 1984" (Washington: Bureau of Justice Statistics, December 1987), p. 3; see also Department of Justice, *Sentencing*

Benefit-cost analyses of corrections programs are in their infancy. The most recent study was based on the largest scientific prisoner self-report survey ever conducted within a single prison system.[42] It estimated that, excluding drug crimes, the median number of crimes committed per prisoner each year was twelve. Using the best available estimates of social costs per crime and annual costs per prisoner, the benefit-cost study concluded that "prison pays" at the margin for most prisoners, and that "more prison beds is a necessary if unfortunate social investment that will probably pay dividends over time."[43]

Still the same benefit-cost study also concluded that, for nonviolent and first-time offenders, imprisonment may be unwise.[44] The crucial question is what fraction of the prison population consists of such petty offenders. A widely cited study reported that the "vast majority of inmates are sentenced for petty crimes," and a national newspaper columnist summarized the study as finding that "80 percent of those going to prison are not serious or violent criminals but are guilty of low-level offenses: minor parole violations, property, drug and public disorder crimes."[45]

But, as Charles H. Logan has demonstrated, the study was seriously flawed, and the journalistic rendering of it completely unfounded. Based on loosely conducted and loosely coded interviews with 154 incoming prisoners in three states, the study used "inmates" to refer to just the entering cohort and not all prisoners, "vast majority" to refer to 52.6 percent, and "petty" crimes to refer to acts that most Americans believe should result in incarceration.[46]

---

and Time Served (Washington: Bureau of Justice Statistics, 1987); and Jacob Perez, *Tracking Offenders, 1987* (Washington: Bureau of Justice Statistics, October 1990), p. 5.

42. John J. DiIulio, Jr., and Anne M. Piehl, "Does Prison Pay?: The Stormy National Debate over the Cost-Effectiveness of Imprisonment," *Brookings Review*, vol. 9 (Fall 1991), pp. 28–35. For complete results of the survey see John J. DiIulio, Jr., *Crime and Punishment in Wisconsin* (Milwaukee, Wis.: Wisconsin Policy Research Institute, December 1990), pt. 2, pp. 11–48. Knowledge about the physical pains, psychological traumas, and economic losses suffered by victims of crime, their families and friends, and the public is increasing. See Albert R. Roberts, ed., *Helping Crime Victims: Research, Policy, and Practice* (Newbury Park, Calif.: Sage Publications, 1990).

43. DiIulio and Piehl, "Does Prison Pay?" pp. 34–35.

44. DiIulio and Piehl, "Does Prison Pay?" pp. 34–35.

45. James Austin and John Irwin, *Who Goes to Prison?* (San Francisco: National Council on Crime and Delinquency, 1990), p. 1; and Tom Wicker, "The Punitive Society," *New York Times*, January 12, 1991, p. A25.

46. Charles H. Logan, "Who Really Goes to Prison," *Federal Prisons Journal*, vol. 2 (Summer 1991), pp. 57–59.

National data analyzed by Lawrence Greenfeld also show clearly that, in 1991, fully 93 percent of state prisoners were serving a sentence for a violent crime or were recidivists. Even in the ostensibly white-collar federal prison system, in the late 1980s, 46 percent of all federal prisoners and 92 percent of the 5,150 prisoners in federal penitentiaries had a history of violence; and, in 1989, 55.6 percent of all federal prisoners had two or more prior convictions.[47]

In sum, the prison population more than doubled in the 1980s as a result of mandatory sentences and the enforcement of tough new antidrug laws. Relative to crime and arrest rates, however, the imprisonment rate remained low in absolute terms and well below its 1960s level. By 1992, it was still true that fewer than one in ten serious crimes and fewer than one in seven arrests for serious crimes resulted in imprisonment. By the same token, most offenders, including drug offenders, still spent less than half of their sentences behind bars. Corrections costs escalated briskly, but the best available benefit-cost analyses suggested that the net of this public investment was positive. Finally, contrary to popular accounts, more than 90 percent of all prisoners were violent offenders or recidivists.

Critics of the second federal war on crime have made four primary arguments: many prisoners, including serious offenders, can be diverted into certain types of community-based supervision programs without a significant threat to public safety and with a significant saving in public money; when informed about such matters as prison crowding, a majority of the public supports a greater use of community-based programs for offenders; imprisonment rates and crime rates do not vary inversely; and legalization of drugs would be more beneficial socially than continued efforts at strict antidrug law enforcement. The best available data furnish little support for the critics' first two contentions. The evidence on the relationship between crime rates and imprisonment rates is mixed, as is the evidence on the likely consequences of legalizing some or all drugs.

Alternatives to Prison

In the 1980s overcrowding behind bars was a less severe problem than overloading on the streets. In many jurisdictions, the increase in the

47. Lawrence A. Greenfeld, *Prisons and Prisoners in the United States* (Washington: Bureau of Justice Statistics, April 1992), p. 16; Department of Justice, "Research Bulletin: Federal Prisoners with a History of Violence" (Washington: Federal Bureau of Prisons, undated), pp. 2–5; and Department of Justice, *1989 State of the Bureau* (Washington: Federal Bureau of Prisons, 1990), p. 55.

use of probation and parole was steeper than the increase in the use of prisons and jails. Nationally, between 1985 and 1990, the number of people in jail or on probation each rose by about 36 percent, while the number in prison increased by 53 percent and the number on parole shot up by 77 percent. In 1990, 62 percent of the more than 4.3 million persons in custody were on probation, and 12 percent of them were on parole. The old idea that prisons were "schools of crime" was succeeded by the idea that the streets are "applied schools of crime," as an important study found that within three years of sentencing, nearly two-thirds of felons on probation would be arrested for a new felony or charged with violating their supervision requirements.[48]

Thus, at the start of the 1990s, about three of every four persons under correctional supervision in this country were under some type of community-based custody. Probation and parole officers found themselves with caseloads that had doubled or tripled in the 1980s and ranged into the hundreds. The officers were unable to supervise most of their charges adequately. And it was virtually impossible to help more than a tiny fraction of offenders to seek drug treatment, find jobs, or enhance their noncriminal life prospects in other ways.[49]

The Katzenbach commission had called for a greater use of alternatives to incarceration but stressed that caseloads should be kept within manageable limits and recommended "an average ratio of 35 offenders per officer."[50] In the 1980s few probation or parole programs featured such a low offender-to-officer ratio, and those that did were styled "intensive supervision programs" (ISPs).

In 1988 ISPs had been tried, or were being established, in forty-five states. Still, by 1990 only about 82,000 probationers and parolees—just over 2.5 percent of the total community-based offender population of 3.2 million—were in any type of ISP.[51] Some ISPs have made use of

48. Louis Jankowski, *Probation and Parole 1990* (Washington: Bureau of Justice Statistics, November 1991), p. 5; and Patrick A. Langan and Mark A. Cunniff, *Recidivism of Felons on Probation, 1986–1989* (Washington: Bureau of Justice Statistics, February 1992).

49. In New Jersey, for example, probation caseloads doubled to 162; in Los Angeles County, they reached nearly 1,000. See *Corrections in New Jersey*; and John J. DiIulio, Jr., *No Escape: The Future of American Corrections* (Basic Books, 1991), chap. 2. See also Howard Goodman, "A Crushing Load for Corrections Officers: Cases Are Doubling, Sometimes Tripling," *Philadelphia Inquirer*, April 20, 1992, pp. A1, A6.

50. President's Commission, *Challenge of Crime*, p. 167.

51. Rhine and others, *Paroling Authorities*, p. 114; and figures for probationers calculated from Jankowski, *Probation and Parole 1990*, pp. 1, 4.

electronic monitoring; others have not. In probation and parole, ISPs have displayed "considerable diversity in goals and purposes, the target population, intake procedures, the methods or conditions of supervision, and program capacity or enrollment."[52] In the typical ISP with or without electronic monitoring, the officer handles thirty-five or fewer cases, and offenders are subject to weekly face-to-face meetings with their supervisor, curfews, drug tests, educational and work standards, community service, restitution, and other such requirements. The typical ISP is thus to be contrasted with routine probation and parole programs in which one officer supervises seventy-five or more offenders and has as little as one face-to-face contact semiannually with each offender.

Naturally, ISPs have been more expensive to operate than regular probation and parole programs, in some cases several thousand dollars more for each offender each year.[53] To place all community-based offenders in an ISP would be prohibitively expensive, and no jurisdiction has contemplated beefing up probation and parole supervision that much. Instead, the hope has been that ISPs could handle high-risk offenders who, if the ISP option were unavailable, would be incarcerated. On average, it costs three times as much to imprison an offender for a year as it does to manage him in an ISP. Thus if ISPs could provide community-based custody for offenders who would otherwise be in prison, and do so with little or no increase in recidivism, they would constitute the ideal intermediate sanction, that is, a humane but no-nonsense punishment that alleviates crowding behind bars, promotes public safety, rehabilitates and reintegrates offenders, saves money, and falls somewhere between loose community-based supervision and full-term incarceration.[54]

The early evidence on ISPs was largely anecdotal but so encouraging that one analyst concluded there was no need to wait for more studies "before moving aggressively to expand the use of ISPs."[55] But all of the most systematic studies have now shown that ISPs fall far short of the

52. Rhine and others, *Paroling Authorities*, p. 115.

53. Joan Petersilia and Susan Turner, *Intensive Supervision for High-Risk Probationers: Findings from Three California Experiments* (Santa Monica: RAND Corp., 1990), pp. 91–93, and Susan Turner and Joan Petersilia, "Focusing on High-Risk Parolees: An Experiment to Reduce Commitments to the Texas Department of Corrections," *Journal of Research in Crime and Delinquency*, vol. 29 (February 1992), pp. 34–61.

54. For a fine general discussion of intermediate sanctions, see Norval Morris and Michael H. Tonry, *Between Prison and Probation: Intermediate Punishments in a Rational Sentencing System* (New York: Oxford University Press, 1990).

55. DiIulio, "Impact of Inner-City Crime," p. 44, and, in general, DiIulio, *No Escape*, chap. 2.

early hopes for them. For example, a recent experimental study of ISPs for high-risk probationers found that, at the end of a one-year follow-up period, about 40 percent of the participants had technical violations and 30 percent had new arrests. The authors concluded that ISPs "are not effective for high-risk offenders" and are "more expensive than routine probation and apparently provide no greater guarantees for public safety." Similarly, a recent experimental study of ISPs for high-risk parolees found that "the ISP results were the opposite of what was intended. . . . ISP was not associated with fewer arrests, even though ISP offenders received more contacts than offenders on routine supervision. . . . ISP supervision turned out to be 1.7 times the cost of routine parole."[56]

The ISPs that were studied did not provide offenders with many social services (job counseling, drug treatment). It is possible that more service-oriented ISPs might succeed where these service-poor ones failed. At this stage, however, the only empirically grounded conclusion is that the programs do not work. Proponents can keep suggesting that ISPs and other alternatives to incarceration "can relieve prison crowding, enhance public safety, and rehabilitate offenders—and all at a cost savings." But the evidence makes it "doubtful that intermediate sanctions can accomplish such grandiose goals."[57]

Remember that poor and minority citizens who live in the places from which most convicted criminals come and to which most of them return bear the costs of experiments with community-based correctional programs. Unfortunately, like other alternatives to incarceration, ISPs allow the criminally deviant to revictimize their socioeconomically disadvantaged neighbors.

Support for Alternatives to Prison

Even if the evidence on ISPs were more encouraging, the public would probably not long support programs that place more offenders back on the streets. Florida and New Jersey were among the states that took the lead in developing ISPs and other intermediate sanctions. Yet the total number of offenders in Florida's ISP programs between 1983 and 1988 (about 10,000) would have amounted to just 4 percent of its total 1989

56. Petersilia and Turner, *Intensive Supervision*, pp. ix, 98; and Turner and Petersilia, *Focusing on High-Risk Parolees*, p. 34.
57. Turner and Petersilia, *Focusing on High-Risk Parolees*, p. 58.

correctional population (266,738). In New Jersey, only 0.6 percent of the state's 1990 corrections population was in any type of ISP program.[58]

The reasons for the stunted growth of ISPs in these states and elsewhere were mostly political. The many blue ribbon reports that endorsed ISPs and other intermediate sanctions were given a polite public reception but not much more. In California, for example, by 1992 the much-publicized 1990 report on inmate population management gathered dust while plans were laid to build fourteen new prisons. In New Jersey the 1990 report on corrections was buried by key policymakers (including those who had sponsored it) and quickly became little more than a rallying point for the state's true believers in intermediate sanctions.

The politics of experimenting with community-based corrections is uniquely treacherous. Elected officials fear that to support even nononsense intermediate sanctions such as ISPs is to risk being cast as soft on crime. For example, the Willie Horton ad led federal, state, and local officials to cut back on prison furloughs even though over 99 percent of all furloughs result in neither a technical violation nor a new crime, and even though some evidence suggests that prisoners who receive furloughs recidivate less and are more likely to get and keep jobs than otherwise comparable prisoners who do not receive them.[59] As the New Jersey report on corrections explained:

> If a welfare-reform program succeeded in getting 99 of every 100 designated persons off public assistance and into a self-supporting job, it would be considered a smashing success, and the architects and legislative sponsors of the program would joust with one another for recognition. If, on the other hand, a penal-reform program resulted in one inmate in 100 committing a highly publicized crime, scathing media commentary and strong public reaction would result in immediate calls for the program's demise.[60]

But critics of the second federal war on crime have asserted that public opinion is far more favorable to community-based corrections than is commonly supposed. A few public opinion polls indicate public willingness to put offenders who are not "dangerous" on probation and parole,

58. Total ISP figure is from DiIulio, *No Escape*, p. 83. Total population figure is from *Correctional Populations 1989*, p. 5; and New Jersey statistic is calculated from *Corrections in New Jersey*, p. 16.

59. DiIulio, *No Escape*, chap. 2, pp. 60–62.

60. *Corrections in New Jersey*, pp. 25–26.

but most polls by far indicate that the public favors incarceration for most crimes under most conditions and believes that most convicted criminals do not serve enough time behind bars and are "let off too easily."[61] Moreover, there is no way of knowing what fraction of the public is aware that already three of every four felons now serving a sentence are not incarcerated, or how much higher public support for incarceration, and political pressures against alternatives, would be if more people were so informed.

Still many supporters of intermediate sanctions have touted studies that, they contend, show that the public, if informed about the ostensible horrors of prison crowding and the supposed benefits of alternatives to incarceration, will support a greater use of probation and parole. Metaphorically speaking, however, the gulf between these studies and scientific survey research is wide enough to hold a 2,000-bed maximum-security prison. Indeed, even after subjecting selected respondents to hours of anti-incarceration propaganda, and despite wording questions in a way that biases results in favor of intermediate sanctions, most respondents in one such study still wanted most offenders to serve time in prison.[62]

The attempt to drum up public support for intermediate sanctions by dramatizing the negative effects of prison crowding may or may not prove effective as anti-incarceration propaganda. But no systematic evidence supports the popular notion that prison crowding is associated with higher levels of cellblock violence, poor inmate health, or other serious problems.[63] Indeed, many of the safest, cleanest, and cost-effective prisons and prison systems in the country have long been among the

61. For example, see Edna McConnell Clark Foundation, *Americans behind Bars* (New York, March 1992), pp. 23–25; and Maguire and Flanagan, *Sourcebook*, pp. 188–91. My reading of this extensive literature is consistent with Mayer, "Shifting Sands of Public Opinion," which finds that American public opinion on crime and punishment has become increasingly conservative since 1965.

62. For example, see John Doble and Josh Klein, *Prison Overcrowding and Alternative Sentences: The Views of the People of Alabama* (New York: Public Agenda Foundation Report, February 1989).

63. On the effects of prison crowding, see Gerald G. Gaes, "The Effects of Overcrowding in Prison," in Michael Tonry and Norval Morris, eds., *Crime and Justice*, vol. 6 (University of Chicago Press, 1985), pp. 95–146; Jeff Bleich, "The Politics of Prison Crowding," *California Law Review*, vol. 77 (October 1989), pp. 1125–80; Christopher A. Innes, *Population Density in State Prisons* (Washington: Bureau of Justice Statistics, December 1986); and James Bonta and Paul Gendreau, "Reexamining the Cruel and Unusual Punishment of Prison Life," *Law and Human Behavior*, vol. 14 (August 1990), pp. 347–72.

most crowded, while some of the most violence-ridden, dirtiest, and costly have long been among the least crowded.[64]

Imprisonment and Crime

There are two widely used measures of crime in the United States. Since 1972 the Bureau of the Census has administered the National Crime Victimization Survey (NCVS) for the Bureau of Justice Statistics. The annual NCVS reports contain data derived from continuing surveys of occupants of a representative sample of housing units in the United States. In the 1990 NCVS report, for example, about 95,000 people 12 years of age or older living in 47,000 housing units were interviewed, and 97 percent of the households selected to participate did so.[65]

According to NCVS data, between 1980 and 1990, the national rate of violent crime (number of victimizations per 1,000 persons 12 years of age or older) declined from 31.0 to 29.6; between 1983 and 1990, it fluctuated between 28.1 and 31.4. Between 1978 and 1988, the national rate of burglary (number of incidents per 1,000 households) dropped from 82.6 to 57.4. During this period, only one rate of criminal victimization—the national rate of motor theft (number of incidents per 1,000 households)—did not decline, beginning and ending at 17.5 following a dip in the intervening years.[66]

The other major crime measure is the Uniform Crime Reports (UCR) compiled by the Federal Bureau of Investigation from state and local police reports. Contrary to the NCVS, the UCR shows that the number of violent crimes per 100,000 resident population increased between 1980 and 1990, from 596.6 to 633.7, and, the UCR records much smaller decreases in the rate of property crime over the same period than does the NCVS.[67]

64. DiIulio, *No Escape*, chap. 1. Bonta and Gendreau ("Reexamining the Cruel and Unusual Punishment," p. 365) observe that the literature "indicates that moderating variables play a crucial role" in determining the consequences of prison crowding. So far as anyone can tell, the key moderating variables relate to prison leadership and management.

65. *Criminal Victimization in the United States, 1990: A National Crime Victimization Survey Report* (Washington: Bureau of Justice Statistics, February 1992), p. iii.

66. Lisa D. Bastian and Marshall M. DeBerry, Jr. *Criminal Victimization 1990* (Washington: Bureau of Justice Statistics, October 1991), p. 4; Department of Justice, *Criminal Victimization in the United States: 1973–88 Trends* (Washington: Bureau of Justice Statistics, July 1991), pp. 68, 77, and pp. 16 (rape), 20 (robbery), 31 (assault), 49 (personal larceny), 68 (burglary), 72 (household larceny).

67. Maguire and Flanagan, *Sourcebook*, p. 353.

By using selected UCR data, some opponents of the second federal war on crime have minimized the crime-reduction effects of the increased use of prisons that occurred in the 1980s. By using selected NCVS data, some supporters of the second federal war on crime have maximized the crime-reduction effects of the increased use of prisons that occurred in the 1980s.[68] But the more one controls for demographic and other variables known to be related to crime rates, the harder it becomes to specify the relationship (if any) between crime rates and imprisonment rates in the 1980s, or, for that matter, in previous decades.

In general, "the evidence is consistent with the view that states (or other jurisdictions) in which the probability of going to prison is high have, other things being equal, lower crime rates than states in which that probability is low"; and "the evidence showing a link between sanctions and crime is somewhat stronger than that showing a connection between economic conditions and crime. But there are various methodological problems that make it hard to be entirely confident that this connection is a causal one—that is, that the higher risk of punishment is keeping down the crime rate."[69]

Common sense says that criminals cannot commit crimes if they are locked up. This common sense can be refined to say that incapacitation "works provided at least three conditions are met: some offenders must be repeaters, offenders taken off the streets must not be immediately and completely replaced by new recruits, and prison must not increase the post-release criminal activity of those who have been incarcerated sufficiently to offset the crimes prevented by their stay in prison."[70]

Just about everything known about crime and imprisonment in the United States suggests that these three conditions normally hold.[71] Using NCVS data, for example, one study concluded that "in 1989 there were an estimated 66,000 fewer rapes, 323,000 fewer robberies, 380,000 fewer assaults, and 3.3 million fewer burglaries attributable to the difference between the crime rates of 1973 versus those of 1989. If only one-half or even one-fourth of the reductions were the result of rising incarceration rates, that would still leave prisons responsible for sizable

68. Edna McConnell Clark Foundation, *Americans behind Bars*, p. 8; and Richard Abell, "Beyond Willie Horton: The Battle of the Prison Bulge," *Policy Review*, vol. 47 (Winter 1989), pp. 32–35.

69. James Q. Wilson and Richard J. Hernstein, *Crime and Human Nature* (Simon and Schuster, 1985), p. 390.

70. James Q. Wilson, *Thinking about Crime*, rev. ed. (Basic Books, 1983), p. 146.

71. Wilson, *Thinking about Crime*, chap. 8 and throughout.

reductions in crime. That possibility must be seriously weighted in debates about America's prisons."[72]

Antidrug Law Enforcement

It is especially important to weigh the incapacitation effect of imprisonment for drug offenders. Between 1980 and 1989, the number of adult arrests for illegal drug sale (or manufacture) increased from 102,714 to 404,275. Over the same period, the number of arrests for illegal drug possession increased from 368,451 to 843,488.[73] Thus in 1989 more than 1.2 million drug arrests were made, representing a 165 percent increase from the less than one-half million drug arrests made in 1980.

In the 1980s the fraction of the nation's corrections population that consisted of persons serving sentences for drug-related offenses (possession or sales) skyrocketed. For example, from 1980 to 1990 the fraction of federal prisoners serving sentences for drug-related offenses rose from 22.7 percent to 54.2 percent. Similarly, between 1970 and 1986, drug offenders were about 10 percent of state prison admissions, but by 1989 they were 20 percent to 35 percent of prison admissions in most states. From mid-1986 to mid-1989, in many states prison admissions for drug offenses more than doubled. In New Jersey, for example, four years after the passage of a tough 1987 drug law, drug arrests nearly doubled and the fraction of the state's prison population in custody for drug offenses increased from 10 to 25 percent. Nationally, in 1979 drug offenders accounted for 6 percent of state prisoners, but by 1991 an estimated 22 percent of inmates were convicted of drug offenses.[74]

Between 1989 and 1990 the number of drug arrests nationally fell from its historic peak of nearly 1.25 million to a little over 1 million.[75] If the number of drug offenders behind bars were to double between 1992 and 1999, as it did between 1980 and 1989, by the year 2000 about half of all prisoners would be drug offenders.

72. Langan, "America's Soaring Prison Population," p. 1573.
73. Department of Justice, *Drugs and Crime Facts, 1990* (Washington: Bureau of Justice Statistics, August 1991), p. 7.
74. The 1980 figure is from Department of Justice, *1989 State of the Bureau*, p. 2. The 1990 figure is from Department of Justice, *1990 State of the Bureau* (Washington: Federal Bureau of Prisons, 1991), p. 7; James Austin and Aaron David McVey, "The 1989 NCCD Prison Population Forecast," *NCCD Focus* (San Francisco: National Council on Crime and Delinquency, December 1989), pp. 4, 5; *Corrections in New Jersey*, pt. 1; and Greenfeld, *Prisons and Prisoners*, p. 14.
75. Snell and Morton, *Prisoners in 1991*, p. 8.

Some evidence shows that drug offenders are displacing other types of criminals behind bars, and no firm evidence shows that stepped-up drug enforcement reduces crime rates. For example, a detailed study found that in the 1980s, Florida "embarked on a policy of incarcerating massive numbers of drug offenders. This policy has accelerated an increase in usage of early release, not only for drug offenders, but also for inmates convicted of violent crimes and those with criminal histories. Despite nearly half a billion dollars spent for prison construction programs, Florida today has the highest rate of prison admissions and the shortest length of stay of any prison system in the country. Furthermore, its already high crime rate has not been reduced but has increased slightly."[76]

In the case of drug offenses, one of the three aforementioned conditions under which imprisonment can be expected to have incapacitation effects may not apply: namely, drug offenders taken off the streets seem to be immediately and completely replaced by other drug offenders.[77]

In the 1980s Robert M. Stutman, former head of the New York office of the Drug Enforcement Agency (DEA), directed a special antidrug operation in New York's Washington Heights neighborhood, one of the first inner-city areas where the use of crack cocaine, crack-related property crime, and crack-financed street gang violence involving expensive weapons had reached epidemic proportions. But Stutman believed the problem was fueled largely by middle- and upper-middle-class persons who purchased crack and other illegal drugs in Washington Heights, making the easy commute by car over the George Washington Bridge from their suburban homes in New Jersey and Westchester County. Stutman persuaded the director of the DEA that this was the case and was authorized to target white visitors to Washington Heights. Eventually, more than a thousand cars were seized by DEA agents, and a few crack gangs were broken up. But as Stutman documents, the operation had almost no effect on the availability of crack in Washington Heights and vicinity. Based on this experience and others, Stutman reasons that the dealers and buyers in the drug trade cannot be arrested or imprisoned in sufficient numbers to make a significant difference in drug abuse or drug-related crime.[78]

76. James Austin, "The Consequences of Escalating the Use of Imprisonment: The Case Study of Florida," *NCCD Focus* (San Francisco: National Council on Crime and Delinquency, June 1991), p. 6.

77. Robert M. Stutman and Richard J. Esposito, *Dead on Delivery: Inside the Drug Wars, Straight from the Street* (Warner Books, 1992).

78. This conclusion is half-supported in a recent drug policy study. See Mark A. R. Kleiman, *Against Excess: Drug Policy for Results* (Basic Books, 1992). Nevertheless, Kleiman argues for increased antidrug law enforcement in the form of stepped-up street-

In light of this record, some critics of the second federal war on crime have recommended the legalization of some or all drugs. Unlike the advocates of the 1960s, the legalization advocates of the late 1980s and early 1990s have waged arguments drawn from comparative history and policy analysis. They have argued the ethical (mainly civil libertarian) case for legalization, but they have not advocated drug use and have stressed the difference between the use and abuse of drugs. The intellectual leaders in the field have attracted a small but influential cadre of public figures who joined them in the call for legalization or argued that legalization was an option that should be debated fairly and fully.[79]

Still legalization remains a political nonstarter. Most citizens who live in low-income neighborhoods where the incidence of drug abuse is high have opposed legalization, as has the general public.[80] While no one who has lived through the cataclysmic international events of the last few years is in a position to dismiss the possibility of radical changes in domestic affairs, no one who understands the American political process would wager ten cents on the proposal.

But the analytical case for legalization cannot be dismissed lightly.[81] Essentially, the case rests on the view that most of the harmful social consequences commonly associated with illegal drugs result not from the drugs themselves, but from the behaviors induced by their illegality. By removing most of the profits from the illegal drug trade, advocates for legalization argue, most of the socially destructive consequences of this trade, including the street violence wrought by inner-city drug dealers, might thereby be drastically reduced.

---

level police work against retail drug buyers—identifying and evicting drug dealers from public housing, investigating and closing stores that are fronts for drug operations, and targeting suburban buyers in inner-city drug markets.

79. The best single example is the widely cited and reprinted article by Ethan Nadelmann, "Drug Prohibition in the United States: Costs, Consequences, and Alternatives," *Science*, September 1, 1989, pp. 939–47. Baltimore's Democratic Mayor Kurt L. Schmoke, U.S. District Judge Robert Sweet, and former Secretary of State George P. Shultz have made public pronouncements in favor of legalization.

80. For example, see the public opinion surveys reported in Maguire and Flanagan, *Sourcebook*, pp. 228–30. Among other findings, the surveys show that in 1989 and 1990, opposition to legalization was strongest among blacks and low-income citizens, and that the same groups were even more worried than other citizens about the effects of legalization on drug use in schools and drug-related crime.

81. The best single antilegalization argument is James Q. Wilson, "Against the Legalization of Drugs," *Commentary*, vol. 89 (February 1990), pp. 23–28; see also William J. Bennett, *The De-Valuing of America: The Fight for Our Culture and Our Children* (Summit Books, 1992), chaps. 3, 4.

As even the strongest opponents of legalization have recognized, data that enable one to systematically evaluate the case for legalizing some or all drugs are sparse.[82] Recently, a multidisciplinary working group of leading experts on drug policy headed by Ethan Nadelmann produced a series of papers that made the case for drug legalization as well it can be made in the absence of such data.[83] As the Nadelmann group recognized, the "most common fear of legalization . . . is that there are millions of Americans for whom the drug prohibition system represents the principal bulwark between an abstemious relationship with drugs and a destructive one. . . . Figuring out, with some measure of confidence, the magnitude and composition of this vulnerable population is among the most important challenges confronting those who take seriously the need to estimate the consequences of alternative regimes."[84]

Opponents of legalization have argued that drug use and abuse in the United States has been on the decline; thus, if there ever was an opportune time for socially risky experiments with legalization, that moment may well have passed.[85] But the Nadelmann group has mustered a great deal of evidence and many novel arguments that support legalization. Analytically, if not politically or morally, the social costs and benefits of antidrug law enforcement efforts are something over which reasonable, policy-oriented people can continue to differ.

Drug Treatment Programs for All Prisoners

Clearly, more time must pass before the second federal war on crime can be declared an abject failure or pronounced a mixed success. But whether one believes that the nation's prison capacity should be expanded or greatly contracted, and whether one supports or opposes strict antidrug law enforcement, there is a case to be made for a stronger federal role in advancing certain types of drug treatment programs for prisoners.

In 1930 the Federal Bureau of Prisons (BOP) was established mainly to manage the burgeoning population of federal prisoners caused by the enforcement of Prohibition.[86] Long before numerous studies had

82 Wilson, "Against Legalization," p. 24.

83. For a summary statement, see Ethan Nadelmann, "Thinking Seriously about Alternatives to Drug Prohibition," *Daedalus*, vol. 123 (Summer 1992), forthcoming.

84. Nadelmann, "Thinking Seriously," p. 23.

85. Bennett, *The De-Valuing*, pp. 122, 149–51.

86. Paul W. Keve, *Prisons and the American Conscience: A History of U.S. Federal Corrections* (Southern Illinois University Press, 1991).

confirmed it, federal corrections officials understood that "drug addiction acts as a 'multiplier' of crime; while criminality often occurs prior to addiction, the onset of addiction results in higher levels of criminal involvement."[87]

In 1966, after several decades of loose experimentation with various types of prison-based drug treatment programs, Congress passed the Narcotic Addict Rehabilitation Act (NARA), which ordered in-prison and aftercare for narcotic addicts who had been convicted for violating federal laws. Unfortunately, this federal effort soon sputtered in the face of research that challenged the efficacy of drug-abuse and other criminal rehabilitation programs. The notion that nothing works in the rehabilitation of criminal offenders gained wide intellectual and political currency, and one jurisdiction after another changed its penal code to reflect this view.[88]

These studies, however, did not demonstrate that nothing works. Instead, they indicated that the effects of many criminal rehabilitation programs were ambiguous, and that the conditions under which programs succeeded were hard to specify, or, to the extent that they could be specified, hard to duplicate widely. In the 1980s, a new and better generation of studies demonstrated that some types of criminal rehabilitation programs worked under some conditions.[89]

87. For example, in a 1991 survey of 395,554 inmates, 40 percent said they were using drugs during the month before the crime, and a quarter said they were under the influence of drugs at the time of the crime. See Susan Wallace, "Drug Treatment: Perspectives and Current Initiatives," *Federal Prisons Journal*, vol. 2 (Summer 1991), p. 32. See also Department of Justice, Office of Research and Evaluation, "Proposal for the Evaluation of the Federal Bureau of Prisons Drug Abuse Treatment Programs" (Washington: Federal Bureau of Prisons, March 1990), p. 5; and Caroline Wolf Harlow, "Drugs and Jail Inmates, 1989" (Washington: Bureau of Justice Statistics, August 1991), p. 1. A 1991 study found that in eighteen jurisdictions, half of 13,120 male arrestees had tested positive for cocaine use. See Joyce Ann O'Neil and Virginia Baldau, *Drugs and Crime 1990: Annual Report* (Washington: National Institute of Justice, August 1991), p. 23. While the relationship of drug abuse and violent crime remains something of a chicken-and-egg question, there is "no doubt that participation in the drug business increases the probability of participation in violent events, both as victim and as perpetrator." See Paul J. Goldstein, "Drugs and Violent Crime," in Neil Alan Weiner, Margaret A. Zahn, and Rita J. Sagi, eds., *Violence: Patterns, Causes, Public Policy* (Harcourt Brace Jovanovich, 1990), pp. 295-303.

88. For an overview, see DiIulio, *No Escape*, chap. 3; and DiIulio, "Getting Prisons Straight."

89. For an overview, see D. A. Andrews and others, "Does Correctional Treatment Work? A Clinically Relevant and Psychologically Informed Meta-Analysis," *Criminology*, vol. 28 (August 1990), pp. 369–404; and Edgardo Rotman, *Beyond Punishment: A New View on the Rehabilitation of Criminal Offenders* (Greenwood Press, 1990).

Among the most efficacious programs, these studies found, were certain types of drug treatment for prisoners. For example, a 1989 study of four programs for drug-involved prisoners with serious criminal histories found that participants' postprogram recidivism rates were lower than for otherwise comparable offenders who had received no such treatment.[90] These successful drug treatment programs had at least five basic features in common:

—Clear statements of the program rules and the consequences of breaking them;

—Obvious concern by program staff about the welfare of participants;

—Participants' regard for staff members as persons worth imitating;

—Preparation of participants for future problems, including family and job problems; and

—Utilization of community resources.[91]

But the fundamental thing these programs had in common was that prisoners were required by law to participate in them. A good deal of evidence suggests that such persons are at least as likely as voluntary participants to respond favorably. As M. Douglas Anglin has observed, "How an individual is exposed to treatment seems to be irrelevant. What is important is that the narcotics addict must be brought into an environment where intervention can occur over time. Civil commitment and other legally coercive measures are useful and proven strategies."[92] Indeed, in a 1990 review of the literature encompassing some eighty studies of corrections-based programs for drug-abusing offenders, Anglin found that appropriate drug abuse treatment in prisons produced a significantly lower recidivism rate than did no treatment.[93]

As these studies show, the longer one stays in a properly structured drug treatment program, the better the chances of a reduction in drug abuse and crime. In voluntary drug treatment programs, dropout rates are notoriously high. But success rates are surprisingly high in prison-based drug treatment programs that provide strict supervision, take

90. Marcia R. Chaiken, *Prison Programs for Drug-Involved Offenders* (Washington: National Institute of Justice, October 1989).

91. Chaiken, *Prison Programs*, p. 2.

92. M. Douglas Anglin, "The Efficacy of Civil Commitment in Treating Narcotics Addiction," in Carl G. Leukefeld and Frank M. Tims, eds., *Compulsory Treatment of Drug Abuse: Research and Clinical Practice*, NIDA Research Monograph Series 86 (Department of Health and Human Services, 1988), p. 31.

93. M. Douglas Anglin, "Ensuring Success in Corrections-Based Interventions with Drug Abusing Offenders," paper presented at the Conference on Growth and Its Influence on Corrections Policy, University of California at Berkeley, May 10–11, 1990, p. 4.

place close to the participant's release-from-custody date, offer meaningful aftercare, and are conducted under conditions of legal compulsion.[94]

In 1990 federal prisons held some 59,000 prisoners, about 47 percent of them with moderate to serious drug abuse problems.[95] On a random and targeted basis, federal prisoners were administered more than 71,000 urine tests, which resulted in only a 1.9 percent detection rate (primarily for marijuana use). Between 1990 and 1992, the federal prison system's drug treatment efforts took shape around four main programs: drug education, drug abuse counseling, comprehensive and pilot residential drug treatment, and transitional services. Some of the key features of these programs were as follows:

—Mandatory forty-hour drug education sessions were provided to all federal prisoners with any history of drug abuse or drug-related crime. By the end of 1992, about 12,000 to 15,000 prisoners will have experienced these sessions.

—Counseling services (Alcoholics Anonymous, group therapy, stress management, prerelease planning) were available at most prisons. The agency planned to make such counseling available on an ongoing basis to any inmate who requested it at any point during his or her incarceration.

—Eleven federal prisons had a total of 609 inmates in intensive, 500-hour residential drug abuse programs involving 280 hours of counseling, 100 hours of wellness training, and supervised aftercare. Three federal prisons offered 1,000 hours of such treatment to a total of 199 inmates. The agency planned to expand the treatment to thirty-one prisons reaching a total of nearly 4,000 prisoners by the end of 1992.

—Throughout the system, transitional aftercare services were available to prisoners in two six-month components, each of which included family counseling, assistance in identifying and obtaining employment, and random urinalysis. One component was provided in the agency's community corrections centers; the other component was provided as postrelease treatment in conjunction with the Probation Division of the Administrative Office of the U.S. Courts.

94. In the case of prison-based programs, "close" to the release date means nine months to a year before parole eligibility; see Anglin, "Ensuring Success."

95. Under the BOP's classification scheme, a moderate problem means that the inmate's use of drugs or alcohol had negatively affected at least one "major life area" (school, health, family, financial, or legal status) in the two-year period before arrest; a serious problem means that it negatively affected two or more major life areas in the two-year period before arrest.

In 1990 the federal prison system planned a major evaluation that will analyze the effectiveness of its multidimensional drug treatment regime on in-prison adjustment and postcustody behavior up to five years after release.[96] The dozens of other studies that show how efficacious prison-based drug treatment can be in breaking the drug-and-crime nexus give one every reason to suppose that the results of this evaluation will be positive and should refine our knowledge about what works in prison-based drug treatment programs.

Thus the federal government should pass a new NARA-style law. Ideally, the law would mandate that drug treatment programs of the type being offered to prisoners in the federal system be extended to prisoners in every state correctional system in the country and be fully funded with federal dollars. Many state prison systems do not have objective inmate classification systems. No comprehensive national survey using standardized measures of substance abuse among state prisoners has yet been made. No one doubts that the number of untreated or undertreated inmates is quite high, although it is difficult to know just how many state prisoners have serious but unmet drug treatment needs. It is even harder to assess the methods and quality of prison-based drug treatment programs from one state to the next, but it is clear that the programs vary widely in methods and quality. For example, in 1990 only 11 percent of state prisoners were active in drug or alcohol counseling programs. Corrections officials in many states have expressed the need to expand their drug treatment programs for prisoners but have lacked the funds necessary to train staff, hire specialists, or administer the programs on a day-to-day basis.[97]

With the federal government taking the lead, all federal and state prisoners can get the drug treatment they need. Because the drug treatment needs of prisoners are bound to vary widely, it is difficult to estimate a single per prisoner per year cost and even more difficult to estimate benefits relative to costs.

Between 1981 and 1989, the BOP's drug treatment budget authority increased from $2.9 million to over $4 million. In 1990 and 1991, it increased to $8 million and $9.5 million, respectively. In 1992, as its full menu of drug treatment programs began to come on line, the budget jumped to $21.8 million.[98] Annual drug treatment expenditure averages

96. Wallace, "Drug Treatment."

97. Greenfeld, *Prisons and Prisoners*, p. 17; and Maguire and Flanagan, *Sourcebook*, pp. 626–29.

98. Maguire and Flanagan, *Sourcebook*, p. 17.

about $300 for each prisoner. To serve 800,000 state prisoners similarly would cost about $250 million a year.

This federal expenditure might be worth the cost in lowering recidivism alone. Given the best single estimate of the median number of crimes committed each year by a typical prisoner (12.5), and the most widely used single estimate of the social cost of a typical crime ($2,300), barely 8,700 treated offenders would need to be rehabilitated each year to justify a quarter-billion-dollar annual expenditure.[99] As a bonus, the program would also repair drug-ravaged lives and help make potentially productive taxpayers out of former criminals.

The new NARA act proposed here might be extended to include drug treatment for selected probationers. Some evidence shows that community-based drug treatment required by law for certain individuals can work, and important experiments designed to test key features of such programs are currently under way.[100] At this time, however, in light of the cost, absence of empirical data, and personnel limitations, it would be premature for the federal government to attempt to help meet the unmet drug treatment needs of the nation's nearly 3 million probationers.

For obvious reasons, it is impossible to specify every detail of how the new federal policy on drug treatment in prisons might be worded, financed, and implemented. Even at this stage, however, at least four issues can be anticipated.

First, should prisoner participation in drug treatment programs result in sentence reductions? Some Democratic proponents of expanding drug treatment in the federal system have taken the position that it should.[101] There is no evidence, however, that such "good time" provisions improve prisoner behavior behind bars or make any difference in postrelease behavior.

Second, should the proposal be extended to jail inmates as well as prisoners? Here the best answer is probably no. Most jail inmates are not in custody long enough to provide them with effective drug treatment.

99. The median crime and social cost per crime figures are discussed in DiIulio and Piehl, "Does Prison Pay?" The simple calculation behind the 8,700 figure is as follows: 12.5 crimes times a social cost per crime of $2,300 equals $28,750; 250,000,000 divided by 28,750 equals 8,695.

100. For example, the Vera Institute of Justice, a leading applied criminal justice research organization based in New York City, is conducting a three-year study of the role of legal compulsion in successful community-based drug treatment programs. For an overview, see Debbie Rodriguez, "Perception of Legal Coercion Scale" (Princeton University, Woodrow Wilson School, May 1992).

101. W. John Moore, "Crime Plays," p. 1222.

Moreover, the administrative quagmire of attempting to administer programs in hundreds of local jail systems should give anyone pause.

Third, should prisoners who receive the treatment once but recidivate receive it a second time? No solid evidence exists on the effects of prison-based drug treatment the second time around, but financial considerations would seem to militate against it. And if the programs are legally structured as a privilege, rather than a right or an entitlement, they need not be provided to all prisoners.

Fourth, should a significant effort be made to evaluate treatment? Clearly, such an effort would reveal whether the treatment was working and refine our knowledge about how best to match individuals with given treatments. In 1990 only 4 percent of federal spending on drug control was directed to research and development.[102] Expanded federal support for prison-based drug treatment should include the technical assistance and funds necessary to conduct evaluation research in every state prison system.

It is impossible to know how much political support a new NARA law along these lines might attract. It is encouraging, however, that while the Reagan and Bush administrations emphasized traditional law enforcement measures, they nonetheless supported an expansion in many types of drug treatments, not least of all inside federal prisons.[103] Some key Democratic members of Congress have already called for more of the same measures as well.[104]

Community Policing for All Inner-City Residents

Well before the 1992 Los Angeles riots, the systematic and anecdotal evidence in support of community policing served as a bridge between criminal justice policymakers and experts whose positions on most law enforcement issues were anything but kindred. At the federal level, for example, Democrats in Congress and the Reagan and Bush administra-

102. General Accounting Office, *Drug Abuse Research: Federal Funding and Future Needs*, PEMD-92-5 (January 1992), p. 4.

103. The Bush administration's first two drug plans did call for more drug treatment efforts. The first director of the National Office of Drug Control Policy, drug czar William J. Bennett, never opposed drug treatment; he merely raised serious and, as it turned out, perceptive cautions about the efficacy of some types of treatment efforts. See White House, *National Drug Control Strategy 1990* (Government Printing Office, January 1990); and Bennett, *The De-Valuing*.

104. For example, see W. John Moore, "Crime Plays," p. 1222.

tions joined in numerous small-scale efforts to advance community policing. Advocates of community policing spanned much of the ideological spectrum, from former U.S. Attorney General Edwin Meese of the Heritage Foundation to fellows at the Progressive Policy Institute.[105]

The Los Angeles riots, however, may have helped to put the need for community policing into broader public focus. The unflattering but accurate image of contemporary policing in most big cities is that of police in cruising patrol cars who are physically, organizationally, and psychologically distant from the people of the communities they protect and serve and are "never around" when needed. Or in the understaffed Los Angeles Police Department (LAPD), the image is that of police in helicopters who mechanically swoop down on violence-ridden, drug-infested communities, skypolice people whose faces they can hardly see, then swoop out of the areas, leaving the communities and their troubles untouched.

Like most big-city police departments, since the end of World War II, the LAPD has stressed emergency responses over active patrolling. The community has hardly participated in the planning of police operations; and the police department has been organized primarily along hierarchical paramilitary lines rather than through the use of participative management teams that cut across ranks (captains sit with junior officers) or functional specialties (plainclothes vice officers work with uniformed officers). Like most of its peer departments, the LAPD has not emphasized the need to get officers out of their patrol cars and into direct, personal, and regular communication with the people who live in the places that they police.

In Los Angeles as in other urban areas, over the last half century, big-city policing has evolved into an increasingly high-technology, bureaucratic game of cops and robbers. Officers are hired, trained, and promoted mainly according to how well they follow administrative orders, not how well they solve community crime problems, and how quickly they respond to calls, not how able they are to think and act in ways that prevent the trouble that brings the calls.

Community policing is about transforming contemporary big-city policing into a community-oriented game of "cops and citizens." Community policing means that police patrol on foot as well as in cars, listen to community residents, work with community leaders and groups,

105. W. John Moore, "Crime Plays."

coordinate problem-solving activities with other government agencies, and use their law enforcement authority and organizational resources in ways that the public understands and approves.

Until the 1980s the academic research on policing and the experiences of most police professionals militated against the concept. In the early 1970s, as the notion that nothing works in criminal rehabilitation gained intellectual momentum, a parallel notion about policing took hold. At that time, several big-city police departments experimented with new deployment strategies. The most famous experiment was the preventive patrol study conducted in Kansas City, Missouri.[106] For a year, the city was divided for policing into three areas, each of which received a different level of patrolling. To the surprise of analysts and just about everyone else, criminal activity, reported crime, rate of victimization as measured in a follow-up survey, citizen fear, and citizen satisfaction with the police were about the same in all these areas. Active auto patrol— beats where cars were visible cruising the streets two to three times more frequently than in the control areas—made no difference at all.

But as with the "nothing works" studies of criminal rehabilitation, a generation of better studies soon emerged to vindicate common sense. These studies showed that, while mere increases in auto patrol mattered little, good things seemed to happen wherever police got out of their cars, onto the streets, and into regular contact and communications with citizens in the community. Street crime decreased. The public's fear of crime abated. Officers' morale strengthened. Police-community relations improved.[107]

---

106. George L. Kelling and others, *The Kansas City Preventive Patrol Experiment: A Technical Report* (Washington: Police Foundation, 1974), and George L. Kelling, *What Works—Research and the Police: Crime File Study Guide* (Washington: National Institute of Justice, undated). For a good overview of the experiment in relation to other studies, see Wilson, *Thinking about Crime*, chap. 4.

107. See James Q. Wilson and Barbara Boland, "The Effect of the Police on Crime," *Law and Society Review*, vol. 12 (Spring 1978), pp. 367–90; Herman Goldstein, "Improving Policing: A Problem-Oriented Approach," *Journal of Crime and Delinquency*, vol. 25 (April 1979), pp. 236–58; Herman Goldstein, *Problem-Oriented Policing* (McGraw-Hill, 1990); James Q. Wilson and George L. Kelling, "Broken Windows: The Police and Neighborhood Safety," *Atlantic Monthly*, March 1982, pp. 29–38; William Spelman and John E. Eck, "Newport News Tests Problem-Oriented Policing," *National Institute of Justice Reports* (January–February 1987), pp. 2–8; David H. Bayley, "Community Policing: A Report from the Devil's Advocate," in Jack Greene and Stephen Mastrofski, eds., *Community Policing: Rhetoric or Reality?* (Praeger, 1988), pp. 225–37; Robert C. Trojanowicz and Bonnie Bucqueroux, *Community Policing: A Contemporary Perspective* (Cincinnati, Ohio: Anderson Publishing Company, 1990); Hans Toch and J. Douglas Grant, *Police as Problem Solvers* (Plenum Press, 1991); Reuben M. Greenberg, "Less Bang-

In the 1980s these studies became the underlying social scientific justification for community policing initiatives in New York City, Houston, and many other cities around the country.[108] But as community policing has attracted more public attention, several mistaken impressions about the concept, and how best it might be applied, have gotten into general circulation. At least five points about the origins and efficacy of community policing should guide future policy.

First, community policing was not the brainchild of any one academic analyst or police chief. The idea had been around in one form or another for several decades. The Katzenbach commission's 1967 report, for example, contains a discussion about police in the community and a recommendation "for the creation of a new kind of officer."[109] To date, neither on paper nor in practice has any one ideal model of community policing been set forth. Among academic experts, for example, some have stressed that community policing is predicated on the development of new cooperative relationships between citizens' groups and their district police. Others have downplayed citizens' groups and stressed the need for the police to interact more closely with other government agencies (school boards, human services agencies).[110] Some police have emphasized the crime-control value of community policing tactics, others have stressed the potential of these same tactics for improved community relations.[111]

Second, although it has often been defined as the antithesis of so-called traditional, command and control, or 911 policing, community policing in no way requires a complete overhaul of police bureaucracies, or a complete transformation of basic post-*Miranda* police training techniques and procedures.

Bang for the Buck: The Market-Approach to Crime Control," *Policy Review*, vol. 59 (Winter 1992), pp. 56–60; and Mark H. Moore, "Problem-Solving and Community Policing: Old Wine in New Barrels?" in Michael Tonry and Norval Morris, eds., *Crime and Justice*, vol. 15 (University of Chicago Press, forthcoming), pp. 99–158. See also the monographs produced by Mark H. Moore of Harvard University's John F. Kennedy School of Government, Program in Criminal Justice, *Perspectives on Policing* (Washington: National Institute of Justice, June and November 1988), especially nos. 2, 3, 4, 5, and 9.

108. For a short list of the initiatives undertaken, see Kelling, *What Works*.

109. President's Commission, *Challenge of Crime*, pp. 97–103.

110. For example, compare Moore, "Problem-Solving and Community Policing," with Goldstein, *Problem-Oriented Policing*. As it happens, those who downplay the role of citizens' groups are more apt to refer to the concept as "problem-solving policing" rather than community policing.

111. For example, compare Greenberg, "Less Bang-Bang," and George James, "Having to Sell as New an Old Idea: The Cop on the Beat," *New York Times*, October 9, 1991, pp. B1, B7.

Third, contrary to views going back several decades, good policing does not require officers to have advanced degrees or college diplomas.[112] Federal bills to advance community policing have often been coupled with efforts to attract recent college graduates or student-interns into a police corps. The estimated annual cost of such programs has ranged as high as $1.7 billion.[113]

But from the 1978 study by the National Advisory Commission on Higher Education for Police Officers to the present, absolutely no evidence has been found to support the idea that college-degree holders make better police officers.[114] By extension, there is no reason to believe that increasing the number of college graduates in uniform is necessary to implement community policing programs effectively. Moreover, veteran officers have been deeply suspicious of community policing ventures.[115] To link community policing initiatives with federal efforts to pin badges on college kids (or "kiddie corps" as some veteran officers have called it) might only raise the odds against successful implementation by stirring unnecessary resentments in the ranks of local police departments.

Fourth, the academic literature strongly suggests that community policing reduces the public's fear of crime, increases its satisfaction with police, and improves police morale. And, in some jurisdictions, community policing has been associated with a reduction in robberies, household burglaries, auto thefts, and drug dealing. The strongest advocates of community policing are police chiefs who have launched it, officers who have worked it, citizens who have experienced it,

112. For example, see "A Bargain for the Nation's Police," *New York Times*, October 17, 1991, p. A26; and Charles B. Saunders, *Police Education and Training: Keys to Better Law Enforcement* (Brookings, 1970).

113. W. John Moore, "Crime Plays," p. 1222.

114. See Lawrence W. Sherman and National Advisory Commission on Higher Education for Police Officers, *The Quality of Police Education* (San Francisco: Jossey-Bass, 1978). In 1990 about 90 percent of all police departments required that new officer recruits have a high school diploma; almost none required a four-year college degree. See Brian A. Reaves, *State and Local Police Departments, 1990* (Washington: Bureau of Justice Statistics, 1992), p. 6.

115. For example, see the following reports on Milwaukee, Houston, New Haven, and New York City: Anne Bothwell, "Tougher Approach Needed to Throttle Crime, Officers Say," *Milwaukee Journal*, September 23, 1991, pp. 1, 8; Heidi Reuter, "Not Everyone Is Sold on Community Policing," *Milwaukee Sentinel*, November 21, 1991, pp. 1A, 8A; "Study Criticizes Community Policing," *New York Times*, August 8, 1991, p. B2; Ralph Blumenthal with M.A. Farber, "Chief with High Profile Uses Streets to Test New Theories," *New York Times*, November 1, 1991, pp. A1, B2; and James, "Having to Sell as New an Old Idea."

academics who have studied it, and journalists who have reported and commented on it.[116]

Still, systematic empirical support for community policing, especially for its efficacy in reducing crime, remains in short supply. It is still impossible to specify the administrative, legal, budgetary, and other conditions under which, other things being equal, given types of community policing strategies have predictable and desirable consequences (reduce crime, reduce citizens' fear of crime, improve police morale, improve police-community relations). That should begin to change, however, as the findings from the ongoing Intensive Neighborhood-Oriented Policing (INOP) project of the National Institute of Justice are compiled.

Begun in 1990, the INOP project was designed to advance community policing by redirecting "police and community resources toward resolving underlying problems that breed crime and drug abuse in a community."[117] Under the terms of the project, the federal government funded community policing initiatives in eight communities. An evaluation of the results of community policing efforts in the INOP sites will be completed by the end of 1992.

Fifth, the federal government, as noted earlier, has already committed itself to community policing through its Operation Weed and Seed program. As currently structured, however, the program does little to strengthen community policing. By way of illustration, consider the early Weed and Seed experience of Trenton, New Jersey.

In Trenton the program was concentrated on four neighborhoods with significant drug-and-crime problems. Small police ministations were set up in each neighborhood. Officers got out of their cars and walked beats, a sight that was new to most community residents. The police worked with local public school officials. Three schools were kept open evenings and weekends as "safe havens," well-policed community centers offering various educational and recreational programs to neighborhood

116. See the works cited in note 107, especially Goldstein, *Problem-Oriented Policing*, Trojanowicz and Bucqueroux, *Community Policing*, Spelman and Eck, "Newport News," and Greenberg, "Less Bang-Bang." Besides the works cited in note 107, see Neal R. Peirce, "The Case for Community Policing," *National Journal*, December 7, 1991, p. 2982; Tina Burnside, "Walking the Beat for Police May Be Coming Back in Style," *Milwaukee Sentinel*, November 21, 1991, p. 8A; and W. John Moore, "Crime Plays," p. 1222.

117. Department of Justice, *Evaluation Plan: 1991* (Washington: National Institute of Justice, June 1991), pp. 19–24, quotation on p. 122. As of this writing, a second INOP project focusing on rural areas is also planned.

residents. In the first year of the program, the weeding resulted in seventy arrests of violent criminals and drug dealers.

The seeding involved seventy members of the New Jersey attorney general's staff, who began a mentoring project for the areas's children, working with local chapters of the United Way, Big Brothers, Big Sisters, and Princeton University alumni. Other state agencies and corporations were encouraged to "adopt a school" and provide whatever support they could to it. The attorney general's staff planned to obtain grants from the federal Department of Housing and Urban Development and the state of New Jersey for use in rehabilitating the infrastructure of the neighborhoods. It also planned to take forfeited property from drug dealers and give it to the community.

Almost everyone familiar with the program sees the positive value in the efforts that were made through mid-1992. Few officers, however, were on the streets to weed. Small numbers and a lack of adequate training and preparation constrained their ability to operate according to community policing precepts. The ability of state and local prosecutors to make federal cases against violent criminals and drug dealers in these neighborhoods was hamstrung because certain federal drug, firearm, and antiracketeering laws did not apply to these criminals. Thus, within months, many of the weeded criminals returned to the neighborhoods. The seeding efforts also fell short partly because the community-based police were too few and too poorly trained.

Under present conditions, the program is "too little weed and too little seed." There are limits to how far any such effort can go without a full-scale commitment to community policing. The federal government needs to target significant aid for the development of community policing within big-city police departments and to change federal drug, firearm, and antiracketeering laws so that they can be applied to street criminals and gangs.

In the 1980s, as the inner-city drug-and-crime problem grew, many police forces contracted.[118] In 1991 hardly a major police force in the country had as many officers as it arguably needed, and none had enough officers to greatly increase the number of officers on foot patrol in its worst neighborhoods. The federal government can and should supply the funds necessary to bring community policing to all inner-city residents.

118. Between 1977 and 1987, the number of sworn officers per 1,000 resident population in fifty-nine large city police departments fell from 2.4 to 2.3, and the total number of officers dropped in fifteen of the fifty largest cities; Maguire and Flanagan, *Sourcebook*, pp. 35, 46.

Leading analysts have suggested that some inner-city neighborhoods "are so demoralized and crime-ridden as to make foot patrol useless."[119] But as some of these same analysts have also suggested, we cannot know whether any of our nation's neighborhoods are "unreclaimable" unless and until far more human and financial resources have been devoted to policing them.[120] Police crackdowns in troubled neighborhoods rarely succeed in reducing crime because criminals quickly move to other locations.[121] But we do not know what would happen if there were, in effect, no place else for them to go. There is every reason to suppose that by doubling or tripling the number of officers on regular duty in and around drug-infested, crime-torn neighborhoods, and by deploying them in accordance with the precepts of community policing, the streets and sidewalks of even the most blighted inner city could be made safe enough for children to play in and adults to walk along.

Even in the heyday of the studies that raised doubts about the relationship between numbers of police and crime rates, no one was seen demanding reductions in police protection for the places where they lived and worked. Indeed, Congress itself clearly values hefty police manpower. In the late 1980s, when 3,855 police officers protected all the other citizens of Washington, Congress had a force of 1,200 just to patrol Capitol Hill.[122] And all over the country, urban businesses and residences that could afford private security services and devices bought them.

Whether or not some inner-city neighborhoods have been underpoliced because of racial or other factors, the federal government can supply the aid necessary to see to it that they become well policed. As Charleston Police Chief Reuben M. Greenberg has written, it is possible to "treat people in public housing as if they lived in a country club or an upscale apartment."[123] Unfortunately, however, it is unlikely that this can be done on the cheap.

To get some sense of what it might cost, a 20 percent increase in the police force of the 222 local police departments that in 1990 served populations of 100,000 or more would cost about $1 billion. These departments had about 182,000 full-time sworn personnel and total

119. Wilson and Kelling, "Broken Windows," p. 38.
120. James Q. Wilson and John J. DiIulio, Jr., "Crackdown: Saving the Next Generation from the Drug-and-Crime Epidemic," *New Republic*, July 10, 1989, pp. 21–25.
121. Lawrence W. Sherman, *Police Crackdowns: National Institute of Justice Reports* (Washington: National Institute of Justice, March/April 1990).
122. John J. DiIulio, Jr., "And Don't Blame D.C.'s Police," *Washington Post*, April 13, 1989, p. A31.
123. Greenberg, "Less Bang-Bang," p. 60.

annual operating expenditures of about $4.7 billion, or around $26,000 for each full-time sworn employee.[124]

The social benefits would almost certainly exceed the costs, as would be evident in reduced criminal victimization, revitalized local economies, and enhanced respect for government. As Mark H. Moore has observed, there is a near-perfect fit between community policing and the needs of the nation's crime-torn, inner-city neighborhoods:

> If there are any areas in which the techniques and structures of community oriented and problem solving policing are likely to be most effective, it is in these domains. Surely an important part of dealing with drugs is learning how to mobilize communities to resist drug dealing. Surely an important part of dealing with violence is dealing with fears. Surely an important part of controlling riots is having networks reaching into the community. If anything, then, these problems give impetus to and provide opportunities for the further development of these ideas as strategies for policing.[125]

Were the federal government to provide such aid, it would be important to ensure that the money goes to police departments, that the funds are spent to institute or expand community policing efforts, and that the localities receiving the funds demonstrate that the additional manpower has been trained and deployed in the neighborhoods that need it, not used to bolster policing in other parts of the community or simply to reduce the local contribution to spending on police. It is unclear what the best intergovernmental grant mechanics of such a program might be. As a first step, therefore, a national commission consisting of U.S. Justice Department officials, local U.S. attorneys, state attorneys general, big-city mayors, and leading police administrators should be convened to study the proposal and devise the most appropriate institutional frameworks and grant formulas.

124. There is no way of knowing precisely how many more police, trained and deployed on the basis of community policing precepts, would be needed to make a dent in the inner-city drug-and-crime problem. But if each of the 222 departments that served populations of 100,000 or more were to increase their forces by just 20 percent, that would mean hiring another 36,000 full-time sworn personnel and spending another $936 million each year. Thus a crude ballpark estimate of the annual federal commitment necessary to begin to realize the potential of community policing as a way of making inner cities livable is about $1 billion annually. Calculated from figures in Reaves, *State and Local Police*, p. 3.

125. Moore, "Problem-Solving and Community Policing," p. 93.

A National Gun Buy-Back Program

As the nation's big-city police know all too well, much inner-city crime, especially the murderous violence wrought by drug-financed street gangs, involves guns. In the 1980s the Fraternal Order of Police became a principal voice in support of strict gun control measures. Between 1981 and 1992, such proposals as a week-long waiting period for the purchase of handguns sparked intense constitutional arguments in Congress and frantic lobbying efforts behind the scenes by groups opposing and favoring gun control. Unfortunately, however, there is little empirical knowledge about the crime reduction effects of such measures. Police and other proponents of gun control measures were unable to muster much systematic evidence in support of their position because such evidence simply did not exist.

In 1981 the Attorney General's Commission on Violent Crime recommended measures that would tighten controls on gun ownership and require states to adopt a mandatory waiting period to allow for a records check to see whether a prospective handgun buyer had a criminal history.[126] This Reagan administration proposal, and the gun control bills that have since been debated in Congress, were commonsense responses to the fact that many crimes, including about 60 percent of all murders, involve firearms. Moreover, in every year since 1972, at least 70 percent of the general public has favored some gun control measures.[127] The movement in favor of gun control that grew up around the efforts of former White House spokesman James Brady, who was shot in the 1981 attempt on President Reagan's life, put the nation's most powerful opposing group, the National Rifle Association, on the defensive.

The question, however, is how efficacious such measures are likely to be in reducing gun-related crime. Nobody knows the number of guns held privately in this country. Some have estimated at least one-fifth of American homes have guns.[128] Numerous federal, state, and local laws already regulate the manufacture, sale, and use of most firearms. What, if anything, additional federal laws would add to the crime reduction effects of the existing battery of state and local laws is simply unclear.

126. Department of Justice, *Attorney General's Task Force on Violent Crime: Final Report* (Washington, 1981), p. ix.

127. Maguire and Flanagan, *Sourcebook*, pp. 204–05, 378.

128. Wilson, *Thinking about Crime*, p. 262.

For example, it is hard to know what the crime reduction effects of week-long waiting periods and other measures would be.

Even a small reduction in gun-related crimes would justify the costs of such laws. In 1991 and 1992 Philadelphia, New York, St. Louis, and other cities offered cash and amnesty to citizens who would turn illegal firearms over to the police or other designated public authorities. By mid-1992, only the most preliminary analyses of the effects of these programs had been completed, and the evidence on their efficacy was quite mixed and very hard to interpret.[129]

The federal government should consider establishing a national gun buy-back program of its own, prefaced by systematic research into the crime reduction effects, if any, of the gun buy-back efforts that have been undertaken to date at the local level. The program should be conducted as an experimental, multiple-site demonstration project along the lines of the research efforts that underwrote the major federal social welfare reform initiatives of the 1980s.[130] The results of the program, which could be called a public health program as well as a criminal justice program, could shed light on broader questions about the relationship between the wide availability of guns and the incidence of crime in this country.

A National Program of Crime-Prevention Research

Of course, in virtually every area of domestic policy, the cry for more and better research has been made so often that it now rings hollow. But for criminal justice, the need is real and the practical benefits could be great. The federal commitment to criminal justice research has been, and remains, trivial, both in absolute terms and compared with what is spent on research in almost every other area of domestic policy. The federal government has spent far more money investigating the effects of smoking on health than on understanding what many citizens rightly view as an equally serious public health problem: criminality. As former

129. Joanne Sills, "An Appeal to Turn in the Guns: Anti-Violence Network Proposes Two-Week Amnesty for Weapons," *Philadelphia Daily News*, June 24, 1991, p. 13; Raol V. Mowatt, "Anti-Firearms Force Goes for Broke: Cash Offer Yields More Guns than Expected," *Philadelphia Inquirer*, July 23, 1991, p. 3B; George James, "Trying to Rid the Streets of Guns, by Buying Them," *New York Times*, November 20, 1991, pp. B1, B5; and Bill Bryan, "Arms Reduction: Gun Buyback Program Ends Today with 7,500 Purchased," *St. Louis Post-Dispatch*, November 13, 1991, pp. 1C, 3C.

130. For an excellent overview of the social welfare demonstration projects, see Richard P. Nathan, *Social Science in Government: Uses and Misuses* (Basic Books, 1988).

director of the National Institute of Justice (NIJ), James K. Stewart, often lamented to NIJ peer review panelists, the federal government spends more on cavity-prevention research than it does on crime-prevention research.

In the 1980s a broadly representative group of the nation's leading criminal justice scholars outlined an ambitious research agenda into the correlates of criminality. If implemented, their research plan could furnish the knowledge necessary to making effective interventions into the lives of persons who are at risk of becoming serious adult criminals. Such research could have benefits that go well beyond the potential to reduce crime. As the group observed, "The high-rate offender tends also to be the failing student, the drunken driver, the unreliable employee, and the abusive or neglectful parent," and "lessons learned about how to prevent crime will almost surely be lessons learned about how to produce better citizens."[131]

Conclusion: Federal Responsibility for Domestic Defense

The twenty-five-year history of federal crime policy is largely a tale of partisan conflict, ideological wrangling, false promises, and shattered hopes. Many of the most disappointing aspects of the first and the second federal wars on crime reflected the fact that, as the Eisenhower commission stressed, the United States has never had a real national urban policy on crime or other domestic priorities.[132] Responding to crime has been, and will continue to be, primarily a subnational responsibility, and there are good constitutional arguments for maintaining this division of responsibilities.

After two wars on crime, the federal government is in a position to shoulder more of the burden for domestic defense. At present, the fraction of the federal budget that goes into criminal justice is trivial, compared with what is spent on other governmental functions (national defense,

---

131. David Farrington and others, *Understanding and Controlling Crime* (Springer-Verlag, 1986), chap. 1, reprinted in James Q. Wilson, *On Character* (Washington: AEI Press, 1991), chap. 13, pp. 188–89.

132. In 1936 Arthur C. Millspaugh of the Brookings Institution called for the administrative rationalization of the nation's criminal justice system. See Arthur C. Millspaugh, *Local Democracy and Crime Control* (Brookings, 1936). Fifty-five years later, another scholar affiliated with Brookings flirted with a kindred proposal. DiIulio, *No Escape*, chap. 5.

education, health care) and in light of the political salience of crime issues.[133]

Even in an era of soaring federal budget deficits, for the federal government to invest an additional $1.25 billion a year or so in criminal justice would hardly bust the federal budget, and by investing in drug treatment for all prisoners and community policing for all inner-city residents, the federal government can make city streets safer, offenders less likely to recidivate, local police more effective, and, in the long run, taxpayers less burdened. And by experimenting with gun control programs and launching a broader research effort designed to enhance our applied knowledge of how to prevent crime, the federal government can begin a third federal war on crime that everybody wins.

133. For example, in fiscal 1988, direct and intergovernmental federal expenditures on all justice activities amounted to just under $8 billion, or 13 percent of all governmental expenditures on crime control; see Maguire and Flanagan, *Sourcebook*, p. 2.

5

ISABEL V. SAWHILL

Young Children and Families

COUNTLESS REPORTS have noted a decline in the fortunes of America's children. The poverty rate among children is increasing, the proportion living with two parents has fallen, and the proportion born out of wedlock has skyrocketed. Reports of child abuse and neglect have increased, as have juvenile crime rates and rates of violent death (table 5-1). Families and children are in trouble, many believe, because of a fundamental reorganization of families brought about by the increased employment of women, rising divorce rates, and more permissive attitudes.

As recently as 1950 the general assumption was that men supported their families, women stayed at home, and marriages endured for a lifetime—or at least until the children were grown. Sex before marriage was taboo (at least for women), and if a pregnancy occurred, adoption or illegal abortion ensured that childbearing outside marriage was a rare event. To be sure, there were exceptions. Among nonwhites, for example, even in 1950, 17 percent of all births were out of wedlock, compared with less than 2 percent among whites.[1] Nonetheless, the norms were clear. But since 1950 profound changes have occurred in each of these measures (table 5-2). These facts are not in dispute. What is in dispute is, first, the consequences for children, and second, the appropriate response.

Some observers contend changes in family functioning have led directly to many problems affecting children, including lower test scores, higher crime rates, greater drug abuse, and more suicides. Others argue that

Richard T. Gill was the discussant for this chapter. I would like to thank Dana Sundblad for research assistance and the following for their comments or advice: Andrew Cherlin, Victor Fuchs, Ron Haskins, Robert Haveman, Loraine Klerman, Kristin Moore, Richard Nelson, Theodora Ooms, Steven Scott, Freya Sonenstein, Barbara Wolfe, and Nicholas Zill.

1. Nicholas Zill and Carolyn C. Rogers, "Recent Trends in the Well-Being of Children," in Andrew J. Cherlin, ed., *The Changing American Family and Public Policy* (Washington: Urban Institute Press, 1988), p. 40.

147

TABLE 5-1. Indicators of Child Well-Being, Selected Years, 1960–91

Indicator	1960	1970	1980	Most recent
Children in poverty (percent)	26.9	15.1	18.3	20.6[a]
Violent death rate (per 100,000 youth aged 15–19)	7.6	14.0	19.1	23.0[b]
SAT scores				
Verbal	477	460	424	424[c]
Math	498	488	466	474[c]
Reports of child abuse and neglect (thousands)	n.a.	60.0	785.1	2,653[a]
Juvenile crime rate (delinquency case dispositions per 1,000 youth aged 10–17)	20.0	32.0	38.3	44.3[d]
Births unintended at conception resulting in a live birth (percent)	n.a.	38.3[e]	31.7[f]	35.3[b]
Infant mortality rate (per 1,000 births)	26.0	20.0	12.6	9.1[a]
Child death rate (per 100,000 children aged 1–14)	200.1	125.8	94.5	76.7[b]
Adults aged 25–29 who have completed 4 years high school	60.7	75.4	85.4	85.9[a]
Income adjusted for family size (dollars)	n.a.	17,101[e]	17,333	18,840[a]
Median maternal age at first birth	21.8	22.1	23.0	23.7
Drug use, youth aged 12–17 (percent using in past month)				
Cocaine	n.a.	0.6[g]	1.4[h]	0.4[c]
Alcohol	n.a.	34.0[i]	37.2[h]	20.3[c]
Marijuana	n.a.	18.5[i]	24.1[h]	10.1[c]
Maternal education (ratio of births by college-educated women to women with less than 12 years of schooling)	n.a.	1:3.6	1:1.7	1:1.2[j]

SOURCES: Children in poverty: Bureau of the Census, "Money, Income, and Poverty Status of Families and Persons in the United States, 1989," *Current Population Reports*, series P-60, no. 168 (1990), p. 59; and *Overview of Entitlement Programs, 1992 Green Book, Background Material and Data on Programs within the Jurisdiction of the Committee on Ways and Means*, Committee Print, House Committee on Ways and Means, 102 Cong. 2 sess. (Government Printing Office, 1992), p. 1072 (hereafter *1992 Green Book*).

Violent death rate: Center for the Study of Social Policy, "1992 Kids Count Data Book" (Washington, 1992).

SAT scores: National Center for Education Statistics, *Digest of Education Statistics, 1990* (Department of Education, 1990), tables 8, 94.

Child abuse: Bureau of the Census, *Statistical Abstract of the United States, 1991* (Department of Commerce, 1991), table 305; and author's calculations from data in Paul Taylor, "Rise in Child Abuse, Foster Care Laid to Failed Drug Policies," *Washington Post*, April 1, 1992, p. A21.

Juvenile crime: *1960, 1970:* Frank Furstenberg and Gretchen Condran, "Family Change and Adolescent Well-Being: A Reexamination of U.S. Trends," in Andrew Cherlin, ed., *The Changing American Family and Public Policy* (Washington: Urban Institute Press, 1988); *1980, 1986:* Bureau of the Census, *Statistical Abstract of the United States*, 1991, table 330.

Births unintended and infant mortality (for ever-married women aged 15–44 only): *1973, 1982:* W. F. Pratt and M. C. Horn, "Wanted and Unwanted Childbearing in the United States, 1973–1982," *Advance Data from Vital and Health Statistics*, no. 108 (Hyattsville, Md.: National Center for Health Statistics, 1985), pp. 4–5; *1988:* L. B. Williams and W. F. Pratt, "Wanted and Unwanted Childbearing in the United States, 1973–1978," *Advance Data from Vital and Health Statistics*, no. 189 (Hyattsville, Md.: National Center for Health Statistics, 1990), pp. 4–5.

Child deaths: National Center for Health Statistics, *Vital Statistics of the United States, 1988*, vol. 2: *Mortality* (Department of Health and Human Services, 1988), table 1-D; and *Vital Statistics, 1960*, vol. 2: *Mortality*, table 1-D.

High school completion: National Center for Education Statistics, *Digest of Education Statistics, 1990*, tables 8, 94.

Income adjusted for family size: *1992 Green Book*, table 47, p. 1376. Figures derived by multiplying average pretax adjusted income for given year by $5,797 (poverty threshold).

Drug use: *1992 Green Book*, table 35, p. 1128.

Maternal age at first birth: National Center for Health Statistics, *Vital Statistics of the United States*, vol. 1: *Natality* (various years).

Maternal education: Nicholas Zill, "Recent Trends in the Well-Being of Children," in Cherlin, ed., *Changing American Family*, p. 49. The number of states reporting data on mothers' educational attainment each year varies.

n.a. Not available.

a. 1990. b. 1988. c. 1991. d. 1986. e. 1973. f. 1982. g. 1972. h. 1979. i. 1974. j. 1985.

TABLE 5-2. Indicators of Family Change, Selected Years, 1950–91
Percent unless otherwise specified

Indicator	1950	1960	1970	1980	Most recent
Children younger than age 18 in single-parent families	7.4	9.1	11.9	19.7	24.7[a]
Children living with neither parent	5.0[b]	3.2	2.9	3.6	2.5[c]
Births out of wedlock	3.9	5.3	10.7	18.4	27.1[c]
Labor force participation by women with children younger than age 18	21.6	30.4	42.4	56.6	66.6[d]
Total fertility rate (ages 15–44)	3.08	3.65	2.48	1.84	1.93[a]

SOURCES: Children in single-parent families: *1950:* Bureau of the Census, "Marital Status and Household Characteristics 1950," *Current Population Reports,* series P-20, no. 33 (Department of Commerce, 1951), p. 13; and *1992 Green Book,* table 4, p. 1080.

Children living with neither parent: *1950:* James A. Sweet and Larry L. Bumpass, *American Families and Households* (Russell Sage, 1987), p. 264; House Select Committee on Children, *U.S. Children and Their Families: Current Conditions and Recent Trends, 1989,* 101 Cong. 1 sess. (GPO, 1989), p. 53; and *1989:* Bureau of the Census, *Statistical Abstract of the United States, 1991,* table 70.

Births out of wedlock: Bureau of the Census, *Statistical Abstract of the United States, 1953* (Department of Commerce, 1953), table 61; and *1992 Green Book,* chart 1, p. 1074.

Labor force participation: *1992 Green Book,* table 1, p. 935.

Fertility rate: *1950:* Bureau of the Census, *Historical Statistics of the United States, Colonial Times to 1970* (Department of Commerce, 1975), table B-11; *1960:* Andrew Cherlin, "American Fertility, Marriage, and Divorce," in *World Population: Approaching the Year 2000,* Annals of the American Academy of Political and Social Science, vol. 510 (July 1990), p. 148; and *1970, 1980, 1988:* Bureau of the Census, *Statistical Abstract of the United States, 1991,* table 86. The mean number of siblings per child was 1.45 in 1990. This is higher than 0.93 (1.93 − 1.0) because the greater numbers of children in larger families weights the averages toward the experience of the children in these families.

a. 1990. b. 1940. c. 1989. d. 1991.

these changes, although troublesome, have done less damage than commonly assumed. The consequences associated with more frequent divorces and the growing time pressures associated with women's wholesale entry into the labor force should not be lightly dismissed, but the divorce rate peaked around 1980 and growth in the labor force participation rate of mothers has slowed. Moreover, in many respects children are better off than they have ever been (table 5-1). The typical child is more likely to have been planned by his or her parents, has a better chance of survival through infancy and childhood, completes more years of schooling, has more material goods, and has fewer siblings with whom to compete for the time and attention of parents. These parents in turn are older, better educated, and if married, more likely to be happily married than in the convention-bound 1950s. At the same time, for some children, mostly those in single-parent families at the lower end of the income scale, the trends have not been so felicitous. Whatever has happened to the average child, the disparity in early childhood experiences has widened as some families have been able to adjust to new choices and conditions while others have not.

Although wholesale attempts to turn back the family clock are unrealistic (as well as unappealing to many adults, women in particular), some tempering of the pace of family change, some reassessment of its consequences, and much more attention to the consequences for the increasing number of children growing up in poor families are in order. Changes in the family have had relatively modest effects on children from middle-class and upper-class families but devastating effects on children from lower-class families, especially in minority communities.

Whether any governmental policy can turn this situation around is in doubt; however, government financial support for low-income working parents, additional funding for preventive health care and preschool education, and greater efforts to prevent early childbearing and enforce the child support obligations of absent parents have the greatest chances of success. Beyond these, some experimentation with welfare policies and with parent education and family support programs may also be useful, although there is no guarantee that they will succeed.

The Role of the Family

Families are the preeminent influence in the lives of children, and good parenting is essential to their healthy development. Unfortunately, little is known about the quality of interactions between children and their parents. One exception is the Home Observation for Measurement of the Environment (HOME) scale, which measures the quality of the physical environment, the regularity and structure of household routines, the availability of intellectual stimulation, and the degree of emotional support provided by parents. On this scale 11 percent of all children aged 3 to 5 years have deficient home environments, while 59 percent have supportive home environments. Among poor children, 24 percent live in deficient homes and 35 percent in supportive homes. Somewhat surprisingly, emotional support is even more lacking than intellectual stimulation in poor homes.[2] Another indicator of the importance of parents is the time and money they invest in their children, and these are enormous. Out-of-pocket expenditures by families (roughly $484 billion) exceeded spending on children by governments at all levels in fiscal year

2. Nicholas Zill and others, *The Life Circumstances and Development of Children in Welfare Families: A Profile Based on National Survey Data* (Washington: Child Trends, 1991), tables 7, 8.

1989 ($314 billion). In addition, parents made sacrifices for their children in the form of forgone earnings among mothers (an estimated $668 billion).[3] (Regardless of the year cited, all figures in this chapter are expressed in 1992 dollars.)

If the family is so critical to the well-being of children, one should look to changes in the family as a possible source of some of the adverse trends shown in table 5-1. Various explanations have been suggested for the diminished well-being of children. One is demographic change, which has produced more working mothers and more single-parent families. A second is changes in the economy that have contributed to rising poverty rates among families with children. Other explanations include changing attitudes about sex and marriage, the rising influence of television, and a social welfare system that has undermined the stability of the family. Although none of these explanations can be dismissed, the evidence suggests that the growth of single-parent families has been the most troubling for children, if for no other reason than the fact that almost half (44 percent in 1989) of such families are poor.[4]

Demographic Change and the Well-Being of Children

The explosion of new opportunities for women in the 1960s and 1970s contributed to a number of fundamental changes in the family: more divorce, more two-earner couples, and lower fertility. Although the revolution in women's roles was not the only factor producing these changes, it was very important, and the ramifications are still being felt.[5]

3. Estimates derived using data from David M. Betson, "Alternative Estimates of the Cost of Children from the 1980–86 Consumer Expenditure Survey," IRP special report 51 (University of Wisconsin, Institute for Research on Poverty, December 1990); Thomas J. Espenshade, *Investing in Children: New Estimates of Parental Expenditures* (Washington: Urban Institute Press, 1984); *Overview of Entitlement Programs, 1991 Green Book, Background Material and Data on Programs within the Jurisdiction of the Committee on Ways and Means*, Committee Print, House Committee on Ways and Means, 102 Cong. 1 sess. (Government Printing Office, 1991) (hereafter *1991 Green Book*); and Bureau of the Census, "Money Income of Households, Families, and Persons in the United States: 1990," *Current Population Reports*, series P-60, no. 174 (Department of Commerce, 1991).

4. Bureau of the Census, "Poverty in the United States: 1988 and 1989," *Current Population Reports*, series P-60, no. 171 (Department of Commerce, 1991), p. 6.

5. Researchers agree that there is a problem in sorting out cause and effect in this area. For example, more opportunities for women have made it less costly for them to divorce and more costly for them to have children, but more divorce and fewer children have also increased the tendency for women to work. Although causation runs in both directions,

Two of these changes—more single parents and working mothers—are worrisome because they imply that parents spend less time with their children. A third, the reduction in family size, is good news because it provides an opportunity for parents to interact more with each child. All these changes have been massive (table 5-2). Currently, two-thirds of mothers are in the paid labor force, compared with one-fifth in 1950, and 25 percent of children live in single-parent families, compared with 7 percent in 1950. If these trends continue, 60 percent of all children born in the 1990s will spend some time in a single-parent family before they reach age 18.[6] (There is no discernible trend in the proportion of children living with neither parent, as shown in table 5-2.) Finally, the fertility rate has plummeted. The average child born in the 1950s or early 1960s had 3 or 4 siblings; the average child in 1990 has 1.4, a number expected to fall further for those born in this decade.[7]

The increased employment of women and the growing numbers of single-parent families mean that the time parents have to spend with children fell by ten hours a week for white families and twelve for black families between 1960 and 1986.[8] Women's time spent in unpaid work fell 30 percent, a decline partially offset by a small increase in men's unpaid work between 1965 and 1985. The big reported drop for women was in domestic work rather than in child care, but distinguishing one from the other is difficult.[9]

---

the best research suggests that the primary source of change has been women's increased earnings potential. See Suzanne M. Bianchi and Daphne Spain, *American Women in Transition* (New York: Russell Sage Foundation, 1986). For evidence that declining fertility is related to the changing status of women, see William P. Butz and Michael P. Ward, "The Emergence of Countercyclical U.S. Fertility," *American Economic Review*, vol. 69 (June 1979), pp. 318–28.

6. Frank F. Furstenberg and Andrew J. Cherlin, *Divided Families: What Happens to Children When Parents Part* (Harvard University Press, 1991).

7. Data on numbers of siblings are available for the 1980s in Bureau of the Census, "Marital Status and Living Arrangements," *Current Population Reports*, series P-20 (Department of Commerce, various years). For earlier years, estimates were derived from Judith Blake, *Family Size and Achievement* (University of California Press, 1989), p. 277. Siblings per child will differ from fertility per woman because the population of children is disproportionately made up of the offspring of more fertile women.

8. Victor R. Fuchs, "Are Americans Underinvesting in Children?" in David Blanken-horn, Steven Bayme, and Jean Bethke Elshtain, eds., *Rebuilding the Nest: A New Commitment to the American Family* (Milwaukee: Family Service America, 1990), p. 66.

9. Data are from time-use diaries. See Jonathan Gershuny and John P. Robinson, "Historical Changes in the Household Division of Labor," *Demography*, vol. 25 (November 1988), pp. 537–52. In another article, Robinson shows that the average mother spent eight

Even if parents spend less time with children, the quality may have improved, if for no other reason than that parents are better educated (the data for mothers are in table 5-1.) Not only do college-educated mothers spend twice as much time with each child as grade school–educated mothers (with the high school–educated falling somewhere in between), but they also put more time into such stimulating activities as reading to, talking with, and teaching their children.[10]

What do we know about the consequences of more single parents, more working mothers, and lower fertility? Research suggests that the growth of single-parent families has been the most troubling for children. Children in these families generally fare worse than those living with both parents. They are more likely to drop out of high school, become the heads of single-parent families themselves, and have a lower socioeconomic status as adults. It is unclear whether the cause is family structure itself or factors associated with it, but attempts to take account of other factors (including the lower incomes of such families and the tendency for initially troubled families to be the ones most likely to break up) have not eliminated all the effects.[11]

With the exception of infants, children of working mothers do not seem to fare consistently better or worse than other children. Moreover, the effects tend to vary with the age, sex, and race of the child, the socioeconomic status of the family, the reasons for the mothers' working, and the quality of substitute care.[12] There is some evidence that maternal

---

hours a week taking care of children in 1965. By 1975 this had dropped to seven hours, and by 1985 it had climbed back to nine. See John P. Robinson, "Caring for Kids," *American Demographics*, vol. 11 (July 1989), p. 52.

10. C. Russell Hill and Frank P. Stafford, "Parental Care of Children: Time Diary Estimates of Quantity, Predictability, and Variety," in F. Thomas Juster and Frank P. Stafford, eds., *Time, Goods, and Well-Being* (University of Michigan Press, 1985), pp. 471–92.

11. Sara S. McLanahan, "The Two Faces of Divorce: Women's and Children's Interests," IRP discussion paper 903-89 (University of Wisconsin, Institute for Research on Poverty, December 1989); and Furstenberg and Cherlin, *Divided Families*.

12. Cheryl D. Hayes and Sheila B. Kamerman, eds., *Children of Working Parents: Experiences and Outcomes* (Washington: National Academy Press, 1983); and Cheryl D. Hayes, John L. Palmer, and Martha J. Zaslow, eds., *Who Cares for America's Children? Child Care Policy for the 1990's* (Washington: National Academy Press, 1990). Extensive research on this matter has not been definitive because it has been impossible to adjust for all of the factors that might affect children, especially those that are related to a mother's decision to work. For example, if women who work are disproportionately more able than other women, their children may do as well as the children of nonemployed women, despite the mothers' reduced time commitment to childrearing. But if women who choose to work are inherently less nurturing, or less committed to their children, any negative effects on their children's development could mistakenly be attributed to their employment.

employment in infancy retards cognitive and behavioral development, probably because very young babies need to bond with at least one caring adult. However, after the first year or so, maternal employment or out-of-home care do not seem harmful.[13] Indeed for poor children, a high-quality, out-of-home experience, as in Head Start, is clearly beneficial, at least in the short run.

The sharp drop in fertility rates has undoubtedly been good for children. Those from smaller families have greater verbal ability, go further in school, and eventually achieve higher socioeconomic status. Research suggests the baby boom cohort might have gained half a year of additional education if fertility rates had been as low as they have been for the baby bust cohort. Indeed, the effects on educational attainment are large enough to offset most of the disadvantages created by the increase in single-parent families during this period.[14] Some of the beneficial effects of smaller family size are undoubtedly associated with more careful planning by parents. Children who are wanted by their parents should fare better than those who are not, and the greater availability of contraception and abortion since the early 1970s has reduced the number of unintended pregnancies that result in a live birth (table 5-1).

One final factor that may have contributed to the deteriorating well-being of children is greater family mobility, which some observers assume left families more isolated and lacking in social supports. The facts only partially support this view. Geographic mobility among children has actually decreased since the 1950s and 1960s. However, the overall decrease, which includes short moves within the same county, masks a modest increase in interstate moves, especially in the 1950s and 1960s, lending some credence to the idea that families now live farther away from relatives and friends.[15]

13. Nazli Baydar and Jeanne Brooks-Gunn, "Effects of Maternal Employment and Child-Care Arrangements on Preschoolers' Cognitive and Behavioral Outcomes: Evidence from the Children of the National Longitudinal Survey of Youth," *Developmental Psychology*, vol. 27 (November 1991), pp. 932–45.

14. Blake, *Family Size and Achievement*. Of course, there is always the possibility that the studies have not adequately adjusted for the fact that the decision to have fewer offspring may be correlated with parental IQ or other difficult-to-measure factors that also produce positive outcomes for children. Nonetheless, the findings seem reasonably robust and the effects are quite large, even after adjusting for family background variables, including (in at least one study), parental IQ.

15. Larry Long, "Americans on the Move," *American Demographics*, vol. 12 (June 1990), pp. 46–49; and Bureau of the Census, *Current Population Reports*, series P-20, nos. 36, 118, 210, 377, 456 (Department of Commerce, various years).

The Economic Position of Families with Children

The income of the average middle-class family with children increased by 11 percent between 1973 and 1990 (table 5-1).[16] At the same time, the distribution of income has become less equal and the poverty rate among families with children has risen. Incomes of the poorest 40 percent of all families have fallen, with almost all the drop concentrated among the poorest 20 percent.[17]

Although one-fifth of children are poor in any one year, not all are equally disadvantaged. Many live in families that are temporarily down on their luck or at the beginning of their careers and will later move up the economic ladder. Thus only 10 percent or so are persistently poor for, say, six years.[18] However, 38 percent of black children are persistently poor; only 5 percent of white children are. A very small but growing percentage of all children—1.3 percent in 1980—live in the kind of troubled neighborhoods where female-headed families, welfare dependency, dropping out of school, and male joblessness are commonplace.[19]

Income and Family Structure

What has produced the increased incidence of poverty among children? As a first approximation, the rapid growth in the number of children living in single-parent families can explain virtually all of the growth since 1960.[20]

16. Although standard census data show little improvement since the early 1970s in the income of families with children, they are somewhat misleading because they are not adjusted for the fact that families today are smaller than in the past and that each child potentially has more resources at his disposal. Almost nothing is known about the distribution of income within families. It is simply assumed that as parental income rises, some of this increase benefits the children.

17. Data on after-tax income adjusted for the receipt of various government benefits are available only since 1979, but they reveal a similar picture of growing inequality. *1991 Green Book*, pp. 1192, 1217.

18. Greg J. Duncan and Willard Rodgers, "Has Children's Poverty Become More Persistent?" *American Sociological Review*, vol. 56 (August 1991), pp. 538–50, table 1. Using a variety of different measures, the authors find no consistent increase in the persistence of poverty among children between the 1970s and the 1980s.

19. Troubled neighborhoods are defined as census tracts where all four of the indicators are at least one standard deviation above the mean for the nation as a whole. Erol R. Ricketts and Isabel V. Sawhill, "Defining and Measuring the Underclass," *Journal of Policy Analysis and Management*, vol. 7 (Winter 1988), pp. 316–25.

20. For data on child poverty rates by family structure, see David J. Eggebeen and Daniel T. Lichter, "Race, Family Structure, and Changing Poverty among American Children," *American Sociological Review*, vol. 56 (December 1991), pp. 801–17; and

Of course, poverty may be a cause and not just a consequence of changes in family structure (or both may be explained by some third factor such as personal characteristics that produce problems both at home and on the job.) Put a little differently, some of the children in single-parent families would undoubtedly have fallen into poverty even if their parents had married or remained married.[21] A recent Census Bureau report shows that children from two-parent families that later split had a mean family income that was only 83 percent of those from families that did not split, suggesting that low income is one precursor of family instability. After the split, the income of mothers and children plummeted to 59 percent of the income of intact families with children, suggesting that, in addition, changes in family composition make an independent contribution to economic hardship.[22] The reasons for this decline include the lower earnings of women and the failure of non-resident parents (overwhelmingly fathers) to support their children. Similarly, many never-married teenage mothers initially come from poor families, but having a child further reduces their chances of escaping poverty.

The increase in single mothers is especially pronounced among blacks. The most important factor has been a declining marriage (or remarriage) rate. Sixty-four percent of all black children are now born to unwed mothers (compared with 18 percent of whites) and 51 percent live only with their mothers (compared with 16 percent of whites). The decline in marriage rates could be related to the difficulty that young men are having supporting a family. Some scholars argue that the growth of female-headed families in the black community has mirrored the drop

Peter Gottschalk and Sheldon Danziger, "Family Structure, Family Size, and Family Income: Accounting for Changes in the Economic Well-Being of Children, 1968–1986," IRP discussion paper 934-91 (University of Wisconsin, Institute for Research on Poverty, September 1989, rev. December 1990). Eggebeen and Lichter find that child poverty rates would have been one-third, or 6.3 percentage points, less in 1988 if family structure had not changed since 1960 (p. 801). Gottschalk and Danziger find that changes in family structure increased the child poverty rate by 12.9 percentage points for black children and 3.0 points for white between 1968 and 1986. The actual child poverty rate decreased by 5.4 percentage points between 1960 and 1988 and increased by 4.7 percentage points between 1970 and 1988.

21. Mary Jo Bane, "Household Composition and Poverty," in Sheldon H. Danziger and Daniel H. Weinberg, eds., *Fighting Poverty: What Works and What Doesn't* (Harvard University Press, 1986), pp. 209–31.

22. Bureau of the Census, "Family Disruption and Economic Hardship: The Short-Run Picture for Children," *Current Population Reports*, series P-70, no. 23 (Department of Commerce, 1991), table C.

in the pool of employed men.[23] However, the relationship is not strong enough to explain more than about 20 percent of the changes in black family structure since 1960. Neither the drop in labor force participation among young black men nor changes in their earnings can carry the full burden of explaining these trends, although they appear to have played some part.[24]

The Effects of Income on Children

Granted that more children are poor, what effect does more or less income have on their lives? This question is surprisingly difficult to answer. It is generally assumed that more family income improves the lives of children, and certainly persistent poverty or low family income is associated with lack of success in school and in the job market.[25] However, the reasons remain unclear. Income may be simply a convenient marker for other variables, such as good genes or competent parenting, that matter more. Or it may confer on parents a sense of efficacy, self-esteem, or standing within the community (especially if it is earned income) that indirectly benefits children. Finally, income can obviously provide additional material goods or reduce stress in a household with direct implications for the welfare of children. From a policymaking

23. William Julius Wilson and Kathryn M. Neckerman, "Poverty and Family Structure: The Widening Gap between Evidence and Public Policy Issues," in Danziger and Weinberg, eds., *Fighting Poverty*, pp. 232–59.

24. David T. Ellwood and Jonathan Crane, "Family Change among Black Americans: What Do We Know?" *Journal of Economic Perspectives*, vol. 4 (Fall 1990), pp. 65–84; Robert D. Mare and Christopher Winship, "Socioeconomic Change and the Decline of Marriage for Blacks and Whites," in Christopher Jencks and Paul E. Peterson, eds., *The Urban Underclass* (Brookings, 1991), pp. 175–202; Daniel T. Lichter and others, "Race and the Retreat from Marriage among American Women: A Shortage of Marriageable Men?" (University of Pennsylvania, Population Research Institute, May 1992); and Saul D. Hoffman, Greg J. Duncan, and Ronald B. Mincy, "Marriage and Welfare Use among Young Women: Do Labor Market, Welfare, and Neighborhood Factors Account for Declining Rates of Marriage among Black and White Women?" paper prepared for the 1991 annual meeting of the National Economic Association.

25. Martha S. Hill and Greg J. Duncan, "Parental Family Income and the Socioeconomic Attainment of Children," *Social Science Research*, vol. 16 (March 1987), pp. 39–73; Greg J. Duncan, "The Economic Environment of Childhood" (University of Michigan, Survey Research Center, July 10, 1989), p. 19; Jeanne Brooks-Gunn and others, "Do Neighborhoods Influence Child and Adolescent Behavior?" Social Research Council, Committee for Research on the Urban Underclass, February 21, 1992; and Robert Haveman and Barbara Wolfe, "On the Determinants of Children's Wellbeing and Economic Success: A Research Perspective," working paper 26 (New York: Russell Sage Foundation, January 1992).

perspective, the mechanism involved is critical. If stress or lack of material goods is the problem, the appropriate response is to just give people income, any kind of income, and children will be better off. If income is a marker of something else, publicly provided income support will have little effect. And if income from work provides self-esteem, earned income is better than welfare, and policy should be oriented toward helping people succeed in the labor market.

Research on these matters is far from adequate, but it has shed some light. The extra income provided to families that participated in the negative income tax experiments of the 1970s increased the probability of high school graduation, raised infant birth weights in at-risk pregnancies, and may have improved the educational performance of young children. However, for the most part the results were disappointing.[26] More recent studies suggest that earned income has more beneficial effects than welfare.[27]

To summarize, although the income available to children has on average not diminished in recent decades, the economic conditions of some children have clearly worsened, primarily because of changes in family structure. Declining earnings of young men, especially those with the least education, played a part, but most growth in single-parent families cannot be explained by purely economic factors.

Cultural Influences

Some observers believe that changes in the family have been caused by shifting cultural attitudes, including a devaluation of obligations to

26. Eric A. Hanushek, "Non-Labor-Supply Responses to the Income Maintenance Experiments," in Alicia H. Munnell, ed., *Lessons from the Income Maintenance Experiments* (Federal Reserve Bank of Boston, 1986), pp. 106–21; Barbara H. Kehrer and Charles M. Wolin, "Impact of Income Maintenance on Low Birth Weight: Evidence from the Gary Experiment," *Journal of Human Resources*, vol. 14 (Fall 1979), pp. 434–62; Rebecca A. Maynard and Richard J. Murnane, "The Effects of a Negative Income Tax on School Performance: Results of an Experiment," *Journal of Human Resources*, vol. 14 (Fall 1979), pp. 463–76; Charles Mallar, "The Educational and Labor Supply Responses of Young Adults in Experimental Families," in Harold W. Watts and Albert Rees, eds., *The New Jersey Income Maintenance Experiment*, vol. 2: *Labor Supply Responses* (Academic Press, 1976), pp. 163–84; and Steven F. Venti and David A. Wise, "Income Maintenance and the School and Work Decisions of Youth," Harvard University, Department of Government, March 1984.

27. Robert Haveman, Barbara Wolfe, and James Spaulding, "Childhood Events and Circumstances Influencing High School Completion," *Demography*, vol. 28 (February 1991), pp. 133–57; and Mary Jo Bane, "How Much Does Poverty Matter?" paper prepared for the 1992 Annual Conference on Security for America's Children.

others and an increased emphasis on self-fulfillment and individual rights. These changes, it is argued, are occurring in virtually all advanced countries as the result of greater affluence that has brought with it more questioning of established rules and social norms and a greater emphasis on the right of all people to choose their own life styles. The result has been less marriage, more sex and childbearing outside marriage, and more employed women. Greater choice for adults has meant less uniformity in the living arrangements of children.[28] If these arguments are valid, no change in government policy will do much to improve the well-being of children. Only more responsible sexual behavior among the unmarried and greater willingness on the part of married parents to sacrifice on behalf of their children will make a difference.

Attitudes have certainly changed in the past two decades. In 1969, 68 percent of the public condemned sexual relations before marriage; only 33 percent did so in 1990. Disapproval of work outside the home by married women has declined from 80 percent in 1930 to 20 percent in the late 1980s. All fifty states have adopted no-fault divorce laws. Although sentiment favoring liberalized divorce laws diminished somewhat after the mid-1970s, tolerance for divorce as the appropriate solution to an unhappy marriage is surely higher than it was in the 1950s.[29]

Whether changes in attitudes have driven changes in behavior is not clear. The initial rise in the divorce rate in the early 1960s, for example, occurred before attitudes began to change in the late 1960s.[30] Similarly, the increase in the number of women working outside the home was

28. This summary draws heavily on Daniel Yankelovich, "The Affluence Effect," Brookings Seminar on Values and Public Policy, 1991–92; David Popenoe, *Disturbing the Nest: Family Change and Decline in Modern Societies* (New York: Aldine de Gruyter, 1988); and Popenoe, "The Family Condition of America: Cultural Change and Public Policy," Brookings Seminar on Values and Public Policy, 1991–92. Also see Barbara Ehrenrich, *The Hearts of Men: American Dreams and the Flight from Commitment* (Garden City, N.Y.: Anchor Press, 1983); David Blankenhorn, "Does Grandmother Know Best?" *Family Affairs*, Institute for American Values (Spring–Summer 1990); Peter Uhlenberg and David Eggebeen, "The Declining Well-Being of American Adolescents," *Public Interest*, no. 82 (Winter 1986), pp. 25–38; and Frank F. Furstenberg, Jr., "Good Dads, Bad Dads: Two Faces of Fatherhood," in Cherlin, ed., *The Changing American Family and Public Policy*, pp. 193–218.

29. Yankelovich, "Affluence Effect," pp. 71–72, 40; and Andrew J. Cherlin, *Marriage, Divorce, Remarriage* (Harvard University Press, forthcoming).

30. This phenomenon is particularly well illustrated in one study of 900 mothers who were interviewed between 1962 and 1977. Their initial attitudes about divorce had no impact on the respondents' later likelihood of divorcing, but the stability of their marriages did affect subsequent attitudes. Cherlin, *Marriage, Divorce, Remarriage*, p. 48.

probably induced by growing employment opportunities and real wages in traditionally female occupations for most of this century, whereas the shift in attitudes about women's roles is a relatively recent phenomenon. Although changes in attitudes may be as much a consequence as a cause of changes in behavior, once established they undoubtedly help reinforce behavior that was once considered unacceptable.[31] So, initial changes in economic conditions or public policy can have larger effects than a simple behavioral model might assume.

At the same time, change is not limitless. A new cultural equilibrium will eventually be established in which people will probably have far more individual choice, but in a context of some shared values about the importance of family commitments. Moving to that equilibrium, however, can engender a great deal of cultural confusion that temporarily inflicts significant costs on society, children in particular.

The lack of commonly accepted rules and institutional supports during this period has put a premium on individual skill and flexibility in managing the transition. Better-educated, higher-income adults with access to private safety nets of all kinds have managed the transition more successfully than less advantaged adults for whom the new emphasis on satisfying personal relationships is likely to be an abstraction in any case. For example, there is no evidence that most of these new attitudes (as opposed to the behaviors that have accompanied them) have permeated inner-city communities. Marriages there are still based on expectations that men will be providers and women childrearers.[32] However, the economy has made these expectations obsolete even for the middle class, for whom two-earner families and delayed childbearing are now the rule. Trying to recreate the old arrangements at the bottom of the economic ladder is not realistic. Rather one must hope that the new views will eventually permeate the ranks of the poor. While two married earners and delayed childbearing would not solve all the problems for poor children, they would help. Cultural trickle-down is not the problem; it is, at least in part, the solution.

The increasing geographic isolation of the poor, especially minorities, may inhibit this process. The civil rights revolution permitted many black

31. Cherlin, *Marriage, Divorce, Remarriage*; and Irwin Garfinkel and Sara S. McLanahan, *Single Mothers and Their Children: A New American Dilemma* (Washington: Urban Institute Press, 1986).

32. For some ethnographic evidence on these assertions, see Elijah Anderson, "Neighborhood Effects on Teenage Pregnancy," in Jencks and Peterson, eds., *Urban Underclass*, pp. 375–98.

middle-class families—in which there have always been working wives
and few children—to move out of the inner city, leaving their former
neighborhoods devoid of role models and community institutions that
might have contributed to a more successful cultural transition.[33] The
result is that an increasing proportion of poor minority children are
living in neighborhoods where teenage pregnancy, single-parent families,
welfare dependency, and an absence of male role models are commonplace.[34] Social norms and peer pressures in these communities work
against staying in school and delaying childbearing.[35]

Television

Television has become a pervasive influence in children's lives. The
number of households with a television set increased from 9 percent in
1950 to 98 percent in 1990. Preschoolers watch television 1,383 hours
a year, one-quarter of their waking lives. Grade school children watch
1,095 hours, almost as much time as they spend in school. But how does
this affect their behavior, attitudes, abilities, and health?[36]

Studies do not find a significant relationship between the amount of
TV viewing and later test scores. The amount of viewing does affect
school achievement, but the effects disappear once one adjusts for the
fact that less able children and those from more disadvantaged families
watch much more television than other children do. Although television's
deadening effects on learning are not borne out by research, its potential
benefits are manifest. "Sesame Street," "Mister Rogers' Neighborhood,"

33. William Julius Wilson, *The Truly Disadvantaged: The Inner City, the Underclass,
and Public Policy* (University of Chicago Press, 1987).

34. Ronald B. Mincy, Isabel V. Sawhill, and Douglas A. Wolfe, "The Underclass;
Definition and Measurement," *Science*, vol. 248 (April 27, 1990), pp. 450–53.

35. Rebecca L. Clark and Douglas A. Wolfe, "Do Neighborhoods Matter? Dropping
Out Among Teenage Boys," paper prepared for the 1992 Annual Meeting of the Population
Association of America; Brooks-Gunn and others, "Do Neighborhoods Influence Child
and Adolescent Behavior?"; Jonathan Crane, "The Epidemic Theory of Ghettos and
Neighborhood Effects on Dropping Out and Teenage Childbearing," *American Journal of
Sociology*, vol. 96 (March 1991), pp. 1226–59; and Christopher Jencks and Susan E.
Mayer, "The Social Consequences of Growing Up in a Poor Neighborhood: A Review,"
in Michael McGeary and Lawrence Lynn, eds., *Inner City Poverty in the U.S.* (Washington:
National Academy Press, 1990).

36. The best review of the literature is Aletha C. Huston and others, *Big World, Small
Screen: The Role of Television in American Society* (University of Nebraska Press, 1992),
p. 6. This section draws heavily on their work.

and other special educational programming have been a clear success. Children who watch these programs learn letters, numbers, vocabulary, and other cognitive skills, and are more likely to demonstrate nurturance, empathy, task persistence, and imaginativeness in interactions with other children and adults. Similarly beneficial gains have been reported for a number of different educational programs and for children from a wide variety of social backgrounds.

The amount of violence depicted on television is staggering: five violent acts an hour in prime time and four or five times that many in children's Saturday morning programming. In both the United States and other countries, researchers find that watching violence on television leads to aggressive behavior, and the effects often last into adolescence and beyond. The National Institute for Mental Health concluded that the magnitude of the effects was as large as for any other variable that has been measured.[37] Thus increases in violent behavior (see table 5-1) may reflect the spread of television into most homes during the 1950s and 1960s. Findings for the other possible effects of television on child development are either inconsistent or not well researched, but television seems to be as important an influence on some behaviors as changes in the family. Of course, the two may interact if busy parents use television as a substitute for other family activities. And, as experts note, parental monitoring and interpretation of what children see on television is critical.

Government may also have a role to play. It can limit the length, frequency, and content of advertising to protect children from messages that exploit their vulnerability and their inability (before age 8 or so) to distinguish advertising from programming. It can also allocate more money to fund age-appropriate educational programs and require stations to broadcast this kind of programming as part of their licensing agreements. Although restrictions on advertising and guidelines for children's programming were eliminated in 1984 as part of a general effort to deregulate the broadcast industry, in 1990 Congress enacted the Children's Television Education Act, which establishes the principle that the broadcast industry has a social responsibility, limits advertising during children's programs, allows broadcasters to cooperate in curbing depictions of violence, and establishes a National Endowment for Children's Television.

37. National Institute of Mental Health, *Television and Behavior: Ten Years of Scientific Progress and Implications for the Eighties*, vol. 1: *Summary Report* (1982) as cited in Huston and others, *Big World, Small Screen*.

Welfare Policies

The welfare system has been widely blamed for the breakdown of the family, especially in inner cities. But welfare benefits have been falling in real terms since the early 1970s, while divorce, separation, and out-of-wedlock births have continued to increase. Moreover, a large body of research shows that effects of the welfare system cannot explain more than perhaps 10 to 15 percent of the observed changes in family composition. For these reasons, recent state efforts to link welfare benefits to changes in marriage and childbearing are unlikely to have much impact. Still, many people are not fully convinced by the evidence because of the difficulty of sorting out the influence of welfare from other factors and the failure to account for the possibility that welfare may take a long time to influence behavior and that behavior itself may influence attitudes. Also, only the variation in benefit levels can be studied, while it may be the very existence of the program that is relevant.[38]

The Role of Government

Whatever the reasons for the declining fortunes of America's children, many contend that government has a responsibility to ensure better chances for them. Two of the most critical areas of traditional governmental responsibility are health care financing and elementary and secondary education, topics beyond the scope of this chapter. But aside from restructuring the education and health care systems, what can government do? Current debate focuses on proposals in three areas: expanding effective services for young children or their families in preschool education, nutrition, and preventive health care; providing additional income support to families with children, primarily through the tax system; and using government policies to encourage parental responsibility. Before considering these strategies in more detail, current government outlays for programs that primarily serve children need to be reviewed.

Spending on Children's Programs

Estimates of recent federal and readily identifiable state and local outlays on programs for children are shown in table 5-3. In some

38. Isabel V. Sawhill, "Poverty in the U.S.: Why Is It So Persistent?" *Journal of Economic Literature*, vol. 26 (September 1988), pp. 1073–1119; and Robert Moffitt, "Incentive Effects of the U.S. Welfare System: A Review," *Journal of Economic Literature*, vol. 30 (March 1992), pp. 1–61.

programs children do not constitute all the beneficiaries, so the age distribution of program recipients has been used to calculate children's share of total outlays (for example, 12 percent of medicaid outlays flow to children.[39] The table shows that

—State and local spending on children is at least three times greater than federal spending because outlays for education are so large and schools are primarily a state and local responsibility.

—The federal government spent about $67 billion on children in fiscal year 1989. The biggest expenditures were for income support, primarily dependents' and survivors' benefits under social security and aid to families with dependent children (AFDC), nutrition (primarily food stamps and school lunches); and education.

—Almost two-thirds of these federal outlays are in means-tested programs, suggesting that they disproportionately help poor children.

—The federal government also provides $44 billion a year in assistance to families with children in the form of tax subsidies, or, more important, exemptions for dependents.

Real federal outlays for children's programs declined 4 percent between fiscal 1978 and 1987 (programs serving the elderly increased 52 percent).[40] The biggest percentage increases in spending on children were for child support enforcement, foster care, education for the handicapped, and immunization programs. The biggest dollar increases were for food stamps, special supplemental food programs for women, infants and children (WIC), medicaid, and education for the handicapped. These increases were offset by real decreases in dependents' benefits under social security, vocational or compensatory education, and employment and training services.

Expanding Effective Programs for Children

In combination with the deterioration of many indicators of children's well-being and the increasing inequality of their prospects, the decline in federal spending on children has prompted bipartisan calls for renewed investments in early childhood programs.

39. These data are from Jason Juffras and C. Eugene Steuerle, "Public Expenditures on Children, Fiscal Year 1989," paper prepared for the National Commission on Children, Airlie, Va., November 1990. A more detailed discussion of the estimates is contained in their paper.
40. *1991 Green Book*, p. 1344.

TABLE 5-3. Estimated Public Expenditures on Children,
Fiscal Year 1989
Billions of 1992 dollars

Program and type	Amount	Program and type	Amount
Federal expenditures		*Health*	
Income support		Medicaid	4.69
Social security[a]	13.73	Maternal and child health	0.62
Aid to families with dependent		Immunization	0.16
children	8.31	Family planning	0.16
Child support enforcement	1.07	National Institutes of Health	0.12
Refugee assistance	0.17	Infant mortality	0.02
Railroad retirement	0.10	Subtotal	5.78
Veterans' benefits	0.07	*Social services*	
Subtotal	23.45	Social services block grant	1.52
Nutrition		Foster care and adoption	1.52
Food stamps	7.81	Head start	1.39
Child nutrition[b]	5.16	Child welfare	0.28
Women, infants, and children	2.19	Juvenile justice	0.07
Commodity supplemental food	0.07	Older American volunteers[c]	0.06
Special milk	0.02	Adolescent family life	0.01
Subtotal	15.25	Other social services	0.17
Education		Subtotal	5.01
Compensatory education	4.74	*Housing*	
Education for the handicapped	2.13	Section 8 leased housing	
Chapter 2 block grant	1.10	assistance	3.63
Impact aid	0.86	Public and Indian housing	1.06
Vocational education	0.83	Homeownership and rental	
Bilingual and immigrant education	0.18	housing assistance	0.25
Indian education	0.08	Subtotal	4.95
Other education	0.37		
Subtotal	10.28		

In 1985 a report from the Select Committee on Children, Youth, and Families listed eight programs, which, on the basis of the best evidence available, produce cost-effective results for children and their families (the five most relevant to younger children are listed in table 5-4). The 1990 update of this report added four additional program areas, the most significant for present purposes being home visiting. Most of the programs deliver preventive health care of one kind or another to disadvantaged families, often with counseling, outreach, or other services included. Head Start provides a preschool education for children 3 to 5 years old from low-income families.

The committee's findings have been cited by business leaders, journalists, children's advocates, private foundations, and scholars, and have

TABLE 5-3 *(continued)*

Program and type	Amount	Program and type	Amount
Training		Exclusion of survivors and	
Job Training Partnership		dependent care benefits	0.53
Act (title II-A)	0.90	Exclusion of employer-provided	
Summer youth employment	0.81	day care	0.29
Job Corps	0.84	Exclusion of foster care payments	0.03
Subtotal	2.56	**Total tax expenditure programs**	**43.69**
Total federal expenditure		**Total all federal programs**	**110.63**
programs	**66.95**	**State and local expenditures**	
Federal tax expenditures[d]		State elementary and secondary	
Dependent exemption[e]	27.14	education	101.75
Earned income tax credit[f]	4.41	Local elementary and secondary	
Dependent care credit	5.52	education	90.49
Exclusion of employer health		State medicaid	3.62
insurance	5.13	State and local AFDC	6.86
Exclusion of public assistance		State foster care	1.12
benefits	0.26	**Total state and local programs**	**203.83**
Exclusion of food stamp and			
housing benefits	0.26		
Exclusion of disability benefits	0.11		

SOURCE: C. Eugene Steuerle and Jason Juffras, "Public Expenditures on Children, Fiscal Year, 1989," in *Beyond Rhetoric* (Washington: National Commission on Children, 1991), table 11-1, p. 315.

a. Benefits to children come through dependents' and survivors' benefits.

b. Includes school breakfast and lunch, child care, and summer feeding programs.

c. Through this program older Americans volunteer as foster grandparents to at-risk children and work on problems such as literacy and drug abuse prevention.

d. Figures are outlay equivalents.

e. Technically, this is not treated as a tax expenditure, but like the taxpayer exemption, as the nontaxability of the first dollars of income.

f. Includes both the reduced tax liability of EITC recipients and the refundable earned income credits that many families receive.

created growing support for an expansion of such programs as Head Start, WIC and medicaid. However, as table 5-4 shows, most programs still serve only a modest proportion of all those who are (or arguably should be) eligible.

The select committee's interpretation of the evidence on effective programs has not gone unchallenged. As the programs have garnered increasing political support, they have been scrutinized more closely.[41] Nowhere has this debate been more heated than in the case of Head Start.

41. Ron Haskins, "Beyond Metaphor: The Efficacy of Early Childhood Education," *American Psychologist*, vol. 44 (February 1989), pp. 274–82; Enid Borden and Kate Walsh O'Beirne, "False Start? The Fleeting Gains at Head Start," *Policy Review* (Winter 1989), pp. 48–51; Douglas J. Besharov, "A New Start for Head Start," *American Enterprise*,

TABLE 5-4. Selected Cost-Effective Programs for Children

Program or intervention	Budget authority, fiscal 1992 (billions of dollars)	Savings in future expenditures per dollar invested	Percent of target population served
Special supplemental food program for women, infants and children (WIC)	2.6	3.00	50–60
Prenatal care	n.a.	3.38	75
Childhood immunization	0.3	10.00	80–88[a]
Preschool education (Head Start)	2.2	6.00	30
Compensatory education	6.7	4.90	50

SOURCE: House Select Committee on Children, Youth, and Families, *Opportunities for Success: Cost Effective Programs for Children Update, 1990,* 101 Cong. 2 sess. (GPO, 1990).
n.a. Not available.
a. Ages 1–4, 80 percent; age 5–14, 88 percent.

Early enthusiasm for the program stemmed from long-term follow-ups of children enrolled in about a dozen early education projects begun in the 1960s. Studies found that a preschool experience (part time for one or two years) produces short-term gains in IQs and in reading and mathematics achievement but that these gains fade by third grade. The experience did, however, make it less likely that the children would be placed in special education classes or would need to repeat a grade. An initially more successful adjustment to school among disadvantaged children seemed to produce more positive attitudes and cumulative progress as each successful learning experience built on the previous one. One study that followed 123 children to age 28 even found reductions in dropout rates, arrest rates, teenage pregnancy, use of welfare, and joblessness during late adolescence. A benefit-cost analysis showed that preschool education can be an excellent investment for taxpayers, saving $4.75 in spending on special education, public assistance, and crime for every $1.00 spent.[42]

Generalizing these findings to Head Start is risky because the early model projects often had greater funding, higher-quality staff, more

vol. 3 (March–April 1992), pp. 52–57; and George G. Graham, "WIC: A Food Program That Fails," *Public Interest,* no. 103 (Spring 1991), pp. 66–75.

42. David P. Weikart, "Children, Child Care and the Role of Quality Early Childhood Education Programs" (Ypsilanti, Mich.: High/Scope Educational Research Foundation, September 11, 1986); and John R. Berrueta-Clement and others, *Changed Lives: The Effect of the Perry Preschool Program of Youths Through Age 19* (Ypsilanti, Mich.: High/Scope Press, 1984).

emphasis on parental involvement, and other characteristics difficult to maintain in a national program, especially as it attempts to serve more and more children. Moreover, the cumulative progress that produces long-term benefits may not be possible without continuing attention and follow-up in the early grades. For these or other reasons, evidence of success is weaker when a large number of Head Start projects are included in the evaluations.[43]

If expanding a program dilutes its effectiveness, the obvious solution is to focus on maintaining quality (perhaps using the results achieved in smaller demonstrations as a standard of performance). The kinds of changes needed in the Head Start program include devoting more funds to improving program quality through teacher training, higher salaries, and improved curriculum and making the program a full-day, year-round experience to accommodate the needs of working parents. In addition, Head Start could be extended to younger children, parental involvement could be increased so that parents develop the skills to teach their children themselves, and follow-up activities for the children could be provided in the early grades.[44] Finally, given high employment rates among the mothers of preschoolers, making Head Start available to everyone, with fees tied to income, is an option that should be explored.

The issues raised in this review of Head Start's success are likely to hold true for other "successful" programs. The evidence is always mixed, the interventions are typically brief, long-term follow-up data are scarce, and it is risky to assume that what is accomplished in small demonstrations by trained and dedicated people will be replicated when the program becomes national in scope. At the same time, it would be a mistake to conclude that a program does not work just because it has not been adequately evaluated. A lack of positive findings may simply reflect insufficient evidence to prove anything one way or the other. Most programs for children—the select committee listed about 125 in 1990 (table 5-3 includes 39)—fall into this category. We simply do not know whether they work. In these cases, one must weigh the risk of doing something and having it not work against the risk of doing nothing and missing an opportunity to improve lives. It can be just as costly to not fund a potentially successful program as it is to fund a potentially unsuccessful one. The select committee's list is not infallible, but it would not be a bad place to start in thinking about investments in the next

43. Ruth Hubbell McKey and others, *The Impact of Head Start on Children, Families and Communities: Head Start Synthesis Project, Executive Summary* (GPO, June 1985).
44. I am indebted to Richard Murnane and Frank Levy for their ideas on this section.

generation. An important caveat is that attention must be paid to the quality of the services delivered and not just the number of children served. The history of social program funding in the United States is one of doing too little for too many with the result that in the end no one benefits.

A reasonable program might devote an additional $1 billion in spending to preventive health and nutrition services. This could include $200 million for WIC, $100 million for immunizations, which have been declining among preschoolers, $500 million for community or school-based health services for underserved urban and rural populations, and $200 million to make home visiting available under medicaid, thereby permitting better outreach and coordination of services for low-income families.

In addition, Head Start should be gradually expanded to cover all eligible three- and four-year-olds, with sufficient funding for more full-day, full-year slots, more training and salary increases for teachers, and more services to children after they enter school. The total cost, if fully phased in by fiscal 1997, would be about $6 billion.

A final subject that has been getting increased attention is the coordination of services for children and their families. The large number of categorical programs with different eligibility rules, funding methods, and regulatory and reporting requirements is a nightmare for service providers and families alike. At the federal level alone, fifteen congressional committees have some jurisdiction over children and five executive branch departments have significant responsibilities, although the Department of Health and Human Services is clearly dominant.[45] This bureaucratic morass is replicated at the state level. Local providers confront a maze of rules and regulations that divert time from serving clients; bewildered families must negotiate myriad programs, offices, and paperwork to secure assistance.

Experts have argued for years that it is results that matter, not program inputs. Accordingly, providing more flexibility to service providers while insisting that they be held accountable for achieving certain results has obvious appeal. However, this would require agreeing on and measuring desirable child outcomes. Also, the new enthusiasm for integrated services needs to be tempered with a realization that some specialization in service

45. HHS accounts for half of all federal spending on children. See Isabel V. Sawhill, "Toward More Integrated Services for Children: Issues and Options," Statement before the Subcommittee on Children, Family, Drugs, and Alcoholism, Senate Committee on Labor and Human Resources, 101 Cong. 1 sess. (May 7, 1991).

delivery is both efficient and effective. Health care professionals cannot help a parent find a job; day care workers or teachers cannot help children with severe emotional problems. And psychiatrists do not know the eligibility requirements for AFDC. Similarly, collective location of services in a school, housing project, or neighborhood may not be realistic beyond the simplest kinds of counseling and drop-in services such as day care. In short, current program categories are not entirely irrational.

With these caveats, it would make sense to "decategorize" some federally funded children's programs so that states can experiment with more effective ways of delivering services.

Additional Income Support for Families with Children

Children and their families can also be helped simply by providing them with more income. This strategy has had broad political support in recent years. Liberals like it because it attacks what they think are the causes of crime, delinquency, school failure, lower productivity, and other social ills.[46] Conservatives like it because it bypasses government bureaucracies and puts money directly into the hands of parents. If it is accomplished by bigger tax credits or deductions for families with children, government may even shrink.[47]

For these reasons, proposals to provide additional tax relief to families with children mushroomed in the early 1990s. The bipartisan National Commission on Children, chaired by Senator Jay Rockefeller, called for a $1,000 refundable tax credit for all children through age 18 (to replace the dependent exemption) at a net five-year cost of $200 billion.[48] The administration's fiscal 1993 budget proposed to increase the personal exemption for children younger than 18 from $2,300 to $2,800 at a five-year cost of $18.5 billion. And the Senate tax bill enacted in early 1992 created a nonrefundable $300 tax credit for children younger than 16 available to families with adjusted gross incomes less than $47,500 (phased out between $47,500 and $60,000) at a five-year cost of $28 billion.[49] In general, tax credits are more progressive than tax

46. See, for example, National Commission on Children, *Beyond Rhetoric: A New American Agenda for Children and Families, Final Report* (Washington, 1991), p. 80.

47. Because only 35 percent of all families include children younger than 18, politics also sometimes demands that tax relief be broadened to include all families. The proposal passed by the House in 1992 fell into this category.

48. National Commission on Children, *Beyond Rhetoric*, p. 80.

49. *Budget of the United States Government, Fiscal Year 1993*, pt. 2, p. 9.

exemptions because credits are worth the same dollar amount at every level of income. Refundable credits are more progressive than nonrefundable ones because they extend relief to low-income families with limited tax liabilities or none.

Tax relief for families with children has a number of merits in addition to its obvious political appeal. First, the value of the exemption for dependents has not kept pace with inflation or the growth of real incomes in the past four decades. If it had, the exemption would have been $7,800 in 1990 rather than $2,050.[50] Second, the United States is the only major industrialized country without a children's allowance, which partially explains its higher rates of child poverty.[51] Third, unlike welfare or other more targeted programs, a children's tax credit carries less stigma and involves fewer disincentives to work or marry. Finally, many people believe that raising children is too expensive and difficult a task, and too important for society as a whole, to be shouldered by parents alone; they contend that it should be a collective responsibility.

Although these arguments are appealing, tax relief for families with children does have drawbacks. First, not everyone agrees that the costs of raising children should be socialized. At issue is the extent to which families without children should be expected to subsidize those with them. Second, lower taxes on families with children are not necessarily the best way to increase the well-being of children: as noted earlier, beyond a certain minimum the effects of income on children's lives appear modest and uncertain. Moreover, most children are economically better off than they have ever been. Although giving parents more income might reduce the stresses of family life and help children, it is not a cost-effective use of government funds. There is good reason to think that a billion dollars spent on Head Start or prenatal care would be more effective than a billion in tax credits for middle-class parents. Moreover, whatever the effects of added income, they are likely to be greatest if assistance is concentrated on low-income children; and it is low-income children who have fared the worst in the past several decades.

The traditional form of support for poor children—public assistance— is both antiwork and antifamily. One solution is to expand the earned

50. C. Eugene Steuerle and Jason Juffras, "A $1,000 Tax Credit for Every Child: A Base of Reform for the Nation's Tax, Welfare, and Health Systems," Changing Domestic Priorities policy paper (Washington: Urban Institute, April 1991).

51. Timothy Smeeding, Barbara Boyle Torrey, and Martin Rein, "Patterns of Income Poverty: The Economic Status of Children and the Elderly in Eight Countries," in John L.

income tax credit (EITC), a measure that is more consistent with work and family values. The EITC could be expanded to eliminate poverty (as officially measured) among full-time workers with one or two children for about $9 billion a year by fiscal 1997, a fraction of the cost of some of the tax relief proposals described earlier. The family-size adjustment and extra credit for children younger than a year old that were introduced in 1990 have made the EITC less like a wage subsidy and more like a welfare program. In addition, they have complicated the administration of the program and made it less likely that low-income families will claim the credit.[52] For both reasons, the family-size adjustment and extra credit for infants should be eliminated.

Tax relief for families with children must compete not just with an expansion of effective services for children, but also with efforts to reduce the deficit. Some argue that as long as these tax proposals are paid for by increased taxes on the wealthy or reduced defense spending, they cannot add to the deficit. But this argument misses the point. If these same funds were devoted to deficit reduction rather than to tax relief, all families would eventually benefit. Productivity and earnings would grow at a faster rate, adding to family income across the board. Tax relief can reallocate funds from families without children to those with them, and from higher-income families to lower-income ones, but it cannot make families as a whole better off.

Budgetary Implications of Expanding Programs for Children

Young children and their families would benefit from additional spending in a number of areas (table 5-5). A reasonable expansion of preventive health care services, especially those for hard-to-reach populations in rural areas or inner cities, would cost $1 billion. Another $6 billion, phased in over five years, could be devoted to expanding Head Start to include all low-income children aged 3 to 5 while preserving quality and providing more full-day, full-year slots so that mothers now on welfare can work. Increasing income support to working poor families

Palmer, Timothy Smeeding, and Barbara Boyle Torrey, eds., *The Vulnerable* (Washington: Urban Institute Press, 1988), pp. 89–119.

52. Although the data are not very good, 80 to 90 percent of eligible families receive the EITC, at least partly because in the past the Treasury automatically computed it for them. With the introduction of the 1990 reforms, the filing process has become more complicated.

TABLE 5-5. Costs of Expanding Federal Programs for Young Children and Their Families, Fiscal Year 1997
Billions of dollars

Program	Proposed fiscal 1992 budget authority	Cost of proposed increase in fiscal 1997
Preventive health care		
WIC	2.6	0.2
Immunizations	0.3	0.1
Community or school-based services	0.5	0.5
Home visiting	0	0.2
Preschool education		
Head Start	2.0	6.0[a]
Income supplements for the working poor		
Earned income tax credit	6.7[b]	9.4[c]
Family planning		
Title X, Public Health Service Act	0.4	0.2
Total	12.5	16.6

a. Includes full funding, improving quality, providing more full-day, full-year slots.
b. Scheduled to increase to $14.6 billion by fiscal 1994.
c. The proposal is for a credit rate of 35 percent on earnings up to $8,940 for a maximum of $3,129. At earnings above $14,080, the credit is reduced by 20 cents for each dollar earned, phasing out completely at earnings of $29,725. There is no adjustment for family size.

would cost $9.4 billion by fiscal 1997, an amount that would bring a mother with a full-time minimum-wage job and two children up to the poverty line.[53] Finally, restoring real outlays on family planning services (discussed in the next section) to 1980 levels would require an additional $200 million.

The total additional budget for these purposes is $16.6 billion in 1997 when all changes are fully in effect. Not all the funds would need to be new. Opportunities exist to reduce spending in some programs of lower priority, such as the school lunch program. Consolidating some services and emphasizing evaluation and greater accountability for results could produce further efficiencies.

Encouraging Parental Responsibility

Some parents fail to provide adequate nurture, discipline, and moral education to their children, but it is not clear what government can or

53. There is no adjustment for family size. After taxes and child care expenses, the family would still be poor unless the head earned a little more than the current minimum wage of $4.25 an hour, but this should be much more likely by 1997.

should do about the problem. The president and other leaders can use the bully pulpit to convey the importance of parental responsibility, but short of playing Big Brother, government's role is limited. Nevertheless, government can take some steps.

Reducing Teenage Childbearing

Most adolescents are not financially or psychologically ready for parenthood. Children of teenage parents are more likely to have poor health, do poorly in school, suffer from behavior problems, and become teenage parents themselves.[54] These bad outcomes may reflect characteristics of young mothers that predispose them to become teenage parents in the first place and not the timing of the birth per se. One recent study found few differences between sisters who had children at an early age and those who delayed parenthood, suggesting that the deprived circumstances or family background shared by both siblings is what produces poor outcomes. If so, efforts to reduce early childbearing, rather than the conditions that give rise to it, may do little good.[55] However, a more recent study based on a larger and more nationally representative sample of sisters suggests that the social and economic benefits or delayed childbearing are still sizable.[56]

Teenage mothers are at high risk of long-term welfare dependency. About half (and three-fourths of single teenage mothers) receive AFDC benefits some time during the five years after they give birth.[57] Total outlays for AFDC, food stamps, and medicaid for families started by a teenage birth were $25 billion in 1989. If one were to include housing subsidies, foster care, special education, and other social service programs,

54. Sandra L. Hofferth, "Social and Economic Consequences of Teenage Childbearing," in Sandra L. Hofferth and Cheryl D. Hayes, eds., *Risking the Future: Adolescent Sexuality, Pregnancy, and Childbearing*, vol. 2 (Washington: National Academy Press, 1987), pp. 123–44; and Frank F. Furstenberg, Jr., Jeanne Brooks-Gunn, and Lindsay Chase-Lansdale, "Teenaged Pregnancy and Childbearing," *American Psychologist*, vol. 44 (February, 1989), pp. 313–19.

55. Arline T. Geronimus and Sanders Korenman, "The Socioeconomic Consequences of Teen Childbearing Reconsidered," *Quarterly Journal of Economics*, forthcoming.

56. Saul D. Hoffman, Frank Furstenberg, Jr., and E. Michael Foster, "Re-evaluating the Costs of Teenage Childbearing," paper prepared for 1992 meeting of Population Association of America. Most of this research has focused on outcomes for mothers rather than their children, but earlier studies suggested that most of the adverse consequences for children are the result of what happens to their mothers.

57. Congressional Budget Office, *Sources of Support for Adolescent Mothers* (September 1990), p. xvi.

TABLE 5-6. Sexual and Childbearing Activity of Women Aged 15 to 19, Selected Years, 1970–88

Percent

Activity	1970	1980	1985	1988
Sexually active before marriage	29	42	44	52
Become pregnant	9.5[a]	11.1	10.9	11.3
Have an abortion	1.9[a]	4.3	4.4	4.4
Give birth	6.8	5.3	5.1	5.4
Give birth out of wedlock	2.2	2.8	3.1	3.7

SOURCES: *Facts at a Glance* (Washington: Child Trends, January 1992); Stanley Henshaw, "U.S. Teenage Pregnancy Statistics" (New York: Alan Guttmacher Institute, April 1992), p. 3; and Bureau of the Census, *Statistical Abstract of the United States, 1991*, table 92.
a. 1972.

the costs would be even larger.[58] Clearly, saving even a small proportion of these costs would be worthwhile.

The challenge can be better understood after reviewing trends in teenage childbearing. Sexual activity among women aged 15-19 has increased steadily during the past several decades (table 5-6). Until the 1980s this did not translate into increases in the birthrate among young women because of the greater use of both contraception and abortion. Since 1986, however, the birthrate has begun to rise as the proportion of the adolescent population that is sexually active continues to expand without commensurate increases in the use of contraception or abortion. Although the AIDS epidemic might have been expected to change these behaviors, it does not seem to have had much effect. Most teenage pregnancies are unintended, and a rising proportion of teenage births is to unwed mothers.

One way to reduce early childbearing is to provide more information about sexuality, including the use of contraceptives by those who are sexually active, and about life options. Another is to motivate adolescents to practice abstinence. Finally, although the primary objective is to prevent early pregnancy, many believe that access to either abortion or adoption should be available for those who experience an unintended pregnancy. Unfortunately, sophisticated evaluations of most programs that have tried to reduce early pregnancy or childbearing do not exist.[59] Nevertheless, some observations seem warranted.

58. *1991 Green Book*, p. 974.
59. This lack of knowledge has persisted because service providers are uninterested in evaluation, evaluation research has no status in the academic community, and neither the federal government nor most foundations have insisted on rigorous evaluations or provided the funding for them. See Kristin Moore's comments in Theodora Ooms and Lisa

—Sex education, now required or encouraged by most states and available in nine of ten large school districts, has increased reproductive knowledge and resulted in more effective use of contraception. No consistent effects on sexual activity or early pregnancy have been found.

—Efforts to promote abstinence have succeeded in delaying the onset of intercourse, but the effects are measured in months rather than years, and the validity of this result has been questioned.[60]

—Family planning clinics, which serve a million teenagers a year, have increased teenagers' contraceptive use and reduced unwanted births.[61]

—Clinics are increasingly located in schools. School-based clinics provide a broad range of health services in addition to family planning; only a few dispense birth control information or devices. A recent evaluation of these programs has raised doubts about their effectiveness.[62]

—Life options programs are designed to provide disadvantaged teenagers with counseling, decisionmaking skills, educational opportunities, job training, employment, or other services to give them a greater stake in their futures and motivate them to defer having children. The programs vary widely, but they tend to be much more expensive than family planning clinics and have not consistently reduced the incidence of early childbearing.[63]

What stands out is that contraceptive services reduce unintended pregnancies and are cost effective. School-based clinics cost about $125 a person a year; contraceptive services perhaps $75 for clinic visits and

Herendeed, *Teen Pregnancy Programs: What Have We Learned? Meeting Highlights and Background Briefing Report* (Washington: Family Impact Seminar, May 26, 1989), p. i.

60. Douglas Kirby and others, "Reducing the Risk: Impact of a New Curriculum on Sexual Risk Taking," *Family Planning Perspectives*, vol. 23 (November–December 1991), pp. 253–63.

61. Sandra L. Hofferth, "The Effects of Programs and Policies on Adolescent Pregnancy and Childbearing," in Hofferth and Hayes, eds., *Risking the Future*, vol. 2, p. 218.

62. An evaluation of six school-based programs found no increases in sexual activity and no significant reductions in pregnancy or births among sexually active students in schools with clinics compared to those without them. However, this finding could be the result of the placement of most clinics in high-risk neighborhoods. See Douglas Kirby and Cynthia S. Waszak, "An Assessment of Six School-Based Clinics: Services, Impact and Potential," Center for Population Options, Washington, 1989.

63. This review of the literature draws on Cheryl D. Hayes, ed., *Risking the Future*, vol. 1; Hofferth and Hayes, eds., *Risking the Future*, vol. 2; Janet B. Hardy and Laurie Schwab Zabin, eds., *Adolescent Pregnancy in an Urban Environment: Issues, Programs, and Evaluation* (Baltimore: Urban and Schwarzenberg, 1991); Ooms and Herendeen, *Teen Pregnancy Programs*; and Sandy L. Hofferth, "Programs for High Risk Adolescents: What Works?" *Evaluation and Program Planning*, vol. 14 (1991), pp. 3–16.

Never see of the teen father mentioning of the responsibility

prescriptions. On average, a family begun by a woman aged 15 to 17 is estimated to cost the public $21,000 during the first twenty years of her child's life. If half these costs could be saved by encouraging adolescents to delay childbearing and complete their schooling, and if only 1 out of every 100 teenagers served did avoid childbearing, the investment would still be reasonable for taxpayers.[64]

There are a number of different sources of funding for family planning services: medicaid, the Maternal and Child Health and Social Services block grants, title X of the Public Health Service Act, and state sources. During the past decade, despite increases in the number of women at risk for an unwanted pregnancy, real public expenditures for family planning services dropped by one-third.[65] In light of this, a one-third increase by fiscal 1997, or about $200 million in additional funds, would be a reasonable goal.

The potential of contraception to reduce teenage childbearing is illustrated by the experience of Western European nations, where sexual conduct is more openly discussed and contraceptives are more readily available. Adolescents in these countries are no less sexually active than U.S. adolescents, but both abortion and birthrates are much lower, primarily as the result of more successful contraceptive practices. If sexually active American teenagers were as successful as those in the Netherlands at avoiding pregnancy, 87 percent of current abortions and a similar proportion of teenage births in the United States could be avoided.[66]

In the meantime, half of all pregnancies among U.S. adolescents are terminated by abortion. After climbing in the 1970s, the proportion has declined slightly since 1980, perhaps because of the increasingly restrictive climate for abortion in recent years.[67] Only thirteen states and the District

---

64. At $100 a teenager, it costs $100 million to serve 1 million. But if the program is successful only in 1 out of 100 cases, it can still delay childbearing for 10,000 teenagers and save more than $100 million (10,000 x $21,000 ÷ 2). Cost estimates from Hayes, ed., *Risking the Future*, vol. 1, pp. 160, 186; and *1991 Green Book*, p. 975.

65. Rachel Gold and Daniel Daley, "Public Funding of Contraceptive, Sterilization, and Abortion Services, 1990," *Family Planning Perspectives*, vol. 23 (September–October 1991), pp. 204–12.

66. *1991 Green Book*, p. 965; and Isabel V. Sawhill, "Where Have All the Fathers Gone?" *Policy Bites*, no. 2 (August 1990).

67. Stanley K. Henshaw, "Abortion Trends in 1987 and 1988: Age and Race," *Family Planning Perspectives*, vol. 24 (March–April 1992), pp. 85–86. For evidence that, after controlling for other factors, states or counties with more restrictive abortion policies have a substantially higher rate of births to unwed mothers, see Shelly Lundberg and Robert D. Plotnick, "Effect of State Welfare, Abortion, and Family Planning Policies on Premarital

of Columbia currently fund abortions for poor women and, under regulations proposed by the Reagan administration and upheld by the Supreme Court, clinics receiving federal funds are prohibited from providing information or counseling on abortion. A nationwide ban on the availability of abortions would produce 75,000 more births to teenagers and cost an extra $500 million a year in income assistance for such families.[68] More likely is a partial ban with wide variations among states. The youngest and poorest women would bear the brunt of these restrictions because they are the least likely to be able to pay for an abortion or travel to a state with less restrictive policies.

For those who are opposed to abortion, adoption is an important alternative. However, the number of women choosing to put babies up for adoption has decreased since the 1950s because of the legalization of abortion, attempts to keep pregnant adolescents in school, and a reduction in the stigma associated with out-of-wedlock births. Less than 4 percent of the babies of unwed adolescents are put up for adoption, and those are disproportionately from white, affluent families.[69] Black teenagers rarely use adoption, perhaps because of the black community's greater acceptance of childbearing at a young age and the lack of black adoptive homes.

Programs funded by the Office of Adolescent Pregnancy Programs are required to mention adoption in counseling adolescents, and numerous public and private agencies handle adoptions (although there is a shortage of residential centers for pregnant teenagers planning to relinquish their children).[70] Thus it is not so much that alternatives to abortion are lacking as that young women are disinclined to use them.

Educating and Supporting Parents

Even if every child were wanted and were born to mature parents, some children would still receive inadequate care. Being a good parent is a challenge, made more difficult perhaps by the loss of informal sources

Childbearing among White Adolescents," *Family Planning Perspectives*, vol. 22 (November–December 1990), pp. 246–51; and Hofferth, "Programs for High Risk Adolescents."

68. Estimates derived from data in Theodore J. Joyce and Naci H. Mocan, "The Impact of Legalized Abortion on Adolescent Childbearing in New York City," *American Journal of Public Health*, vol. 80 (March 1990), pp. 273–78.

69. Brenda W. Donnelly and Patricia Voydanoff, "Factors Associated with Releasing for Adoption among Adolescent Mothers," *Family Relations*, vol. 40 (October 1991), p. 404; and *Facts at a Glance* (Washington: Child Trends, November 1988).

70. Donnelly and Vodyanoff, "Factors Associated with Releasing for Adoption."

of information and support from relatives and neighbors. Can good parenting be taught or otherwise fostered by efforts to support families?

Parent education programs have a long history. Some have focused on middle-class or well-educated families, others on groups with special needs. During the 1960s parent education was optimistically endorsed as a way of breaking the cycle of poverty in high-risk families. More recently, it has been implemented for all families through the public school system in Missouri and Minnesota. Parent education has also become a key element in family support programs, which focus on the whole family and the need to provide services, including parent education, health screening, child care, and referral to other services tailored to the needs and cultural diversity of particular low-income families. Kentucky, Maryland, and Connecticut have developed comprehensive family resource and support programs, and many smaller programs have sprung up in other states. Although the federal government is currently conducting a demonstration and evaluation of these more comprehensive approaches, to date there is considerable enthusiasm but little hard evidence of their effectiveness.

Some smaller projects have been carefully evaluated. One program from the mid-1960s, the Parent Child Development Centers, served low-income families with children younger than age 3. At the end of three years, mothers were interacting more positively with their children, and children had gained in cognitive, language, and other skills relative to those in a control group. Similarly, a home visitation program in Elmira, New York, and Project Redirection, a comprehensive service program for disadvantaged teenagers, have reported an improvement in parenting skills among participating mothers compared with those in a control group.[71] Although the research base in this area is thin, such efforts are a promising way to prevent damage to young children in high-risk environments.

Collecting Child Support

The dramatic rise in both divorce and out-of-wedlock childbearing along with rising welfare costs has focused attention on the need to

71. Paul R. Dokecki, Erwin C. Hargrove, and Howard M. Sandler, "An Overview of the Parent Child Development Center Social Experiment," in Ron Haskins and Diane Adams, eds., *Parent Education and Public Policy* (Norwood, N.J.: ABLEX Publishing, 1983), pp. 80, 98; David L. Olds and others, "Preventing Child Abuse and Neglect: A Randomized Trial of Nurse Home Visitation," *Pediatrics*, vol. 78, no. 1 (1986), pp. 65–

collect more financial support from absent parents. The hope is that responsibility for supporting children will be returned to parents, thereby saving welfare costs and possibly discouraging childbearing among those unwilling to make a long-term commitment to their biological offspring.

Current levels of support are very low. Only 37 percent of families with a mother but an absent father received any child support in 1989; the average amount was $3,386.[72] Moreover, the level of assistance has varied little in the past decade. Total child support received in 1989 was $12.7 billion, 69 percent of the amount legally due. Thus perfect enforcement of current awards would produce an additional $5.8 billion. However, many women do not have awards at all, and the awards that do exist are generally a small proportion of the father's income. If child support awards were obtained in every case, established at the standard prevailing in Wisconsin or Colorado, updated annually, and paid in full, an additional $29 billion to $36 billion in collections would be available nationwide.[73] These figures are of course hypothetical, but they suggest the potential that exists.

The gap between actual and potential child support has led to many efforts in recent years to strengthen child support enforcement, starting with legislation in 1975 and culminating in the Family Support Act of 1988, which requires that states make greater efforts to identify both parents at birth, that they normally use a state-developed formula or guideline to set awards, and that all new awards be collected through automatic wage withholding beginning in 1994.

One reason that the trends in expected child support payments have not been more favorable in the face of greater enforcement efforts is that the proportion of all single mothers who have never been married increased from 19 to 30 percent between 1978 and 1989, and it has been particularly hard to establish awards for them.[74] If paternity can be established in more cases and child support awards enforced, younger men might behave more responsibly.

78; and Denise F. Polit, "Effects of a Comprehensive Program for Teenage Parents: Five Years after Project Redirection," *Family Planning Perspectives*, vol. 21 (July–August 1989), pp. 164–69.

72. Bureau of the Census, "Child Support and Alimony: 1989," *Current Population Reports*, series P-60, no. 173 (Department of Commerce, 1991), pp. 7, 15.

73. Donald T. Oellerich, Irwin Garfinkel, and Philip K. Robins, "Private Child Support: Current and Potential Impacts," IRP discussion paper 888-89 (University of Wisconsin, Institute for Research on Poverty, August 1989).

74. *Current Population Reports*, series P-60, no. 173.

Concern about deterioration in men's sense of family responsibility has led to proposals to further strengthen child support by federalizing the system and using the IRS to make collections of child support as automatic as taxes. Another proposal would require mothers to cooperate with the authorities in locating fathers and establishing awards, but in return they would be assured a publicly provided minimum benefit if the father had insufficient income to support his children. Proponents believe the assured benefit, in combination with a mother's earnings from a job and the earned income tax credit, would help reduce poverty and welfare dependency among single parents and their children. Opponents, however, see the proposal as welfare by another name. If personal responsibility is to be emphasized, it would be a mistake to offer an assured benefit before a much more adequate system for establishing and collecting awards is in place. The overriding objective should be to return financial responsibility for children to parents, not to further socialize their costs. If this goal can be accomplished, there may be some merit in further supplementing the incomes of parents who have little ability to support their children. Whether this is best accomplished through child support assurance, an earned income tax credit (available to absent fathers as well as mothers), or other means will remain a matter of debate, but once again an expanded EITC has much to recommend it.

Linking Welfare Benefits to Responsible Family Behaviors

Concern about the growth of single-parent families has produced a flurry of interest in modifying the welfare system at the state level in ways that would reward marriage and discourage childbearing. For example, a New Jersey law denies additional benefits to mothers who have children while on welfare but, under certain conditions, allows a woman to remain on welfare after marrying. Similar proposals have been made in California and Wisconsin. The federal government is encouraging state experimentation with the welfare system and plans to provide waivers to make this possible if the proposals are budget-neutral and the experiments rigorously evaluated.

Research suggests that welfare benefit levels have not had much impact on marriage or childbearing rates. However, the only good evidence available is from the income maintenance experiments of the 1970s, which found that extending benefits to two-parent families does not stabilize families.[75] The effects on childbearing are also likely to be limited. Even if the cap on benefits for additional children were to change behavior, it would probably affect only the one-third of AFDC children who are actually born on welfare.[76]

In sum, these experiments are not likely to produce the hoped-for effects, and they could produce hardship for some current welfare recipients. They are also likely to divert state attention from implementing the Family Support Act of 1988, designed to move welfare mothers toward economic self-sufficiency. At the same time, given the dramatic increases in children born out of wedlock and the high proportion that are poor, further experimentation with the existing welfare system as a device for learning more about the problem would not be unreasonable.

Conclusions

This chapter has considered three approaches to improving children's lives. The first, providing additional income to families with children, assumes that society places numerous stresses on parents, many of which are made worse by lack of income. These stresses are most severe for low-income families, and tax relief for them—desirable on grounds of equity alone—has a better chance than nontargeted assistance of improving children's lives. Broader tax relief for middle- and upper-income families with children is not a good investment. These same funds would be better devoted to some combination of deficit reduction and an expansion of effective programs for children.

The second strategy, expanding service programs for children, assumes that there are programs with a demonstrated capacity to make a difference in the lives of children and that these programs compensate for some well-known deficiencies in family functioning. Expanding a few programs carefully would be a good use of currently scarce resources. It would represent an investment in the future with a rate of return that is, from

75. Glen G. Cain and Douglas A. Wissoker, "A Reanalysis of Marital Stability in the Seattle-Denver Income Maintenance Experiment," IRP discussion paper 857-88 (University of Wisconsin, Institute for Research on Poverty, January 1988); General Accounting Office, *Welfare Reform: Projected Effects of Requiring AFDC for Unemployed Parents Nationwide*, HRD 88-88BR (May 1988); and General Accounting Office, *Unemployed Parents: An Evaluation of the Effects of Welfare Benefits on Family Stability*, PEMD-92-19BR (April 1992).

76. This is a preliminary unofficial estimate from the Congressional Budget Office.

everything we know, more than competitive with alternative uses of the same funds.

The third strategy, encouraging parental responsibility, assumes that parents who are fully and competently involved in raising their children are the most essential element in producing better lives for children. Although many single parents are doing an excellent job, much of the increased poverty among children and the other adverse effects they endure is directly related to the growth of single-parent families. Regardless of family type, what may be most significant in the lives of children is a growing inequality of prospects related to their family circumstances. The problem is that no one knows how to fix the family. Reducing early out-of-wedlock childbearing, educating parents and potential parents, enforcing their financial responsibilities, and making sure that government policies are consistent with the goal of parental responsibility are useful steps but will only work if there is a more general commitment to the task.

RICHARD J. MURNANE
AND FRANK LEVY

6

Education and Training

FOR MOST PEOPLE, a healthy economy is one that produces rising living standards and mass upward mobility.[1] From this perspective, the U.S. economy is ill. Average earnings are growing very slowly, a problem America has had since 1973, and earnings inequality has grown rapidly since the late 1970s.[2] Improved schools and better worker training are part, but only part, of the solution to these problems.

Slow earnings growth means little economic progress across generations.[3] In the twenty-five years between 1948 and 1973, the average earnings of 40-year-old men who worked full time almost doubled, from $18,910 to $35,500.[4] In the succeeding thirteen years, the average earnings of 40-year-old men working full time fell 4 percent, to $33,971 in 1989 (all comparisons are in 1990 dollars).[5]

The increase in inequality appears most sharply in growing earnings differences among young workers with different amounts of education (table 6-1). Young male high school graduates working full time earn about 15 percent less today than their counterparts a decade ago. Young college graduates earn 7 percent more. The earnings gap between high

John H. Bishop was the discussant for this chapter. We would like to thank the Spencer Foundation and the Consortium for Policy Research in Education for support of the research upon which this chapter is based. We also appreciate the comments many colleagues provided on earlier versions.

1. By mass upward mobility we mean that families see significant economic progress in their lifetime and can reasonably expect that their children will live better than they did.

2. By the late 1980s, however, the rate of increase in inequality appears to have leveled off.

3. Slow growth also limits the gains any single worker sees in his or her own life.

4. In census terminology, these figures represent the median individual income of men who work year-round and full time.

5. Similar statistics for older men and for most women would have shown modest growth; statistics for younger men would have shown a slightly sharper decline. Some of the poor performance of money income can be explained by the growth of fringe benefits. With an adjustment for these, earnings for men aged 35 to 44 would have grown by 2 percent a decade instead of the earlier 15 to 20 percent.

TABLE 6-1. Individual Earnings of Year-Round Full-Time Workers
Aged 25 to 34, by Selected Levels of Education, 1979–89
Constant 1990 dollars

Workers and years of education	1979	1989	Percent change
Men			
12 years	26,947	22,979	−14.7
16 years	30,506	32,965	7.3
Women			
12 years	15,774	16,029	1.6
16 years	22,289	25,046	12.3

SOURCES: Authors' tabulations from Bureau of the Census, Current Population Survey demographic file for 1979;
and Current Population Reports for 1989.

school and college graduates has opened from 13 percent to 43 percent.
Among younger women, high school graduates working full time earn
about what their counterparts did ten years ago. Their high school–
college earnings gap has also expanded, from 41 percent to 56 percent.

Earnings growth slowed because labor productivity has grown slug-
gishly. From 1973 to 1979, growth in labor productivity averaged an
anemic 0.9 percent a year, less than one-half its previous long-run average.
From 1980 to 1990, productivity growth revived slightly to an average of
1.2 percent a year.[6] In the 1970s, productivity slowed in all sectors of the
economy. In the 1980s, it grew rapidly in manufacturing but not at all in
services. Productivity in mining and construction decreased.[7]

During the 1970s, the impact of stagnant productivity was largely confined to the domestic economy. The problems usually associated with
globalization—large trade deficits, heavy import competition, loss of manufacturing jobs—did not appear. Although stagnant productivity weakened American competitiveness, the United States compensated by permitting the exchange value of the dollar to fall. The cheaper dollar meant that
U.S. producers could sell their products abroad at ever-lower prices even

6. Economic Report of the President, February 1992, table B-44. One can reasonably
ask why wages were stagnant when productivity was rising, albeit slowly. A partial answer
is that consumer prices (used to adjust wages for inflation) were rising more quickly than
the general price level (used to adjust GNP for inflation and to produce estimates of labor
productivity).

7. One can point to a variety of causes of the productivity slowdown—weak labor force
skills, of course, but also myopic management and scarce capital. Although these factors
may depress long-run productivity growth, each changes gradually, so they are unlikely to
have caused a sudden slowdown. It is important to note that other industrialized countries
experienced sharp productivity slowdowns (from higher initial levels) at the same time.

though they were not making substantial efficiency gains.[8] The result was a continually balanced trade position with the rest of the world.

During the first half of the 1980s, the process was reversed. A fall in private saving and a rise in the budget deficit drove up interest rates and caused the exchange value of the dollar to increase. U.S. exports became more expensive and foreign imports cheaper, and the weak competitive position of U.S. firms was exposed. As the decade progressed, the dollar's value began to fall again, but American firms continued to be under pressure for many reasons. An important one was the large increase in the ratio of debt to equity among many firms, exacerbated by a wave of leveraged buyouts. This pushed managers to lower costs simply to meet much higher interest charges.

Firms responded to these pressures to cut costs in a number of ways. One common method of adjustment was to cut costs while retaining the same technology and organization of work. Companies demanded wage and benefit concessions from workers, speeded up production lines, and transferred production to countries where wages were lower. The resulting reduction in the number of semiskilled jobs was partly responsible for the falling incomes of younger male high school graduates.[9] But this response did not change the skill requirements for workers who did retain their jobs.

A second possible response was to introduce new technology of a kind that reduced the number of workers needed and permitted the substitution of relatively unskilled labor for relatively high-priced skilled labor. When successful, this strategy reduced skill requirements and, again, reduced wages.[10]

A different and, we believe, much rarer response was to invest heavily in improving product quality and to reduce costs by redesigning production processes. This strategy often includes redesigning jobs so that workers undertake a variety of tasks, sometimes in teams, instead

8. The cheaper dollar also made foreign imports to the United States increasingly expensive, which also helped domestic producers by reducing import competition.

9. There were other factors involved, including a surge in the supply of such men. For a full discussion, see Frank Levy and Richard J. Murnane, "U.S. Earnings Levels and Earnings Inequality: A Review of Recent Trends and Proposed Explanations," *Journal of Economic Literature* (September 1992), forthcoming.

10. There are differing evaluations of the effectiveness of this strategy. For a sample of contrasting views, see Paul Adler, "New Technologies, New Skills," *California Management Review*, vol. 29 (Fall 1986), pp. 9–28; and Henry M. Levin, Russell Rumberger, and Christine Finnan, "Escalating Skill Requirements or Different Skill Requirements?" paper prepared for a June 1990 conference on changing occupational skills held at Brown University.

of carrying out one narrowly defined task. This response, which is difficult to carry out successfully, requires increased worker skills and training, and the companies that have chosen this strategy have paid the relatively high wages needed to attract and retain workers with the requisite abilities (including the ability to learn new skills).

All three responses raised manufacturing productivity, but only the third increased earnings for most employees. Why haven't more firms adopted this option? The investments required are typically large and immediate, while gains accrue only in the long term. Giving more discretion to line workers may encounter resistance from supervisors whose status is reduced. Despite these and other obstacles, adopting high skill–high wage technologies must be one important means to a better economic future.[11]

This strategy can be used only if new labor force entrants can analyze information and make thoughtful decisions. But it also requires good management and capital. Improved education alone may simply produce large numbers of underemployed, disaffected people. Similarly, it makes little sense to talk about better training for workers without talking about better management. Unless management sees the need to upgrade workers' skills, training simply will not take place. But unless able workers are available, adopting new technology will be excessively costly, even with good management. It is this fact that is the principal link between schools, training, and America's economic future.

Improving education involves restructuring of its own: changes in the organization of schools and the incentives offered students and educators to excel. In fact, the task of restructuring companies and that of restructuring schools share many features. For both, restructuring takes time and involves risk. Ideas that look good on paper usually do not work the first time; but with persistence and adaptation, practices may be found that produce the improvements needed.

The analogy between businesses and schools is not perfect. Because companies generally have equal access to raw materials, the quality of their output provides a good measure of their production skills. But different schools serve students with widely differing nutrition and

11. Our discussion to this point has focused on manufacturing, but anecdotal evidence suggests the current recession is also putting similar pressure for restructuring on parts of the service sector. Here, too, different companies have responded in different ways, some of which raise skill requirements while others do not. For a discussion of these responses, see National Center on Education and the Economy, *America's Choice: High Skills or Low Wages* (Rochester, N.Y., 1990).

health levels and preparation for learning, characteristics that affect achievement. Student achievement thus reflects differences in student backgrounds as well as in the effectiveness of schools.

Another difference between schools and businesses concerns equity. Our society accepts that affluent families are better fed and housed and have more consumer goods than poor families. But almost every state constitution guarantees every child access to good schooling. This means that the educational system must be judged by how well it serves all children, not just those from affluent families. These equity concerns do not reduce the imperative of finding ways to improve the quality of American education, but they do complicate the design of ways to ensure accountability for educational reform.

Preparing Youth for Productive Work Lives

Four problems are often cited as evidence that American students are poorly prepared for productive work in the economy. Too many students leave high school before graduating. Many do poorly in the transition from school to work. Many have difficulty reading. And many lack mathematics and science skills. How significant are these problems?

High Student Dropout Rate

One-quarter of American young people leave school without a high school diploma.[12] Among young Latinos, the most rapidly growing group in the American student population, the dropout rate is especially high: roughly two out of five leave school without a diploma.[13] Although school dropouts have always fared less well in the labor force than have workers with more education, changes in the economy have especially limited the opportunities of male dropouts. Earnings for male high school graduates aged 24 to 34 fell by 20 percent from 1971 to 1987, but earnings of dropouts fell by 30 percent, leaving most of them unable to support a family.[14] Moreover, most dropouts are excluded from attending college, increasingly the path to a middle-class job.

12. Chester E. Finn, Jr., "The High School Dropout Puzzle," *Public Interest*, no. 87 (Spring 1987), p. 5.

13. National Council of La Raza, *Hispanic Education: A Statistical Portrait 1990* (Washington, October 1990), p. 36.

14. Author's tabulations from Bureau of the Census, Current Population Survey, March demographic files. For a discussion of alternative methods of computing dropout rates, see National Center for Education Statistics, *Dropout Rates in the United States: 1989*, NCES 90-659 (Department of Education, September 1990).

Half of all dropouts—more than 500,000 a year—do eventually earn a high school equivalency diploma by passing the General Educational Development (GED) test, which is used in all fifty states.[15] No one would dispute the importance of providing dropouts with a second chance, but for men at least, holders of the GED fare no better in the labor market than dropouts who do not earn one.[16] The evidence is somewhat more encouraging for female holders of GED credentials, but they still earn considerably less than high school graduates.[17]

Finding ways to motivate students to stay in school is a critical challenge facing the educational system. At the same time, it is a mistake to view the dropout rate solely as an indicator of the quality of American education. Rather the rate reflects to a large extent the structure of economic opportunities in the country, because youth from low-income families are particularly at risk of dropping out.[18]

The Transition from School to Work

In every society young people change jobs more often than older workers do and experience more unemployment. In part these patterns reflect voluntary behavior as young people try out different jobs. In the United States, however, the period of job instability for many is protracted and extends to the years when family responsibilities demand stable employment. In 1988 more than one-third of men aged 29 to 31 had held their jobs less than one year. In contrast, less than 10 percent of men aged 29 to 31 in Germany in 1985 had held theirs for less than one year.[19]

15. Authors' estimate based on Finn, "High School Dropout Puzzle," p. 8.

16. Stephen V. Cameron and James J. Heckman, "The Nonequivalence of High School Equivalents" (University of Chicago, Department of Economics, June 1991).

17. See Timothy Maloney, "Estimating the Returns to a Secondary Education for Female Dropouts," discussion paper 737-91 (University of Wisconsin, Institute for Research on Poverty, February 1991). Another dropout pattern is that the proportion of black youth aged 16 to 24 who hold a high school diploma or a GED has increased from 73 percent in 1969 to 86 percent in 1989. Although this undoubtedly reflects progress, the significance of the change for their earnings potential depends on how much of the change reflects an increase in the proportion of black youth who graduate from high school. Until 1988, the Current Population Survey did not distinguish conventional high school diplomas from alternative credentials.

18. Sara S. McLanahan, "Family Structure and the Reproduction of Poverty," *American Journal of Sociology*, vol. 90 (January 1985), pp. 873–901.

19. Paul Osterman, "Is There a Problem with the Youth Labor Market and If So How Should We Fix It?" (Massachusetts Institute of Technology, Sloan School of Management, July 1991), pp. 10–12.

Employment instability is costly. Male high school graduates aged 29 to 31 who held the same job for three years or more earned an average hourly wage of $11.15 versus $6.68 for those who had held their jobs for less than one year. Among the reasons for the differential is that workers with short spells of employment often get less training from their employers than do long-term workers, and workers with more training tend to be paid higher wages.[20]

Young people from minority groups experience particular difficulty in finding employment. Just 29 percent of black high school dropouts aged 16 to 24 who were not enrolled in school were employed in 1990, compared with 57 percent of white dropouts. For high school graduates not enrolled in school, 56 percent of blacks and 79 percent of whites held jobs.[21]

Thus while young people in every society have difficulty in making the transition from school to stable employment, the problem seems particularly severe in the United States, especially for minority group members and high school dropouts.[22]

Inadequate Literacy

The National Assessment of Educational Progress has claimed that 30 percent of adolescents and young adults in the United States lack basic literacy skills, including the ability to use reading to collect information from different parts of a document to make sense of an unfamiliar task.[23]

Case studies suggest that to an increasing extent poor literacy skills hamper labor market entrants in finding and holding jobs that pay enough to support a family. Thomas Bailey, for example, reports that textile companies formerly recruited mechanics from the ranks of machine operators, who usually had little education. Informal on-the-job training

20. Osterman, "Is There a Problem," p. 11. Another reason that length of time on a job is positively related to wages is that the least able workers experience the greatest difficulty in obtaining a stable job. See Lori G. Kletzer, "Returns to Seniority after Permanent Job Loss," *American Economic Review*, vol. 79 (June 1989), pp. 536–43.

21. Osterman, "Is There a Problem," p. 51.

22. Although the youth employment record of the United States is much poorer than the records of Germany and Japan, the United States is not the only country where young people have difficulty finding employment. For example, the youth unemployment rate during the 1980s was very high in the United Kingdom.

23. Richard L. Venezky, Carl F. Kaestle, and Andrew M. Sum, *The Subtle Danger: Reflections on the Literacy Abilities of America's Young Adults* (Princeton: Educational Testing Service, 1987), p. 22.

was adequate to teach them the skills they needed. But in recent years the companies have introduced looms with microprocessors and other electronic components. Repairing these machines requires that mechanics follow complicated manuals and updates provided by manufacturers, and literacy skills are much more important in making repairs.[24] Our own case studies of firms in the insurance and automobile industries support Bailey's finding that literacy skills are increasingly important in securing jobs that pay enough to support a family.[25]

Weak Performance in Mathematics and Science

American students score much lower than students in most other industrialized countries on comparable tests of mathematics and science knowledge. Although differences in the composition of the test-taking sample in each country explain some of the variation, American children have mastered less of the science and mathematics measured on the tests than students in other countries have.[26]

Comparisons of test scores from various countries are not the only evidence that many American students leave high school without adequate mathematical problem-solving skills and knowledge of science. The 1990 National Assessment of Educational Progress (NAEP) reported that only 56 percent of American 17-year-olds "can compute with decimals, fractions, and percents; recognize geometric figures; solve simple equations; and use moderately complex reasoning."[27] Only 43 percent of 17-year-olds have "some detailed scientific knowledge and can evaluate the appropriateness of scientific procedures."

Why do American students do so poorly? Recent analysis suggests that differences in the amount of time devoted to mathematics instruction

---

24. Thomas Bailey, "Education and the Transformation of Markets and Technology in the Textile Industry," technical paper 2 (Columbia University, Conservation of Human Resources, April 1988).

25. We are not arguing that literacy skills are increasingly important in obtaining a job irrespective of wage level. During the 1980s the American economy generated a large number of jobs, especially in service industries, that required few skills. These jobs paid very low wages, however.

26. For informative discussions of the difficulties in making reliable inferences from cross-national comparisons of achievement, see Elliot A. Medrich and Jeanne E. Griffith, *International Mathematics and Science Assessments: What Have We Learned?* (National Center for Education Statistics, January 1992); and Iris C. Rotberg, "I Never Promised You First Place," *Phi Delta Kappan*, vol. 72 (December 1990), pp. 296–304.

27. Ina V. S. Mullis and others, *Trends in Academic Progress* (Department of Education, November 1991), p. 456.

and the time students spend on homework and other school practices explain less of the variation in average test scores across countries than do the percentage of families living in poverty, the percentage living in female-headed families, and other home circumstances.[28] The NAEP data also illustrate the link between socioeconomic status and test scores. Black and Latino students score lower than white students on average, and children whose parents went to college score higher than children whose parents did not.

The low test scores of U.S. children and the very low scores of children from minority groups reflect, in part, the courses they take. A recent study compared the mathematics achievement test scores of Japanese and American eighth graders. Japanese students, all of whom study algebra by the eighth grade, scored considerably higher than American students. But many of the American eighth graders had not taken algebra, and those who did scored as well as their Japanese counterparts. This suggests that test score differences both among and within countries reflect not only a student's circumstances—for example, whether he or she lives with both parents—but also how much the student is expected to learn and what the student is taught.[29] Improving the circumstances of disadvantaged children and providing all students with a challenging curriculum may be critical to increasing the science and mathematics knowledge of American children.[30]

How crucial to productivity and earnings is it that all American labor force entrants, high school graduates as well as college students, learn mathematics and science? We do not know. Some evidence suggests that scores on tests of mathematics are positively related to effectiveness in carrying out a wide range of jobs and that proficiency in applying arithmetic to practical problems is positively related to the probability that people will be fully employed.[31] The reason may be that ability to

28. Richard M. Jaeger, "'World Class' Standards, Choice, and Privatization: Weak Measurement Serving Presumptive Policy," paper prepared for the 1992 annual meeting of the American Educational Research Association.

29. Ian Westbury, "Comparing American and Japanese Achievement: Is the United States Really a Low Achiever?" *Educational Researcher*, vol. 12 (June–July 1992), pp. 18–24. This study attempts to control for differences in student ability in making these comparisons.

30. For an informative discussion of other differences between countries that affect educational performance, see David K. Cohen and James P. Spillane, "Policy and Practice: The Relations between Governance and Instruction," *Review of Research in Education*, vol. 18 (1992), pp. 3–49.

31. John H. Bishop, "A Strategy for Achieving Excellence in Secondary Education: The Role of State Government," paper presented at the 1991 Council of Chief State School

solve mathematical problems is a good indicator of ability to follow directions, a critical skill in many jobs.

No comparable evidence shows that knowledge of science is strongly related to job performance for Americans not working in scientific fields. The case for giving science prominence in a required curriculum for all students must rest on other grounds.[32] Two arguments seem compelling. First, lack of preparation in science denies students access to well-paying technical careers.[33] Second, instruction in hands-on science, not just learning facts, may expand job opportunities for students in companies using advanced managerial practices. The skills learned would include the ability to work in teams, identify problems, collect evidence, and draw conclusions.[34] Unfortunately, hands-on science instruction is not the norm in many American schools.[35]

Improving American Education

The history of educational reform efforts in the United States is replete with dropout-prevention programs and compensatory education programs to improve reading and mathematics skills. Typically these programs have had little effect on what teachers and students do in their classrooms and on what parents expect their children to accomplish.[36]

Officers Summer Institute, Okoboji, Iowa, figs. 3–6; and Francisco L. Rivera-Batiz, "Quantitative Literacy and the Likelihood of Employment among Young Adults in the United States," *Journal of Human Resources*, vol. 27 (Spring 1992), pp. 313–28.

32. See American Association for the Advancement of Science, *Science for All Americans: A Project 2061 Report on Literacy Goals in Science, Mathematics, and Technology* (Washington, 1988).

33. For information on salaries paid to recent college graduates with various undergraduate majors, see College Placement Council, *College Placement Council—Salary Survey* (Bethlehem, Pa., various issues). Among 1991 college graduates, students with a bachelor's degree in engineering or computer science received salary offers of $30,000–$35,000 compared with $20,000–$23,000 for students with a general liberal arts degree.

34. Kazuo Koike, *Understanding Industrial Relations in Modern Japan* (St. Martin's Press, 1988).

35. Data collected in surveys by the Research Triangle Institute and the National Assessment of Educational Progress show that science teaching relies heavily on lectures and textbooks and devotes little time to hands-on work that involves students in investigation and problem solving. See Iris R. Weiss, *Report of the 1985–86 National Survey of Science and Mathematics Education* (Research Triangle Park, N.C.: Research Triangle Institute, 1987); and Lee R. Jones and others, *The 1990 Science Report Card: NAEP's Assessment of Fourth, Eighth, and Twelfth Graders* (Washington: National Center for Education Statistics, 1992).

36. Edward Pauly, *The Classroom Crucible* (Basic Books, 1991), chap. 6.

This is not coincidental; governments find it much easier to raise budgets than to change the core instructional program.[37] Yet precisely because these programs do not change what students and teachers do every day, they have had little effect on student achievement and school completion.

Two new strategies for improving American education go beyond "more of the same." The first tries to change the way teachers and students in individual schools interact. The second tries to reform the system, the rules under which schools operate.

School-Based Reforms

In recent years school reformers such as James Comer, Henry Levin, Theodore Sizer, and Robert Slavin have developed principles to improve the education offered to American children, especially disadvantaged children. Each has formed partnerships with the faculties of specific schools to change the way teachers interact with each other and with students.[38] One shared principle is the belief that every student can achieve a great deal in school and that the expectation of significant accomplishment along with the support needed for success must be a part of every student's school experience. A second principle is that teaching is so complex and involves such intense interactions with students that all teachers will encounter problems. Support must be provided, whether in the form of tutors, a mental health team, or collaborations with other teachers. A final principle is that no single blueprint for change will work everywhere. Each participating school, guided by general principles and aided by an outside reform team, must work out its goals and a plan for achieving them that fits the strengths and priorities of its faculty and the needs of its students. Because these differ from school to school, reform programs in individual schools will differ widely. Moreover, the reforms will evolve as faculty and students experiment, drop what does not work, and build on promising practices.

Despite the lack of rigorous evaluations verifying their effectiveness, school-based reform efforts are appealing because they attempt to improve the quality of the daily school experience of all children attending a particular school, especially children from poor families. Indeed, many

37. For an informative discussion of government attempts to change what happens in school classrooms, see Richard F. Elmore and Milbrey W. McLaughlin, *Steady Work: Policy, Practice and The Reform of American Education* (Santa Monica: RAND Corp., 1988).

38. These partnerships have expanded to include school districts and, in Sizer's case, states.

of the initiatives are taking place in schools serving high concentrations of such children. For this reason, government policies to bring about systemic reform should support school-based reforms.

Systemic Reforms

Many state and federal policymakers have embraced systemic reform to accelerate changes in the quality of education provided in all schools. Most visions of systemic reform combine six elements: creating standards, improving incentives, strengthening connections between school and work, increasing accountability, building capacity, and "leveling the playing field."[39]

Creating standards. A lack of clarity about what American children should learn hampers educational reform efforts. Without clear standards for what children should know, parents find it difficult to evaluate the quality of education their children are receiving. Students moving from one school district to another or even from one school to another in the same district experience different curricular emphases. Teacher training institutions receive little guidance about the types of instruction aspiring teachers should master. Staff development efforts lack clear goals toward which teachers should strive. Textbook publishers, lacking guidance about learning goals, find it most profitable to develop texts that are consistent with current teaching practices. The desire to change these situations provides the impetus for developing a set of national standards describing the skills and knowledge American children at each grade level should possess.

The most tangible product of the effort to set such standards is *Curriculum and Evaluation Standards for School Mathematics*, produced by the National Council of Teachers of Mathematics (NCTM). This effort is notable because it demonstrates the possibility of agreement on specific standards. The NCTM project also demonstrates how great an effort is required to gain agreement on standards: it took eight years to complete, in large part because of extensive consultations with interest groups and many rounds of professional review. But consultation and review were wise practices; they appear to account for the warm reception the mathematics standards have received. Developing meaningful standards, a critical part of systemic reform, must therefore be expected to

39. Marshall S. Smith and Jennifer O'Day, "Systematic School Reform," in Susan H. Fuhrman and Betty Malen, eds., *The Politics of Curriculum and Testing* (New York: Falmer, 1991), pp. 233–67.

take years of sustained effort. Efforts are now under way to develop standards in geography, history, science, English, and work readiness.[40]

Setting standards also requires creating ways to assess how well students meet the new standards. Many states are developing new assessment strategies, some working alone, many working with the New Standards project, a privately funded effort to develop assessments in mathematics, literacy, and work readiness. The New Standards assessments will be based on portfolios, projects, and performances and will differ significantly from multiple choice tests that tend to be unrelated to the details of curriculum and learning goals. The New Standards assessments will be designed around the material in the newly developed national standards. Local discretion in using the assessments will be encouraged. Teachers will help design their school's instructional approach and will promote comparability in standards by evaluating random samples of students' work in other schools. The project's goal is to develop assessments, tied to national standards, that will raise expectations for what students should learn, while encouraging school faculties to introduce school-based reforms.[41]

Efforts to set standards and develop assessment techniques face several problems. First, there is little coordination among the states. Of course, independent attempts to set standards do provide new ideas, but coordination among states and professional associations would ensure a much greater influence on curriculum development, textbook content, teacher training, and what ultimately happens in classrooms.

A second problem is designing assessments that accurately measure how well students master the material described in national standards. This measurement is made harder when, as now, a growing number of students lack English proficiency. The measurement is also made harder if the assessments are used in a "high-stakes" manner in which assessment

40. Some projects are led by professional associations, in many cases with federal government support; others have been initiated by states. For information on setting standards, see the National Council on Education Standards and Testing, *Raising Standards for American Education: A Report to Congress, the Secretary of Education, the National Goals Panel, and the American People* (Washington, 1992); and the Secretary's Commission on Achieving Necessary Skills, *Learning A Living: A Blueprint for High Performance* (Department of Labor, April 1992).

41. See *The New Standards Project 1992–1995, A Proposal* (University of Pittsburgh, Learning Research and Development Center, and National Center on Education and the Economy, Rochester, N.Y., January 1992); and Lauren B. Resnick, "Performance Assessment and Educational Quality," paper prepared for the April 1992 meeting of the American Educational Research Association.

scores influence the careers of students or the reputation of the school. When assessments are used in this way, students and teachers have strong incentives to beat the test rather than learn skills.[42] But if assessments are used only to get a general picture of the performance of an educational system, with no consequences for students or teachers, incentives to learn new skills are weakened. Not surprisingly, the role of assessments in systemic reform is the subject of heated debate.[43]

Increasing incentives. Analysts agree that high school students' lack of incentives to take demanding courses and work hard in school partly explains the inadequate basic skills of many labor force entrants. Although the years of formal education that people complete has become an increasingly important determinant of earnings, differences in cognitive skill levels among labor force entrants with the same amount of formal education play little part in determining initial wages. One reason is that American employers find they cannot get reliable information quickly on the skills of high school graduates applying for jobs. Thus they cannot base hiring decisions on the quality of applicants' academic preparation. Knowing this, students have little incentive to master difficult material.[44] This attitude hampers teachers' efforts to challenge them and results in a destructive accommodation under which students and teachers make few intellectual demands on each other.[45] Parents may be willing participants in these accommodations: they are told their children are doing well and are not pressured to see to it that their children study hard.[46]

42. For a thoughtful description of these issues, see Robert L. Linn, "Technical Considerations in the Proposed Nationwide Assessment System for the National Education Goals Panel" (University of Colorado, Boulder, Center for Research on Evaluation, Standards, and Student Testing, July 1991); and Richard Shavelson, Gail P. Baxter, and Jerry Pine, "Performance Assessments: Political Rhetoric and Measurement Reality," *Educational Research*, vol. 21 (May 1992), pp. 22–27.

43. For more discussion, see Office of Technology Assessment, *Testing in American Schools: Asking the Right Questions*, OTA SET-519 (February 1992).

44. See Bishop, "A Strategy for Achieving Excellence in Secondary Education." See also James E. Rosenbaum, "What If Good Jobs Depended on Good Grades?" *American Education*, vol. 13 (Winter 1989), pp. 10–43.

45. See Arthur G. Powell, Eleanor Farrar, and David K. Cohen, *The Shopping Mall High School: Winners and Losers in the Educational Marketplace* (Houghton Mifflin, 1985).

46. Evidence consistent with this comes from a recent NAEP mathematics study. The test supplemented its usual mathematics questions with questions asking students how well they thought they were doing in mathematics. State-by-state averages showed that students in low-scoring states believed they were doing well while students in high-scoring states thought they were doing only moderately well.

College-bound students may also shirk hard courses and hard work. A national poll of college freshmen reports that 70 percent are attending their school of first choice.[47] Even allowing for some exaggeration, this suggests that many colleges do not require high grades and rigorous high school coursework for admission. Many students have been able to attend college after devoting their high school years to jobs and leisure rather than to study.

These arguments are compelling, but they rest more on a chain of logic than on empirical evidence. In fact, the evidence that does exist is ambiguous. On the one hand, the percentage of high school graduates who go to college has been very sensitive to the difference between the earnings of college graduates and those of high school graduates. This supports the relevance of financial considerations to students' academic decisions. On the other hand, many students drop out of high school even though dropouts fare considerably worse than high school graduates in the labor market. Also, a federally funded program that offered summer and weekend jobs to disadvantaged students and school dropouts who returned to school increased employment rates but did not increase the graduation rate of either group.[48] The implication of this evidence is that although incentives are important, it is not obvious which incentives matter most to students or how students will respond to particular incentives.

In recent years various private organizations with connections to employers have developed proposals to increase incentives for students to work hard in school. The programs typically have two parts: students complete assessments that provide information about their skills, and a central clearinghouse then makes this information available to potential employers.[49] Many of these proposed plans focus on improving the flow of information about candidates for entry-level jobs in a single metropolitan area.

Recently the Bush administration has proposed that high school seniors take American achievement tests in five core subjects. Taking the

47. See Alexander Astin and others, *The American Freshman* (University of California, Los Angeles, Graduate School of Education, 1992).

48. Judith M. Gueron, *Lessons from a Job Guarantee: The Youth Incentive Entitlement Pilot Projects* (New York: Manpower Demonstration Research Corporation, 1984).

49. Christina M. Salerno, "A Report to the Public and Employers: A Review of Projects to Provide Better Signalling of High School Competencies" (Cornell University, Center for Advanced Human Resource Studies, 1992).

tests would be voluntary, but employers and postsecondary educational institutions would be encouraged to use the results in making employment and admission decisions.[50] As with the other plans, the intent is to provide students with incentives to work harder in school, but the evidence is lacking on just what student responses will be.

Students do need incentives to work hard. The challenge is to get the incentives right. Many tests currently in use result in students learning lists of facts and little else. The hypothesis is that performance-based assessments tied to new learning standards will induce students to master skills that will matter in their lives. But this is uncharted territory.

Strengthening connections between school and work. The traditional argument for providing occupational instruction to students who do not plan to go to college is that it will teach them some specific skills and the behaviors that employers value. But recent studies have shown that many students also learn cognitive skills such as mathematics more effectively when the subject is taught in the context of real world problems connected to career options than when it is taught simply as an academic subject.

The advantages of such "situated learning" have spurred efforts to develop vocational programs that integrate learning academic material with preparation for particular occupations.[51] There are several models for such integration.[52] One is the career academy, an idea that stems from a program for disadvantaged youth begun in Philadelphia in 1969. Each academy is organized as a school within a school to provide concentrated activity and support for participating students. Each also has an occupational theme. Curricula are designed to blend academics and vocational material to capture students' interest. Local employers provide mentoring for students and internships in the academy's occupational field. Finally, students are held responsible for attendance and completing homework; failure to comply jeopardizes a student's place in the program. The programs thus combine strong support with

50. Department of Education, *America 2000: An Education Strategy* (1991).

51. See, for example, Lauren B. Resnick, "Learning in School and Out," *Educational Researcher*, vol. 16 (December 1987), pp. 13–20. For a discussion of the value of work-based learning, see Stephen F. Hamilton, *Apprenticeship for Adulthood: Preparing Youth for the Future* (Free Press, 1990).

52. These descriptions are taken from Thomas Bailey and Donna Merrit, "School to Work Transition and Youth Apprenticeship in the United States," paper prepared for the Manpower Demonstration Research Corporation, New York, May 1992.

significant incentives for students to learn and achieve.[53] A number of school districts are developing career academies as a way to keep disadvantaged students in school. California, which currently has forty-seven state-supported academies, plans to increase the number substantially in the next few years.[54]

Technical preparatory ("tech prep") programs provide a second model. They coordinate the curriculum of the last two years of high school and two years of community college, preparing students to work in a cluster of related occupations. The goal of the program is to facilitate completion of high school, entry into community college, and completion of an associate's degree. By providing entry to postsecondary education, the tech prep model may enable more occupational mobility and thus attract more students than traditional apprenticeship programs.

The academy and tech prep programs appear to be promising ways to improve the school-to-work transition, and initiatives in many states seek to make them available to more students. So far, however, they serve only a small percentage of students. Little research has evaluated the effectiveness of particular approaches.[55]

Increasing accountability. Taxpayers asked to pay for school reform want assurances that increased expenditures actually improve the quality of education. This has made accountability a critical element of systemic reform. Although there are many definitions of accountability, pressures now favor outcome-based accountability, in which performance is assessed at regular intervals and actions are taken to improve schools and districts that perform poorly.[56]

A number of problems must be faced in developing valid measures of outcomes. What aspects of performance should be measured? Although businesses can be reasonably assessed in terms of profitability, schools

53. See Bailey and Merritt, "School to Work Transition"; and Charles Dayton and others, "The California Partnership Academies: Remembering the 'Forgotten Half,'" *Phi Delta Kappan*, vol. 73 (March 1992), pp. 539–45.

54. Dayton and others, "California Partnership Academies," p. 543.

55. There have been no random assignment studies of school-to-work transition programs. There have been nonexperimental evaluations of career academies, however. For example, see David Stern and others, "Benefits and Costs of Dropout Prevention in a High School Program Combining Academic and Vocational Education: Third-Year Results from Replications of the California Peninsula Academies," *Educational Evaluation and Policy Analysis*, vol. 11 (Winter 1989), pp. 405–26.

56. For a discussion of alternative definitions of accountability, see Linda Darling-Hammond and Carol Ascher, *Creating Accountability in Big City Schools* (Columbia University, Teachers College, March 1991).

are supposed to help students develop many skills, some more difficult to measure than others. Narrow measures of accountability can create incentives to focus instruction on them and neglect the others.[57] As the adage goes, what you test is what you get. One proposed solution is for parents, teachers, and the principal of each school to agree on what will be measured and then negotiate performance goals with the school board.[58] An alternative adopted by South Carolina is to collect data on multiple indicators of performance, including student attendance and dropout rates, as well as measures of student skills.[59]

A second problem is that student achievement typically reflects family backgrounds as well as the effectiveness of instruction. As a result, comparing the average achievement of students in one school with those in other schools often does not provide a valid measure of a school's performance. It also sets up bad incentives. For example, schools can improve their performance ratings by dissuading low-achieving students from entering, or by encouraging them to stay home on the testing days. Also, teachers may avoid working in schools serving disadvantaged children, who typically score lower than middle-class children on most school performance measures. A solution proposed for this problem is to define performance in terms of progress on each outcome measure. Much needs to be learned, however, about how to do this reliably.[60]

Finally, what actions can be taken to induce poorly performing schools and districts to improve, and perhaps reward, the especially effective schools? This problem is difficult since schools may perform poorly because of inadequate funding, poor hiring practices, lack of teacher training, corruption, and many other reasons; and different causes of poor performance require different remedies. States are experimenting with ways to tailor the remedy to the source of deficiency. For example, Kentucky's Education Reform Act of 1990 specifies that a school in which the percentage of successful students declines by more than 5

57. "Teaching to the test" also produces an artificially high estimate of student achievement. See Daniel M. Koretz and others, "The Effects of High-Stakes Testing on Achievement: Preliminary Findings about Generalization across Tests," paper prepared for the 1991 annual meeting of the National Council on Measurement in Education.

58. Carnegie Forum on Education and the Economy, *A Nation Prepared: Teachers for the 21st Century* (New York: Carnegie Corporation, 1986).

59. Division of Public Accountability, *What Is the Penny Buying for South Carolina?* (South Carolina Department of Education, December 1, 1990).

60. For a discussion of these issues, see Robert H. Meyer, "Educational Performance Indicators and School Report Cards: Concepts," revision of a paper prepared for the 1991 meeting of the Association for Public Policy Analysis and Management.

percent will be declared a school in crisis. These schools must develop an improvement plan, but they become eligible for state funds to implement it. They are assigned a distinguished educator from another district who has the power to transfer or dismiss personnel. And students are allowed to transfer from a school in crisis to a successful school, even if the successful school is in a neighboring district.[61] Other states have adopted other strategies.[62] Only with time will it be possible to learn which measures of accountability are most effective in leading to remedies for poor performance and encouraging superior performance.

Building capacity. Accountability requires that school systems create the conditions under which teachers can change the way that they teach. This is analogous to asking a business to restructure its work. Businesses that have succeeded in restructuring work have invested heavily in continuous training for their employees. Although it is expensive, they found training enabled employees to undertake new tasks and assume new responsibilities for quality control. Businesses also found it necessary to restructure their work environments. Fifteen years ago, U.S. auto workers were told to keep the production line moving even if it meant that defects were not corrected. Some plants that have successfully converted to what is sometimes called the Toyota method of producing automobiles have ordered workers to stop the line whenever defects are spotted. In this and other ways, workers are given the means of controlling the processes that result in defects and are made responsible for eliminating them.

Many of the same lessons hold for schools. It will not be easy for teachers who have long used particular instructional techniques to change the way that they teach. Science teachers who have emphasized memorizing facts will find it difficult to learn to teach by helping students organize and carry out their own experiments. Incentives to make this change will help, but they must be accompanied by detailed curriculum guidelines and extensive training and support.[63] Similarly, teachers cannot be expected to be responsible for student progress toward newly defined goals without the resources and the autonomy to devise good instructional

61. *The Kentucky Reform Act of 1990: A Citizen's Handbook* (Frankfort, Ky.: Legislative Research Commission, September 1991).

62. See Susan H. Fuhrman and Richard F. Elmore, "Takeover and Deregulation: Working Models of New State and Local Regulatory Relationships," CPRE research report RR-024 (Rutgers University, Consortium for Policy Research in Education, April 1992).

63. For evidence on the difficulties involved in helping teachers change their methods, see the articles in *Educational Evaluation and Policy Analysis*, vol. 12 (Fall 1990).

plans and carry them out. To teach science by having students do experiments requires good facilities, time to plan and set up equipment, and control over a budget sufficient to purchase materials. Many school districts are a long way from meeting these conditions.[64]

Curriculum redesign and teacher training will be particularly important in improving school-to-work transition programs. Tech prep and academy programs require curricula that teach academic subjects in the context of occupation-related problems. Teachers will have to know not only their own academic discipline but also a considerable amount about the occupations for which students are preparing. It takes talented teachers with the time to develop or adapt integrated curricula to make these programs work.

Where will the teachers be found who have the talent and skills to help students master new national educational standards? There are many already in the schools, but not enough. During the next fifteen years teachers hired during the baby boom years will retire. This turnover means large numbers of talented teachers must be recruited at a time when the labor force will be growing slowly and competition for talented college graduates will be stiff. But the turnover also provides the opportunity to upgrade the quality of the teacher corps dramatically.

Continuing past practices will not improve the quality of teachers. In the late 1960s, college graduates with high IQs were only slightly less likely than graduates with average IQs to become teachers. By the 1980s the high-IQ graduates were only one-fourth as likely to become teachers. Those high-IQ graduates who did enter the classroom were much more likely than other new teachers to leave after one or two years.[65]

The explanation for these patterns is straightforward: money and job opportunities. In previous generations, women and minority college graduates had few good career opportunities. Teaching was thus a relatively attractive occupation, even for the most academically talented. But by the 1980s, teaching salaries had declined both absolutely (net of inflation) and relative to salaries in other occupations, and opportunities in other occupations had increased. The result is that schools will need to pay more for talented college graduates in the 1990s than they did in the 1960s, when large numbers of new teachers were last hired.

64. For a description of the working conditions that hinder effective teaching, see Susan M. Johnson, *Teachers at Work: Achieving Success in Our Schools* (Basic Books, 1990).

65. For an extensive discussion of teachers' career patterns, see Richard J. Murnane and others, *Who Will Teach? Policies That Matter* (Harvard University Press, 1991).

As part of systemic reform, some states have instituted policies to lure skilled graduates into teaching. State-financed salary increases have reversed the 20 percent decline in real salaries that occurred during the 1970s, returning the average starting salary (in constant dollars) approximately to its 1972 level. These increases are important because competitive teaching salaries increase the number of college graduates who want to become teachers and the number of years they stay in the classroom.[66]

Working conditions as well as salaries must improve if schools are to hire college graduates with good alternative career opportunities. Most critically, schools must be reorganized to give teachers the discretion, time, and resources to plan and implement high-quality instructional programs. The school-based reforms initiated by Theodore Sizer and others provide promising models for changing school organizations and making teaching more attractive to enterprising college graduates.

Competitive salaries and good working conditions are critical to attracting talented people, but they do not guarantee that the graduates will undertake the training needed to learn how to teach. Mandatory training programs are not the answer. This strategy often creates a captive audience for particular training programs and results in instruction that does not improve teaching skills and may deter some talented students from teaching.

Some states are linking licensure to demonstrations of teaching competence, rather than to completion of particular preservice training programs. Performance-based licensing may encourage creative training programs to prepare candidates for the performance-based licensing assessment and attract talented graduates who did not participate in undergraduate teacher training programs.[67] But performance-based licensing systems are as hard to develop as performance-based assessments of student skills. Because licensing examinations are high-stakes tests, students and training institutions may focus on mastering the skills that are part of the assessment and slighting other skills. The tests must reliably measure the skills needed to teach effectively. Still, the problems

66. See Murnane and others, *Who Will Teach?*, p. 8, for teachers' starting salaries from 1972 to 1988 in constant dollars and relative to salaries in other occupations. American Federation of Teachers salary surveys show the average salary for beginning teachers changed by less than 1 percent between 1988 and 1991, remaining between $21,500 and $21,800 in 1991 dollars.

67. See Murnane and others, *Who Will Teach?*, chap. 7, for evidence that alternative licensing programs not requiring undergraduate teacher preparation attract talented college graduates to teaching, including a significant number of minority group members.

caused by conventional regulations that base licensing on completing specified training programs and passing multiple choice examinations on particular subject matter are so serious that performance-based licensing holds real promise.[68]

Leveling the playing field. Encouraging students to work hard in school, in effect, means increasing the importance of school performance in the competition for who gets good jobs. In this competition every student must have an equal chance. Currently, they do not. Twenty percent of American children live in families with incomes below the poverty line. These children are especially likely to come to school with physical and mental problems that hinder learning. A disproportionate number come from groups that have experienced racial or social discrimination. The schools these children attend often lack the resources needed for effective teaching, especially for hands-on science instruction.[69] The poor quality of urban schools helps to explain why black males in their early twenties who attended urban high schools have annual earnings 9 percent lower than those of comparable black youth who attended suburban high schools.[70]

The historical reliance in the United States on local property taxes to finance public education produced enormous disparities in expenditures per pupil both within and among states. Typically districts with large per pupil tax bases had relatively high per pupil spending—often with relatively low property tax rates—while districts with small per pupil tax bases had low per pupil spending and high tax rates. Beginning in the late 1960s, challenges to school finance systems led many state supreme courts to declare unconstitutional the state systems of school finance that depended heavily on the property tax.

In the subsequent revisions of school finance, state revenues were typically substituted for local revenues, especially in property-poor districts. These changes equalized local property taxes but not per pupil expenditures: fiscally strapped communities often used state aid for tax relief instead of school expenditures.[71]

---

68. Murnane and others, *Who Will Teach?*, chap. 7.

69. Jeannie Oakes, *Multiplying Inequalities: The Effects of Race, Social Class, and Tracking on Opportunities to Learn Mathematics and Science* (Santa Monica: RAND Corp., 1990).

70. Edwin A. Sexton and Janet F. Nickel, "The Effects of School Location on the Earnings of Black and White Youths," *Economics of Education Review*, vol. 11 (March 1992), p. 14.

71. Some states, including California, have achieved significant equalization of government funds devoted to public schooling. However, wealthy districts have found ways,

During the 1980s, advocates of school finance reform stopped demanding state aid that communities could use as they chose and began asking for increased school funding in communities that spent little on education. These efforts have foundered in many states because verifying strong connections between expenditures and student performance is difficult. The fear has been that funds may not be used wisely. This in turn has encouraged interest in defining the state role as paying a significant part of the cost of high-quality basic education, including the courses students need to meet newly defined academic standards. A few states such as Kentucky and South Carolina have explicitly tied increased state funding to systemic reform, standards and support for building capacity, and incentives for students and educators to improve performance.

It is too early to tell how much school finance reform coupled to systemic reform can improve the performance of students in low-spending school districts. But these districts are not necessarily those serving large percentages of children from poor families. In fact, urban districts serving poor children often have relatively large tax bases per pupil. This has not prevented severe funding crises in many of them, however, because educational costs are high in big cities, children from poor families often have special educational needs, and schools must compete for municipal funds with other relatively expensive public services such as police and fire protection. School finance reform has thus been a blunt instrument for improving the education of children from poor families.

Thoughtful systemic reform has the potential to improve American education. But if hastily implemented, without reducing the enormous disparities in the quality of education in different schools and without alleviating the poverty that handicaps one in five of the nation's children, systemic reform could threaten the fragile social fabric of the country and destroy what it is supposed to improve.

A Role for Family Choice?

For the Bush administration and some reformers, the centerpiece of school reform is a tax-funded voucher that would allow parents to purchase education at any public or private school.[72] In our judgment,

---

including the establishment of not-for-profit foundations, to maintain atypically high resource levels.

72. Department of Education, *America 2000.*

the case for such vouchers is weak. The potential gains are small, and there is substantial risk that a politically acceptable voucher plan would increase current educational inequalities. Greater parental choice within the public school system would be a step forward; it would improve accountability and might improve student achievement. But the evidence does not support spending public monies on private schools.

Those who support vouchers argue that private schools, freed from public bureaucracies, do a far superior job of raising student achievement. The data do not support this point. It is possible to compare the achievement test scores of students currently in public and in private schools. These comparisons indicate that even the largest estimates of differences in achievement are small relative to the goals for American education. For example, scores from the 1990 NAEP mathematics assessment show that even though private school students tend to come from better-educated families than public school students (and parental education is a strong predictor of student achievement), their average achievement is only marginally better. Among students in the twelfth grade, 55 percent of those in public schools, 46 percent in Catholic schools, and 49 percent in other private schools had not mastered "reasoning and problem solving involving fractions, decimals, percents, elementary geometry and simple algebra," content introduced by the seventh grade.[73] Approximately half the students attending each type of school graduate without strong basic mathematics skills. Simply increasing the number of students attending private schools would do little to improve mathematics achievement.

This finding should not be surprising. The idea of using vouchers to improve student achievement implicitly assumes that parents want a challenging education for their children and recognize that learning difficult material means considerable work. But many parents want to be told their children are doing well. They do not want the conflicts that arise when students are required to sacrifice jobs and leisure to the demands of schoolwork. Private schools, like private producers in other industries, prosper by giving customers what they want.

High School and Beyond survey results also suggest that it is a mistake to assume that private schools have an impact on students' achievement dramatically superior to that of public schools. Even the largest estimate of a private school advantage is small relative to the differences in the

---

73. National Center for Education Statistics, *The State of Mathematics Achievement: NAEP's 1990 Assessment of the Nation and the Trial Assessment of the States* (Department of Education, June 1991).

estimated effectiveness among public schools or among private schools.[74] Which school a child attends is much more important than whether the school is public or private. Thus the challenge is to make more public schools work as well as the best ones do.

Voucher supporters argue that public schools are too constrained by bureaucratic rules that make it hard to use resources wisely.[75] In many cases, such as inefficient teacher-hiring procedures, these charges have merit and changes are needed. It is important to recognize, however, that many rules, such as restrictions on the uses of funds for compensatory education, bilingual education, and the education of learning-disabled children, are attempts to make schools more responsive to the needs of children. Educating these children provides challenges for any school, public or private. Changes in the regulations governing the uses of these funds are needed, but the obligations to serve these children cannot be abandoned.

Would it be possible to design a voucher system that provided high-quality education to all children, including those disadvantaged by poverty or special needs? We do not know; it has never been tried. However, twenty-five years ago the federal government tried to find a community willing to experiment with a system that provided vouchers with higher values for disadvantaged children, mandated that no participating school could charge families more than the value of the voucher, and required schools facing excess demand to allocate half the available places by a lottery. No community wanted to try such a regulated system.[76] But such regulations are essential to protect the educational options of disadvantaged children.

Regulations would also be needed to control fraud in a voucher system. This has been the experience with medicaid, job training in proprietary training schools, and other government programs that pay private firms to deliver services. Regulations enforced by a government bureaucracy can control fraud, but they create a system quite different from the education "market" that advocates of vouchers endorse. Thus

74. John F. Witte, "Private School Versus Public School Achievement: Are There Findings That Should Affect the Educational Choice Debate?" *Economics of Education Review* (forthcoming); and Richard J. Murnane, "A Review Essay: Comparisons of Public and Private Schools: Lessons from the Uproar," *Journal of Human Resources*, vol. 19 (Spring 1984), pp. 263–77.

75. John E. Chubb and Terry M. Moe, *Politics, Markets, and America's Schools* (Brookings, 1990).

76. David K. Cohen and Eleanor Farrar, "Power to the Parents? The Story of Education Vouchers," *Public Interest*, no. 48 (Summer 1977), pp. 72–97.

a system of vouchers that protected the interests of disadvantaged children and controlled fraud would not have a significant constituency, and it is only such a system that would ensure equality of educational opportunity and the efficient use of government resources.

Expanding choices within the public sector through mechanisms other than vouchers can improve educational achievement. First, it can indicate what kinds of school programs parents value. Second, it can support school-based reform by providing justification for faculties to develop distinctive programs. Thus it is useful to expand public-sector choice. However, many local experiments with such programs, including magnet schools, alternative schools, and open enrollments, indicate that the effects are modest and are no substitute for finding ways to improve the core instruction in every school, the task of systemic reform.[77]

Implementing All Elements of Systemic Reform

Systemic reform has the best chance for improving American education if all its elements are implemented. Omitting some would reduce the chance of success and could result in damage to American education. For example, investing in teacher training without a clear sense of the skills that teachers should help students master is unlikely to improve teaching and learning. Developing standards for what students should know without investing in teacher training or developing curricular materials that take account of the new standards will increase student and teacher frustration more than academic achievement. Increasing ties between students' school performance and postschool earnings will increase incentives for students to work hard in demanding courses only if their schools offer demanding courses and these courses are well taught. Increasing incentives for student performance without leveling the playing field could deepen the disadvantages students from low-income families experience in schools and in the labor market and increase income inequality. These examples illustrate the logic underlying systemic reform: many forces have collaborated to weaken American schools and many will have to be coordinated to improve them.

77. Richard J. Murnane, "Family Choice in Public Education: The Roles of Students, Teachers, and System Designers," *Teachers College Record*, vol. 88 (Winter 1986), pp. 196–89.

The Federal Role

Responsibility for elementary and secondary education in the United States has been left primarily to the states, which in turn delegate an extraordinary amount of authority to 15,000 local school districts. As a result, the governance of education is extremely decentralized and the federal role limited. In 1989 the federal government's expenditures for public elementary and secondary education were only 6.2 percent of total expenditures, down from 9.8 percent in 1979.[78]

The contraction of the federal role in elementary and secondary education is unfortunate, especially during a decade when slow economic growth and stagnant earnings have become national problems. Improving the skills of the labor force contributes to solving these problems. Improving the quality of elementary and secondary education should be a national goal, and the federal government should be willing to increase taxes to pursue this goal.

Given the structure of educational governance in the United States, the federal government can improve American education most effectively by supporting systemic reform and promoting the many school-based reform initiatives under way in states and local districts. Federal efforts should focus on four types of activities:

—Promoting high-quality instruction for disadvantaged students;

—Recruiting and training talented teachers;

—Supporting the development of standards and assessment methods and coordinating state reform efforts;

—Sponsoring research and developing a system to monitor the progress of systemic reform.

High-Quality Instruction for Disadvantaged Children

Improving opportunities for the nation's most disadvantaged citizens is a critical federal responsibility. The primary instrument for achieving this goal is title I of the Elementary and Secondary Education Act of 1965, subsequently renamed chapter 1 in the 1981 reauthorization. Chapter 1 was used to support services to 5 million children in 51,000 schools at a cost of $6.1 billion for fiscal year 1991.[79]

78. National Center for Education Statistics, *Digest of Educational Statistics 1991*, NCES 91-697 (Department of Education, 1991), p. 147.

79. Office of Technology Assessment, *Testing in American Schools*, p. 82.

Designing regulations for the use of chapter 1 funds has always been difficult. The goal is to use the money to improve the education of disadvantaged children. For this reason the regulations prevent districts from treating the funds as general aid. Most school districts have found that they could comply most easily by hiring special chapter 1 teachers to instruct eligible children outside the regular classroom during the school day. Thus one type of instruction replaced another, but the time devoted to learning was not increased. Moreover, chapter 1 instruction typically focused on developing the initial reading and computation skills emphasized on the standardized tests used to evaluate program effectiveness. Thus the instruction neglected many aspects of new learning goals, as outlined, for example, in the National Council of Teachers of Mathematics *Standards* volume.

The legislation reauthorizing chapter 1 in 1988 made changes to address these problems. It allowed schools in which at least 75 percent of the students were eligible for chapter 1 assistance to spend the money on schoolwide improvement programs. It also introduced accountability by individual schools and required schools that do not meet state-established standards for achievement to be identified for program improvement. Although the accountability procedures do focus attention on improving students' achievement, they also discourage use of chapter 1 funds for kindergarten and first grade years because the procedures mandate that achievement gains be measured from the end of the first grade. The higher students score on this initial test, the more difficult it is to show subsequent gains. The procedures also create incentives to retain students in the same grade for more than one year.[80]

In 1993 Congress will reauthorize chapter 1 and has the opportunity to stimulate school-based reforms in schools serving large proportions of disadvantaged children. It could thus truly help the one-fifth of the nation's children living in poverty. Congress should enact four reforms in chapter 1. First, funding should be increased from $6.1 billion to $8 billion. The additional funds should go to schools serving high concentrations of eligible children. Second, Congress should encourage the development of schoolwide reforms by permitting them in schools in which at least 50 percent (instead of 75 percent) of the students are eligible for chapter 1. Third, local education authorities should be permitted to negotiate accountability agreements with individual schools

80. Robert E. Slavin and Nancy A. Madden, "Modifying Chapter 1 Program Improvement Guidelines to Reward Appropriate Practices," *Educational Evaluation and Policy Analysis*, vol. 13 (Winter 1991), pp. 369–79.

under which schools would be given several years to demonstrate progress. The achievements could be measured by scores on tests that measure mastery of curricula tied to new achievement standards.[81] Finally, funds should be set aside for the development of the entire faculty, for solving attendance problems, and for teaching parents how to help their children learn more effectively.[82] All these recommendations are aimed at using chapter 1 to make improved schooling for disadvantaged children a central component of systemic reform.[83]

Federal programs to improve education for disadvantaged children can make a difference if they promote real changes in the school experiences of these children. However, it is even more important for the federal government to improve the lives of children outside school. Even the most potentially effective systemic reforms cannot succeed unless more is done to ameliorate the multiple disadvantages that children from poor families bring to school. Chapter 5 in this volume discusses these disadvantages and recommends federal policies to address them.

Recruiting and Training Talented Teachers

Finding talented replacements for the large number of teachers who will retire in the next fifteen years is a daunting challenge. The most difficult task will be to find an adequate supply of teachers skilled in mathematics, chemistry, and physics because graduates trained in these fields are lured by particularly high-paying jobs outside teaching. Finding talented black and Latino teachers will also be difficult. Not only has the proportion of teachers from minority groups not kept pace with the growing proportion of black and Latino children in the student population in the past ten years, but the percentage has fallen.[84]

81. The logic for allowing several years to show progress is that James Comer and other reformers took years just to develop promising schoolwide reform programs. The logic for using tests tied to curriculum standards is to ensure that chapter 1 programs focus on helping disadvantaged children achieve the same learning goals set for all children. See James P. Comer, *School Power: Implications of an Intervention Project* (Free Press, 1980).

82. Many of these suggestions come from Slavin and Madden, "Modifying Chapter 1 Program Improvement Guidelines."

83. Many of the problems that turned up in chapter 1 regulations also turned up in federal special education regulations. The 1990 Perkins Act, which reauthorized federal support for vocational education, increased the percentage of federal funds going to districts serving large numbers of disadvantaged students, mandated integration of vocational and academic curricula, and required that states and districts establish an outcome-based system of accountability. All these provisions could promote systemic reform.

84. Murnane and others, *Who Will Teach?* discusses these problems.

The federal government and some states have used loan forgiveness programs to recruit college students into teaching. These programs have not been particularly effective in attracting students who would not otherwise teach, but there has been no systematic exploration of how strongly college students' decisions depend on variations in the loan forgiveness schedule.[85] The states' alternative licensing programs do appear to attract talented college graduates, but serious questions remain about whether the brief training period provides the skills needed to teach effectively.[86]

What is needed are programs that attract talented college students to teaching, especially minority group members and students with backgrounds in mathematics and science. The programs must provide the recruits with effective training, place them in schools facing teacher shortages, and provide them with the kind of support all teachers need to survive and grow during their first year on the job. To fill that gap we recommend that the federal government fund ten demonstration programs aimed at achieving these objectives. Grants of $16 million ($2 million a year for eight years) should be awarded each winner in an open competition in which universities, not-for-profit groups, school districts, and consortia of these organizations submit proposals. Eight years should be long enough to develop innovative recruiting and training approaches and to observe the teaching performance and early retention rate of program graduates. This grant program would modestly increase the supply of teachers in areas with shortages, but the greatest benefit would be the lessons for states and districts about effective ways to attract and train able teachers.

The Carnegie Commission on Science, Technology, and Government has also advocated using grant competitions to stimulate development and implementation of innovative programs. Currently three-quarters of the $200 million annually appropriated for Eisenhower Mathematics and Science Education programs are distributed to the states, which in turn allocate them to school districts by formula. The districts typically use the money to provide in-service training to teachers, but because districts do not compete for the grants, they have little incentive to use the money creatively. All the Eisenhower program training funds should

85. David M. Arfin, "The Use of Financial Aid to Attract Talented Students to Teaching: Lessons from Other Fields," *Elementary School Journal*, vol. 86 (March 1986), pp. 404–23.

86. Murnane and others, *Who Will Teach?*, chap. 7, discusses alternative licensing programs.

be distributed through grant competitions to encourage effective training and stimulate innovations that can influence the strategies used in the many state-supported in-service training programs.[87]

Setting Standards and Developing Assessments

Although the politics of reform dictate that each state establish its own educational standards, these efforts will be much more effective if the states use widely respected standards as guides. The standards of the NCTM and the American Association for the Advancement of Science are good examples.[88] The federal government should continue subsidizing efforts of professional organizations to develop performance standards in specific subject areas and should fund the coordination of ongoing efforts.[89] The government must recognize that, although rapid progress in establishing standards is desired, extensive public participation and professional review increase the likelihood that the standards will ultimately have a positive influence on what happens in classrooms.

Similarly, improved techniques for assessing student achievement are critical to reform and extremely expensive to develop. States have so far worked on these programs quite independently, which has led to duplication of effort and delays. Failure to coordinate actions stems in part from budgetary stringencies. In many state departments of education, funding for travel and participation in interstate collaboratives is one of the first things cut from strained budgets.

The Council of Chief State School Officers, the College Board, and the Education Commission of the States are trusted by the states and are in a position to organize such coordination but cannot afford to do so. Federal financial support for conferences, travel, and the development of networks of states working on similar types of assessments is an inexpensive, potentially powerful strategy for helping states create a common approach toward systemic educational reform.

87. For more information on this proposal, see Carnegie Commission on Science, Technology, and Government, *In the National Interest: The Federal Government in the Reform of K-12 Math and Science Education* (New York, February 1991), pp. 37–37.

88. National Council of Teachers of Mathematics, *Curriculum and Evaluation Standards for School Mathematics* (Reston, Va., 1989); and American Association for the Advancement of Science, *Science for All Americans*.

89. The federal government has recently provided funding to the National Academy of Sciences to produce national science standards, drawing from the efforts of the states, the AAAS, the National Science Teachers Association, and other organizations.

In addition to these coordination efforts, the federal government should support private organizations working with states to develop new strategies for assessing the performance of teachers and students. Among the promising efforts are the New Standards project and the work of the National Board for Professional Teaching Standards (NBPTS). The New Standards project is working with seventeen states to develop performance-based assessments of student achievement. This effort may have a marked impact on the attention teachers devote to hands-on science and using mathematics and reading skills to solve problems. The NBPTS is working with states to develop means of assessing teachers' skills. The results may improve licensing practices and thereby attract more talented college graduates into teaching. While the success of neither of these efforts is guaranteed, adequate funding is critical to learning whether performance-based assessments of student and teacher skills can play important roles in improving American education.

Finally, the federal government should coordinate its own activities that influence elementary and secondary school education. Sixteen federal agencies and eight congressional subcommittees, for example, are currently concerned with mathematics and science education. Coordination will not be easy because the fragmentation and overlapping stem from longstanding fears that a strong national government would dictate local school practice.[90] Coordination efforts are not glamorous and do not win votes, but they will reduce the conflicting messages that federal policies often send school districts and increase the effectiveness of federal programs in improving American education.[91]

Sponsoring Research and Developing a Monitoring System

While analysts tend to agree on the need for systemic reform and on its elements, they do not agree on ways to achieve it. For example, some analysts believe that national achievement tests would cause students to put forth more effort and would make educators more accountable. Critics argue that high-stakes testing would narrow teaching and learning and result in neglect of some important skills.[92] Others argue that high-stakes testing will further handicap students from low-income families

90. See Cohen and Spillane, "Policy and Practice."
91. For ideas on ways to coordinate federal education policies, see Carnegie Commission on Science, Technology, and Government, *In the National Interest.*
92. Office of Technology Assessment, *Testing in American Schools.*

because they will be denied access to high-quality courses and teaching. Advocates respond that the new high-stakes tests will be better than the commercial standardized tests used in the 1980s, so that teaching to the tests will promote meaningful achievement. Some also believe that the tests will improve course offerings and the quality of teaching in urban schools by highlighting the inadequate performance of poor children attending them.

The variety of experiments with testing taking place in school districts and states creates valuable opportunities to learn more about the consequences of particular strategies. Funding research on the consequences of these experiments is an important federal activity.

In addition, the federal government should sponsor research and random assignment demonstrations to discover the most effective strategies for implementing systemic reform. For example, it could sponsor research on the consequences of voluntary tests for high school seniors, with the scores being made available to potential employers upon request. Researchers could explore whether employers used this information to make hiring decisions. They could also explore how much the new arrangements affected student effort and teachers' allocations of instructional time. Random assignment evaluation could also be used to investigate how much various school-to-work transition programs improved participants' subsequent job experiences. Yet another subject would be the effect on instruction in chapter 1 programs of substituting performance-based assessments of student achievement for standardized tests. These and many other questions remain unanswered as states embark on education reforms. By sponsoring research, the federal government can influence state reform efforts and increase the potential for their success.

Finally, the federal government should support the development of measures to monitor the progress of systemic reform, particularly the extent to which disadvantaged children receive the instruction they need to master the skills described in national standards. Although the federal government should fund the creation and maintenance of a monitoring system, a private organization protected from political whims should do the work. One strategy would be to make the system part of the National Assessment of Educational Progress.[93]

93. For a discussion of the need for and possible content of an educational indicator system, see National Center for Education Statistics, *Education Counts: An Indicator System to Monitor the Nation's Educational Health* (Government Printing Office, 1991).

Making Systemic Reform Work

Systemic reform of the nation's schools will take a long time, even with sustained efforts toward agreed goals. Progress will be impossible if the goals change every time the balance of power in Congress or the party controlling the White House changes. Bipartisan support for long-term educational reform is necessary for success and always difficult to sustain. The recognition that American education badly needs improving means that chances for sustained bipartisan support are better than in the past. But the federal government must not get involved in specific, highly politicized initiatives that jeopardize coalition building. This is one more reason why federal funding for private school vouchers, an extremely divisive proposal, should be avoided.

Worker Training

Better schooling has a significant long-term role in improving labor force skills. But its immediate impact on worker skills is smaller than it was in the past. In 1960, at the height of the baby boom, there were 59 million U.S. children under age 16, nearly as many as were in the 69-million-person labor force. The number of young people turning age 18 each year was equal to 5 percent of the labor force, and so better schools could improve average labor force skills rather quickly. Today, the number of children younger than age 16 is slightly lower—58 million— while the labor force stands at 125 million.[94] In the near term, then, improving the skills of those already in the labor force has at least as much potential as better schooling for boosting productivity.

As it does for primary and secondary education, the federal government plays a modest role in the nation's job training, with its greatest impact on programs aimed at low-income workers such as the Job Training and Partnership Act. The state and local role in training is also relatively modest: the state supports economic development activities and community colleges that are often a source of technical and vocational education. Most training is supplied by individual private companies that train their own employees.[95] This structure leads to the economists' standard

94. Authors' calculations from data in *Economic Report of the President, February 1992,* tables B29, B30.

95. We include both companies that provide direct training and those that purchase training from community colleges and other outside institutions.

question: If training is so valuable, why doesn't the private sector provide enough of it?

The most frequent answer begins with a company's fear that it will train workers only to lose them to another that may offer a higher wage because it did not pay for training. Small firms that have limited opportunities for internal advancement are most vulnerable to this kind of raiding. Thus training is more likely to be undertaken by large companies, especially those that practice a full employment model of labor relations in which a company emphasizes job security and creates avenues of promotion for its employees. Employees, for their part, expect to remain with the firm and to undertake the training that advancement requires.[96] The company knows it will recoup its investment because trained employees will remain awhile.

But the 1980s witnessed extensive restructuring, particularly by manufacturing firms. One by-product was to reduce the number of firms that could make such long-term employment guarantees. Even IBM, Aetna, AT&T, and others that used to offer a job for life have laid off large numbers of employees in the face of competitive pressures. The average size of plants has also shrunk in the past fifteen years, which may signal a long-term trend.[97]

Programs that train disadvantaged workers have also been ignored by business because they have not demonstrated consistent successes of a kind that would make them attractive to employers.[98] Most evidence comes from government-sponsored training programs for welfare recipients and others with weak basic skills. Some programs directed at women have been fairly successful at helping them to obtain higher-paying jobs. The record of programs for adult men is mixed, although some recent programs have led to earnings gains. Programs aimed at teenagers have produced very limited gains.[99] Few programs have improved skills enough

96. For a comparison of the full employment model and other models of labor relations, see Peter B. Doeringer and others, *Turbulence in the American Workplace* (Oxford University Press, 1991).

97. Steve J. Davis and John Haltiwanger, "Wage Dispersion between and within U.S. Manufacturing Plants, 1963–86," *Brookings Papers on Economic Activity, Microeconomics* (1991), pp. 115–80.

98. Gary Burtless, "Public Spending on the Poor: Historical Trends and Economic Limits," paper prepared for the conference, "Poverty and Public Policy: What Do We Know? What Should We Do?" Madison, Wis., 1992.

99. Many of these evaluations have been done by the Manpower Development Research Corporation. For a summary, see Judith M. Gueron and Edward Pauly, *From Welfare to Work* (New York: Russell Sage Foundation, 1991).

for workers to compete for "good jobs," ones that pay $7.00 an hour or more. Thus private employers are reluctant to train such workers on their own. Still, the programs often save the government more than they cost (in reduced welfare benefits, for example).

The third, and perhaps most important, reason the private sector has provided too little training is its slowness in adopting high-wage, high-skill technologies. Inadequate training in statistical process control provides a case in point. Statistical process control is a set of procedures by which workers can monitor the quality of their production. Traditionally, the typical manufacturing worker has had no such responsibility—quality has been the responsibility of inspectors at the end of the assembly line—and has had no need to know statistical process control. But modern manufacturing requires workers to monitor quality so as to "get it right the first time."[100] It follows that only those companies willing to modernize will invest in teaching statistical process control.

While current federal training efforts are modest, the federal government is positioned in ways that states and private firms often are not. Attempts to expand federal training must take account of this if money is to be spent wisely. In particular, business will pressure any government to pay for training that it might otherwise pay for itself. States and cities often compete with one another to attract new firms and find it difficult to resist this pressure. But the federal government is better positioned to resist and to spend on projects that would otherwise be ignored. Two kinds of projects stand out: broad skills training by employer consortia or associations and training of disadvantaged workers.[101]

An employer consortium offers a way for smaller firms to share training costs and reduce the loss when a trained worker jumps to another company. Consortium training usually does not replace training by an individual firm; instead it provides broader skills that provide a useful base for further training. The Massachusetts Machine Action Project (MAP), a consortium of metalworking firms, trains workers to set up and run various machines (though workers may need additional training on the particular machine of a new employer), to read blueprints,

---

100. An example of such a modern assembly process is the Toyota automobile assembly process. See James P. Womack, Daniel T. Jones, and Daniel Roos, *The Machine That Changed the World: The Story of Lean Production* (Harper, 1991).

101. Rosemary Batt and Paul Osterman, "A National Framework for Employment and Training Policy: Lessons from Local Initiatives, A Report to the Economic Policy Institute" (Washington: Economic Policy Institute, September 29, 1991).

and to apply principles of quality control.[102] Federal funding to help form such consortia fills an important gap in current training efforts.[103]

The federal government is already heavily involved in training disadvantaged workers, an involvement that will have to continue. Not only do many firms believe it is not cost effective to train disadvantaged workers, but their caution often becomes the states' caution. Because training activities are part of a state's economic development program, the state is concerned that an emphasis on disadvantaged workers may cause companies to locate elsewhere. Thus the responsibility for training disadvantaged workers is left in the hands of the federal government. These programs have built a modest record of success, and they should be expanded. To the extent that training, per se, has limited effects, an intensified effort will need to provide public service jobs with pay near the minimum wage.

What A Better Trained Labor Force Can and Cannot Do

We end this chapter with a caveat. Systemic educational reform, if successful, would improve the basic skills of new entrants to the labor market and presumably reduce the premium that companies must pay to attract workers with these skills. But this alone will do little to spur productivity growth. After all, in the late 1970s, productivity barely increased even though highly educated and relatively low-priced labor force entrants were abundant. We mention this not to downplay the importance of improving American education but to make clear that productivity growth will require not only workers with the basic skills to respond rapidly to training and to learn new tasks on the job. It will also take a dramatic increase in the number of businesses committed to using workers in new ways.[104]

In summary, the evidence supports two conclusions. Improving the skills of the labor force is necessary to increase productivity, and this is

102. Batt and Osterman, *National Framework*, p. 162.

103. Ideally, one would want such consortia to become institutionalized so that they could continue to respond on their own to changing market conditions.

104. For an extended exposition of this contention, see Paul Osterman, *Employment Futures: Reorganization, Dislocation, and Public Policy* (Oxford University Press, 1988); and National Center on Education and the Economy, *America's Choice! High Skills or Low Wages.*

an important reason for making the sustained investment needed to promote all the elements of systemic reform. At the same time, simply improving the skills of labor force entrants will not increase productivity very much. If productivity growth is to accelerate, the private sector must invest more heavily in research and development, in new equipment, and in reorganizing production so as to make better use of workers' skills.

7

LINDA R. COHEN AND
ROGER G. NOLL

Research and Development

THE UNITED STATES stands at a crossroads in science and research policy. The federal government now spends more than $70 billion on research and development (R&D).[1] Now that the cold war has ended and the world economy has become increasingly integrated, the government is forced to consider reorienting research policy away from national security and toward enhancing the productivity and international competitiveness of American industries.

This chapter examines how federal R&D programs might be restructured to serve new purposes. Civilian R&D policy is difficult to assess because the array of R&D programs and the institutions that support them are so heterogeneous. A comprehensive assessment requires more than determining whether the federal R&D budget is the right size. It would also have to ascertain whether the government is properly allocating the budget between fundamental and applied research, across technologies, and among research institutions.

We cannot hope to address all of these issues in a life's work, let alone a single chapter. Instead, we focus on a few issues in R&D policy: the conceptual argument for government research support, the historical pattern of R&D in the United States and the effect federal policies have had on this distribution, and the kinds of R&D activities the United States supports in comparison with those in other advanced industrialized countries. We examine programs that support the development of new technologies for the private sector, focusing on how the government sets priorities and organizes its commercial R&D projects. Finally, because

Richard R. Nelson was the discussant for this chapter. The authors also want to thank W. Edward Steinmueller for helpful comments on an earlier version and Jane Edsell for administrative support. Roger Noll thanks the John and Mary Markle Foundation for research support.

1. American Association for the Advancement of Science, Intersociety Working Group, *AAAS Report XVII: Research and Development FY 1993* (Washington: AAAS, 1992), p. 49.

most basic research, and even a growing share of commercially oriented R&D, is undertaken in universities, we examine how the federal government is managing this relationship.

We conclude that although the United States appears to underinvest in R&D, there is no compelling reason for it to invest a great deal more to keep the country prosperous. The main problem is not *how much* it invests, but how it sets priorities and how it manages what it spends. Federal programs for the development of new commercial technologies have been largely unsuccessful because the government does not make good decisions about what to support, and because it is too inflexible and unadaptive in its conduct of R&D programs. Federal management methods to ensure accountability in spending federal R&D dollars are extremely wasteful and reduce the productivity of research organizations. Moreover, the new emphasis on federally subsidized R&D joint ventures, such as Sematech, does not represent a plausible, effective solution to this problem. These problems are not insurmountable, but if the government hopes to deal with them it will have to rethink its role and reorganize many R&D programs and institutions.

Rationale for R&D Policies

Although the federal government has supported civilian R&D programs since the early nineteenth century, it has usually pursued narrow policy objectives rather than economic growth and international competitiveness.[2] In some cases, the rationale for federal involvement has been to improve productivity in a politically important industry, as was the case with agricultural R&D programs in the nineteenth century and the ill-fated supersonic transport (SST). However, most of its programs have been "mission oriented" to produce a new technology that would help government achieve a programmatic objective that was at best only indirectly linked to the economic performance of an industry. In almost all cases, mission-oriented projects have been related to national security issues, either by creating a new defense technology or by advancing commercial applications of technologies that are also used in defense, such as nuclear power and spacecraft. Even in the late 1970s after the OPEC oil embargo, the energy R&D programs that sought to improve the performance of the energy sector were justified in part on the basis of national security.

2. See David C. Mowery and Nathan Rosenberg, *Technology and the Pursuit of Economic Growth* (Cambridge University Press, 1989).

The view that the government should play a broad role in supporting R&D grew out of the experiences of World War II. Defense concerns in the late 1930s gave rise to major R&D efforts in aircraft, rocketry, computers, electronics, nuclear energy, and other technological fields. In addition, academic scientists and engineers made important contributions to the development of new defense-related technologies by creating and applying new knowledge in basic science. These experiences demonstrated that government-sponsored R&D, whether fundamental research in universities or commercial projects in industry, could produce significant benefits to society. Consequently, after the war the government continued to support research not only in the defense sector, but also in industries that were closely related to defense, such as computers and nuclear energy. In addition, it created the National Science Foundation to expand the nation's capabilities in scientific research and education in universities.

During the postwar period, the scope and magnitude of government R&D gradually expanded. The most important new programs were in the area of biomedicine and energy. Older programs that had served primarily defense objectives—notably, spacecraft, microelectronics, and aircraft—were broadened to serve explicitly commercial purposes. Despite this broadening, the government never took the obvious next step: to develop a systematic and coherent civilian R&D policy. Americans are skeptical of national economic planning, and a comprehensive R&D policy emphasizing national economic growth is definitely a form of national plan. Nevertheless, the rationales for many of the mission-oriented and commercial projects undertaken since World War II easily translate into a case for a broad commercial R&D policy. Moreover, now that the cold war is over, it will probably be more difficult to call on national security to justify supporting both weapons development and commercial R&D that is linked to defense industries. Meanwhile, other industrialized countries—notably Japan—have gone further than the United States in developing a coherent civilian R&D policy. For all of these reasons, the United States is now being forced to rethink its approach to civilian R&D.

The basis for a more comprehensive approach to R&D policy lies in the link between research and economic growth. Economic research provides good evidence that most of the growth in per capita income in the United States and other industrialized societies is due to technological progress—to advances in knowledge that increase the productivity of labor and other resources.[3] With increasing international competition in numerous industries, the policy debate has been extended to encompass competitiveness: if the U.S. is to maintain high and growing per capita income, it must improve the productivity of its workers. If R&D is responsible for a substantial part of the advances in knowledge, more R&D can produce more rapid economic growth and a more competitive domestic industrial base.

The less obvious reason for government to support R&D is that otherwise there would be too little of it. Here the issue is whether R&D is a public good that creates improvements in economic well-being that are not captured (or appropriated) by the organization undertaking it. If businesses invest in R&D to earn greater profits from it, and if some of the returns accrue to someone else, firms will generally invest in R&D less than is socially optimal. However, a great deal of the research takes place at nonprofit institutions, especially universities, and much of it is financed by private philanthropy. Furthermore, the extent of spillovers is open to question. It is conceptually possible, therefore, that total private investment is not suboptimal. A recent survey of the economic research on this issue concludes that the spillover value of R&D is actually quite large, if imprecisely measured.[4] Research indicates that between one-third and two-thirds of the economic benefits of R&D are not captured by the organization that performs it, so that the average social return to R&D investments is about double the returns to risky investments in physical capital.

The simplistic policy conclusion to draw from these findings is that the government could improve the nation's economic performance by paying a 50 percent subsidy for all R&D, thereby offsetting the benefits that accrue outside the R&D performer's organization. The problem is

3. Important contributions to this literature include Moses Abramovitz, "Resource and Output Trends in the U.S. since 1870," *American Economic Review*, vol. 46 (May 1956, *Papers and Proceedings, 1955*), pp. 1–23; Robert M. Solow, "Technological Change and the Aggregate Production Function," *Review of Economics and Statistics*, vol. 39 (August 1957), pp. 312–20; Raymond Vernon, ed., *The Technology Factor in International Trade* (National Bureau of Economic Research, 1970); Edward F. Denison, *Accounting for United States Economic Growth, 1929–1969* (Brookings, 1974); and Edward F. Denison and Jean-Pierre Poullier, *Why Growth Rates Differ: Postwar Experience in Nine Western Countries* (Brookings, 1967).

4. Zvi Griliches, "The Search for R&D Spillovers," Working Paper 3768 (Cambridge, Mass: National Bureau of Economic Research, 1991). See also Frederic M. Scherer, "Inter-Industry Technology Flows and Productivity Growth," *Review of Economics and Statistics*, vol. 64 (November 1982), pp. 627–34; and Edward F. Denison, *Accounting for Slower Economic Growth: The United States in the 1970s* (Brookings, 1979).

that such a policy is also highly inefficient when the spillover benefits of R&D differ substantially among technologies. For example, some basic scientific research is not aimed at solving any particular practical problem, and the kinds of innovations that will flow from it are almost impossible to predict. For this work to have practical significance, its results must be available to others seeking solutions to practical problems. Once the results are made widely available, however, the original research performer is unlikely to capture a significant fraction of their value. Instead, the organizations making use of it, and their customers, will be the primary beneficiaries.

The degree to which the innovator derives the social benefit of innovation varies greatly even among commercial R&D ventures. New products and production processes differ in the extent to which they can be copied by others, and hence in the incentive they will give a firm to be an innovator rather than a copier. In some industries market prices— for final product or inputs—may not reflect true social values. Prices usually exclude environmental effects, may be set in imperfectly competitive markets, or may reflect a degree of impatience or risk aversion that is inappropriate for social decisions. If prices do not reflect true economic values, firms face distorted incentives for making R&D investments.

The immediate conclusion is that government R&D policy is more efficient when it focuses on the types of R&D for which spillovers create the most problems. This is a somewhat more sophisticated version of the statement that government R&D policy should "pick winners"— only here the issue is not just to identify R&D projects that are likely to be commercially valuable, but to identify valuable projects that are likely to receive too little attention from the private sector because they have large spillover benefits.

A policy that provides targeted support for areas of R&D exhibiting the greatest spillover benefits is not without drawbacks. First, when R&D support is targeted, competition may dwindle. If the most efficient way to pursue R&D in an industry is to undertake a single project through one firm or a consortium, the program may create a monopoly. Second, targeted R&D support is easily distorted by the political system. Elected political officials are unlikely to welcome the decline of a major industry, particularly in their district, and so may attempt to prop it up by subsidizing its R&D excessively. Conversely, an emerging technology, because it is not yet in use, may have no advocates to pressure political officials to support it. Third, the public sector faces considerable difficulty tailoring management systems to effective R&D projects. Government procurement and expenditure policies usually contain exacting safeguards to protect against fraud and abuse since the public tends to be skeptical about the overall efficiency of government. But such safeguards create serious problems for research programs, which require a great deal of managerial flexibility and creativity owing to their uncertainty. In the best of circumstances, some will fail and others will experience cost overruns or produce results that do not conform to the original plan. Safeguards against abuse are not consistent with management practices that are most appropriate for dealing with these characteristics of R&D.

In general, efficient R&D policies are hard to design because trade-offs have to be made among several conflicting objectives. There is a relatively strong case for supporting fundamental R&D that broadens society's technological base and for widely disseminating the results to maximize their spillover value. Substantial efficiencies are theoretically possible from targeting particular technologies for assistance; in practice, however, the government may not be able to identify them, channel support to the most promising areas, or manage them efficiently.

R&D Priorities in the United States

The amount and type of R&D performed in the United States results from many uncoordinated decisions rather than a comprehensive policy. Within the federal government, numerous agencies, working through different congressional committees, develop largely unrelated plans, while coordinating institutions—such as the Office of Management and Budget, the Office of Science and Technology Policy, the National Science Foundation, the Federal Coordinating Council on Science, Engineering and Technology (FCCSET), and the budget committees of Congress—do not attempt anything approaching comprehensive, economywide R&D planning. Consequently, to refer to R&D priorities in the United States is misleading. What we mean by this term is a combination of the explicit priorities the government follows when selecting which R&D to support and the implied priorities in the actual distribution of R&D effort throughout the economy.

This section examines the historical trends in the amount and distribution of R&D in the United States and in other advanced, industrialized societies. These data reveal three key facts. First, during the past fifteen years, the fraction of R&D accounted for by the private sector, and hence reflecting primarily private priorities, has grown substantially in the United States. Second, nearly all of the federal R&D effort goes

TABLE 7-1. U.S. R&D, by Source of Funds, Selected Years, 1960–89[a]

Billions of 1990 dollars

Year	Federal	Industry	University	Total
		Source of funds		
1960	37.27	19.26	0.86	57.38
1963	45.65	22.23	1.14	69.01
1966	52.74	27.67	1.56	81.96
1969	49.43	33.22	1.88	84.52
1972	44.88	33.25	2.16	80.29
1975	40.30	35.21	2.24	77.76
1978	43.64	41.03	2.55	87.22
1981	46.93	50.50	2.80	100.22
1984	55.60	60.17	3.34	119.11
1987	64.27	63.63	4.46	132.36
1989	65.74	67.14	4.96	137.85

SOURCE: National Science Board, *Science and Engineering Indicators—1989*, NSB-89-1 (Government Printing Office, 1989), table 4-2, pp. 264–65.

a. Totals may not add because numbers have been rounded.

to defense, health, and energy. Third, the United States spends about the same fraction of GNP on R&D as other nations, but it is the only one that focuses its R&D resources so extensively on these areas. Hence the central policy issue for the United States is not whether it spends enough on R&D, but whether it allocates and manages its R&D budget appropriately. Because of the importance of national security issues in the formulation and conduct of R&D, we conclude this section with an extended look at the role of the Department of Defense (DOD) in civilian R&D.

Spending for research and development in the United States has increased steadily over the past fifteen years and now amounts to more than $150 billion a year.[5] Fueled by increases in military spending and, later, the space race, real federal expenditures climbed rapidly after World War II and into the 1960s, but dropped in the first half of the 1970s with the completion of the Apollo program and the conclusion of the Vietnam war. Federal spending then accelerated again in the mid-1970s and by 1984 had returned to its 1966 level.

Tables 7-1 and 7-2 illustrate the changes in the composition of R&D. Since 1966, most of the increase in R&D spending has been in the private sector, where real spending on R&D more than doubled. The share of total R&D performed by industries now exceeds 70 percent. R&D spending by universities (from foundations, gifts, nonprofit organizations,

5. AAAS, *AAAS Report XVII*, p. 59.

TABLE 7-2. U.S. R&D, by Performer, Selected Years, 1960–89
Billions of 1990 dollars

Year	Federal	Industry	Nonprofit	FFRDC	University	Total
	Performer					
1960	7.36	44.82	1.20	1.54	2.76	57.68
1963	9.29	51.46	2.20	2.16	4.40	69.50
1966	12.16	58.71	2.77	2.38	6.48	82.49
1969	11.62	60.75	2.89	2.41	7.38	85.05
1972	13.03	55.51	2.42	2.14	7.47	80.86
1975	11.92	53.83	2.84	2.20	7.59	78.37
1978	12.45	60.87	3.06	3.14	8.45	87.97
1981	11.84	72.79	3.23	3.49	9.62	100.96
1984	14.18	87.57	3.69	3.82	10.57	119.82
1987	15.05	95.91	4.02	4.71	13.55	133.25
1989	15.47	99.98	3.88	4.88	14.58	138.77

SOURCE: National Science Board, *Science and Engineering Indicators—1989*, table 4-2, pp. 264–65.

and university sources) also increased rapidly, although it accounts for a small share of total R&D expenditures (table 7-2). Likewise, research at federally funded research and development centers (FFRDCs) tripled between 1960 and 1989. Total federal R&D increased by two-thirds during the 1960s but has remained relatively constant since then.

Whereas real R&D expenditures have grown, R&D spending as a fraction of GNP seems to have stabilized since the mid-1980s. The share of GNP devoted to R&D increased during the early 1980s and currently accounts for slightly less than 3 percent of GNP. This proportion is about the same as in Japan and West Germany and slightly more than in France and the United Kingdom (table 7-3). (Because of differences in accounting practices, classification systems, and estimation methods, it is difficult to draw reliable conclusions from the small differences in R&D effort among these countries.)[6] Likewise, the role of government in national R&D effort, while larger in the United States than in some other countries, is not dramatically different. The government now accounts for about 45 percent of total R&D in the United States in comparison with 36 percent in Germany and 54 percent in Italy. In contrast, the government's share is only 20 percent in Japan, although this figure is misleading because of the coordinating functions of the

6. For example, both Germany and Japan include all expenditures on universities as part of civilian R&D, whereas only some of these expenditures are so counted in the United States. If the general support for universities is omitted, the share of GNP devoted to civilian R&D falls to 2.6 percent in Japan and 2.4 percent in Germany.

TABLE 7-3. R&D as a Percentage of GNP, by Source of Funds, Selected Countries, 1988

Country	Source of funds				
	Government	Industry	Higher education	Other	Total
France	1.17	0.99	*	0.14	2.30
West Germany	1.01	1.83	*	0.03	2.87
Japan	0.58	2.03	0.26	0.03	2.90
United Kingdom	0.86	1.10	*	0.24	2.20
Sweden	1.18	1.86	*	0.03	3.07
Italy	0.76	0.59	*	0.06	1.41
United States	1.29	1.40	0.08	0.03	2.80

SOURCES: National Science Foundation, *International Science and Technology Data Update*, NSF 91-309 (Washington, 1991), pp. 7, 17.
* Less than 0.01 percent.

government through the Ministry of Finance and the Ministry of International Trade and Industry.

As these comparisons show, the United States does not appear to lag behind other countries in either overall R&D effort or government support for R&D. Indeed, because the U.S. economy is so much larger than the other advanced economies, and because R&D is to some degree a domestic public good, R&D efforts theoretically can produce more domestic economic benefit in the United States than in these other countries. Of course, as trade barriers tumble and the world economy becomes more integrated, foreign spillover benefits from R&D increase, so the relative advantage of the large U.S. domestic economy diminishes.[7] Nevertheless, the data provide no reason to believe that inadequate overall R&D effort is a source of poor economic performance or declining international competitiveness in the United States.

The U.S. government controls national R&D policy in three ways: through tax policy, through direct expenditures, and through the creation of institutional environments that encourage private investment in R&D (which are discussed below). Since 1981 the federal government has subsidized private R&D through preferential tax treatment. The federal tax code allows firms a 25 percent credit for increases in their R&D expenditures. Thus a substantial share of the increase in industry spending since 1980 can be considered off-budget federal financing (see table 7-4). However, R&D tax credits amount to a modest share of total

7. See P. A. David, David C. Mowery, and W. Edward Steinmueller, "Economic Returns from Basic Scientific Research," *Economics of Innovation and New Technology*, vol. 2, no. 2 (1992).

TABLE 7-4. The Federal R&D Tax Credit, 1981–91
Millions of 1982 dollars

Year	Outlay equivalent of federal tax credit	Revenue loss
1981	220	16
1982	640	415
1983	969	590
1984	3,106	1,276
1985	2,179	1,493
1986	2,004	594
1987	2,300	1,580
1988	1,020	740
1989	1,255	903
1990	1,233	846
1991	1,220	839

SOURCE: National Science Board, *Science and Engineering Indicators—1991*, NSB-91-1 (GPO, 1991), p. 334.

industry R&D expenditures. Certainly, the tax subsidy is nowhere near large enough to offset the difference between private and social returns to R&D.

In its direct expenditures, the federal government divides R&D into three categories: basic (which has no particular application in mind); applied (which attempts to create new technological know-how to solve a specific practical problem); and development (which brings new technologies to the level of practical use). Since 1980, development and basic research have supplanted applied research. Two-thirds of federal R&D now goes for development. Basic research surpassed applied work in 1987 and currently accounts for about 18 percent of federal expenditures (table 7-5).

In recent years federal R&D research support has shifted to defense and health. During the 1980s nearly the entire increase in development was accounted for by the DOD. National Aeronautics and Space Administration (NASA) expenditures doubled over this period, mainly because of the construction of the fifth shuttle orbiter and, more recently, the work on the space station. The R&D budget of the Department of Energy (DOE) declined in the first half of the 1980s, but recovered in the late 1980s and by 1992 had nearly returned to its 1980 peak. DOE activities have shifted from energy-related work to defense and basic science. In health, the emphasis has been on basic research. The Department of Health and Human Services (HHS) is now the biggest source of funds for basic research. HHS and NASA were also the only

TABLE 7-5. U.S. Federal Spending for R&D, by Category and Agency, 1980, 1985, 1989
Millions of 1990 dollars

Agency	1980			1985			1989		
	Development	Basic	Applied	Development	Basic	Applied	Development	Basic	Applied
DOD	11,719	540	1,721	26,623	861	2,307	34,151	947	2,407
DOE	3,476	523	754	2,825	943	1,198	2,956	1,267	959
HHS	447	1,763	1,570	423	3,233	1,796	531	4,240	2,276
NASA	1,624	559	1,051	1,544	751	1,033	2,342	1,374	1,700
NSF	13	815	90	0	1,262	97	0	1,708	122
DOA	47	276	382	38	445	466	32	471	486
Other	967	474	1,445	811	769	1,515	631	764	1,588
Total	18,233	4,950	6,923	32,226	8,264	8,315	40,611	10,771	9,416

SOURCE: National Science Board, *Science and Engineering Indicators—1989*, table 4-6, pp. 272-73.

TABLE 7-6. U.S. Federal R&D, by Budget Function, 1981–90
Billions of 1990 dollars

Year	Budget function						Total
	Defense	Energy	Health	Space	Science	Other	
1981	25.67	4.88	5.40	4.34	1.76	3.72	45.76
1982	28.91	3.95	5.07	3.39	1.78	3.31	46.40
1983	31.45	3.25	5.42	2.69	1.97	3.37	48.16
1984	35.61	3.14	5.81	2.80	2.20	3.71	53.26
1985	39.79	2.82	6.40	3.22	2.44	3.88	58.54
1986	42.46	2.63	6.40	3.33	2.45	3.79	61.05
1987	43.59	2.29	7.30	3.78	2.68	3.99	63.62
1988	43.34	2.30	7.65	3.98	2.83	4.04	64.13
1989	42.22	2.53	8.04	4.78	3.12	4.22	64.89
1990	44.51	2.34	8.27	6.18	3.47	4.29	69.06

SOURCE: National Science Board, *Science and Engineering Indicators—1989*, table 4-16, p. 285.

agencies to receive real increases in applied research appropriations during the 1980s.

Energy spending, omitting DOE expenditures for atomic defense research and physical science (mainly for the superconducting super collider), declined by two-thirds in real dollars during the first term of President Ronald Reagan (table 7-6). Since 1985, spending for energy research has been constant, although the emphasis has shifted from nuclear technologies to coal research, which has received steadily increasing support in the past five years. As a result, expenditures in this area are now as large as they were during the energy research heyday of the late 1970s. As a share of all federal R&D, defense spending peaked in 1986, and has been declining slowly since, but in 1990 still accounted for 64 percent of all federal R&D. Both space and basic science spending experienced significant real increases, with spending on major new space procurement projects (the fifth shuttle and the space station) roughly equaling the decline in defense.

The United States spends far more on defense and health and far less on civilian industrial technology than other advanced, industrialized nations (table 7-7). Despite some highly publicized projects, the share of U.S. R&D going to energy is only about half the level in Germany and one-sixth that in Japan. Because so much of the U.S. effort is devoted to defense weapons systems, which presumably have a small spillover value to the rest of the economy, the share of U.S. R&D that is commercially relevant is considerably less than in some other countries. If defense R&D is subtracted from the total, the U.S. share of GNP for nondefense

TABLE 7-7. R&D Appropriations, by Socioeconomic Objective,
Selected Countries, 1987[a]

Percent

Socioeconomic objective	Country				
	France	Germany	Japan	United Kingdom	United States
Agriculture	3.6	2.0	4.0	4.2	2.3
Industry	10.6	15.3	4.8	8.7	0.2
Energy	6.7	8.7	23.2	3.5	3.6
Infrastructure	3.2	1.9	1.8	1.5	1.8
Environment	0.4	3.3	0.5	1.0	0.5
Health	3.6	3.2	2.4	4.3	11.9
Advancement of knowledge	26.6	43.8	50.8	20.2	3.6
Civil space	5.9	4.9	6.1	2.7	6.0
Defense	34.1	12.5	4.5	50.3	68.6

SOURCE: National Science Board, *Science and Engineering Indicators—1989*, table 4-22, p. 289.
a. Columns may not add to 100 percent because some categories have been omitted.

R&D drops to about 2 percent, whereas Japan and Germany remain at 2.9 and 2.7 percent, respectively. However, focusing on the so-called civilian share of R&D expenditures in the United States understates the importance of defense to civilian R&D. As Lewis Branscomb observes, defense polices and institutions have shaped U.S. R&D policy since World War II.[8] Consequently, the shift in defense policy brought on by the demise of the Soviet Union ranks as the most important challenge (and opportunity) for U.S. R&D policy in the past fifty years.

Three aspects of the relationship between defense policy and nondefense R&D deserve special attention: the relationship between defense issues and nondefense federal R&D programs, the extent of commercially relevant R&D performed under the defense R&D budget, and the relationship between DOD procurement and industrial research. Our discussion necessarily only scratches the surface of these issues. Nevertheless, it underscores the magnitude of the challenge facing government in supporting the R&D enterprise should defense policy significantly change.

With the notable exception of health, most federal R&D supported by the government has some connection with defense. Historically, a political coalition to support an R&D program could rarely be organized unless it included defense proponents. From 1946 through the mid-1980s, an important justification for federal support for civilian nuclear

8. See L. M. Branscomb, "Does America Need a Technology Policy?" *Harvard Business Review*, vol. 20 (March–April 1992), pp. 24–28.

power research was to ensure domestic control of the technology, deemed essential for pursuing U.S. nonproliferation goals. Space exploration was justified on the grounds that rocket technology had both military and civilian applications and it could keep the United States abreast or ahead of the Soviet Union. The enormous increase in expenditures on science, authorized by the National Defense Education Act of 1958, stemmed from a security-based response to Sputnik. Similarly, the boom in energy research in the wake of the second oil crisis was authorized under the Defense Production Act of 1979.

Whether the government will accept civilian justifications for new technology programs is uncertain. For example, Sematech failed to win congressional approval as a Commerce Department activity, although it emerged successful (and unchanged) from the Defense Advanced Research Project Agency (DARPA) as a national security imperative. DARPA supports a score of programs with immediate commercial applications; however, from 1987 to 1992 attempts to establish a civilian counterpart agency all failed.

Civilian technology alone rarely has the political appeal to command a majority in Congress, for several reasons: innovation occurs years after the research is initiated; the research results are uncertain; and the ultimate beneficiaries of research are seldom identifiable. The electoral structure of government causes politicians to seek programs that produce benefits quickly, to shy away from risky investments, and to concentrate resources on well-identified, politically powerful groups. The commercial goals of R&D programs may be controversial because a successful program has the potential to hurt some firms that competed successfully before the innovation. Furthermore, many in the United States are ambivalent about whether government should attempt to direct commercial activities. As a result of all these factors, R&D efforts typically need to contribute to other goals besides commercial innovation in order to gain congressional approval. In the past national security has been one of the least controversial justifications for developing a new technology, so that a winning political coalition often could be created by marrying defense purposes to a commercial project.

DOD-sponsored research contributes to the development of civilian technology both indirectly (through spillovers) and through direct support of civilian applications. Of the $13.3 billion the federal government spent on basic research in fiscal 1992, $1.2 billion was characterized as "defense" support (provided through either the DOD or DOE). In addition, the DOD funds fundamental research that is only loosely related to defense through its "technology base" program, which received $4.2 billion in fiscal 1992.[9] According to the president's budget, this program "supports a wide range of scientific disciplines, including mathematics, chemistry, biochemistry, meteorology and solid state physics" and has led to numerous civilian applications from navigation systems to cellular telephones.[10] The DOD Independent Research and Development (IR&D) program, which in 1987 amounted to $2.1 billion, provides support for defense contractors.[11] Although most IR&D payments are probably used for defense-related projects, some of it goes into generic research that may ultimately have civilian applications. In addition, nearly all of DARPA's budget supports commercially relevant research; the agency received $1.6 billion in fiscal 1992.[12]

Several important industries are directly supported by DOD research programs. The DOD budget includes numerous civilian R&D initiatives: $232 million for the High Performance Computing Initiative, $449 million for the Advanced Material and Processing Initiative, $180 million for the National Aerospace Plane, and $100 million for Sematech.[13] DARPA's portfolio includes high-definition television ($75 million), X-ray lithography techniques for integrated circuit production ($60 million), and "precompetitive technology development" ($60 million).[14]

These programs and projects overlap, and the defense budget is not available in a form that permits an accurate estimation of the amount directed to civilian applications. We estimate that $7 billion to $8 billion of the DOD research budget is primarily civilian. This figure constitutes only about 15 percent of defense R&D, so that substantial defense R&D cuts could be accommodated without any impact on civilian innovation. But $8 billion also amounts to nearly 40 percent of federal civilian R&D expenditures. Hence a significant cutback on DOD research could have an enormous impact on federal support for civilian R&D.

Changes in defense policy will affect the relationship between DOD and its civilian contractors. In 1992, Secretary of Defense Richard B. Cheney told Congress that the 1990s will be a "decade of development,

9. *Budget of the United States Government, Fiscal Year 1993*, pt. 1, p. 127.

10. *Budget of the United States Government, Fiscal Year 1993*, pt. 1, p. 127.

11. National Science Board, *Science and Engineering Indicators—1989*, NSB-89-1 (Government Printing Office, 1989), app. table 4-14, p. 284.

12. AAAS, *AAAS Report XVII*, p. 50.

13. *Budget of the United States Government, Fiscal Year 1993*, pt. 1, pp. 102, 103, 111; and "Sematech: Model Project Gets Mixed Reviews," *Science*, March 20, 1992, p. 1501.

14. AAAS, *AAAS Report XVII*, p. 76.

more than of production."[15] The administration's new acquisition strategy emphasizes technology demonstration and prototype evaluation, and accordingly the DOD plans to increase funds for research on new and advanced technology. The American Association for the Advancement of Science reports that "this new emphasis on R&D . . . has been accompanied by actual and proposed procurement terminations—over 100 weapons systems within the last two years."[16] The problem with this strategy, as pointed out by Deputy Secretary of Defense Donald Atwood and a number of academic observers, is that federal procurement exerts a powerful stimulus on private investment in R&D.[17] Despite cost-based accounting practices, once a weapons system enters procurement, the lead contractor has considerable monopoly power in its dealings with DOD. William Rogerson estimates that about 4 percent of the value of a procurement contract is composed of payments in excess of production costs.[18] But this does not imply monopoly profits. Because a procurement contract is awarded on the basis of a design competition, applicants dissipate the excess payments at the design stage through private investment in R&D. Frank Lichtenberg estimates that one dollar in current government sales stimulates nine cents of private R&D. He concludes that fully half of the increase in industrial R&D in the early 1980s was due to the buildup in weapons acquisitions.[19]

The critical feature of the acquisition process is that it establishes a prize: procurement profits awarded to the most successful R&D program. DOD procurement provides an incentive system that solves the market failure problem in R&D. Indeed, Rogerson argues that because the R&D effort is unobservable to a federal agency—a classic principal-agent problem—the prize mechanism is the only efficient way to support R&D. Thus increasing direct federal R&D subsidies at the expense of procurement amounts to pushing rather than pulling on the proverbial string and is doomed to fail.

15. Quoted in AAAS, *AAAS Report XVII*, p. 70.

16. AAAS, *AAAS Report XVII*, p. 72.

17. For Atwood's remarks, see AAAS, *AAAS Report XVIII*, p. 71. See also Edwin Mansfield, *Technology Change* (Norton, 1971).

18. William P. Rogerson, "Profit Regulation of Defense Contractors and Prizes for Innovation," *Journal of Political Economy*, vol. 97 (December 1989), pp. 1284–1305.

19. Frank R. Lichtenberg, "The Private R&D Investment Response to Federal Design and Technical Competitions," *American Economic Review*, vol. 78 (June 1988), pp. 550–59.

A sobering historical episode illustrates the problem: it concerns the fate of aircraft R&D when the country demilitarized after World War I.[20] In the absence of security imperatives, Congress insisted that the government retain the rights to designs emanating from competitive R&D projects, and that once a winning design was identified, the DOD should hold a competitive bid for production. In one case in which the design rights for a bomber were kept by the government, the winner of the design competition subsequently lost the production contract because it attempted to amortize the development expense in its bid: "Deprived of his airplane, [the designer] no longer had any incentive to improve that particular design. Worse yet, deprived of a profitable production contract as a means of reimbursing his earlier investment, [he] was soon unable to finance further development work. . . . The statutes intended to protect the public's interest, here operated to the reverse effect and retarded the pace of research and development."[21] The Army Air Corps attempted to evade the incentive problem by padding procurement contracts. When the evasion became public, it drew the ire of Congress, detailed in hearings in which defense contractors were characterized as "rapacious" and "fraudulently abscond[ing] with obscene profits at the taxpayers' expense."[22] The dilemma was never resolved, but ultimately became moot as the country resumed a rapid military buildup before World War II.

The important lesson of defense R&D is that the new defense environment threatens to reduce the civilian R&D effort. If the defense R&D budget is cut, the commercial spillovers from weapons research plus civilian R&D support from the defense agencies will obviously decline. The changes in procurement practices are likely to cause a further reduction in private R&D; and as political support for defense R&D falls off, other civilian R&D activities that have benefited from their loose tie to national security will suffer. These conclusions do not imply that defense R&D and procurement must be maintained at recent levels in order to save U.S. R&D; but they do imply that, without a major refocusing of civilian R&D strategies, a decrease in defense R&D will

20. See Thomas L. McNaugher, *New Weapons, Old Politics: America's Military Procurement Muddle* (Brookings, 1989), chap. 2. We are indebted to William Rogerson for calling our attention to this account.

21. Irving B. Holley, Jr., *Buying Aircraft: Matériel Procurement for the Army Air Forces* (Washington: Office of the Chief of Military History, 1964), p. 85; quoted in McNaugher, *New Weapons*, p. 26.

22. McNaugher, *New Weapons*, p. 28.

reduce both publicly and privately financed civilian R&D. Unless the United States overcomes its political resistance to supporting civilian R&D without a strong national security justification, the gap in civilian R&D between the United States and its principal international competitors is likely to widen.

The Allure of Bigness

Throughout the postwar era, federal R&D programs have tended to waste funds on very large facilities and projects. In the case of basic research, the federal government has been most generous to projects requiring either federal laboratories or large on-campus research facilities. The construction of the superconducting super collider, for example, would give the United States a large experimental facility for high-energy physics research at each point of the compass: in California, Illinois, New York, and Texas. The Departments of Defense, Energy, and Health and Human Services and the National Aeronautics and Space Administration all have several large research facilities scattered around the nation engaged in the full spectrum of work from fundamental scientific research through demonstration and performance tests intended to facilitate the adoption of new commercial technologies.

The poor record of the federal government in supporting large commercial R&D projects is well known.[23] Briefly, the federal government does not do a particularly good job of identifying directions of commercially relevant R&D. Yet administrations of both parties have persistently tried to "pick winners" in certain industries. The history of commercial R&D in the energy sector is especially instructive. In the 1950s, the federal government began supporting the development of commercial light-water nuclear reactors. Then, in the 1970s, it tried to develop a commercial breeder reactor. Retrospectively, the decisions to push for the commercial adoption of both technologies were made too soon, perhaps a reasonable mistake, but the push continued after evidence accumulated showing nuclear power to be economically unattractive and

23. Comprehensive case studies of a wide range of federally financed technology development programs can be found in Richard R. Nelson, ed., *Government and Technical Progress: A Cross-Industry Analysis* (Pergamon Press, 1982); Walter S. Baer, Leland L. Johnson, and Edward W. Merrow, *An Analysis of Federally Funded Demonstration Projects: Executive Summary*, Research Report R-1925-DOC (Santa Monica: RAND Corp., 1976). See also our recent book, *The Technology Pork Barrel* (Brookings, 1991), which examines several of these projects and provides explanations for them.

dubious on safety grounds. A similar case is the government's effort to develop synthetic fuels from coal, which began as a small program in the early 1960s seeking a solution to the decline of the coal industry in West Virginia and Kentucky. In the 1970s the program exploded into a multibillion-dollar response to OPEC. Despite the failure of nearly every test facility, the program continued to grow. For a few years, the Reagan administration vastly reduced its scope, citing it as a prototypical example of the kind of wasteful interventions that President Reagan sought to curtail, but by the second half of his administration the program had been revived. In 1992 it was supporting forty-two plants, spending more money than ever before, and planning a substantial expansion.[24] To this day, it has not developed an economically attractive technology for making synthetic fuels from eastern coal. In similar fashion, the government is busily investing in follow-up programs to such commercial disasters as the space shuttle and the supersonic transport.

Big-ticket R&D projects are not a trivial part of the federal R&D budget. The budget proposed by the president for fiscal 1993 contained the following items: $350 million for the magnetic fusion reactor, $640 million for the superconducting super collider, $500 million for synthetic fuel from coal, $250 million for the National Aerospace Plane, $2.25 billion for the space station, $53.2 million for NSF's science and engineering research centers, and $400 million for the Earth Observation Satellite System.[25]

Even direct research support for universities tends to get bundled into large institutional grants. In the 1960s, the National Science Foundation began to award "institutional development grants" to help universities build competence in specific areas of research. During this period, the government also gave grants for constructing research facilities. Eventually this practice was eliminated because government agencies could not make such grants strictly on a project's merits because they faced political pressure to distribute these grants "equitably" among states and regions. For about ten years, the government managed to stay out of the big grant business, but in the 1980s it reentered. First, Congress began inserting line items to support particular facilities at designated universities, and then the National Science Foundation began to support engineering research centers, which initiated joint research between universities and business on ways to improve manufacturing technology.

24. Department of Energy, *Clean Coal Technology Demonstration Program: Program Update 1991*, DOE/FE-0247P (February 1992), p. 2.
   25. *Budget of the United States Government, Fiscal Year 1993.*

This precedent was then used to create science research centers for fundamental research and to build supercomputing centers on university campuses.

The allure of big projects is not difficult to understand. Elected political officials succeed because they put together winning coalitions, in part by advocating policies that are beneficial to the constituencies served by these coalitions. R&D facilities are an almost ideal economic base for a community: relatively nonpolluting, they employ large numbers of highly skilled, highly paid people. With the growth of the environmental movement in the United States, which has called into question many other forms of federal construction projects (highways, dams, and the like), it is not surprising that elected political officials would want to provide visible benefits to constituents through large federal grants for research facilities.

In one sense, the local popularity of research facilities meshes nicely with the argument that, all else equal, the private sector will underinvest in R&D. But the political attractiveness of these projects has little to do with the economic rationale for government support. R&D facilities used as mechanisms for promoting local development create a number of political problems.

First, once a facility is built and in operation, it is difficult to close or even substantially reduce. The local popularity of the facility is not related to whether it succeeds in producing more research benefits than costs. Instead, it is popular because its costs are the principal source of local benefits. Hence government R&D projects are difficult to kill or scale back if they begin to fail and thus are allowed to live on several years or more past the time when it would make sense to abandon them.

Second, the most politically attractive form of support for research is not necessarily the most efficient, since larger, more concentrated projects not only provide visible economic benefits to many citizens in a community but put the role of political representatives on display. In contrast, small grants are not likely to receive any public attention or to have been influenced much by elected politicians, so the local community is unlikely to base political support on whether it receives them.

Third, the management strategy that is politically most attractive can be inefficient. R&D is inherently uncertain, in that it explores uncharted technical waters to ascertain whether something novel and useful can be found. In most cases, there are many interesting lines of research for achieving a given purpose, and none is so clearly superior that a rational decisionmaker would explore only that option. Hence the best strategy is usually to pursue several lines of research simultaneously and to winnow out the approaches that are producing poor results as more is learned. The unpredictability of this process has several political ramifications. To begin with, the best policy is likely to be to cut off some projects—which means inflicting losses on the communities in which they are located. Another problem is that the best policy may produce a technology that makes some firms, or entire industries, obsolete. The communities that are homes to the losers will urge the government to prevent their projects from failing—in the first instance by keeping them alive longer than they should, and, second, by using its other policies, such as regulation and procurement, to create a market for commercial technologies that otherwise would fail. In addition, the government will tend to favor certain kinds of institutional arrangements for pursuing R&D. For example, the cooperative industry projects that focus on a single path of technical development are attractive because they minimize the chance that a project will be canceled or that it will produce an innovation that upsets relative competitive advantages within an industry.

These classic pork barrel effects on R&D projects do not reflect some failure of character or courage on the part of elected officials. The most altruistic member of Congress will not succeed in achieving the most meritorious public purposes without obtaining political support for them or without setting up a politically durable institutional structure for carrying them out. Exhorting members of Congress and the president to pay no heed to the distributive concerns of their supporters ignores an enduring reality of representative democracy and, therefore, an inherent feature of R&D policy in the U.S. system. Rather, R&D policies should be designed in the expectation that distributive politics cannot be ignored.

New R&D Institutions

Current federal policies for commercial innovation encourage research joint ventures (RJVs), groups of private firms that join together to address a defined set of research problems. The philosophy behind this strategy is that joint RJVs can overcome market failures, so federal financial participation can be small and industry—not government—can decide which specific technical options to pursue. The government sent a strong signal of approval for RJVs to industry in 1984 by relaxing certain antitrust laws. In addition, it has actively promoted RJVs through programs that coordinate private activities and provide financial support.

A novel program is the advanced technology program (ATP), initiated in 1989 at the National Institute of Standards and Technology. The ATP provides partial support to consortia undertaking generic precompetitive research. While this program has a modest budget ($50 million in fiscal 1992), it is the philosophical centerpiece of the new policies designed to help firms succeed in international competition through technological advances.[26] Another strategy of particular interest to the cash-strapped national laboratories is the cooperative research and development agreements (CRADAs), whereby government agencies or labs undertake research for industry consortia or individual firms. CRADAs were first authorized for agencies in 1986 and for federal laboratories in 1989. By 1992 more than 1,500 CRADAs were active, with an estimated value of $323 million.[27] In addition, the government shares costs for several big-ticket programs, including the national aerospace plane (NASP) and Sematech. These programs encompass both generic research and product development: NASP for hypersonic aircraft and Sematech for semiconductor manufacturing technology.

It is too early to provide a definitive assessment of the RJV experiment, but because RJVs represent a new philosophy and because they specifically address problems with the conduct of research by industries that face foreign competition, the economic rationale and political attractiveness of this collection of activities merit further discussion.

RJVs can improve research in three ways. First, they may circumvent the incentive problems individual firms encounter in conducting research that is not appropriable. Second, an RJV may cut costs by taking advantage of economies of scale or scope that are unavailable to a single firm or by avoiding the duplication of effort in competing firms. Third, an RJV can speed the diffusion of a new technology by facilitating the dissemination of research results among firms and agencies or between the federal government and firms.

However, RJVs can be expected to foster innovation only under certain conditions that usually make RJVs unattractive either to firms in the industry or to the government. We conclude that RJVs are not a panacea for the country's declining international competitiveness and they will probably have only a limited role in U.S. R&D policy.

26. Office of Technology Assessment, *Competing Economies: America, Europe, and the Pacific Rim, Summary*, OTA-ITE-499 (GPO, 1991), p. 22.

27. National Science Board, *Science and Engineering Indicators—1991*, NSB-91-1 (Government Printing Office, 1991), p. 102; and *Budget of the United States Government, Fiscal Year 1993*, pt. 1, p. 130.

The argument that RJVs will generally be beneficial rests on a narrow vision of the nature of research in competitive industries. Uncertainty about the promise of alternative paths of technological development leads to diversity in R&D projects. An R&D policy that restricts research options reduces both expenditures and the likelihood of producing a successful innovation. In the United States, industries composed of several competitive firms tend to have higher rates of measurable technological progress, including patent filings, counts of important inventions, and productivity growth. These studies lend credence to the view that reducing the number of independent research approaches reduces technological progress.[28]

The key to a successful RJV program is to focus on industries in which firms do little research because the technology is not appropriable or because research is subject to economies of scale or scope not present in production. However, in industries with these characteristics, firms may have no incentive to join an RJV. In a competitive industry, innovations that are widely adopted cause either a price reduction or an improvement in product quality that does not increase profit margins. The benefits of R&D are captured by consumers or downstream industries. An RJV will speed dissemination of an innovation—indeed, that is one of its social benefits. In doing so, however, it curtails the ability of innovators to derive even short-run profits from an innovation. Recognizing this effect of an RJV, firms will face a disincentive to organize one.

A different problem arises when an RJV pursues research that would be quickly disseminated (copied) in its absence. In this case, each firm prefers to have others join the consortium and do the research, which the firm can then use for free. This of course, is the standard free-rider problem, which the RJV in general does not solve.

Potential members have an incentive to join an RJV in three cases. If the benefits of the technology are not appropriable, the government can simply pay for the R&D. If the costs to the participants are almost zero, even a consortium that produces technologies with mostly spillover benefits will be attractive to the companies. But if the industry is international, an RJV will produce at best a transitory benefit for the

28. For comprehensive discussions of this issue, see Richard R. Nelson, Merton J. Peck, and Edward D. Kalachek, *Technology, Economic Growth, and Public Policy* (Brookings, 1967); Morton I. Kamien and Nancy L. Schwartz, "Market Structure and Innovation: A Survey," *Journal of Economic Literature*, vol. 13 (March 1975), pp. 1–37; and Jennifer F. Reinganum, "Practical Implications of Game-Theoretic Models of Innovation," *American Economic Review*, vol. 74 (May 1984, *Papers and Proceedings, 1983*), pp. 61–66.

domestic industry, since foreign competitors will be able to free ride on the innovations produced by the consortium. Hence a significant degree of appropriability is necessary for an RJV to have a lasting effect on the international competitiveness of a domestic industry.

An RJV can also avoid the free-rider problem when it produces research that has significant appropriable benefits. In this case, the consortium can generate profits for the joint venturers by licensing the technology at a royalty rate that prevents the competition from forcing prices down to production costs. The role of the government here is limited, for firms already have an incentive to create an RJV on their own. An RJV would fail to emerge on its own only if the degree of appropriability of the technology is too low to allow the costs of collaborative research to be recaptured through royalties. Then, the government can encourage the venture by subsidizing it.

Finally, the free-rider problem does not arise if members are able to capture benefits because they collectively or individually exert market power. For example, if consortium members are regulated utilities, they do not compete in product markets. The more troubling circumstance is when the consortium provides a mechanism for collusive price control or division of markets. In this case an RJV can be socially attractive only if it can achieve savings without reducing the diversity of the projects. Government involvement here is primarily regulatory to ensure that the RJV is not used to create monopoly profits that exceed the incentives necessary to undertake the research. In this case, by assumption, the industry does not face international competition.

Proposals for forming a government-sponsored RJV therefore need to be evaluated on a case-by-case basis, and RJVs intended to promote international competitiveness inevitably require the financial participation of the government. Consequently, whether a government-supported RJV makes sense depends on whether the expenditure component of the government's involvement can be reasonably efficiently managed. In particular, one must examine whether the RJV is prone to the pork barrel influences described earlier. The stability of an RJV, like that of other federal efforts to develop new technologies, is only partially related to the economic or technological success of the program. Past technology development programs that involved large federal expenditures and industry participation (such as the programs for breeder reactors and synthetic fuels, both of which started out with at least 50 percent industry cost sharing) demonstrate that failures are difficult to kill. Indeed, an RJV is likely to have even more difficulty making efficient program modifications. Firms are an important source of critical information about a program's performance. To the extent that an RJV includes all domestic firms in an industry, such information may be muted.

The potential usefulness of the RJV policies is further limited by their political attractiveness. Experience to date suggests that RJVs have significant political liabilities. The problems of the Sematech consortium are a case in point. The administration suggests that Sematech's problems are unique,[29] but we find them to be inherent in programs designed to enhance the international position of competitive domestic industries.

In the mid-1980s, U.S. firms stopped manufacturing dynamic random access memory chips for sale to other companies.[30] The loss of U.S. capacity was of concern for reasons of both security and competitiveness. Because integrated circuits (ICs) are used extensively in advanced weapons systems, domestic capacity, particularly for the most advanced chips, was deemed vital to national security. The competitiveness argument is related to both the IC industry and to the role of ICs as "technology drivers." Loss of the IC industry would hasten or exacerbate the loss of market share in a range of electronic products. Sematech was part of a set of federal responses, which included trade as well as R&D policies.[31]

The original intent of Sematech was to develop the sorts of technology that produce the biggest theoretical social benefits from an RJV. Sematech planned to investigate generic and "precompetitive" aspects of manufacturing process technology that were expected to be of value to all IC manufacturers and would not interfere with their competition in the product market. Furthermore, the program would pursue R&D exhibiting economies of scale and scope.[32]

The process technology program did not work out. Sematech constructed a model chip fabrication plant at its headquarters in Austin, Texas, but the plant was never used for demonstration production runs that would investigate learning economies in manufacturing. IBM, the largest chip manufacturer among Sematech members, objected to the quantity of chips that were to be produced at the plant, apparently out

---

29. *Budget of the United States Government, Fiscal Year 1993*, pt. 1, p. 97.

30. David C. Mowery and W. Edward Steinmueller, "Prospects for Entry by Developing Countries into the Global Integrated Circuit Industry: Lessons from the U.S., Japan, and the NIEs" (Stanford University, Center for Economic Policy Research, 1991).

31. General Accounting Office, *Federal Research: The SEMATECH Consortium's Start-up Activities*, RECD-90-37 (November 1989).

32. See Congressional Budget Office, *The Benefits and Risks of Federal Funding for Sematech* (September 1987); and Congressional Budget Office, *Using Federal R&D to Promote Commercial Innovation* (April 1988).

of concern that it would be pressured to buy the chips and thus would have to substitute them for chips it produces internally. Member firms also stated that production lines are unique to each company and each type of chip being manufactured, so they could learn little from the plant's operation.

Experience with the fabrication plant bears out the observations made above. In an RJV, innovations need to be transferable to sponsoring companies. If the innovation can be transferred to sponsoring companies, it can probably also be transferred to nonmembers. Sematech is composed of a relatively small fraction of the industry. Thus, if the consortium generated innovations that were not amenable to licensing (virtually any process innovation), members could expect nonmembers (both domestic and foreign) to adopt the innovations as well. Because this industry is highly competitive, an industrywide innovation would most likely push the price down or force firms to increase the quality of computer chips without a commensurate increase in profits. As the Sematech experience demonstrates, a fraction of firms in a competitive industry will not choose to conduct generic research, even when it is subsidized by the federal government.

The consortium attempted to solve the problem by focusing on technology that would be appropriable by Sematech members. Sematech allocated over a third of its R&D budget to manufacturers of IC production equipment to develop better equipment for the semiexclusive use of Sematech members.[33] The details of contracts are proprietary, but Sematech's plan states that it provides "preferential availability of all funded equipment, systems, materials, supplies and chemicals to members, assuring them a return on their investment."[34] According to magazine reports, the basic deal is that Sematech members are to get first use of the new technology, either contractually (equipment manufacturers are not allowed to sell the equipment to nonmembers for a year) or through various arrangements whereby Sematech members have the exclusive right to "test" the equipment in their fabrication plants.[35] The equipment, of course, can be licensed, patented, and protected.

33. Congressional Budget Office, *Using R&D Consortia for Commercial Innovation: SEMATECH, X-ray Lithography, and High-Resolution Systems* (July 1990), p. 23.

34. "SEMATECH—1991 Update," Technology Transfer doc. 9101044A–GEN (Austin, Tex.: SEMATECH, 1991).

35. Brink Lindsey, "Dram Scam," *Reason*, vol. 23, no. 9 (1992), pp. 40–48.

Until recently, the Sematech consortium was happy with this arrangement, although it left three other groups somewhat disgruntled: the equipment manufacturers that did not receive Sematech contracts, some equipment manufacturers that did, and IC firms that are not members of Sematech.

Those that did not get contracts claim that Sematech is laundering federal dollars into a "picking winners" scam, a charge that is politically unnerving to Sematech's ideological proponents. The so-called winners think of Sematech as a downstream cartel that has appropriated an excessive share of the returns to their innovations. Unfortunately for Sematech, these firms can counter its legal authority. Semi-Gas, one of the winners, discovered that even though it was not allowed to sell Sematech-sponsored equipment to Sematech's competitors, it could sell itself. In 1990 the Matheson Company, a subsidiary of Nippon Sanso, offered $23 million for Semi-Gas, which had been purchased three years earlier for only $5 million. Opponents of the sale claimed this increase in value was entirely due to Semi-Gas's association with Sematech.[36]

The loudest complaints about Sematech's equipment strategy have come from domestic IC firms who are not members. Their self-appointed spokesman, T. J. Rodgers, the chief executive officer of Cypress Semiconductor, has testified at virtually every congressional hearing on Sematech. His complaints are that Sematech is an anticompetitive cartel, that its membership fees discriminate against small firms, and that the federal government's RJV policy is unfair to entrepreneurs.[37] He may be successful in limiting the extent to which Sematech can appropriate equipment innovations. Sematech is now planning to allow sales of the new equipment to all domestic semiconductor firms.

The key point of this history is that when an RJV—or any government program—is of benefit to only a fraction of the domestic industry at the expense of the remainder, it generates political controversy. Traditional government R&D policies that relied on contracting offer numerous examples of programs that floundered because of such controversy. For

36. *Foreign Acquisition of Semi-Gas Systems*, Hearing before the Subcommittee on Science, Technology, and Space of the Senate Committee on Commerce, Science, and Transportation, 101 Cong. 2 sess. (GPO, October 10, 1990).

37. See, for example, his congressional testimony, "The American Semiconductor Industry: Winners or Whiners?" in *Legislation Concerning Production Joint Ventures*, Hearing before the Subcommittee on Antitrust, Monopolies and Business Rights of the Senate Committee on the Judiciary, 101 Cong. 2 sess. (GPO, July 17, 1990). See also Graeme Browning, "Techies in Cahoots," *National Journal*, July 6, 1991, pp. 1687–90.

example, NASA's satellite program was canceled in 1973 even though it had been one of the most successful commercial technology development programs undertaken in the postwar era. Firms that lost the contract to develop the next generation of geosynchronous satellites raised approximately the same arguments described here and succeeded in killing the program.[38] The Army Air Corps procurement policy following World War I suffered precisely the same problem. A contract announcement inevitably inspired complaints by losing firms, who lobbied their congressmen to examine, shave, and preferably terminate winning proposals.[39] RJV policy for industries that are competitive at the production level faces a dilemma: to be attractive to firms, RJVs need to be relatively exclusive; that is, a sufficient number of firms need not adopt the innovation in order for prices to remain high enough for participating firms to reap profits. But if the noninnovating share of the industry includes domestic as well as foreign firms, political controversy can be expected to ensue.

Equipment R&D has been less appropriable by Sematech members than they hoped. Not surprisingly, the consortium fought the sale of Semi-Gas. A pack of outraged senators joined it to complain that the sale undermines the whole point of Sematech: to enhance the competitiveness of American industry relative to that of Japan. The first line of defense was the Exon-Florio amendment, which directs the president to block sales of U.S. assets that would "impair national security." The president declined to do so in the case of Semi-Gas. The technical justification offered by William Rudman, deputy under secretary of defense for trade security policy, was that "the Exon Florio statute . . . requires that determinations be made on a case-by-case basis. It does not provide a legal basis for the protection of an entire industrial sector or technological base from foreign acquisition."[40]

The Semi-Gas experience is a small example of what can happen in the absence of an integrated R&D policy. The problem is essentially twofold. First, federal agencies can veto each other's efforts when they jointly but separately control policy. Second, in the United States different governmental organizations frequently respond to separate interests. The congressional committees that authorize and appropriate funds to Sematech attempted to protect the investment the government and member firms had in Sematech by blocking the Semi-Gas sale. At

38. Cohen and Noll, eds., *Technology Pork Barrel*, chap. 7.
39. McNaugher, *New Weapons*, chap. 2.
40. *Foreign Acquisition of Semi-Gas Systems*, Hearing, p. 24.

the same time, the agency responsible for invoking the Exon-Florio amendment interpreted the proposed sale in the context of security issues and perhaps overall trade strategy. Regardless of the appropriateness of the decision, it undermined the RJV strategy. The outcome is thus an apparent contradiction of federal purpose.

Sematech's authorization expires in fiscal 1993, so Congress will decide its fate in 1992. Two of its original fourteen members have announced that they will pull out,[41] and the president has proposed cutting its budget by 20 percent. We expect that future research activities conducted by Sematech are unlikely to include the sort of generic activities for which it was organized. If Congress insists that any appropriable innovations Sematech discovers be made available to its competitors, the joint venturers are likely to lose interest in participating in the consortium. Sematech's troubled history suggests that RJVs are not the models for future technology policy.

The national aerospace plane stands in sharp contrast to Sematech.[42] Unlike Sematech, NASP is likely to receive a significant increase in federal funds. NASA's proposed budget includes an increase from $20 million to $80 million, on top of the Air Force's contribution of $180 million. NASP is organized as an extreme version of a joint venture.[43] Participating firms have formed a "team" that fully shares all results and that has separated the profit-sharing agreement from any firm's contribution to the research effort. Yet both its members and the government are satisfied with the program, citing numerous generic results related to aircraft materials, engines, fuels, and flight simulation methods, as well as designs for the X-30, the hypersonic plane that forms the centerpiece of the program.

NASP diverges from Sematech in three critical ways. First, all domestic firms interested in the technology are members. Consequently, if the research results are not as promising as we have suggested here, we—and Congress—have no way of finding out at this point. Second, the

41. See Andrew Pollack, "A Chip-Industry Defection," *New York Times*, January 12, 1992, sec. 3, p. 12, and Pollack, "A Founding Member Leaves Sematech Chip Consortium," *New York Times*, January 7, 1992, pp. C1, C2.

42. See Linda R. Cohen, Susan A. Edelman, and Roger G. Noll, "The National Aerospace Plane: An American Technological Long Shot, Japanese Style," *American Economic Review*, vol. 81 (May 1981, *Papers and Proceedings, 1980*), pp. 50–53.

43. "Teaming Agreement Stresses Equality among Five NASP Prime Contractors," *Aviation Week and Space Technology*, vol. 133, no. 18 (1990), pp. 38–39; AAAS, *AAAS Report XVII*, p. 178; and *Budget of the United States Government, Fiscal Year 1993*, pt. 1, p. 111.

U.S. aerospace industry is internationally dominant. No significant competitors, either domestic or foreign, will free-ride on nonappropriable technology that the consortium generates or will complain about potential appropriable results. Third, the chief purchaser of NASP technology is likely to be the federal government. As with other defense procurement contracts, a prize awaits firms that sell the technology to the government, and the government can use procurement to make the program a success.

Our comparison of these programs suggests that the small scale of other federally sponsored RJVs may be the result of inherent problems in the strategy rather than the newness of the programs. For example, the advanced technology program has received far less in federal appropriations than its sponsors had hoped. Both the administration and the Senate authorized $100 million a year for the program; however, only $10 million was appropriated in 1990, $36 million in 1991, and $50 million in 1992.[44] We suspect that the small appropriations reflect the difficulties in federal participation in commercial RJVs.[45] Our overall assessment is somewhat gloomy. RJVs may have a role to play in technology policy, and we outline below conditions that appear most favorable for their success. However, they appear unlikely to play a significant role in improving the international competitiveness of U.S. industries.

University-Sponsored Research

Beginning in the early 1980s, a long history of placid, mutually supportive relations between universities and the federal government started to unravel under a stream of news stories about university mismanagement of federal research funds. The first such "scandals" involved faculty, who were charged with falsifying research results and misusing federal research funds. The battle escalated in 1989 when federal auditors, and later members of Congress, attacked universities for spending the government's money inappropriately and even illegally. Many universities reimbursed

44. *Budget of the United States Government, Fiscal Year 1993*, pt. 1, p. 115; and OTA, *Competing Economies*, p. 22.

45. Because they offset some operating costs at national laboratories (although only a small fraction), CRADAs have a particular political appeal. The chief policy question regarding CRADAs is whether the benefits of technology transfer from the laboratories to industry or the economies of scope in the conduct of research available to laboratories but not to industry are large enough to offset potential problems in the use of the labs to conduct proprietary research. Resolving this issue is premature at this point and beyond the scope of this chapter.

the government for controversial expenditures, and virtually all universities are designing more comprehensive auditing systems for monitoring costs to be charged to the government. The purpose of this section is to shed some light on the origins of the controversy, its implications for federal research policy, and how it might be resolved.[46]

Federal support for universities should be evaluated according to the contributions university research makes to national goals. As is the case with other research programs, federal support for universities is intended to contribute to economic growth and to assist in developing new technologies for the public sector. In addition, university research support may affect the way engineers and scientists are prepared to undertake more practically relevant work in later employment, thereby indirectly affecting national goals. As a practical matter, assessing the national benefits of university research is quite difficult. University research and education tend to be general and foundational, and therefore to have a very long-run effect that is difficult to measure. Nevertheless, because the current controversies about universities have raised important questions about the proper size and scope of federal support, some assessment, albeit crude, of this performance is essential for making intelligent policy decisions.

The federal government has played a key role in the rise of the American research university by providing universities with substantial funds for basic research. In 1991 more than half the research funds spent by universities, or over $8 billion, came from the federal government.[47] (The table below shows the source of university research funds in 1988.)[48] While other nations support universities with public funds, elsewhere government support for research tends to be directed at either government laboratories (as in Europe) or industrial research facilities (as in Japan).

Source	Percentage of all research funds
Federal government	60
State and local government	9
Universities	18
Industry	7
Other	7

46. Stanford University was prominently involved in these disputes. One of the authors is a faculty member at Stanford. The views expressed here are his own and not those of Stanford University.

47. National Science Foundation, *Federal Funds for Research and Development: Fiscal Years 1989, 1990, and 1991* (Washington, 1991), p. 143.

48. National Science Board, *Science and Engineering Indicators—1989*, p. 297.

A major consequence of strong federal support for university research is that in the United States teaching and research are integrated. In other countries, few universities rank among the best research institutions, and many of the best research scholars in science and engineering do not teach. For example, in a recent study of molecular biology and neurobiology, the top-ranking institutions in the world, measured by total publication and total scientific citations per paper, were roughly equally divided between U.S. universities and European institutions.[49] Of the forty institutions on the four "top ten" lists, twenty-two are universities and eighteen are nonteaching facilities. The United States accounts for eighteen of the universities and seven of the nonteaching facilities, while four universities and eleven nonteaching facilities are in Europe.

Because university research funds are spread over many institutions in the United States, the dominance of the United States in basic research is greater than is revealed in the "top ten" lists. U.S. institutions account for about 40 percent of the world's scholarly publications in clinical medicine, biomedical research, biology, earth and space sciences, engineering, and mathematics, 30 percent in physics, and 22 percent in chemistry. The United States also ranks first in citations per published paper in all fields except mathematics, where it is second to the United Kingdom. In all scientific fields taken together, citations per paper are 40 percent higher in the United States than in any other country.[50] Finally, the United States leads the world in training research scholars and annually attracts hundreds of thousands of students from Europe and Asia.

While the scientific productivity of U.S. research universities is impressive, the link between basic research and economic productivity is not well understood. Edwin Mansfield has undertaken the most extensive work to date to evaluate the effects of university research on the national economy. One of his findings is that U.S. companies find basic research more profitable than do Japanese companies, even though both countries do about the same amount. He also finds that U.S. companies devote substantially more R&D effort to inventing new products and processes, as compared with making improvements on old products and processes.[51]

---

49. *Science*, vol. 256 (April 24, 1992), pp. 460, 468.

50. National Science Foundation, *International Science and Technology Update*, NSF-91-309 (Washington, 1991).

51. Edwin Mansfield, "Industrial R&D in Japan and the United States: A Comparative Study," *American Economic Review*, vol. 78 (May 1988, *Papers and Proceedings, 1987*), pp. 223–28.

Mansfield interprets these results as indicating that U.S. universities are better at training scientists and engineers who are capable of producing commercially valuable research that is original and fundamental. Mansfield has also investigated the extent to which the quality of U.S. research universities translates into economic payoffs to American industry.[52] His conclusions are preliminary, but suggest that academic research plays a major role in bringing new, valuable products to market in a wide range of industries.

The history of federal support for university research provides many examples in which universities played an important role in attaining national technological and economic objectives. The federal government began pursuing national R&D objectives through grants to universities in the nineteenth century, when it established extremely successful agricultural research programs in the land grant colleges.[53] Shortly before World War II, universities became increasingly involved in federal research projects. The first generation of computers was developed at Harvard, the Massachusetts Institute of Technology, and the University of Pennsylvania in the 1940s, and nuclear weapons technology grew out of research at the University of Chicago and other universities. After World War II the government institutionalized its relationship with universities, first, by giving several universities the responsibility for managing the government research laboratories that had developed weapons during the war, and second, by creating the National Science Foundation, the main purpose of which is to support research projects in universities.

Because the early ventures with universities were widely regarded as a great success, federal support for university research became increasingly generous. By the 1960s, all major research universities were growing financially dependent on federal grants and contracts. No university can now realistically expect to be a major center of research without substantial federal support. In addition, almost every leading research university has become the manager of a federal laboratory, the budgets for which are not included in the total given above for support for university research.

Federal research support for universities takes two forms. The first is institutional support, which provides funds to a university to establish

52. Edwin Mansfield, "Academic Research and Industrial Innovation," *Research Policy*, vol. 20 (February 1991), pp. 1–12.
53. See Bruce L. R. Smith, *American Science Policy Since World War II* (Brookings, 1990).

or to operate a research facility. The second is project support, in which a university faculty member proposes to investigate a particular research question and asks the government to pay part of the costs.

Institutional support consists of large contracts or grants to provide infrastructure for research and sometimes teaching in a particular field. One example is a management contract to operate a federal laboratory, in which the government pays for the facilities and the management expenses, usually providing only a small additional budget for research projects. Some of the research laboratories of the Department of Energy (such as the Lawrence Laboratories) and of the National Aeronautics and Space Administration (such as the Jet Propulsion Laboratory) fall into this category. Another example is an institutional grant to a university to build competence in an area of research. The engineering and science research centers of the National Science Foundation fall into this category. The research conducted in these facilities is usually financed by separate project grants and is usually carried out by staff scientists, university faculty, and subcontractors.

Project grants typically involve "cost sharing" in that not all of the university's resources devoted to the project are compensated by the government. For example, most of the time spent by a faculty researcher working on the project is not reimbursed by the government. As a result, the total cost to the government of a sponsored research project is normally much higher if the project is carried out in a company or a federal research lab, rather than a university.

In contrast to institutional support, project grant support has no natural way to cover the costs of the facilities, equipment, and management associated with the research project unless it is carried out in facilities receiving institutional support. Since about 1970, the federal government has helped pay for these institutional costs of research by adding an indirect cost item to every project grant received at a university.[54] The approach taken was borrowed from the method of reimbursing federal contractors for overhead costs. The federal government issued some general, often vague rules on how to separate the institutional costs of federally sponsored research from other activities, and then left it largely to the universities to develop accounting systems to estimate these costs.

54. Bruce L. R. Smith and Joseph J. Karlesky, *The State of Academic Science: The Universities in the Nation's Research Efforts* (New York: Change Magazine Press, 1977), pp. 200–23.

Indirect cost rates doubled between 1970 and the mid-1980s, when they stabilized at about 70 percent at leading private research universities and nearly 50 percent at leading public universities. The primary causes of the increase were additional depreciation and maintenance on buildings and equipment, higher utility prices, and growth of universities' administrative bureaucracy.

The growth in capital costs was due in part to the replacement of institutional facilities grants by indirect cost recovery. The government decided to pay for capital facilities through add-ons to research grants rather than by separate facilities grants. This category of indirect costs accrues only to private universities, because facilities purchased from government funds (federal, state, or local) are not eligible for indirect cost recovery. This exclusion accounts for the majority of the difference in indirect cost recovery rates between public and private universities. Utility bills rose because the real price of energy increased over the period and because ever-more sophisticated research equipment consumed more energy. Finally, university bureaucracy grew in part because of regulatory requirements regarding government-sponsored research, including audit safeguards.

The controversies over indirect cost recovery in the early 1990s operate at two levels. The most visible controversy involves expenditures that call into question the propriety of university decisionmaking and accounting procedures. Examples are social events hosted by university administrators, retreats of university administrators and trustees at expensive resorts, and other seemingly frivolous expenditures. In practice, the visible scandals involved small expenditures, typically less than 1 percent of indirect cost recovery, which the universities returned voluntarily for political and public relations purposes.

The deeper, and financially far more significant, issue surrounding indirect cost recovery is that the premise of the system of federal reimbursement for research is under question. Federal agencies responsible for overseeing the contractual relationships with universities are not simply rewriting the rules to keep yachts, flowers, junkets, and silk sheets out of the government's budget. They are trying to cut payments for indirect costs across the board and are imposing more rigorous accounting methods.

For example, consider the changes with respect to administrative overhead. Federal officials are replacing the methods for estimating the administrative costs of sponsored research with a much more elaborate auditing system. The system installed at Stanford University to audit expenditures for federal sponsored research is estimated to increase the accounting costs of the university by $15 million to develop and $4 million a year to maintain, although some of these costs would have been incurred anyway.[55] At the same time, the Office of Management and Budget has proposed capping the indirect cost of administration at 26 percent of the direct costs of a grant.[56] One cannot simultaneously lower the maximum allowable expense and increase administrative requirements without forcing universities to absorb a much larger fraction of the costs of government-sponsored research.

Another illustrative example is the treatment of libraries. Major research universities have extensive library collections, and some have indirect costs for libraries that exceed 5 percent of the direct costs of research grants. Recently the federal government has challenged these estimates. To please government auditors, the University of Chicago recently surveyed all library users about the purpose of their visit, where they were employed, and whether they worked on a sponsored research project. The costs attributed to sponsored research were set equal to library costs multiplied by the share of library use accounted for by Chicago personnel who were working on a sponsored research project. This method produces perverse incentives. Most fundamentally, to allocate the fixed costs of a library collection among the categories of users is arbitrary. A research university with a strong library, such as Chicago, attracts users from throughout its community—business, public schools, other colleges and universities. Once a scholarly work is acquired for a research project, it costs virtually nothing if library students use it for class papers and faculty assign it in courses. But the cost allocation method favored by the government encourages universities to prevent such uses to maximize the fraction of costs paid by the government.

The library story points to another controversial aspect of the new approach to cost reimbursement, the assumption that teaching and research can be separated in a research university. This point of view is at variance with the uniquely American system of combining research and education. The most effective form of research training takes place not in classrooms, but in laboratories and offices, where students talk about and participate in research as part of their education. To divide

55. By contrast, Stanford's average annual reimbursement to the federal government for 1981–88 in response to the indirect cost controversy was less than $1.1 million. Private communication from Robert L. Byer, Stanford vice president for research.

56. 56 Fed. Reg. 50228 (1991).

the cost of a lab or an office in proportion to the time spent teaching and doing research rewards faculty and universities who seal off their research activities from students. This is the system that foreign students seek to escape when they apply to attend U.S. universities.

If the government's actions to cut the costs of university research seem arbitrary, the fact remains that the system of indirect cost recovery that was in place until the early 1990s had serious flaws. The spirit of the system was sensible: to give universities funds to cover infrastructural costs roughly in proportion to the success of the university in obtaining federally sponsored research projects. Throughout most of the postwar years, federal research support was sufficiently generous that many universities received a substantial income from federal research grants. In addition, supporting infrastructure through add-ons to small project grants insulates government from constituency pressures to turn these grants into a form of pork barrel.

The weakness of the indirect cost recovery system is that it is a form of cost-plus contracting, which blunts the incentives of universities to be careful about incurring indirect costs. Private universities face an incentive to raise unlimited money for new research facilities. If a philanthropic organization or individual can be induced to pay for a new facility, the university can be paid twice—once through the contribution to build it, and a second time through indirect cost recovery. Likewise, if the university adds accountants and procedures to generate better estimates of the actual costs of sponsored research and to audit the activity of researchers, the university collects twice—once through the higher estimates of indirect costs, and again for the accounting system that produces the estimates.

The new cost accounting rules fail to address the incentive problems that exist in cost-based reimbursement. Moreover, the new method is worse because it creates new sources of inefficiency—such as requiring elaborate accounting systems that cost many times more than the errors they avoid, and inducing universities to close libraries to students and businesses in order to maximize the government's financial contribution.

The government has a precedent for dealing with this problem: medicare cost reimbursement for hospitals, adopted in 1983. Previously, medicare paid hospitals on the basis of cost reimbursement and witnessed ever-escalating hospital prices. The new system sets a fixed price for each type of hospital service, based on nationwide costs, so that hospitals now have financial incentives to reduce medical costs. The analog for indirect cost reimbursement is to set a fixed national rate for indirect costs that would not require audit justification and that would not depend directly on essentially arbitrary allocation schemes for attributing joint costs between sponsored research and other uses. Because this system would save a large university millions of dollars in record keeping, it could both reduce the cost of sponsored research to the government and increase dollars for research purposes.

This proposal amounts to a form of price cap regulation, and has three major complications. First, overhead rates among research universities differ. At a minimum, the rate would probably need to differ between public and private universities. Some universities have lower indirect cost rates because they cover part of their administrative overhead through management fees from federally financed laboratories. Rates also vary because differences in the age of capital plant cause differences in maintenance and depreciation charges.

Second, because a national uniform rate will be more visible and financially significant, it may be more difficult to change than individually negotiated rates. If so, universities may face financial problems later because scientific equipment and facilities for cutting-edge research are becoming increasingly costly. One possibility for avoiding some of the problems associated with cost changes is to index the rate to the major categories of expenses. The approach has been used successfully by utility regulators in adjusting electricity rates to reflect variability in fuel costs for electric generation.

Third, due to the heterogeneity of universities and the likelihood of generally rising capital costs for research, the agency responsible for setting a national uniform rate is likely to be pressured to make exceptions. Some pressure is likely to come from political leaders, just as they now seek to influence the geographic distribution of expenditures for large, visible research facilities.

Despite these problems, the advantages of a fixed indirect cost rate over the current system are large. Administrative expenditures devoted to documenting cost-based indirect cost recovery are so large that even an imperfect fixed rate system is likely to be both cheaper for the government and more financially attractive to universities than the present system.

The current controversy surrounding university finances raises a fundamental issue: whether the United States wants to have the structure of research universities that it enjoys at present. The government may now believe that federally sponsored research at U.S. universities has somehow failed—that the money could be spent more productively elsewhere. Judging from the scientific productivity of U.S. academics and the strong desire of foreigners to attend U.S. universities, this possibility seems remote but cannot be ruled out.

The budget pressures on the federal government offer a more plausible explanation for the current crisis. During the past twenty years, the government has been increasingly interested in supporting highly visible research projects. The congressional practice of "earmarking"—that is, requiring funds to be awarded to specific institutions or even researchers— is on the rise in R&D appropriation bills. A recent study by the Office of Science and Technology Policy identified 566 earmarks in 1992 R&D appropriations for facilities and research, totaling $993 million, an increase of 23 percent over 1991.[57] R&D earmarking is a natural result of the shrinking discretionary share of the federal budget. Members of Congress have always attempted to promote projects that could be represented as a direct personal benefit from the representative to constituents. As opportunities for providing constituent benefits drop elsewhere, discretionary categories that are not conducive to earmarking, including overhead charges on university grants and contracts, will be under greater pressure for budget cuts.

A more troubling possibility is that university support may be suffering from a structural decline in support for science as defense investments fall in national priority. Education has benefited financially from its connection to national security goals, particularly at universities where research produced advances leading to new weapons systems. Unless science is seen as an equally important mechanism for furthering other national goals, such as economic growth, university support is unlikely to remain at its current level.

Regardless of the appropriate magnitude of federal support for university research, it makes no sense to starve all research universities at levels of reimbursement that are not adequate for maintaining research facilities. Whereas the government can pursue this strategy for a while without many ill effects, within a few years the quality of research will decline as universities become unable to pay for new facilities and the administrative infrastructure needed to support sponsored research. If consolidation of university research is the objective, a better strategy is to support each research project adequately but reduce the number of projects—and thereby the number of universities that attempt to be strong in research and graduate education.

57. *Budget of the United States Government, Fiscal Year 1993*, pt. 1, p. 139.

Assessing R&D Policy

The U.S. government faces several major decisions about future federal support for R&D. Although international comparisons suggest that the United States is probably not underinvesting in R&D, the composition of the R&D budget needs some serious rethinking.

At the top of the list for assigning new priorities is defense-related R&D in the post–cold war era. National security policy has a pervasive impact on the conduct of R&D in the United States. The most fundamental connection is that in the past, security concerns were almost always part of the justification for civilian science and technology programs. If the United States is to maintain federal subsidies for R&D at their present level—and continue on a par with other major industrialized nations—it will have to accept alternative justifications as equally valid. In addition, a reduction in the DOD budget has two immediate implications for domestic civilian R&D. Several leading high-technology industries have benefited from defense R&D. A reduction in this support could weaken their international competitive position. Nevertheless, defense R&D, because it involves so much more than support for these industries, can be cut a great deal without necessarily harming them.

A large reduction in defense procurement contracts is likely to cause a sharp decrease in private R&D, because defense contractors respond to profits from procurement by increasing their efforts in design competitions. The right lesson to draw here is that profit incentives have a powerful impact on private decisions. The wrong lesson is that creating a monopoly industry structure yields the appropriate incentives. The DOD strategy works for two reasons: first, because the prize of a defense contract exists, and second, because the design stage of weapons programs is highly competitive. Without competition, the profits in a weapons contract become an industry subsidy rather than a reward for successful innovation. Lichtenberg finds that while competitive government contracts yield a very large increase in private R&D, noncompetitive contracts have no significant R&D spillovers. This result suggests that considerable caution should be exercised in government programs that foster collaboration in R&D. For example, the Federal Communication Commission is currently establishing standards for high-definition television (HDTV) that will probably yield considerable wealth to the holder of the approved patents. The FCC's strategy of encouraging a design competition among firms, with the prize an approved standard, encourages private R&D. However, the government's policy of encouraging team efforts and cross-licensing agreements among firms investigating HDTV technology has merit only if economies of scale or scope in research offset the potential disincentive effects of collaboration.

The second highest priority for reallocation in the federal R&D budget is health-related research. If high-tech biomedical industries are the most promising businesses of the twenty-first century, the United States is well placed to dominate the field. We offer no evidence to question the future economic and human importance of biomedical technology, but we do wonder whether the emphasis it has received during the past twenty years is fully deserved. Many of the technologies that have been developed in recent years have been adopted extensively only in the United States, through the atypically permissive attitude Americans have toward medical care expenditures. The United States is now spending about 14 percent of GNP on medical care, and the fraction continues to grow as rapidly as it has for the past twenty-five years (see chapter 2). Much of this expenditure has little effect on the duration or the quality of life. Thus the health benefits of so much biomedical research may not be worth the costs. Policymakers must seriously consider whether the biomedical field has too many researchers and too many medical research projects in comparison with other lines of research that seem to have a higher social payoff.

If some of the R&D budget is reallocated, the federally supported R&D joint ventures developed during the 1980s provide the obvious, ready institutional structure for rechanneling defense and health dollars into other high-technology industries and areas of basic research. The conceptual arguments for targeted federal R&D support seem to apply most aptly to generic, technology-based research. But thus far, the federal government has not used the right institutional and financial arrangements in setting up generic research centers, and it has not focused federal research on areas that most clearly fit the rationales for government assistance. Generic research centers must be created with a strategy that fully comes to grips with a fundamental dilemma. Industry must participate in both project selection and R&D in order to cause the most rapid and complete diffusion of new technology. But, left to its own choices, an industry consortium will favor projects that serve its primary function—which is to maximize industry profits. As a result, it will choose research strategies that are appropriable to the innovators, that facilitate collusion, and that allow firms jointly to reduce parallel, competing lines of technology development and overall R&D efforts.

Thus far, each side of the technology policy debate about generic research centers and RJVs has tended to ignore the valid claims of the other. But if the arguments of both sides have validity, the solution must have the following characteristics:

—Generic centers must focus on efforts that, for reasons of appropriability and scope economies, no firm or small consortium of firms would do by itself.

—RJVs must include the entire industry so as to avoid having the government favor some firms at the expense of others.

—Unless the domestic industry is already dominant in the world, some aspect of the R&D product must be sufficiently appropriable to delay if not prevent its adoption by foreign producers.

—The government must participate actively in the choice of projects to weed out ones that are inappropriate because they create market imperfections that exceed any realistic economic benefit.

—The government must pay a sizable fraction of the R&D costs so that firms have an incentive to participate in an enterprise that will produce mainly spillover benefits for their customers and for society as a whole.

To date, the government has not adhered to these policies. As a result, the several research centers that it has established are not likely to serve any purpose other than to provide an industrial constituency with a subsidy.

The federal government also needs to develop a better mechanism for allocating funds between large and small projects and for picking among the big projects. The present system is organized along industrial and technological lines. Both the agencies that implement the policies and the congressional committees that oversee them are fragmented, and the trade-offs across technologies, and between commercial projects and other forms of R&D, are considered only at the levels of the Executive Office of the President and each chamber of Congress acting as a committee of the whole. It is not realistic to take the big-project bias out of the federal government. Trade-offs would be given some consideration, and there would be a greater willingness to make some political enemies, if all technology-based research support was assigned to one agency and one congressional committee in each chamber. Support for activities that contribute to the technology base should be institutionally separated from demonstration facilities, such as space shuttles and synthetic fuel plants, to provide some protection against cost overruns and stretchouts for the big-ticket failures eroding financial support for the former.

Finally, the government needs to work out its objectives, and a suitable implementing strategy, in dealing with universities. In the generally sorry picture of American education, the research university is one of the few remaining points of strength. It is the envy of the world and a magnet for foreign students and faculty. Yet it is jeopardized by government agencies that shortchange reimbursement for indirect costs and by excessively prescriptive congressional earmarking for visible research. As a result, the government is spreading dollars too widely, supporting each project too ungenerously to sustain high-quality research, and frittering away too much of the budget on expensive audit and accounting systems. Whether or not university research continues to be supported at past levels, the reimbursement method needs to be changed. A form of prospective reimbursement, based on the price-cap principle, is a far better approach than an audit-intensive, inherently confrontational system of cost reimbursement based on arbitrary accounting formulas.

8

CLIFFORD WINSTON
AND BARRY BOSWORTH

Public Infrastructure

IN AN ERA dominated by laissez faire thinking, public infrastructure investment is one of those rare activities where government has been criticized for doing too little instead of too much. Outlays for publicly owned physical capital have fallen greatly during the past two decades, from 4 percent of gross national product (GNP) in the late 1960s to 2 percent by the 1980s (figure 8-1). Furthermore, several studies have pointed out that the decline in spending for public infrastructure correlates closely with the slowing of productivity growth after 1973. Governments have, therefore, been urged to expand spending on public infrastructure as a means of increasing productivity.

The consensus breaks down on how to raise the money to pay for increased infrastructure spending. Because of the federal budget deficit, federal agencies are reluctant to assume financial responsibility for increasing infrastructure spending. Instead, federal officials urge the states to raise their taxes to finance added outlays. State officials reciprocate by calling on the federal government to provide greater financial resources regardless of the budgetary situation.

Is the federal government missing a significant opportunity to spur economic growth by stonewalling on this issue? We argue that the social returns of investing in public infrastructure are substantial, although not as large as some recent studies suggest. Any returns, however, will be held down because of the inefficiencies that currently plague infrastructure investment.

To maximize these returns, government policies must change to better address the problems connected with the current system. The condition of roads, bridges, and harbors has deteriorated somewhat, but the most costly aspects of the problem are linked with increased congestion in the transportation system. Simply spending more money will not resolve

James M. Poterba was the discussant for this chapter. Research assistance was provided by Karen McClure and Suzanne Smith.

FIGURE 8-1. Net Public Capital Stock and Gross Investment, 1950–91

Percent of GNP

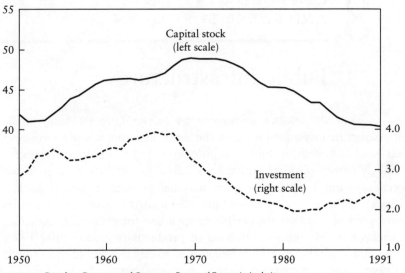

SOURCE: Data from Department of Commerce, Bureau of Economic Analysis.

these congestion problems. Changes are needed in the management of public infrastructure. We therefore propose reforms in pricing and investment policy that could raise the benefits of the current system with little added cost.

The Public Capital Stock

Investment in public infrastructure has fallen at all levels of government—federal, state, and local—over the past two decades. The decline extends across a broad range of different types of capital. Annual investment, however, is a poor measure of the services provided by a public capital stock built up over many decades. Nor do the investment data distinguish between new additions and the replacement of old capital. Thus, for many purposes it is more useful to focus on trends in the stock of public capital. As shown in figure 8-1, however, the capital stock has failed to grow in line with the overall economy, falling as a ratio to GNP from 49 percent in 1970 to 41 percent in 1990.[1]

1. The measures of the public capital considered in this paper include only reproducible physical capital. Thus we do not consider the issues about management of the vast government investment in land and natural resources. All references to levels of past

TABLE 8-1. Components of the Public Capital Stock, Selected Years, 1960–90

Capital stock	Percent of GNP				1990 stock (billions of dollars)
	1960	1970	1980	1990	
Total public[a]	46.1	48.9	45.3	40.6	2,180.4
Federal	9.4	7.9	6.4	5.5	298.1
Buildings[b]	3.1	2.0	1.5	1.3	70.1
Core infrastructure	0.5	0.6	0.6	0.5	26.3
Highways and streets	0.4	0.4	0.4	0.3	17.2
Other structures[c]	0.2	0.1	0.2	0.2	9.1
Conservation and development	3.9	3.5	3.2	2.6	140.5
Equipment	1.9	1.9	1.2	1.1	61.2
State and local	36.7	41.0	38.9	35.1	1,882.3
Buildings[b]	10.8	12.9	12.4	10.6	575.0
Core infrastructure	24.1	25.7	23.9	21.5	1,143.0
Highways and streets	16.8	17.8	15.5	13.0	693.6
Sewer systems	3.0	3.0	3.5	3.5	184.1
Water supply facilities	2.3	2.3	2.1	2.1	109.6
Other structures[c]	2.1	2.6	2.8	2.9	155.7
Conservation and development	0.4	0.7	0.7	0.6	33.3
Equipment	1.4	1.7	1.9	2.5	131.0

SOURCE: Data from Department of Commerce, Bureau of Economic Analysis.
a. Includes government owned but privately operated as well as government enterprises.
b. Includes educational, hospital, and industrial buildings, as well as office buildings, police and fire stations, courthouses, garages, and passenger terminals.
c. Includes mass transit, airports, and electrical and gas facilities.

Table 8-1 shows a more disaggregate picture of the capital stock. The total nonmilitary stock of structures and equipment was nearly $2.2 trillion in 1990, compared with a private business capital stock of $5.3 trillion. Most public capital (85 percent) is owned by state and local governments. Nearly two-thirds of the capital stock is concentrated in core infrastructure, which includes transportation, water and sewage facilities, and government-owned electric and gas utilities. This core infrastructure might be expected to be most closely related to private-sector output. The second principal category of buildings embraces offices, schools, hospitals, and similar structures. The final small component, conservation and development, consists largely of water resource projects, such as flood and erosion control. Interestingly, the post-1970 decline in public capital investment is reflected in all of these categories.

investment are expressed as a percentage of GNP. The data on the public capital stock and investment are obtained from the Bureau of Economic Analysis of the Department of Commerce and they incorporate the recent revisions to the national accounts.

Part of the falloff in public investment should cause no alarm. In particular, the reduced rate of investment in public buildings can be explained as a rational response to changed circumstances. The very rapid growth in the school population during the 1950s and 1960s initiated a large expansion of educational facilities by state and local governments. School enrollments declined after 1975. The rapid buildup of hospital facilities in the 1960s, fueled by generous federal grants, has resulted in significant excess capacity. The decline in federally owned buildings reflects the depreciation of industrial buildings that were built by the government in World War II and the Korean War but operated by private firms. No one is proposing to replace these structures. Furthermore, there are few arguments in favor of an expansion of investment within the area of conservation and development. Federally financed water resource projects have had notoriously low rates of return and have been dominated by political considerations.

The slowing of growth in the core infrastructure component of the public capital stock, however, is troubling. Investment has fallen as a ratio to GNP from a peak of over 26 percent in the early 1970s to 22 percent in 1990. The reduced investment in this area has stimulated much of the argument that public infrastructure investment has been inadequate. Most expenditures for new construction and maintenance of this capital are the direct responsibility of state and local governments, but they are assisted by large federal grant programs.

Highways and streets account for the biggest share of infrastructure investment by state and local governments (figure 8-2). Adjusted for inflation, highway investment rose continuously from about $10 billion a year in 1950 to over $35 billion in the late 1960s, then fell sharply during the 1970s, and dropped off to less than $20 billion annually by the early 1980s before beginning a recovery to about $30 billion today. Since replacement investment is a rising share of total investment, the slowing of growth in the net capital stock has been even more marked. Investments in water and sewage facilities have gradually increased with a period of rapid upgrading of sewer facilities in the 1970s required to comply with the 1972 amendments to the Water Pollution Control Act. A similar gradual expansion is evident for investments in other structures, which include airports, mass transit, and publicly owned electric and gas utilities. Thus evidence of a decline of investment in the core infrastructure is concentrated in the area of highway construction.

Total costs of public infrastructure include the expense of operation and maintenance as well as investment. Recent trends in total outlays of

FIGURE 8-2. State and Local Government Investment in Core Infrastructure Projects, 1950–91

Billions of 1990 dollars

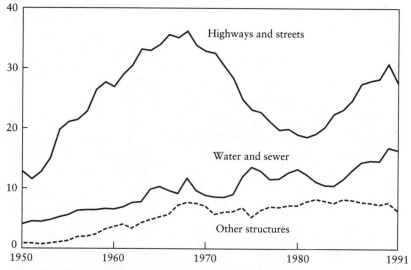

SOURCE: Data from Department of Commerce, Bureau of Economic Analysis.

the federal government and state and local governments on core infrastructure activities are shown in figure 8-3.[2] Federal matching grants for the interstate highway system and the upgrading of the nation's sewage treatment systems grew rapidly during the 1960s and 1970s. Real federal outlays fell in the 1980s. State and local governments' spending out of their own resources remained relatively flat from 1968 to 1985, but has begun to rise again in recent years. Investment outlays accounted for about $55 billion out of total expenditures of $110 billion in 1990.

Investment has declined in part because investment requirements have fallen. The construction of the interstate highway system required a large investment during the 1960s and was largely finished by the early 1970s. Investment in other road systems also fell, however, during a period when the data indicate some deterioration in the quality of the roads and an increase in congestion.

2. The total costs are understated to some extent because the government expenditure data include only the capital investments of publicly owned utilities. Their operating costs are included within the private sector. Federal grants are deducted from the spending of state and local governments in order to eliminate any double counting of expenditures.

FIGURE 8-3. Trends in Core Infrastructure Expenditures, 1960–90

Billions of 1990 dollars

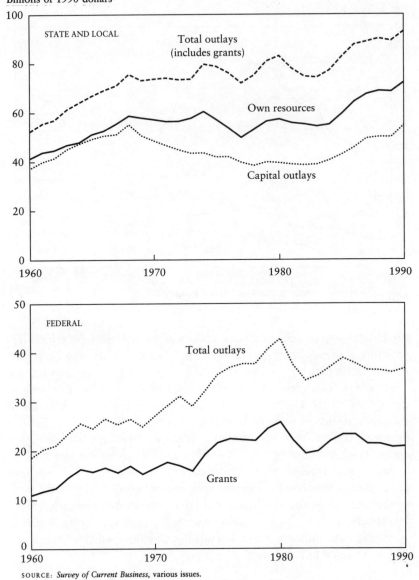

SOURCE: *Survey of Current Business,* various issues.

The more important explanation for falling investment appears to be a lack of revenues. Highway construction is financed largely by dedicated fuel taxes, both federal and state. Those taxes are imposed on a cents-per-gallon basis and did not increase as fast as general inflation (figure 8-4). The federal tax, for example, remained four cents a gallon from 1960 to 1982, a period in which the general price level tripled. Even today's fourteen-cent tax rate is below today's equivalent of the 1960 tax. The gap in the effective tax rate is even greater at the state level. An average tax rate equivalent to the 1960 rate would be twenty-seven cents a gallon compared with an actual average rate of sixteen cents. A decline in effective tax rates is evident for every state. Apparently, voters reacted to the rise in crude oil prices after 1973 by forcing an offsetting reduction in the effective tax rate. Since the mid-1980s, when the inflation-adjusted price of gasoline fell back to pre-1973 levels, voters in some states have begun to accept tax rate increases and investment spending has turned back up.

It is sometimes argued that the lack of infrastructure spending reflects a failure of the federal government to disburse the moneys that have flowed into the trust funds for highways and airports. Yet an inspection of the trust funds shows no significant accumulation of unspent funds, especially considering that the trust funds are not used to cover all federal expenses.

Measuring the Benefits

There is widespread agreement that investments in the public infrastructure offer substantial benefits, and some analysts are convinced that current rates of public investment are very deficient. Increased public investment, however, does divert resources from other uses, requiring lower rates of private investment or public and private consumption. At any time public officials should demonstrate that the benefits of added capital spending exceed the costs. And in the face of widespread public opposition to any tax increase, the pressure to do so is particularly strong. Nor is it enough to show that the benefits are positive. Benefits should exceed the costs by more than the net return from private investment because the increased public investment financed by borrowing is likely to come at the cost of reduced private-sector investment.

Public versus private benefits. Unfortunately, the accurate measurement of the return on investments in the public sector is far more complex than for that in the private sector. In most cases no direct market valuation of the output from public capital is possible. The highway system, for

FIGURE 8-4. State and Federal Vehicle Fuel Tax Rates,
Actual and Adjusted for Inflation, 1960–91

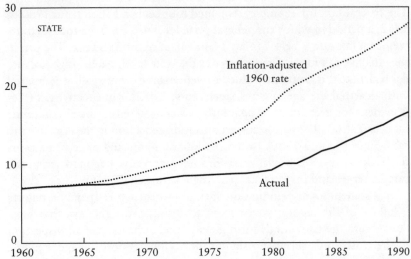

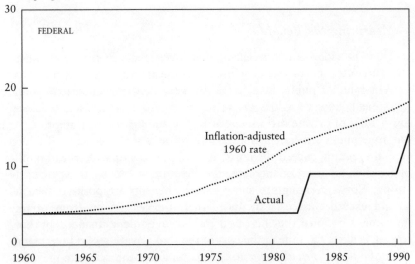

SOURCE: Federal Highway Administration, *Highway Statistics* (Department of Transportation, various years).
Estimate for 1991 state taxes based on national income accounts data.

example, reduces the cost and speeds the movement of goods and services, benefits that are reflected in standard measures of the nation's output of goods and services but are only loosely linked to the prices that users pay. As a result, public investments also generate some important economic distortions. The trucking industry gains from using roads for which it does not pay its full share of the costs related to wear and tear. The rail transport industry, which does not receive similar subsidies, suffers some offsetting losses from the diversion of freight transportation.[3] The existence of the interstate highway system has enabled households and businesses to move to the suburbs, but one of the costs has been urban decay and diminished employment opportunities for the inner-city residents who can not afford an automobile. Furthermore, since infrastructure investments do have significant reallocation effects, an analysis of the local economic benefits of an investment may overstate its aggregate contribution to the economy. Many jurisdictions use such projects, partly financed by federal grants, to lure businesses from other areas.

Finally, only a portion of the services of the public infrastructure supports the economic output of the private sector. Those benefits include lower transportation costs, saving in inventory stocks, and economies of scale in production, marketing, and location. The preponderance of highway travel, however, is accounted for not by trucks moving goods but by private automobiles moving people. Reduction in travel time and increased flexibility in decisions about where to live are consumption gains to American families that are normally not included in general measures of the economy's output of goods and services. The recent investment in sewage treatment facilities, designed to reduce pollution, also produces benefits that are not included in the GNP statistics.

Aggregate estimates. Because the benefits of public investments are so diffuse, it has been very difficult to agree on how to measure their value. The traditional evaluation of the costs and benefits of public investments on a project-by-project basis has been criticized for ignoring some indirect benefits. To deal with the presumed synergistic aspects of infrastructure investments, some analysts have turned to aggregate analysis that correlates growth of public capital with growth of output of the private sector.

Much of the current interest in expanding investment in the public infrastructure has been stimulated by several such studies that suggest

3. Kenneth A. Small, Clifford Winston, and Carol A. Evans, *Road Work: A New Highway Pricing and Investment Policy* (Brookings, 1989). They find that current trucking user charges are below the marginal cost of the damage caused by trucks.

that the benefits provided to the economy are far larger than previously thought.[4] They point out that, while it has been standard practice to take account of increases in private capital per worker in accounting for gains in labor productivity, the contribution of public capital, despite its size, has often been overlooked. They maintain that a dollar of investment in public capital earns an extraordinary return, many times that for private capital. For example, David Aschauer estimates that a $10 billion infrastructure investment would increase private-sector output by $8.5 billion in the first year following its completion, and the rate of return, based on the benefits to private-sector output alone, would be 90 percent for a project with a life of fifty years. This can be compared with a more typical return of 8 to 10 percent for the private sector.[5] With allowances for the noneconomic benefits, the estimated rates of return on public capital are phenomenal and difficult to believe.

Subsequent analysis has concluded that these estimates of the rate of return are flawed and overstated.[6] The aggregate data are dominated by trend factors that make it impossible to obtain reliable estimates of the causal link between public investment and aggregate economic output. It is true that growth in the public-sector capital stock and productivity both slowed after 1970, but that relationship alone is not enough to establish a causal relationship. The research using aggregate data has greatly stimulated interest in the role of the public infrastructure in economic growth; but, by suggesting that large gains can be achieved

4. These papers focus on the link between changes in the aggregate stock of public capital and economic growth in the private sector. David A. Aschauer, "Is Public Expenditure Productive?" *Journal of Monetary Economics*, vol. 23 (March 1989), pp. 177–200; and Alicia Munnell, "Why Has Productivity Growth Declined? Productivity and Public Investment," *New England Economic Review* (January–February 1990), pp. 3–22. For a more complete set of citations to articles on this issue, see Congressional Budget Office, *How Federal Spending for Infrastructure and Other Public Investments Affects the Economy* (July 1991).

5. The example uses Aschauer's output elasticity of 0.24, a capital stock of $1.1 trillion, and business-sector output of $4.2 trillion in 1990. The rate-of-return calculation uses straight-line depreciation, and a fifty-year asset life. The rate of return may be overstated in part because these studies include public-sector capital but not the cost of the labor required to operate and maintain the capital.

6. For a summary of the debate, see CBO, *Federal Spending for Infrastructure*, pp. 24–34, including the citations. The statistical studies encounter a fairly simple problem. The rate of increase in total factor productivity slowed sharply after 1973. The inclusion in the statistical analysis of any variable, such as the public capital stock, with a similar one-time break in its growth rate around 1973 will yield a highly significant statistical coefficient. Unless one can observe multiple episodes of sharp variation in the growth of productivity or public capital, it is difficult to use the correlation to infer a causal relationship.

simply by spending more, it has diverted attention from the issue of how to invest in and manage the infrastructure more efficiently. The overstatement of the returns and resulting debate over research methodology have also undermined the essential point that there are numerous potential public infrastructure projects for which it is widely agreed that the benefits exceed the costs by substantial margins.

Cost-benefit studies. The Congressional Budget Office has summarized a large number of cost-benefit studies of individual investment strategies in the transportation sector.[7] Most of the estimated benefits are in areas, such as reduced congestion, that are only partially included in the GNP statistics. The benefits, though smaller than those estimated in the aggregate studies, are still impressive. Investments required to maintain the current quality of the highway system provide expected annual returns of 30 to 40 percent. Selective expansion of the system in congested areas would yield returns of 10 to 20 percent. Investments to alleviate congestion of the air traffic control system and at major airports would also generate high returns. For both highways and air traffic, the major congestion problems occur only at peak periods. As a result, the investment returns would be much higher were it not for large excess capacity during off-peak periods.

Not all infrastructure projects, however, yield high rates of return. Returns from inland waterway projects are low, especially when one accounts for errors made by the Army Corps of Engineers.[8] The General Accounting Office estimates that the return from capital allocations for public transit and rail has been low in small cities, as shown by the fact that a large fraction of the allocation to these cities went unspent for lack of projects. However, large cities concurrently have experienced a capital shortage.[9] Perversely, the 1991 extension of the federal grant programs increased transit and rail capital allocations for small cities and lowered them for large cities.

Estimating Investment Needs

Since the use of much of the public infrastructure is free, meaningful estimates of investment requirements are hard to come by. In a private

7. Congressional Budget Office, *New Directions for the Nation's Public Works* (September 1988), pp. 14–15.

8. CBO, *New Directions*, pp. 87–90.

9. General Accounting Office, *Budget Issues Analysis of Unexpended Balances at Selected Civil Agencies*, AFMD-86-24 (September 1986), pp. 34, 81.

market it is always possible to compare the revenues from the sale of a product or service with the cost of producing it. Competitive profit-maximizing firms will then expand capacity up to the point of equality between marginal benefits and costs. In the area of the public infrastructure, benefits to users bear little or no relationship to the costs they pay. Without a market test, how can we decide how much to invest and where?

Two methods have been used to estimate resource requirements. The first (ratio to GNP) is a highly aggregative approach based on the simple rule of thumb that the stock of public capital should expand in line with the overall growth of the economy. That is, the public capital stock is projected as a fixed proportion of GNP, and investment needs are the sum of net additions to that stock plus an allowance for depreciation or replacement of existing capital. The use of a fixed ratio to GNP assumes that the public's demand for the services provided by the public infrastructure expands in proportion to the rise in incomes. The major difficulty with such estimates is they implicitly assume that the current pattern of public spending, used as a starting point, is efficient, and that future needs will grow proportionally with national income. In addition, this approach cannot be used to estimate needs at a more disaggregate level because it gives no guidance about where the investments should occur.

The second approach (functional needs assessment) uses engineering data to evaluate the costs of meeting specific standards of performance at the level of individual functional categories. In the case of highways and bridges, for example, on-site inspections are used to assess the current condition of the system, and estimates of future traffic flows are used to project future capacity needs. This measure of investment needs also lacks a market test, and the focus is on estimating the cost of fixing deficiencies rather than evaluating their impact on users. In other words, the procedure provides an estimate of costs, but no measure of benefits. It can become the equivalent of a wish list.

Despite their deficiencies, both of these approaches are suggestive of infrastructure needs. They are illustrated in the following two sections.

Ratio-to-GNP Approach

The implication of a fixed capital-output ratio as a target for investment policy is outlined in table 8-2 for the overall public capital stock and for the category of core infrastructure. Real GNP is projected to grow 2.5

TABLE 8-2. Illustrative Computation of Public Investment Needs

Percent of GNP unless otherwise specified

Investment	Core infrastructure	Total public capital
Low option: Maintain current capital intensity		
Target capital/output	22.0	40.0
Investment needs		
New	0.55	1.00
Replacement[a]	0.60	1.40
Total	1.15	2.40
Current investment rate	1.00	2.20
Additional investment	0.15	0.20
Billions of 1990 dollars	8.0	11.0
High option: Restore 1970 capital intensity		
Target capital/output	25.0	48.0
Investment needs		
New	0.60	1.20
Replacement[a]	0.69	1.70
Increased capital intensity[b]	0.30	0.80
Total	1.59	3.70
Current investment rate	1.00	2.20
Additional investment	0.59	1.50
Billions of 1990 dollars	33.0	83.0
Addendum		
Current investment		
(billions of 1990 dollars)	55.0	130.0

a. The depreciation rate is 0.035 for the total capital stock and 0.0275 for the core infrastructure.
b. The restoration of the existing capital stock to the target ratio to GNP is assumed to spread over a ten-year period.

percent annually in the 1990s.[10] If the goal were to expand the current capital stock in line with the future growth of GNP, net additions to the stock of core infrastructure capital would be equal to the ratio of core infrastructure to GNP (0.22) multiplied by the trend growth of GNP (2.5 percent), or 0.55 percent of GNP. The existing capital stock depreciates at about 2.75 percent annually, requiring replacement investment of another 0.6 percent (2.75 percent times 0.22) of GNP. Thus, maintenance of the ratio of core infrastructure to GNP would require an annual investment rate equal to 1.15 percent of GNP. Since current investment of $55 billion represents about 1 percent of GNP, the country would need to devote an additional $8 billion annually to maintain a constant core infrastructure–output ratio. While the total public capital

10. Congressional Budget Office, *The Economic and Budget Outlook: Fiscal Years 1993–1997* (January 1992), p. 22.

stock is much larger, the gap between current and projected investment is largely concentrated in the area of the core infrastructure. Maintaining the current ratio of total public infrastructure to GNP would only require $11 billion of added investment.

Restoring the ratio of the public capital stock to GNP that existed in the early 1970s is a more ambitious target. The buildup to the higher ratio to GNP is assumed to be spread over a ten-year period. As shown in the lower panel of table 8-2, that goal would require far higher levels of investment. A major source of the added investment is the need to invest at a higher rate for several years in order to raise the current ratio of capital to output (labeled "increased capital intensity" in the table) back to that of 1970. For the core infrastructure, additional annual investment to raise the capital-output ratio to 0.25 would amount to $33 billion, with about half of that being part of a transitional buildup of the stock to the higher ratio to GNP. If the same target were extended to the total public stock, the additional requirements would be $83 billion annually. As mentioned earlier, however, maintenance of the overall public capital stock at the historical peak ratio to GNP has little rationale.

The implication of the projection in table 8-2 is that small increases in public investment would suffice to maintain the status quo, but the costs of more ambitious goals rapidly escalate.

Functional Needs Assessments

Several federal agencies conduct ongoing needs assessments in their specific areas of responsibility. They estimate the cost required to maintain current conditions as measured by some standard of physical condition, safety, or performance. They further estimate the costs of achieving higher standards. Those studies show that any added investment above current levels should be heavily concentrated on highways and that the fundamental problem is congestion, not deterioration of the existing system. Current rates of investment are roughly adequate to maintain the existing condition of the system, whereas an increase of about 50 percent would be required to meet the more ambitious goals. Some of the studies yield very large dollar estimates of the investment needs because they accumulate investment outlays over many years. Expressed as a share of the nation's output over the number of years that they encompass, these estimates are actually consistent with the range of investment requirements presented in the prior section.

Highways and bridges. Highways account for a large fraction of projected investment needs. The Department of Transportation estimates the investment needed to meet specific engineering standards for the nation's highways and bridges over the next twenty years.[11] The standards that receive the greatest emphasis are pavement condition and congestion for highways and functional and structural deficiencies for bridges. Pavement conditions are rated on the basis of serviceability on a scale ranging from poor (0–2.0) to good (3–5); repaving is usually called for at an index of 2.5. The survey statistics provided evidence of a general deterioration of pavement quality in the late 1970s and early 1980s, but in recent years the proportion of the highway system rated as poor has declined.

Instead, the major problem is congestion. Between 1970 and 1990 vehicle-miles traveled rose by 93 percent, while road mileage increased by only 4 percent. Data on lane mileage are unavailable. To the extent that roads have been widened, the 4 percent increase in road mileage understates the growth in the vehicle-carrying capacity of U.S. roads. The problem of congestion is concentrated in urban areas; the proportion of urban interstate mileage classified as congested (capacity utilization rates above 80 percent) during peak travel periods rose from 23 percent in 1975 to 45 percent in 1990.[12] The evidence of congestion is highly localized, however, and the data refer to peak travel periods. The initial response has been to increase the number of lanes within the existing right-of-way; but, when that option is exhausted, the cost of obtaining new right-of-ways will sharply reduce the attractiveness of added investment as a solution to the congestion problem.

Surveys also indicate that 40 percent of the nation's 577,000 bridges are rated as structurally deficient or functionally obsolete.[13] The category of structurally deficient refers to safety and structural inadequacies, whereas functionally obsolete often indicates inadequate capacity. These estimates should be taken with a grain of salt, however. Since state allocations of federal grants are directly tied to their ranking in the survey, states have a strong incentive to find problems. Furthermore, bridges can be judged deficient for reasons that do not indicate any need for added investment. Many of the bridges carry very little traffic, and

11. The latest estimates are contained in *Report of the Secretary of Transportation to the United States Congress, The Status of the Nation's Highways and Bridges: Conditions and Performance*, Committee Print, House Committee on Public Works and Transportation, 102 Cong. 1 sess. (Government Printing Office, 1991).

12. Federal Highway Administration, *Highway Statistics 1990* (Department of Transportation, 1991), p. 175.

13. *Status of the Nation's Highways and Bridges*, Committee Print, p. 153.

alternatives are available. Seven percent of the bridges on the interstate system are rated as structurally deficient, and 21 percent are functionally obsolete. More indicative, the percentage of bridges rated as structurally deficient rose in the early 1980s but has been declining recently with increased spending. Again, the problems are heavily localized with a few states accounting for most of the deficiencies.[14] It is difficult to meet these problems through an expansion of federal aid because the political system demands an even distribution of additional funding.

The Department of Transportation study provides two estimates of highway investment needs: (1) maintaining 1989 conditions and performance and (2) a more ambitious goal of repairing all pavement in the poor category (roughly 10 percent of the current system miles) and sharply reducing the proportion of the system classified as congested. The reduction in congestion projects a 50 percent increase in urban interstate lane-miles and a 44 percent increase for other urban principal arterial roads. Both estimates cover a twenty-year period and incorporate a uniform 2.5 percent annual growth in vehicle-miles of travel. The high estimate also incorporates the investment required to eliminate all existing and future bridge deficiencies. The low estimate maintains the current number of deficient bridges.

The analysis yields the following estimates of investment requirement:[15]

Infrastructure	Maintain 1989 conditions	Improve conditions
	(billions of 1989 dollars)	
Highways	830	1,378
Bridges	84	120
Total	914	1,498

These estimates seem much larger than those of the prior section, but they differ in two respects. First, it is common to convert the twenty-year total to an annual basis simply by dividing by twenty (yielding $46 billion and $75 billion for the two scenarios); but that average will automatically be far above current investment rates. It is more reasonable to compute the rate of investment (share of GNP) required to meet the goal over the twenty-year period of the projections. If the average annual

14. Heywood T. Sanders, "Public Works and Public Dollars: Federal Infrastructure Aid and Local Investment Policy" (San Antonio: Trinity University, Department of Urban Studies, February 1991).

15. *Status of the Nation's Highways and Bridges*, Committee Print, p. 158.

investment is divided by average GNP over the same period and that percentage is applied to today's GNP, the annual cost of maintaining the system would be $35 billion in 1990 and the cost of the improvement scenario would be $58 billion. Second, unlike the data from the national accounts, the estimates of the Department of Transportation include the costs of land acquisition. Including land acquisition, actual capital outlays in 1990 were $35 billion. Thus current investment seems adequate to maintain the system at present levels, while the improvements scenario would require an increase of about 65 percent. This range is similar to the estimates reported earlier of what would be required to return to the capital intensity of the early 1970s.

Investment projections are dominated by the costs of responding to increased congestion; 72 percent of the projected costs of meeting the estimated $400 billion backlog are for capacity expansion, as opposed to 28 percent for pavement improvements. For the high option, two-thirds of the projected highway capital outlays are for capacity expansion.

Water and sewers. The major capital outlays required to achieve the water quality goals of the 1972 Clean Water Act have been made. This is one area in which the level of construction activity has increased over the past two decades. Surveys by the Environmental Protection Agency show remaining needs in the area of wastewater treatment of about $80 billion, a figure that has remained stable throughout the 1980s. Passage of the 1987 Clean Water Act is expected to add about $30 billion as its provisions are phased in over future years. While there are still unmet needs, current investment levels are sufficient to steadily reduce the backlog. Annual investment in water and waste disposal systems, currently running at $9 billion, might be raised by $3 billion to $4 billion in future years.

Aviation. Major airports and the national air traffic control system have become increasingly congested. The Federal Aviation Agency estimates that airport investment of $0.5 billion annually over the next ten years will maintain existing system conditions, and $4.0 billion annually will relieve current and projected congestion.[16] Over half of the $40 billion would be needed for land acquisition, paving, and lighting of added runways. In addition, the new air traffic control system, which is far behind schedule, will continue to absorb over $1 billion annually for most of the 1990s. If added investment in new runways at existing

16. Federal Aviation Administration, *National Plan of Integrated Airport Systems* (March 1991).

airports were selected as the primary method of reducing congestion in the short run, the added capital costs would amount to only $1 billion to $2 billion annually.[17] In any case, the increase in spending above current levels would be small.

Mass transit. The mass transit system, however, is faced with growing problems of excess capacity as individuals continue to move to the suburbs and rely more heavily on the private automobile. A 1988 study by the Congressional Budget Office reported extremely low levels of capital utilization, and the problem appears to be getting worse, not better.[18] The strongest economic argument for increased investment would be to modernize existing systems in older cities such as New York; but that type of spending also generates the least political appeal, and emphasis continues to be placed on a disproportionate distribution of investment funds toward small cities and new systems. A simple expansion of capital outlays has not provided an effective solution to declining usage of mass transit facilities.

In summary, a strong argument can be made for raising investment in public infrastructure, but needs can easily be exaggerated. Current investment is roughly adequate to maintain the quality of the system. More ambitious targets aimed at restoring the capital intensity of the early 1970s have a limited rationale and would require a 50 percent increase in investment. The more detailed functional needs studies reach similar conclusions.

These estimates of investment needs, however, ignore the growing evidence of waste and inefficiency that plague the system. They are based solely on a projection of demand without a weighting of costs versus benefits. In some cases the respondents to the surveys have a strong incentive to overestimate their needs as a means of attracting funds from the federal government. Furthermore, the evidence does not offer much support to the view that the overall system is currently suffering from a failure to maintain most existing facilities. Instead, the most costly aspect of the problem lies with the increased congestion on highways and streets in urban areas. The expansion of supply, however, has repeatedly failed to resolve road congestion. In the short run, the high costs of obtaining new right-of-ways will limit reliance on added roadways. In the long run, new users rapidly recreate congested conditions. They will always do so if they continue to be able to use public facilities without paying

17. CBO, *New Directions*, pp. 69–73.
18. CBO, *New Directions*, pp. 27–54.

for the costs they impose on others. To an increasing extent the nation will be forced to consider other methods of relieving congestion.

Public Infrastructure Inefficiencies

The capital investment needs outlined above are based on the current efficiency of U.S. infrastructure use. But, if infrastructure systems were built and used more efficiently, the capital needs could be greatly reduced.

There are, in fact, three major areas where efficiency could be improved. The first inefficiency is organizational. Operation of the public infrastructure is not subject to competitive market forces to minimize costs and improve quality. Consequently, construction and maintenance of the infrastructure system are often needlessly costly. A second inefficiency arises from the political forces that often channel money into projects with low economic benefits but large political payoffs. Too often, the allocation of funds among alternative projects is not based on an evaluation of their relative costs and benefits.

The third group of inefficiencies arises because use of the public infrastructure is not correctly priced or designed. Described in greater detail below, the problem is well illustrated by the following example. Pick any pothole-riddled, congested two-lane road in an urban area. Suppose public funds are used to widen the road to four lanes and repave it. Benefits will immediately flow from this investment in the form of lower travel time and less vehicle damage. But many travelers who previously avoided the road during peak travel periods will now choose to use it. New businesses and residences will be located near it. Former mass-transit users will be led to buy cars. Before long the road will fill to capacity and again deteriorate, requiring another round of expansion. The cycle has been played out repeatedly in all of America's major urban areas.

This phenomenon, known as Downs's law, reveals two types of economic inefficiencies. The first is that use of the road is not priced efficiently. That is, if vehicles were required to pay tolls based on the costs of congestion imposed on other users and on pavement wear (current charges are based on the gas tax, which does not reflect congestion or damage to the roadway), congestion would be reduced, especially during peak periods, and the road would last much longer.

The final problem is that the roads are not built efficiently. Efficient investment requires that pavement depth and the number of lanes be expanded to the point at which the cost of an additional unit of investment would equal its benefits. Current design standards for road depth and width seldom meet this criterion; thus they generate wasteful investments that lead to poor-quality roads.

By reducing the organizational, political, and economic inefficiencies, the United States could make more efficient use of the current infrastructure, avoid massive new public investment, and prevent the recurrence of periodic infrastructure problems.

The Organizational Environment

Building and maintaining infrastructure is inherently expensive; but, as most homeowners know, unanticipated "extra" costs seem to make every repair or new addition more expensive than planned. These extra costs arise in public investments because government agencies are not faced with the same incentives as private competitive firms. Private firms may choose the contractor they believe will deliver the best combination of quality and minimum cost. Public agencies must invariably choose the lowest-cost bidder. As a result, they write minutely detailed specifications to prevent contractors from substituting inferior materials and construction techniques. Contractors are also encouraged to focus on adherence to the letter of the contract rather than seeking higher-quality, efficient alternatives. Governments emphasize monitored physical design standards, rather than harder-to-measure standards of performance. Furthermore, rather than emphasizing the efficient overall management of the system, government managers are encouraged to set the price in a way that encourages users to demand more services than they are willing to pay for, stimulating further expansion of supply.

Although the inefficiencies have not been measured, it is widely believed that (controlling for quality) annual infrastructure expenditures are several billion dollars higher than they would be under efficient contracting and management.

Privatization is often proposed as a solution to some of these problems. Privatization is quite likely to reduce these inefficiencies, but may create a large deadweight loss from monopoly pricing. The benefits of private markets arise from the combination of private ownership *and* competition. Private monopolies often generate social and economic problems as serious as those described here. Until a convincing case can be made that travelers on roads and through airports throughout the country have alternatives that would prevent the owners of these facilities from setting monopoly prices, privatization should only be pursued on a limited basis.

The Political Environment: Incentives for Inefficiency

Congress authorizes federal expenditures on infrastructure. Congressional decisions are often based on considerations other than cost-benefit analysis. When such analysis is used, estimates of future demand are often overstated. Grant policies often result in unwise investment decisions. And projects that have outlived their usefulness refuse to die. Yet billions of dollars continue to be funneled by the federal government into a system riddled with inefficiencies.

Most recently, the Intermodal Surface Transportation Efficiency Act of 1991 (ISTEA) allocated $155 billion for highway and transit spending for fiscal years 1992–97. Will this money be spent wisely?

In the case of highways, a large share of the funding will be used for maintenance. An increased percentage, however, is earmarked for demonstration projects. The ISTEA designates $6.5 billion, or 5.7 percent of highway funding, to demonstration projects, a fivefold increase over spending on such projects authorized in the 1987 Surface Transportation Act. Demonstration projects approved in the 1991 ISTEA depended solely on successful lobbying and congressional debate and are not subject to any uniform evaluation. This practice seems to flout the major argument advanced to gain passage of the ISTEA: that each project funded will be subjected to rigorous evaluation at the state and local level to determine its overall contribution to the regional transportation improvement plan. This plan is designed to improve regional economic development—a national goal—which in turn justifies continued federal funding.

To estimate the worth of demonstration projects, the General Accounting Office analyzed 66 of the 152 projects approved in the 1987 Surface Transportation Bill at the request of Congress.[19] This study concluded that many demonstration projects would not otherwise be eligible for federal funding (for example, repairing local roads that are not on the federal highway system),[20] and that most demonstration projects were not critical to state and regional highway needs. A further problem is that because of overruns the cost to complete the 66 projects totaled

19. General Accounting Office, *Highway Demonstration Projects: Improved Selection and Funding Controls Are Needed*, RECD-91-146 (May 1991).
20. GAO, *Highway Demonstration Projects*, p. 2.

$1.9 billion, far exceeding the $700 million allocated for those specific projects. Many of these projects therefore were not initiated and the authorized funding remained frozen within federal coffers.[21] Demonstration projects included in the current bill will most likely generate the same problems, as there has been no significant change in policy.

When federal infrastructure funds are confined to specific uses, states and cities have a tendency to favor activities that qualify for a large federal contribution at the expense of activities that could provide greater social benefits. In fact, the highway laws of several states direct officials to select projects to maximize the use of federal funds. Under the 1987 Surface Transportation Act, for example, the federal government funded 80 percent of public transit capital expenses and 50 percent of operating expenses. Brian Cromwell has pointed out that this funding arrangement has influenced local governments to scrap transit equipment prematurely rather than incur the repair costs that would maintain bus and rail cars throughout a cost-minimized equipment life.[22] Similarly, the Congressional Budget Office found that a reduction in federal funding of wastewater treatment led to less overbuilding, shorter construction periods, and lower reserve capacity.[23] In short, the withdrawal of federal funds, up to a point, resulted in more efficient allocation of resources.

The Economic Environment: Pricing and Investment Inefficiencies

The benefits from efficient pricing and investment arise because U.S. infrastructure is characterized by pricing systems that do not reflect economic costs.[24] Investment is based on poor design decisions that have resulted in higher costs of use. Consider the following examples. Currently, the gasoline tax is effectively used to charge all vehicles for congestion and to charge trucks for road wear. But the gas tax bears little relationship to a vehicle's contribution to congestion or road

21. The funding allocated to demonstration projects cannot be redirected to more urgent transportation needs.

22. Brian A. Cromwell, "Federal Grant Policies and Public Sector Scrappage Decisions," Federal Reserve Bank of Cleveland, April 1990. The 1991 ISTEA changed this arrangement to fund both capital and operating costs at 80 percent.

23. Kenneth Rubin, *Efficient Investment in Wastewater Treatment Plants* (Congressional Budget Office, 1985), p. xii.

24. This section summarizes the material in Clifford Winston, "Efficient Transportation Infrastructure Policy," *Journal of Economic Perspectives*, vol. 5 (Winter 1991), pp. 113–27.

damage. Road damage depends on vehicle weight per axle. The damage caused by an axle is defined in terms of the number of "equivalent standard axle loads" (esals) causing the same damage; the standard is a single axle bearing 18,000 pounds. This damaging power rises exponentially to the third power with its load. Thus, for example, the rear axle of a thirteen-ton van causes over 1,000 times as much damage as that of a car. Since trucks and buses cause almost all of the pavement damage, discussion of pavement wear charges is usually limited to them.

A marginal cost pavement wear charge can be assessed by multiplying a vehicle's esal-miles by the marginal cost of an esal-mile. Such a charge would reflect much more accurately the damage caused by vehicles using the road. It would also encourage truckers to shift to trucks with more axles for a given load, thus extending pavement life and reducing highway maintenance expenditures. The fuel tax, by contrast, is perverse. The gas tax rises with a vehicle's axles, since trucks with more axles require larger engines and get lower fuel economy. Oregon has used a weight-distance tax for many years, and recently introduced on a partial basis a trucking tax based on axle weight. Oregon reports that evasion of the tax is no more of a problem than for fuel taxes. Other states are introducing new technologies that permit the weighing of vehicles moving at highway speeds.

A vehicle's contribution to congestion depends on the time of day and roads a motorist uses. A gasoline tax does little to discourage the use of a given road during a particular time of day. The only way to reduce congestion permanently is to set a congestion toll. Recent technological advances and worldwide experimentation have brought societies closer to actually implementing congestion pricing on their roads. Tolls can be assessed without disrupting travelers' journeys or invading their privacy. Toll roads in Texas and Oklahoma, for example, use electronic tax collection as an alternative to toll booths. And creative redistribution schemes have made the idea of congestion pricing more politically appealing. Timothy Hau provides a comprehensive discussion of the actual implementation of congestion pricing.[25]

Congestion pricing could be introduced most easily at airports. The principal cost that an aircraft imposes when it takes off or lands is that it delays other aircraft. In addition, the air traffic control system is overloaded during a few peak hours of the day when airlines and civil

---

25. Timothy Hau, "Congestion Charging Mechanisms: An Evaluation of Current Practice" (Washington: World Bank, March 1992).

aviation schedule a large number of plane departures and arrivals. Currently, the common way of assessing landing fees at airports is by aircraft weight, which has little to do with the delay an aircraft causes. Similar to road transportation, the only way to reduce air transportation delay permanently is to set a congestion toll. The secretary of transportation has called for the implementation of congestion pricing at the busiest airports.

To be sure, the idea of congestion pricing of roads and airports is not new, and, because it has yet to catch on, some have concluded that it is a politically untenable policy. Such views seem premature in view of recent technological advances. It is more encouraging to consider the rising tide of interest in and support for congestion pricing. Favorable editorials, supportive policy conferences, optimistic plans for demonstration projects, and explicit reference to it in the 1991 ISTEA tell only part of the story. The most important part is the increasing support for congestion pricing to be found in government agencies and among elected officials who must deal with the growing problem of congestion in the transportation system. Congestion pricing is no longer a pipe dream of academic economists.

Besides being mispriced, roads and airports have been incorrectly built. Recent research indicates that roads were not made thick enough. If they were more durable, trucks would do less damage to them, and annual maintenance expenses would be reduced. The United States has also lagged behind other countries in the introduction of improved pavement materials. Airports were also underbuilt. Optimal investment in airports calls for many more runways at congested airports. When this is not feasible, other capacity-enhancing mechanisms, such as microwave landing systems, could be introduced.

The net benefits to society from replacing current pricing of and investment in roads and airports by optimal pricing and investment are summarized in table 8-3. Optimal road pricing generates $11 billion in annual net benefits in the form of reduced travel delay and lower maintenance expenditures. Optimal pricing of airport runways generates an additional $4 billion in annual net benefits in the form of reduced air travel delays. Thus society stands to gain roughly $15 billion in annual net benefits from efficient pricing of infrastructure without incurring any increase in capital expenditures.

If optimal pricing of roads and airports is accompanied by optimal investment (that is, roads are built to optimal thickness and airports are

TABLE 8-3. Net Benefits from Optimal Pricing and Investment
in Highways and Airports

Billions of dollars

Item	Net benefits
Highways	
Optimal road wear pricing	5.35[a]
Optimal congestion pricing	5.65[b]
Total net benefits	11.00
Optimal road wear pricing and optimal investment	7.75[a]
Optimal congestion pricing	5.65[b]
Total net benefits	13.40
Increase in annual capital costs from optimal highway investment	1.28[a]
Airports	
Optimal runway pricing	3.82[c]
Optimal runway pricing and investment	11.01[c]
Increase in annual capital costs from optimal runway investment	0.82[c]

SOURCE: For highways, Kenneth A. Small, Clifford Winston, and Carol A. Evans, *Road Work: A New Highway Pricing and Investment Policy* (Brookings, 1989); for airports, Steven Morrison and Clifford Winston, "Enhancing the Performance of the Deregulated Air Transportation System," *Brookings Papers on Economic Activity: Microeconomics 1989*, pp. 61–123.
a. 1982 dollars.
b. 1981 dollars.
c. 1988 dollars.

built with the optimal number of runways), then annual net benefits rise to nearly $25 billion. And the annual increase in capital expenses to reap these benefits is only $2 billion. The federal government should absorb this increase in spending because it will actually improve its budgetary situation in the long run. Because optimal pricing and investment of roads will lower annual maintenance expenses by some $8 billion without significantly affecting revenues, the highway budget will be improved by nearly $7 billion. Under optimal congestion and road wear pricing and optimal investment, urban roads will virtually pay for themselves. In addition, airports will also be financially self-sufficient under optimal pricing and investment.

Efficient pricing and investment complement each other. Efficient pricing improves the efficiency of infrastructure use and lowers the capital requirements of efficient investment. Efficient investment lowers the marginal cost of infrastructure use and softens the distributional effects of efficient pricing. (Indeed, as shown in the original sources noted in table 8-3, the distributional effects of efficient road user and airport pricing and investment are small.) Collectively, efficient pricing and investment generate substantial net benefits. Simply increasing infrastructure spending without efficient pricing and improved design will result in considerable waste because systems will continue to be inefficiently used and built.

An additional advantage of these policies is that they will help resolve financing constraints and the issue of where to invest. Efficient user charges will cover the costs of monitoring and building most facilities and automatically direct the revenues to those portions of the system most in need of expansion. When the optimal user fee is insufficient to cover fixed costs, vehicle registration and similar fees could make up the difference.

Policy Implications

Measuring the returns from public infrastructure investment is extremely difficult. But the aggregate data and evidence from more detailed studies of investment requirements support the view that an increased supply of public infrastructure would generate substantial future benefits. Some recent aggregate studies emphasizing the gains in private-sector productivity exaggerate the returns, however, and ignore big gains that could be realized through a more efficient management of existing assets.

In particular, there is a large variance in the return among alternative infrastructure investments—some projects would generate returns as high as 30 percent, while others fail to cover their costs. Under the current institutional arrangements, additional funds are unlikely to be confined to the projects with the highest returns. Without reforms to the political and institutional system that directs infrastructure spending, a large unqualified increase in infrastructure spending, particularly at the federal level, would be inappropriate.

The first priority of public policy should be improving the efficiency of infrastructure spending and use. Many of the current pressures to boost spending result from congestion of the transportation system rather than from a failure to maintain the existing system. The congestion problem cannot be solved by simply expanding the supply; and, at least in the area of urban highways, that choice would be prohibitively expensive. Efficient pricing and investment would produce immediate benefits at little cost. Some localities are currently exploring such policy reforms. The federal government could accelerate adoption of these policies by requiring that grant requests for infrastructure improvements include a plan to reduce capital needs by efficient pricing and investment.

Although efficient user charges should replace gasoline taxes (and current aircraft landing fees) for purposes of allocating scarce infrastructure, there is still a role for gasoline taxes to help internalize standard emissions externalities. We reject, however, the notion that higher gasoline taxes could substitute for efficient taxes on axle loads and on congestion. The pricing policy advocated here can be achieved easily using current technology, and it does not have to be implemented precisely to generate substantial benefits. For example, Small, Winston, and Evans show that a simple uniform axle weight tax will result in a loss of less than 1 percent of the benefits produced by the optimal marginal-cost tax that varies by type of road. Manipulation of current fuel and other user charges simply will not generate comparable benefits.

A final benefit of an efficient infrastructure policy is that it should spur improvements in government purchases of infrastructure services. The preoccupation with favoring low bids at the expense of quality and ultimately cost is shortsighted frugality but long-range profligacy. Quality and cost should be jointly considered and evaluated as a project progresses. One possible way to promote such an outcome is a "franchise monopoly" arrangement in which long-term contracts with efficient contractors can be developed but are subject to periodic public review and competitive challenge from potential alternative contractors.

To be sure, government will still have to choose the projects to fund. The recent increase in funds allocated to demonstration projects is not an encouraging sign that these choices will become more efficient in the near future. The only way to ensure the selection of projects with the highest net benefits is to force policymakers to provide greater justification and to subject them to greater accountability for their decisions. If politically related inefficiencies are more highly publicized, public pressure may reduce their frequency.

Taken collectively, the proposed measures to reduce the organizational, political, and economic inefficiencies that pervade current infrastructure investments will substantially lower capital needs. Most important, society will be ensured high returns from the investments that are made.

9

CHARLES L. SCHULTZE

Paying the Bills

THE AUTHORS of the preceding chapters identify a number of specific governmental actions or budgetary programs that, on the basis of the best available evidence, they judge to be capable of promoting some important national goals. These proposals, when fully implemented four or five years from now, would add about $90 billion a year to federal budget outlays.

For more than ten years, the federal budget has been in very large deficit, with the federal debt rising steeply as a percentage of gross domestic product (GDP). The large deficits have made it virtually impossible for the executive branch or Congress to seriously consider major new programs or substantial additions to existing ones. And the deadlock between the president and Congress over how to eliminate the deficits shows no sign of ending in the near future. Indeed, a majority of voters, while deploring the deficits, seem disposed to punish candidates who support any of the painful measures actually needed to end them.

Should a nation that is unwilling to pay for existing federal programs undertake new ones? Are the programs recommended in this book important enough to justify adding further to budget deficits and the growth of federal debt? What would be the economic consequences of doing so? Should the new programs be paid for by additional taxes—either general taxes or taxes explicitly earmarked for their support? Should they be financed by spending cuts elsewhere in the budget, particularly the defense budget? Or should these programs be put on the back burner until a political consensus can be reached on a set of budget actions designed both to reduce the budget deficit and to provide for their financing? This chapter explores these issues and concludes with a set of proposals that, if adopted, would simultaneously close the budget deficit and pay for high-priority new programs.

Although other factors created them, the large deficits of the 1980s

The author wishes to thank Charles L. Hornbrook for research assistance.

are now being perpetuated by the steeply rising cost of the government's health care programs. An effective set of health care reforms, incorporating federally imposed expenditure limits on both public and private health expenditures, would not only serve as a desirable end in itself, but would also contribute significantly to eliminating the federal budget deficit. Thus I suggest a new ten-year budget proposal with five components: a health care reform and cost control package; an earmarked value-added tax to pay for part of the federal health care budget; several smaller tax increases, including a proposal to tax social security benefits more like private pensions; a series of expenditure cuts throughout the budget; and increased federal expenditures to fund at least some of the measures recommended in this book. These measures, together with budgetary savings from rigorous health care control and the associated savings in interest payments on the debt, would combine to bring the budget into balance over the next ten years.

The Deficit: Magnitude and Consequences

In 1992 the federal budget deficit, swollen by recession and the bulge of borrowing required for the saving and loan bailout, reached a new peacetime peak of 6 percent of GDP. But even with the saving and loan outlays omitted and the recession over, the budget deficit will still exceed 3 percent of GDP in the mid-1990s. Thereafter, under current budget policies, the deficit will rise gradually, reaching 4.2 percent of GDP, or some $430 billion, by the year 2002.[1]

Huge deficits like this are harmful to the economy not because they threaten a major cyclical catastrophe—rapid inflation followed by steep recession—but because they erode the nation's long-term growth. The large deficits from 1982 to 1990 coexisted with declining unemployment and low inflation. Tough monetary policy by the Federal Reserve and the resulting high real interest rates restrained demand and spending in some sectors of the economy sufficiently to offset the inflationary pump-priming effect of large budget deficits.

Deficits damage the economy because in normal times—outside of recession—each dollar the federal government borrows to finance its budget deficit absorbs private saving that would otherwise have been available to increase the nation's productive wealth, at home or abroad.

1. Congressional Budget Office, *An Analysis of the President's Budgetary Proposals for Fiscal Year 1993* (March 1992), p. 148.

Large and sustained budget deficits mean that the nation must either reduce its investment at home or borrow overseas. Over the past decade, the United States did some of both as private saving fell and the government deficit soared. Domestic investment declined and, by running a large trade deficit, the nation borrowed resources from abroad. Both alternatives depress the growth of national living standards. Reducing domestic investment retards growth in the productivity of American workers. Borrowing abroad increases debt service payments to foreign lenders.

Large budget deficits have been particularly harmful in recent years because they were coupled with a fall in the private saving rate, from a little over 9 percent of national income in the decades before 1980 to less than 7 percent now. Budget deficits of the current size drain off more than half the shrunken volume of private saving.

The Deficit's Origins and What Sustains It

It is widely believed that the "deficit problem" arose because budget discipline broke down in the 1970s and 1980s, leading to a large growth in federal spending, and that the deficit is sustained because of pressure on Congress from various special interest groups who have successfully blocked major expenditure cuts. At first glance the raw budget numbers seem to support that view. In 1979, the last high-employment year before the big surge in deficit spending, federal revenues amounted to 19.1 percent of GDP (see table 9-1). In 1990, revenues were 18.9 percent of GDP, and, as currently projected by the CBO, they will be 19.0 percent in 1997. (I use the year 1990 because the 1992 results are distorted by the recession.) Relative to the size of the economy, revenues have been flat. But expenditures rose from 20.7 percent of GDP in 1979 to 21.9 percent in 1990 and are projected to reach 22.4 percent in 1997. Flat revenues combined with rising spending seem to be the main explanation for the rise in the budget deficit, which was already 1.7 percent of GDP in 1979.

On closer examination, however, the data in table 9-1 suggest that the forces at work have been quite different and far more complex than this simple story. Major reforms of the social security system enacted in 1977 and 1983 sharply raised social security taxes, not only to cover current modest increases in social security spending but also to build up surpluses in the social security trust fund. But in the 1980s, taxes to support the rest of the government's activities—its general operating

TABLE 9-1. Federal Budget Expenditures, Revenues, and Deficits,
Fiscal Years 1979, 1990, 1997[a]

Percent of GDP

Budget component	1979	1990	1997
Expenditures	20.7	21.9	22.4
Social security	4.3	4.6	4.8
General operating budget	16.4	17.3	17.6
Health care[b]	1.7	2.7	4.4
Net interest	1.8	3.4	3.6
Subtotal	3.4	6.1	8.0
All other	13.0	11.2	9.6
Defense	4.8	5.5	3.6
Civilian	8.2	5.8	6.0
Revenues	19.1	18.9	19.0
Social security	4.0	5.2	5.3
General operating budget	15.1	13.7	13.7
Surplus or deficit	−1.7	−3.0	−3.4

SOURCES: Author's calculations based on data from Congressional Budget Office, *The Economic and Budget Outlook: Fiscal Years 1993–1997* (January 1992); *Budget of the United States Government, Supplement, Fiscal Year 1993*; and Congressional Budget Office, *An Analysis of the President's Budgetary Proposals for Fiscal Year 1993* (March 1992). Numbers have been rounded.

a. For 1990 and later years, the expenditures and deficits in this table, and throughout the rest of this chapter, exclude the deposit insurance outlays associated with the saving and loan bailout. There are large positive expenditures in 1989–94, and negative expenditures are projected for later years as the government sells off the assets it has taken over.

b. Excludes administrative costs and the inflow of part B medicare premiums, both of which are included in the "all other" civilian category.

budget—were cut by as much as social security taxes were raised. Revenues to support this general operating budget fell by 1.4 percentage points as a share of GDP. As a consequence, the rising surplus in the social security trust fund would have been matched by a growing deficit in the government's general operating budget even if there had been no increase in the expenditure share.[2]

The expenditure share of the general operating budget did increase from 1979 to 1990 and will remain at that level in 1997. But the startling

2. To be precise, the "general operating budget" ought to exclude the revenues and expenditures of the medicare trust funds as well the social security retirement and disability funds. But in order to highlight the role of rising health care outlays in driving up the overall budget deficit, I have kept medicare within the general operating budget and combined its outlays with those of the medicaid program. Also, strictly defined, the outlays of the general operating budget should include the interest payments from the general fund to the social security trust funds, and those same payments should also be included in the revenues of the trust fund. But in the published budget data the "net interest" category subtracts those intragovernmental payments to avoid double counting; otherwise the expenditure and revenue components of the overall budget would add to more than the total. For simplicity, and at no cost to the accuracy of the basic story being told, I have used the official net interest payments concept as part of the general operating budget.

fact that emerges from table 9-1 is the magnitude of the rise in expenditures for two items: health care (medicare and medicaid) and interest payments on the federal debt. Together their expenditure share rose by roughly 2.5 percentage points from 1979 to 1990 and will rise another 2 percentage points by 1997—four times more than the growth in total operating expenditures.

Federal spending for health care costs has been driven up mainly by the same factors as those pushing up private health care spending: prices rising faster than general inflation, and rapidly rising use of expensive medical technology. According to a recent study by the Department of Health and Human Services, total health care spending in the nation rose by 169 percent over the 1980s.[3] General inflation accounted for 57 percentage points of that rise and population growth for another 10 percent. The rest of the growth—56 percentage points—was accounted for by a rise in medical care prices greater than general inflation, the spread of high-cost, high-tech medical techniques, and an increased per capita use of medical care services.[4] The projections for 1997 assume that these factors of rising relative prices and increasing per capita use of medical services will continue.[5]

During the 1980s the sharp growth of health care costs, the rise in defense spending, and the reduction in taxes outside the social security system overwhelmed a sizable reduction in all other civilian outlays, whose share of GDP fell by 2.4 percentage points. The consequent string of large budget deficits, together with the high interest rates that characterized the decade, pushed up interest payments on the debt sharply. And over the next five years the continuing projected growth in health care costs will outweigh the decline in defense spending that is already under way. Growth of the federal debt will slightly outpace GDP, and federal interest payments as a share of GDP will continue to edge up.

In sum, a comparison of 1997 with 1979 shows a sharp and continuing

3. Sally T. Sonnefeld and others, "Projections of National Health Expenditures through the Year 2000," *Health Care Financing Review*, vol. 13 (Fall 1991), pp. 1–27.

4. The overall rise in health care spending is larger than the sum of the individual items because the various factors interact with each other; for example, the rise of 10 percent in the population has to be applied not only to the per capita amount of services used in 1980 but to the much larger use of services in 1990.

5. In the last few years, in addition to the factors pushing up health care spending generally, the federal government's outlays were boosted by an unusually large rise in medicaid spending—partly because of the recession, partly because of legislated additions to the rolls, and partly for other reasons. The projections foresee a continuation of some special cost-raising factors, but at a slower pace.

TABLE 9-2. Budgetary Costs of New Programs, Fiscal Year 1997

Billions of 1997 dollars unless otherwise specified

Program	1997
Social programs	27
Infrastructure	4
Health care (employer alternative)	60
Total	91
Percent of GDP	1.1

growth in health care costs, a reduction in general operating revenues, and a self-perpetuating growth of interest on the debt, which in combination will overwhelm a large reduction in the aggregate of all other spending, including defense. The result is an enlarged federal deficit that will grow still more unless policy is changed.

Budgetary Costs of the Recommended Programs

As explained in Henry Aaron's chapter on health care, none of the three main options for achieving universal health insurance will add more than about 4 percent to national health care spending. Two of these options, however, would switch much of what are now private expenditures to the federal budget and require very large tax increases, in the hundreds of billions of dollars. Aaron himself recommends an option that builds on and extends employer-based health insurance to all workers and their families at an annual cost to the federal budget of $35 billion (rising to $60 billion by 1997). This outcome minimizes income redistribution associated with health care reform. The budget financing plan developed in this chapter incorporates this alternative.

Table 9-2 summarizes the additional budget expenditures required to pay for the proposed programs in 1997, when all the programs are fully in effect.[6] The largest items of budget expenditures are the costs (at fiscal 1997 levels and prices) of extending health insurance to those now not covered ($60 billion), expansion of the earned income tax credit ($9 billion) and the Head Start program ($6 billion), both recommended in Isabel Sawhill's chapter on children and families, the program for the

6. The budget estimates in the table assume that the capital costs of building additional housing units for the homeless, as recommended in chapter 3, are spread out over four years. The estimate of the federal cost of the infrastructure program is based on an additional $3 billion in highway and airport investment and $4 billion in sewer and water investment (in 1997 prices), with an average federal cost share of 50 percent.

homeless ($7 billion), and infrastructure investment ($4 billion). The total increase in outlays would come to $91 billion in 1997 ($78 billion in today's prices), a formidable sum for a government facing a large and continuing budget deficit.

Economic Aspects of Financing New Programs

When workers are unemployed and plants are idle, the government can increase spending without any real economic cost. By calling upon unused resources, government can hire people to run new programs, undertake new construction of houses or highways, or provide additional cash benefits that will increase consumption by the poor without having to divert resources away from the production of other goods and services for consumers, investors, or exporters or from other government programs. But recession is not the normal state of the U.S. economy. And so, in planning long-run public programs, one has to assume that if the government expands its purchases of goods or services or provides additional cash benefits so that some group of private citizens can consume more goods or services, somewhere else in the economy purchases of goods and services for consumption, investment, exports, or other government programs will have to be reduced.

If public or private consumption is reduced, consumers bear an immediate cost. If public or private investment is reduced, the nation's stock of productive capital will grow more slowly, the growth of output per worker will slacken, and consumers will suffer an even larger loss in the future. If resources are directly or indirectly diverted from export production to government, the trade deficit will rise, the nation will have to borrow more from abroad, and again future consumption will suffer as the country has to pay debt service to foreigners.

The relevant costs of a new or expanded government program are thus the goods and services that have to be forgone elsewhere in society, either immediately as current consumption falls or later because of reduced investment or greater foreign borrowing. The way in which the additional government expenditures are financed is important precisely because alternative means of financing divert the necessary resources from different sectors of the economy. There are three ways to provide the financing.

1. *Tax increases.* Where the resources come from depends on the kind of taxes being increased. Most broad tax increases mainly reduce consumption. But an income tax increase also lowers the after-tax return

from dividends, interest, and capital gains. It may therefore lower not only consumption but also saving and investment. Economists do not agree on how significantly an increase in income taxes will reduce saving and investment. In my judgment, the effect is not large, but neither will it be zero. In contrast, a broad sales tax or a value-added tax imposed on consumption will reduce only consumer purchases. Increasing excise taxes on such things as gasoline or tobacco will particularly reduce the consumption of those items.

2. *Reducing other government expenditures.* If new or expanded programs are financed by a reduction in entitlement programs, current consumption by those receiving the reduced entitlement will fall. Public consumption, such as defense, can be reduced. On the other hand, reducing public investments that have a substantially positive rate of return will slow the growth of national income by placing the burden of the new programs on consumers in the future.

3. *Deficit financing.* If, in a period of high employment, new or expanded programs are financed by increases in the budget deficit, total spending in the economy will threaten to become excessive and inflationary pressures will mount. The Federal Reserve will have to restrict the growth of money and credit and push up interest rates sufficiently to reduce spending elsewhere in the economy, thereby making room for the added federal outlays.

A rise in interest rates reduces spending on residential construction and on business investment. The cut in private capital formation will slow economic growth, and future living standards will suffer. And the future losses will exceed what it would have cost to cut back consumption today. A rise in American interest rates will also tend to raise the exchange value of the dollar as foreign investors bid for dollars to invest in high-yield American securities. The increase in the dollar's exchange value will discourage American exports by making them more expensive for foreigners and correspondingly will make foreign imports cheaper for Americans. Production will fall and resources will be freed up in exporting industries and in import-competing domestic industries. The resulting trade deficit will be financed by an inflow of foreign lending and other capital, on which debt service will have to be paid in future years. And the payment of that debt will reduce future disposable income and consumption.

In summary, appropriate tax increases or government spending cuts can draw the resources for the new programs principally from current consumption, public and private. The nation bears the costs today.

Deficit financing, on the other hand, leads to higher interest rates, which reduce domestic investment and exports and raise imports. That route postpones the loss of consumption but only by making the loss larger in the future.

How the Current Situation Restricts Choices

The programs proposed in this book would help the country in two ways. First, some would improve the desperate lot of the nation's most disadvantaged people. A decent society ought to be willing to devote to that purpose the small fraction of national income that is proposed. But this generation should pay for its own good deeds. It should not attempt to escape the costs of its benevolence by transferring them to future generations through deficit finance and the consequent reduction in domestic investment and increase in foreign borrowing. These programs should be financed by higher taxes or spending cuts elsewhere in the budget (in a way that would not harm the people needing help).

Second, some of the proposed programs are themselves public investments and should raise future national income. But financing such programs by additional deficit spending reduces private investment or raises foreign borrowing by almost as much as the increase in public investment. Such a course boosts economic growth only if the rate of return to new public investment exceeds that of the private investment it displaces or is greater than the cost of foreign borrowing. Even when private investment is high, borrowing to pay for public investment could be dangerous, since opening the doors to deficit financing of public investment would encourage the proponents of virtually every kind of federal spending to define it as an investment and insist that it really has a very high payoff in raising future national income. But with private investment depressed, as it is today, public investments financed through deficits would cut an already shrunken private investment share and would be unlikely to do much to speed the pace of economic growth.

Channeling the budget saving from further reductions in the defense budget to the proposed social or infrastructure spending is not an appropriate way to finance the spending. That budget saving could be used to reduce the projected budget deficits and thereby raise sorely needed private investment. In a similar vein, even if it were politically possible to enact a general tax increase to finance the proposed federal social and infrastructure programs, that action would probably reduce the possibility of enacting another tax increase later on as a means of reducing the deficit. And so again, the public programs would have been financed at the risk of preempting a tax increase that could have been used to reduce the deficit and increase private investment.

A Combination of Tax Increases and Spending Cuts

These considerations suggest that deficit reduction and financing of high-priority public programs should be tackled simultaneously through a program of tax increases and expenditure cuts. Out of every $5 billion that can be realized from expenditure cuts and tax increases, an explicit decision could be made to use, say, $4 billion for deficit reduction and private investment expansion and $1 billion for high-priority federal programs. In this way neither important objective would preempt the other, and indeed the constituency for the necessary painful measures might be broadened.

Three types of measures are available to pay for a joint program of deficit reduction and selected program expansion: cuts in defense spending, cuts in civilian spending, and tax increases.

As a starting point, it is highly likely that in the relatively near-term future the payroll tax for the hospital insurance part of medicare will have to be raised. Projections by the CBO and the social security trustees imply that the fund will begin running a deficit in the mid- or late 1990s. I have assumed a payroll tax increase beginning then and yielding $35 billion by the year 2002. The overall budget deficit would be reduced to about $390 billion (3.8 percent of GDP) in that year.

Potential Defense Spending Cuts

In 1992 defense spending—exclusive of the outlays associated with the Gulf War—will be about $295 billion. The 1990 budget agreement sets separate ceilings through 1993 on discretionary spending in three categories: defense, international, and domestic. But for 1994 and 1995, the agreement set only an overall ceiling for the sum of the three categories. These ceilings require cuts in the real value of discretionary spending over the next three years. The CBO has projected total discretionary spending beyond 1995 on the assumption that from then on spending rises no faster than inflation. These assumptions underlie the expenditure projections in table 9-1 and throughout this chapter.

If nondefense discretionary spending is held constant in real terms from 1993 onward, by 1997 defense spending will have to be cut almost

TABLE 9-3. Alternative Defense Budgets, Fiscal Years 1992, 1997
Billions of 1992 dollars

Budget proposal	1992	1997
Baseline	295	239
Administration 1993 budget	295	242
Option A	...	200
Option B	...	180

SOURCES: Author's estimates based on Testimony of John D. Steinbruner before the House Budget Committee, 102 Cong. 2 sess., February 13, 1992; and *Budget of the United States Government, Fiscal Year 1993.*

20 percent, or about $55 billion below its current level, to meet the budget agreement target (see the top line of table 9-3). The administration's 1993 budget recommends cuts that would bring the budget to about that figure (second line in table 9-3).

In recent testimony before Congress, Brookings Senior Fellow John D. Steinbruner argued that several attractive defense strategies for the post–cold war era would permit substantially larger cuts in the defense budget.[7] Option A (third line in table 9-3) would accelerate the downsizing of the American military posture to reflect the disappearance of the Soviet threat but would continue reliance on collective security arrangements with U.S. allies and others. A substantial reduction in strategic forces, numbers of military personnel, and the procurement of conventional weapons would be possible, eventually leading to a defense budget about 40 percent below the present level.

According to Steinbruner, an even larger restructuring of national security objectives and military budgets could be realized if the United States could successfully negotiate international agreements to reduce the offensive capabilities of all major armed forces around the world. In that case, the potential threats faced by the United States—and everyone else—would be greatly reduced, making possible an even greater reduction in defense budgets everywhere. U.S. defense spending under that alternative (option B) would fall an additional $20 billion by 1997, again leading to even lower numbers later (fourth line in table 9-3).

In 1997 prices, defense spending could be cut below the baseline projections by about $47 billion in the first alternative and by $70 billion in the second. Because the second alternative, however attractive, hinges on the successful negotiation of a complex set of international agreements, I will assume the first alternative.

7. Testimony of John D. Steinbruner before the House Budget Committee, 102 Cong. 2 sess., February 13, 1992. I have assumed a slightly slower phasing in of his defense budget.

TABLE 9-4. Civilian Budget Expenditures, Fiscal Years 1979, 1990, 1997

	Billions of dollars			Percent of GDP		
Expenditure	1979	1990	1997	1979	1990	1997
Total (excluding net interest)	345	711	1,190	14.2	13.0	15.2
Entitlements	248	567	977	10.2	10.4	12.4
Health care[a]	41	149	346	1.7	2.7	4.4
Social security	103	247	374	4.2	4.5	4.8
Means tested	27	59	101	1.1	1.0	1.3
Other	78	113	156	3.2	2.1	2.0
Discretionary	123	202	290	5.1	3.7	3.7
Offsetting receipts	−26	−58	−77	−1.1	−1.1	−1.0

SOURCES: Author's calculations based on CBO, *Analysis of the President's Budgetary Proposals for Fiscal Year 1993*; and *Budget of the United States Government, Fiscal Year 1993*.
a. See table 9-1, footnote b. Medicare part B premiums are included in "offsetting receipts."

Potential Civilian Spending Cuts

By 1997 federal civilian spending (excluding interest on the debt), will amount to about $1.19 trillion dollars, or 15 percent of GDP (table 9-4). The most dramatic change has occurred and will continue to occur in health care spending. Of the 2.7 percentage-point increase in health care spending as a ratio of GDP from 1979 to 1997, two-thirds will be squeezed out of other civilian spending and only one-third added to the spending total (which, as shown in the first line of table 9-4, rises by only 0.8 percentage point over the period). This suggests that the executive and Congress have kept a tighter rein on such spending than most people realize. The means-tested entitlement programs—principally food stamps, welfare, and housing subsidies—never were very large and remain close to 1 percent of GDP, edging up a little by the end of the period. Social security outlays also increase slightly as a percentage of GDP. But all other spending, for both entitlement and discretionary programs, will decline from 8.3 percent of GDP in 1979 to 5.6 percent by 1997, a one-third reduction relative to the size of the economy.

These programs can be cut further. Ripe targets include agricultural subsidies (1997 value, $10 billion); compensation for low-rated veterans' disabilities ($2.4 billion); higher user charges for federal airways and waterways and for use of the radio spectrum ($4.4 billion); NASA's space station and advanced rocket ($3 billion); and some reduction in the federal government's $87 billion civilian and military retirement benefits.[8] Cuts in these programs and small miscellaneous cuts elsewhere can yield perhaps $20 billion in annual budget saving by 1997. But given the relatively tight rein held on most civilian programs outside of health care and social security in recent years, and the likelihood of some legitimate need for future expansion in a few of these federal programs, there is limited potential for significantly greater cuts. Health care and social security remain the main areas to examine for potential budget saving.

Social security benefits. The immense popularity of the social security program makes it highly resistant to benefit cuts. One might argue that the huge growth in the aged population eligible for social security benefits starting in 2010 warrants a reduction in benefits. That is exactly what Congress did in 1983 when it not only raised social security taxes but scheduled a gradual reduction in benefits, beginning in 2001. But whatever one thinks about the level of benefits, there is little justification for the favorable tax treatment now given to those benefits. Benefits are untaxed for couples with incomes below $32,000, and only one-half of benefits are taxed above that threshold. If social security benefits were taxed in the same way as private pensions, about 85 percent of the benefits would be subject to taxation, and there would be no special threshold other than the personal exemptions and deductions to which all taxpayers are entitled.[9] Should the private pension approach be adopted and the current thresholds cut in half, additional revenues of about $17 billion could be realized by 1997. Although this is a revenue increase rather than an expenditure cut, it represents the fairest way to reduce net social security benefits. It still treats low-income social security beneficiaries better than other taxpayers. The remaining threshold, and the combination of personal exemptions, the standard deduction, and a low 15 percent bottom tax bracket would eliminate or minimize the burden on the low-income elderly.

8. Congressional Budget Office, *The Economic and Budget Outlook: Fiscal Years 1993-1997* (January 1992), table 3.3; and Congressional Budget Office, *Reducing the Deficit: Spending and Revenue Options* (February 1992).

9. Recipients of private pensions may deduct an amount based upon their contribution to the plan (on which taxes were paid at the time the contribution was made). But taxes are levied on the amount of the pension representing the employer's contribution and any interest or dividend earnings from the pension fund. On average, for current social security beneficiaries, their own payroll tax contributions account for 15 percent or less of the benefit payment while the contributions of employers and government account for 85 percent. In future years the average percentage of benefits representing employee contributions will rise.

Whatever the pros and cons of further reductions in social security benefits, the permanent elimination or reduction in the value of cost of living allowances is a poor way to go about it. Newly retired beneficiaries now receive a benefit tied both to their past wages and a general wage index for the economy as a whole. Thereafter that initial benefit is indexed to the consumer price index (CPI), preserving its purchasing power in the face of inflation. If 2 percentage points were subtracted from the cost of living allowance each year, when inflation was 5 percent benefits would be raised by only 3 percent. The benefits of new retirees would not be affected; initial benefits would rise each year in line with economywide wages, as they now do. A person one year into retirement would suffer a 2 percent reduction in the real value of the retirement benefit. But the older the retiree became, the greater the erosion of the benefit. An 85-year-old, retired for twenty-three years, would suffer a 36 percent loss of purchasing power. If benefits should be reduced, it should not be in a way that increases the burden as retirees age.

Medicare and medicaid. There is one reform in the medicare program that, although politically difficult, has much to recommend it and would produce significant budget savings. When the medicare program was first introduced, it was designed so that half of the cost of physicians' services (part B) would be paid by the federal government and half would be borne by beneficiaries in the form of premium payments. But Congress has refused to raise the premium in line with rising costs. As a consequence, beneficiaries' premiums now cover less than 25 percent of the program costs. A gradual increase in the premiums, bringing them up to a 35 percent coverage ratio, would lower the federal budget contribution to the program by $9 billion in 1997. At a relatively modest cost the medicaid program would cover the extra costs for poor households, and an appropriate change in the income tax laws could insulate the near poor from any additional burden.

Health Care Cost Controls

For some years now the federal government has been attempting to realize budgetary savings by reducing the growth of costs in its own health care programs. While some of the reforms were highly desirable and have been adopted by private health insurers—for, example, the prospective payment system for hospitals—it is doubtful that much further progress can be made in this direction without fundamental reforms to reduce the growth of health care costs in the nation as a whole. Indeed, tough limits on payments to physicians and hospitals for medicare and medicaid result in a shifting of costs to the private sector with a consequent rise in insurance premiums. And federal payments to physicians for serving medicaid patients have fallen so far behind fees for other patients that the quality and availability of such services is suffering. More and more medicaid patients have to use the emergency rooms of big-city hospitals as their principal source of health care.

Further large budgetary savings in federal health care programs will depend on the adoption of basic health care reforms that include tough cost controls and expenditure limits applying to both private and public health care services. As chapter 2 makes clear, effective cost controls would entail major changes in the structure of the health insurance industry, restrain the growth of salaries for physicians and other health care providers, and eventually force the country to make some painful decisions about which health care procedures yield benefits too small to justify their costs. Health care providers, insurers, and patients would all have to give up something.

But effective cost containment measures would yield a very important side benefit: a substantial reduction in the growth of the federal budget for health care, now projected by the CBO to rise at a frightening 12 percent a year. About 2 percentage points of the projected growth in federal health care expenditures will be due to the increase in the eligible population; 3.6 percentage points, to the assumed rise in general inflation; and a little less than 6 percentage points, to "excess" growth in spending stemming principally from the rise in relative prices for medical care, new technology, and increased use of services. If tough health care cost controls and other reforms could be imposed that would gradually shrink the 6 percent annual excess to 3 percent by 1997, federal expenditures for health care in 2002 would be $86 billion (14 percent) lower than the CBO projection, and the dollar saving in the private sector, through lower insurance costs and other health care outlays, would be even larger.

Federal budget savings of these magnitudes would also gradually reduce the federal debt and the interest payments on that debt, lowering the budget deficit still further. In the example worked out above, the annual saving in interest on the debt after ten years would amount to $20 billion. Together, the reductions in health care costs and interest payments would cut the budget deficit projected for that year, from $390 billion to $284 billion.

Wishing, of course, will not make all of this come true. Only determined, sometimes painful, and politically controversial cost controls will be effective. A budget financing program that relied upon flabby and easily avoidable controls over health care costs would be a charade.

Tax Increases

Even successful health care cost controls combined with feasible spending cuts elsewhere in the budget will not be enough to eliminate the budget deficit and finance part or all of the programs recommended by the authors of this book. Tax increases will also be needed.

The history of American budget policy reveals that general tax increases were often imposed to pay for declared or undeclared wars, while earmarked taxes were initiated and often increased to pay for such popular programs as social security and highway building. But voters and their representatives have been extremely reluctant to support general tax increases to finance civilian spending by the federal government. Until the 1930s the federal government spent only 1 percent of GDP for purposes other than paying for present or past wars—military spending, veterans' benefits, and interest on the debt accumulated in wars. The exigencies of the Great Depression led to an increase in non-war-related spending to about 4 to 6 percent of GDP. Spending then held at or below that level until the mid-1950s. Thereafter civilian spending (as a share of GDP) began to rise.[10] It was financed, however, not by general tax increases, but by the gradual reduction of defense spending from 11 percent right after the Korean War to 5 percent in 1980. General taxes were raised in the 1980s, and in the budget agreement of 1990, to recoup part of the losses from the large 1981 tax reduction. On balance, however, the historical record has to make one pessimistic about the prospects for securing large general tax increases to finance either deficit reduction or new civilian programs.

In contrast, American voters have frequently been willing to support tax increases earmarked for high-priority uses. In polls, American citizens have indicated by substantial margins that they would be willing to pay an increased tax for purposes they valued highly—for example, the environment and medical care. Responding to a poll is hardly the same as supporting an actual tax increase, and some polls suggest that the magnitude of the tax increases respondents are willing to pay is quite

10. Civilian spending as defined in tables 9-1 and 9-4 includes outlays in veterans' benefits and interest. For a discussion of the historical record, see Charles L. Schultze, "Is There a Bias toward Excess in U.S. Government Budgets or Deficits?" *Journal of Economic Perspectives*, vol. 6 (Spring 1992), pp. 25–43.

small compared with the size of program costs. Nevertheless, the poll results are consistent with the historical record.

Some conservatives have supported the concept of earmarked taxes since they explicitly confront voters with the price of the public goods they are receiving. Such taxes, it is argued, may both increase the likelihood of intelligent choices by voters and give politicians and bureaucrats greater incentives for providing the goods efficiently.[11] A proliferation of spending programs tied to earmarked taxes would swamp voters with too much information and limit the flexibility of government, but selective use of such taxes would avoid that problem.

Public finance specialists have long objected to earmarked taxes out of a concern that spending would tend to grow as fast as the revenues from the tax, whether or not there was a good case for such expansion. Whenever the fund into which the earmarked tax is placed begins to build up a surplus, those who particularly benefit from the program will press for additional spending on the ground that the government is collecting revenues under false pretenses and not using them for the purpose intended. Highway and airline interests have made these arguments when there were surpluses in the highway or airways trust fund.

There is at least one major area of federal spending in which it is highly unlikely that the revenues from an earmarked tax would outrun revenues: federal health care programs. The revenues from an earmarked addition to the income tax, a special payroll tax, or a newly established value-added tax would grow approximately in line with GDP. However, even with the toughest of cost controls, federal health care spending is likely to grow faster than GDP. A special tax, earmarked for some part or all of those programs, would not incur the objection raised above. Federal health care costs would thus be an ideal candidate for financing through an earmarked tax.

The cost of providing medical care for the poor (medicaid) should continue to be paid out of general revenues, since those outlays are highly redistributive and probably ought not to be financed by a special earmarked tax. The costs to be covered by an earmarked tax might therefore include two elements: the $40 billion of expenses for part B of medicare now paid for out of general revenues and not covered by the hospital insurance payroll tax and the expanded beneficiary premiums recommended earlier, and any additional budgetary costs incurred to

11. See James Buchanan, "The Economics of Earmarked Taxes," *Journal of Political Economy*, vol. 71 (October 1963), pp. 457–69.

extend health insurance to those who do not now have it ($35 billion for fiscal 1992, as estimated in chapter 2).

Although many kinds of taxes could be levied and earmarked to finance these costs, there are three chief possibilities: an addition to the current payroll tax, an increase in income taxes, or a new value-added tax (VAT). The average payroll tax is already stiff, now amounting to 15.3 percent, half paid by employers and half by employees. Most economists believe that the tax, including the part initially levied on employers, is ultimately borne by workers. The payroll tax will have to be raised early in the next century to begin paying for the surge of retirees that will start then. A further addition to that tax does not recommend itself as the best way to collect the earmarked revenues.

Of the two remaining alternatives, a special supplement to the income tax would be most attractive from the standpoint of income distribution, since the well-to-do would pay more than a proportionate fraction. But from the standpoint of minimizing the unfavorable supply-side effects of taxes, a value-added tax would be superior. By 1997, even with successful cost controls beginning to be effective, it would take approximately a 15 to 20 percent increase in personal income taxes to raise the necessary revenues. If a special surcharge of that amount were levied, the top marginal rate would be raised to about 37 percent. It is hard to find convincing evidence that this would have a large depressing effect on private saving, but some impact might well be felt. A VAT would have no such effect. Similarly, the disincentive effect on labor supply from a tax increase of the size indicated is likely to be modest. Nevertheless, some economic research suggests the disincentive would be larger with a progressive income tax than with a VAT. All in all, a VAT would be the best choice for an earmarked tax to pay for federal health care costs.

A valued-added tax would raise consumer prices by an amount roughly equal to the tax. In the year the VAT was imposed, the increase would show up in the consumer price index and therefore in the cost of living allowances for social security benefits, federal employees' retirement benefits, and other indexed benefit programs.[12] In order to prevent these beneficiaries from completely escaping their share of the tax burden, it would be appropriate to reduce the cost of living allowance in that year, eliminating at least the bulk of the increase due to the VAT. On the other hand, it would be desirable to reduce the burden of the added tax

---

12. The revenue estimates of the VAT have been calculated net of any associated increases in federal spending due to higher prices.

TABLE 9-5. Proposals for Earmarked Value-Added Tax
for Health Care

Proposal	1977	2002
Scenario A (with cost savings)		
Revenues (billions of dollars)	119	194
VAT tax rate (percent)	4.0	5.1
Scenario B (without cost savings)		
Revenues (billions of dollars)	128	226
VAT tax rate (percent)	4.4	5.9

SOURCE: Author's estimates, derived by adjusting the net yield of a 5 percent broad-based VAT as given in Congressional Budget Office, *Reducing the Deficit: Spending and Revenue Options* (February 1992), p. 335.

on the poor through such devices as an increase in welfare payments or a refundable earned income tax credit. That would cost money and raise the deficit. The added costs of shielding the poor may be somewhat larger than the gain from reducing the cost of living allowance, leaving a net budget cost of perhaps $10 billion.

Table 9-5 indicates the additional revenue and the tax rate that would be required to cover both the federal government's general revenue contribution to medicare and the additional costs of extending health insurance to the uninsured. Estimates are provided to illustrate two different scenarios: (A) a rigorous set of cost controls is adopted, which, after being phased in over the next several years, reduces the growth of health care costs by 2 percentage points a year (lowering the annual growth of health care costs in the federal budget from 11.6 to 9.6 percent a year); and (B) no reduction in cost growth. Both scenarios assume that beneficiary premiums are raised to cover 35 percent of the cost of physicians' services (part B of medicare). The calculations assume that the VAT is applied broadly to almost all consumer goods. However, an alternative could easily be substituted with narrower coverage (for example, excluding food and private medical care costs) and a correspondingly higher rate.

The legislation creating and earmarking the VAT should be written so that adjustments in the tax rate must be enacted periodically (say, every two years) to cover the costs of the health care programs it finances. This requirement would reinforce pressures to control costs. Failure to hold down health care costs would require increases in the VAT and create a political constituency for cost control. Even with a 2 percent reduction in the annual growth of health care costs, as assumed in scenario A, an increase in the value-added tax rate would still be required within five years after the new tax had been introduced. Moreover, any attempt by groups representing the elderly to pressure Congress into holding down beneficiary premiums in the face of rising costs—as has been the history of the past two decades—would run into widespread opposition because it too would lead to an increase in the tax rate.

A value-added tax falls least heavily on the rich. A recent CBO study estimates that a 3.5 percent broad-based VAT would impose burdens ranging from 2.3 to 3.2 percent of the incomes of the middle three-fifths of the income distribution, but only 1.5 percent on the top one-fifth of families.[13] Some people who report high incomes in a particular year are enjoying windfalls that overstate their long-run position in the income distribution. Nevertheless, under a VAT upper-income families would bear a below-average burden in paying for the nation's health care needs and reducing the deficit. As a consequence, I propose that the top marginal income tax rate be raised from 31 to 34 percent, yielding about $10 billion by 1997. This would affect couples with taxable incomes over $89,250 in 1993; since the tax code is indexed, this threshold would rise each year with inflation.

The Budgetary Results

If all the budgetary and financing measures suggested in this chapter were adopted, and if health care cost controls could shave 2 percentage points from the growth of health care costs (as assumed above in scenario A), the budget could be gradually brought into virtual balance over the next ten years, and modest sums would be available to finance new or expanded programs such as those proposed in this book.

The elements of this financing plan are shown in table 9-6. Elements that reduce the budget deficit are shown as positive numbers; those that raise the deficit are shown as negative numbers. The cost controls are assumed to take effect gradually between now and 1996. Most revenue increases and expenditure reductions are phased in between 1994 and 1997.

Several items in table 9-6 need special comment. If cost controls take effect as assumed, the increase in the hospital insurance payroll tax, assumed to be necessary in the original baseline budget projection, could be avoided, and the revenue from that payroll tax increase would not be forthcoming; that shows as a negative entry in the table. The cost of

13. Congressional Budget Office, *Effects of Adopting a Value-Added Tax* (February 1992), pp. 34–36.

TABLE 9-6. Financing New Programs and Balancing the Budget
Billions of current dollars

Element	1997	2002
Original budget deficit[a]	−265	−390
Health care reforms		
Saving from cost control	21	86
Value-added tax	119	194
Increased part B premiums	9	23
less: Extension of health insurance	−56	−86
less: Decreased hospital insurance tax	...	−35
Other budget changes		
Increase top marginal rate (31 to 34 percent)	10	11
Tax social security benefits	17	21
Defense budget cuts	47	85
Civilian budget cuts	20	25
less: New programs	−25	−35
Shield poor from VAT	−7	−10
Interest "bonus" (lower debt)	25	105
Total changes	180	384
New budget deficit	−85	−6

a. Assumes the enactment of an increase in the hospital insurance payroll tax; see text.

shielding the poor from the VAT is net of the budgetary savings from partially disallowing the effect of the VAT on cost of living allowances. The interest "bonus" reflects the fact that the proposed measures would slow and eventually halt the growth in the federal debt and produce major savings in annual interest payments. In addition, the eventual elimination of the budget deficit and the accompanying rise in national saving would lower interest rates, producing additional reductions in federal expenditures for interest on the debt. If interest rates fell by 1 to 2 percentage points—a restrained estimate of the consequences of eliminating the budget deficit—substantial additional saving in expenditures would be achieved by 2002. For conservatism, however, I have not included in table 9-6 the expenditure saving from these potential interest rate reductions.

In 1989 total tax collections in the United States by all levels of government were 30.1 percent of GDP. This was about the same as the tax burden in Japan and lower than that in other major industrial countries, including Germany (38.1) and the United Kingdom (36.5).[14]

14. *Comparison of the Tax Systems of the United States, The United Kingdom, Germany, and Japan*, Committee Print JCS-13-92, Joint Committee on Taxation, 102 Cong. 2 sess. (Government Printing Office, 1992), p. 5. On a different basis of measurement,

TABLE 9-7. The Budgetary Effects of Failing to Reduce Health
Care Cost Growth[a]

Billions of current dollars

Effect	1997	2002
Loss of cost saving	− 25	− 100
Higher value-added tax	9	32
Higher health insurance payroll tax	...	35
Higher part B premium	2	8
Additional cost of shielding the poor	− 1	− 2
Increased interest payments	− 2	− 7
Change in budget deficit	− 17	− 34

a. Minus sign denotes increase in deficit.

The tax increases contemplated in this chapter—the health care VAT, the increased tax on social security benefits, and the higher top personal income tax rate—would ultimately amount to 2.2 percent of GDP. The United States would still be a relatively low-tax country.

Table 9-7 shows the consequences for the financing scheme if cost controls failed to slow the rise in health care costs. Only part of the higher health care costs (those affecting the medicaid program) would show up in a higher budget deficit. Under the financing arrangements proposed above, all of the other cost increases—for medicare and for the new program of subsidies for employer health insurance—would require higher taxes. The VAT would have to be raised by almost 1 percentage point in 2002, and a higher payroll tax for hospital insurance would have to be imposed. Again, linking health care spending to an earmarked tax strengthens incentives for cost control. And because the higher costs would require higher taxes and premiums, the deficit would grow less than the extra health care spending. The budget would be in deficit, but by less than 0.5 percent of GDP.

At the present time there is a temptation for the president and Congress, in an effort to achieve budget economies, to impose ceilings on physicians' fees and hospital reimbursements in medicare, and especially medicaid, so low as to generate the unwanted consequences outlined earlier in this chapter: health care providers recoup by shifting costs to private insurers, and physicians become increasingly unwilling to accept medicaid patients. Political incentives to control federal health

government revenues in the United States in 1989 were 31.8 percent of GDP, compared with 33.4, 45.0, and 40.2 percent in Japan, Germany, and the United Kingdom, respectively. *OECD Economic Outlook*, vol. 51 (June 1992), table R-16.

care costs can have undesirable side effects. But if a comprehensive set of cost controls is in place, on the private as well as the public sector, such cost shifting is much less feasible. The additional political incentives to control budgetary costs that are built into the earmarked tax scheme are less likely to produce unwanted consequences.

In sum, the health care financing mechanism proposed here would have the very desirable feature of confronting citizen-taxpayers with the fundamental choices they have to face: to what extent do they wish to pay for virtually unlimited access to highly expensive medical technology, and how much are they willing to ration that access in order to have more money for other things?[15]

Conclusion

Earlier chapters stressed the potential benefits of new social and investment policies for the nation. While those chapters identified some initiatives that could be taken without additional federal spending, they outlined others that would require significantly higher outlays. This chapter, on the other hand, opened by stressing the benefits of higher private investment and economic growth that could be gained by reducing the federal budget deficit. The chapter then sketched a series of measures that could both finance the new policy initiatives and shrink or eliminate the budget deficit.

The budget deficit has stifled discussion of domestic policies that might add to government spending. Because it has persisted for so long, it has assumed an almost demonic image in the minds and statements of many commentators and elected officials. This view is needlessly apocalyptic. The deficit was created by a series of specific policies adopted in the early 1980s; it has been intensified by high interest rates and by large interest payments on the debt, both caused in part by the deficits themselves and by rapidly rising health care costs. This chapter has shown that a series of cuts in spending on both defense and domestic programs, including entitlements, and tax increases earmarked for health care, combined with interest savings from a reduction in growth of the federal debt, can pay for the initiatives proposed here and for deficit reduction. With the imposition of tough and effective cost controls on

15. Henry Aaron recently proposed an earmarked value-added tax as part of a national health care reform plan. Aaron, *Serious and Unstable Condition: Financing America's Health Care* (Brookings, 1991), pp. 147–48.

health care spending, the tax increases would be moderate and the deficit would be eliminated. Without effective cost controls, the tax increases would be larger and a small deficit would remain. But even in the latter case the nation's long-run welfare would be substantially improved.

No herculean effort is required to pay for the new initiatives and the deficit reductions proposed in this book. But elected officials must be willing to propose, and the electorate to support, some steps that both so far have avoided.